D0253751

*The Business of
the Japanese State*

Cornell Studies in Political Economy

EDITED BY PETER J. KATZENSTEIN

Power, Purpose, and Collective Choice: Economic Strategy in Socialist States, edited by Ellen Comisso and Laura D'Andrea Tyson

The Political Economy of East Asian Industrialism, edited by Frederic C. Deyo

Politics in Hard Times: Comparative Responses to International Economic Crises, by Peter Gourevitch

Closing the Gold Window: Domestic Politics and the End of Bretton Woods, by Joanne Gowa

The Philippine State and the Marcos Regime: The Politics of Export, by Gary Hawes

Pipeline Politics: The Complex Political Economy of East-West Energy Trade, by Bruce W. Jentleson

The Politics of International Debt, edited by Miles Kahler

Corporatism and Change: Austria, Switzerland, and the Politics of Industry, by Peter J. Katzenstein

Small States in World Markets: Industrial Policy in Europe, by Peter J. Katzenstein

The Sovereign Entrepreneur: Oil Policies in Advanced and Less Developed Capitalist Countries, by Merrie Gilbert Klapp

International Regimes, edited by Stephen D. Krasner

The Business of the Japanese State: Energy Markets in Comparative and Historical Perspective, by Richard J. Samuels

Europe and the New Technologies, edited by Margaret Sharp

Europe's Industries: Public and Private Strategies for Change, edited by Geoffrey Shepherd, François Duchêne, and Christopher Saunders

National Styles of Regulation: Environmental Policy in Great Britain and the United States, by David Vogel

Governments, Markets, and Growth: Financial Systems and the Politics of Industrial Change, by John Zysman

American Industry in International Competition: Government Policies and Corporate Strategies, edited by John Zysman and Laura Tyson

The Business of the Japanese State

Energy Markets in Comparative and Historical Perspective

Richard J. Samuels

CORNELL UNIVERSITY PRESS

Ithaca and London

All coalmining photographs in Chapter 3 appear by courtesy of the Japan Coal Association; the mine drawings of Yamamoto Sakubei are reproduced with the permission of Chikuhō Bunko. All oil industry photographs in Chapter 5 appear by courtesy of the Nippon Oil Corporation.

Copyright © 1987 by Cornell University

All rights reserved. Except for brief quotations in a review, this book, or parts thereof, must not be reproduced in any form without permission in writing from the publisher. For information, address Cornell University Press, 124 Roberts Place, Ithaca, New York 14850.

First published 1987 by Cornell University Press.

International Standard Book Number (cloth) 0-8014-2022-9
International Standard Book Number (paper) 0-8014-9462-1
Library of Congress Catalog Card Number 87-5230
Printed in the United States of America
Librarians: Library of Congress cataloging information
appears on the last page of the book.

The paper in this book is acid-free and meets the guidelines for
permanence and durability of the Committee on Production Guidelines
for Book Longevity of the Council on Library Resources.

*To my mother and
to my late father*

Contents

Preface   ix

1. States, Markets, and the Politics of Reciprocal Consent   1

2. State-owned Energy Corporations in the Industrial
   Democracies   23

3. A Political History of the Japanese Coal Industry   68

4. A Political History of the Japanese Electric Power Industry   135

5. A Political History of the Japanese Oil Industry   168

6. A Political History of Alternative Energy in Japan   228

7. The Business of the Japanese State   257

Notes   291
References   331
List of Acronyms   351
Index   353

Preface

One is unlikely to read a major business publication these days without finding some reference to Japanese industrial policy. Japanese bureaucrats are routinely given as much credit as Japanese businessmen, sometimes more, for understanding, anticipating, and capitalizing upon market opportunities. The Japanese state looms large in any account of the Japanese economic miracle.

Nevertheless, I begin this book with a puzzling observation. Although Japan is reputed to be among the strongest, smartest, and most centralized states in the industrial world, it is nearly alone among the industrial democracies in the extent to which it depends on private firms and private capital markets, rather than public firms and public investment, to sustain economic growth. Moreover, Japan is widely characterized as precariously dependent on imported raw materials. Crude oil and coal are only two of the many commodities that the Japanese produce hardly at all. Surely then, in energy markets at least, Japan should have both the incentive and the capacity to intervene in the same way that European states do—through state ownership.

But when we examine patterns of ownership in the energy markets of the industrial democracies, we find that no nation has less state ownership of electric power or coal than Japan and that only Japan and the United States rely entirely upon private firms for the refining and sale of petroleum products. Like the United States, but unlike virtually all other advanced industrial nations, Japan has no national oil champion, no national electric utility, and has not nationalized its once considerable coal industry. The natural questions are "Why?" and "So what?"

State ownership matters very little in Japan, it is widely thought, because economic policy makers are too smart to believe in it: as Japanese bureaucrats can rule more effectively by guiding private firms and by capturing the efficiency of private markets for public ends, why should they bother with state ownership?

This book rejects the conventional view of bureaucratic prescience and control. It explains that Japanese energy policies are market-conforming by emphasizing the constraints upon rather than the power of the Japanese economic bureaucracy. Its analysis is built upon an examination of several hundred years of coal market transformations and a century of similar market restructuring in oil and electric power. There is simply no evidence to support the prevailing view of a Japanese bureaucracy that purposefully chooses policies to anticipate and conform to the demands of the market.

This is not the oft-told story of "guided free enterprise," "state-led capitalism," or "bureaucratic dominance." Instead, it is a story framed by a process of "reciprocal consent," in which firms give the state jurisdiction over markets in return for their continuing control of those markets. Reciprocal consent is not a new idea, of course, but an elaboration of ideas that have enjoyed a certain currency in political science and especially Japanese studies, where interactions among elites, especially bureaucrats and businessmen, have attracted much attention. By "reciprocal consent" I refer not to consensus as a cultural norm but to the transactional nature of Japanese government-business relations, which is enduring because of the political stability of Japan's national institutions.

In short, we learn that the Japanese state negotiates more than it leads, and we learn why these negotiations prevent the Japanese state from adopting the competitive, commercial role in energy markets it has so often sought.

This book is about states and markets. It is a study of how businessmen and bureaucrats in general, and the Japanese in particular, attempt to organize their economies. One purpose is to identify and explain the various roles of the state in structuring domestic markets and to further the comparative analysis of relations between business and government. Another purpose is to re-specify these roles and relationships in Japan. By identifying limits to state capacity in the most likely case, Japanese energy, we learn an important lesson: we can most profitably test attributions of state autonomy and state strength from the often ignored perspective of the market itself.

In September 1982 I was in a Denver hotel room the night before presenting a paper to the American Political Science Association on the subject that I later developed into this book. I was startled by a telephone call from Washington, D.C., where it was already two o'clock in the morning. The call came from a Japanese government official, one of MITI's eyes and ears on energy-related issues in the United States. As a courtesy I had sent him a copy of my working paper. He was quite agitated because in one section I had noted, on the basis of an interview with one of his colleagues (whose anonymity I had preserved), that relations between MITI and private electric utilities were less than harmonious. As this position "did not represent official MITI policy," he "requested" that I retract references to business-government conflict in Japan. The reader will soon learn that I did not.

Although it is a curious way to begin a book, I mention this incident for two reasons. First, that phone call seemed to confirm popular conceptions of the fears, paranoia, and arrogance of Japanese bureaucrats. Years of field research in Japan had not prepared me for this experience. But second, and more important, I can happily report that in subsequent years of research and interviews in Japan, Europe, and the United States, never again was I confronted by anything but enthusiastic cooperation, from bureaucrats as well as from businessmen.

The cooperation that mattered most directly, I suppose, was financial and institutional. I am grateful for generous financial support from the Japan-MIT Endowment for Energy Policy Studies under the auspices of the MIT Center for International Studies with the assistance of the Center for Energy Policy Research and Energy Laboratory of MIT. A Mitsui Career Development Professorship provided me with additional resources, most notably time, to complete this book. Support for foreign research came from the Social Science Research Council and from the Fulbright Commission. These grants made it possible for me to work first in Rome with Umberto Colombo at the National Commission for Atomic and Alternative Energy Sources, then in Tokyo with Ikuta Toyoaki at the Institute for Energy Economics (IEE). Both gentlemen graciously placed the considerable resources of their institutes at my disposal. I thank in particular Andrea Aparo, Danielle Mazzonis, Fernando Scaduto, Cesare Silvi, and Maria Steffek for making our stay in Rome so pleasant. In Tokyo there are simply too many friends to list, but I must mention Tomitate Takao, Suzuki Shinji, Kimura Tōru, Tanaka Norio, and Sakakibara Sakura of the IEE. Government officials were free with their data; researchers were free with their ideas and analyses; and scholars, journalists, and corporate officials always found time to talk with me. In both cities I surely took more than I could give.

The cooperation that mattered best was personal. I am grateful to many friends and colleagues, old and new, who encouraged me throughout the half-dozen years it took to transform an idea into a book. I offer special thanks to the following scholars who carefully read parts of the manuscript: Faneuil Adams, Jr., Morris Adelman, Gary Allinson, Suzanne Berger, John Campbell, Harvey Feigenbaum, John Freeman, David Friedman, Martha Harris, Laura Hein, John Ikenberry, Chalmers Johnson, Peter Katzenstein, Ellis Krauss, Jeanne Kirk Laux, Michael Lynch, Thomas Neff, T. J. Pempel, Lucian Pye, Theda Skocpol, and

Raymond Vernon. Thanks are also due to Greg Nowell for reliable research assistance, Laura Hastings for preparing the index, and Eva Nagy for flawless and unflappable secretarial support. The chance to rewrite under the editorial supervision of Roger Haydon and Peter Katzenstein for Cornell University Press was a reward all its own.

Finally, I thank my wife, Debbie, and our sons, Brad and Alex, who tramped off across continents and oceans for a year on a wonderful adventure together. This book is dedicated to my mother and to my late father, who made part of the journey with us.

RICHARD J. SAMUELS

Cambridge, Massachusetts

*The Business of
the Japanese State*

CHAPTER ONE

States, Markets, and the
Politics of Reciprocal Consent

This book is about states and markets, a relationship about which so much is known and so little is understood. I start from the curious fact that the Japanese state, reputed to be among the strongest, smartest, and most centralized in the industrial world (and faced with resource constraints second to none) is nowhere a direct, commercial participant in energy markets. Despite a pervasive regulatory presence, Japan has no European-style national oil champion, no national electric utility, and no state-owned coal mines.

In energy, as in other sectors, the Japanese state is a pervasive market player without a commercial market presence. Japan has a state-owned oil firm that does not explore, produce, transport, refine, or sell oil; it has part ownership in an electric utility that is prohibited from selling power to end-users; and it has not owned a coal mine in more than a century. By the mid-1980s the Japanese government had even divested holdings in the few businesses in which it had enjoyed a commercial stake: the salt and tobacco monopoly, telecommunications, and national railways.

The near absence of state ownership distinguishes Japan from most of Western Europe. The Europeans build national champions with state equity, the Japanese restructure private markets. One question is why they do so. Another is whether it matters. The evidence in this book fails to support the widely held view that it does not matter whether the Japanese state is a commercial participant in markets. Japanese state planners prefer regulation to ownership, it is often argued, because regulation affords greater flexibility without compromising state authority. They prefer market-conforming policies to market-displacing policies because they believe the market is a policy instrument most efficiently controlled by indirect means.

I suggest a different explanation for the nature and extent of state intervention in the Japanese market place. In three hundred years of coal and one hundred years of oil and electric power development, direct state intervention has always mattered. Regulation has often been the planners' second choice in Japanese industrial policy; regulation, even when it is most extensive, has depended upon the cooperation and preferences of private actors.

Japan is a singular case of public policy without public ownership. The Japanese state is a market-conforming player not because it is strong enough to control by other means, nor because it is smart enough to appreciate the efficiency of the market, but because in the development of Japanese commerce and industry powerful and stable private actors emerged who established enduring alliances with politicians and bureaucrats. These same actors vigilantly checked market-displacing intervention. As a result the Japanese state, when it intervenes, usually attempts to reproduce shifting market structures, and it does so by fortifying the position of existing firms.

These market-conforming actions cannot prevent significant transformations of market structure in Japan. These shifts help explain the pervasiveness of the Japanese state in the economy. Because there is no end to market instability, there is no end to efforts by the state and firms alike to order markets. As a consequence, intervention by the Japanese state is paradoxical—the Japanese state is pervasive in the economy because, as we shall see, private actors have learned how to limit and enhance state power simultaneously. They surrender jurisdiction to retain control.

The point at issue is not why the state is so pervasive in the Japanese economy but why firms find a pervasive state so congenial. The answer lies in the ways that private interests have institutionalized their access to public goods. I thus conclude that the market place and state structures are as fully the product of negotiation and opportunity in Japan as they are elsewhere. This analysis challenges assumptions of bureaucratic dominance and state-led capitalism in Japan. It suggests, rather, a comparative framework of "reciprocal consent." The state often helps structure market choices, but public/private negotiations invariably structure state and market choices alike. By incorporating Japan, this framework suggests the need for caution in the application of models of state-society relations which stress the autonomy and capacity of the democratic state. For the politics of reciprocal consent, negotiation and compact are the core of business-state relations.

CRITICAL ISSUES AND EMPIRICAL QUESTIONS

Three related theoretical issues have become central to studies of business-government relations in the industrial democracies. The first concerns the identity of the modern state and its relative autonomy. The second concerns state capacity. The third centers upon questions of change and development. Each issue suggests a different set of empirical questions about the politics of business-government relations. But attention to state structures and public policy, I believe, while it is critical for analysis of markets, can also be excessive. It can misdirect inquiry by understating the preferences of market players. This book builds upon evolving, relational approaches to states and markets to direct our attention as much toward the market as toward public policy and the state.

State Identity and State Autonomy

Identifying state structures should in theory be easy. Most Western social scientists have long accepted Max Weber's notion of the state as the monopolist of the legitimate use of coercion. Differences emerge, however, in assigning the state a central place in political analysis. Weber's notion is linked on the one hand to fundamental disagreements about what constitutes legitimacy and coercion and on the other to disputes about state autonomy. Until recently these disagreements remained unexplored, largely because behavioral approaches to political analysis led many away from the study of institutions altogether.

For what seemed good reasons, a prewar political science that had focused exclusively upon legal-formal attributes of states was replaced by one that viewed terms such as state, sovereignty, and government as undesirable reifications. The first postwar generation of political scientists did not ignore bureaucracies but preferred to focus upon systems, actors, and goals. The dominant intellectual force was the political sociology of Talcott Parsons and his associates (ironically, for they took many of their initiatives in Weber's name). This approach had become so entrenched by the late 1960s that J. P. Nettl was led to fire the opening fusillade in an effort to "bring the state back in."[1]

The perception that behavioral approaches may have gone too far now dominates discussions of state and society. Similarly, classical liberals and traditional Marxists have been criticized for their shared identification of the state as the reflection of societal demands. Liberals focus upon markets and society, seeing fragmented, diffuse, overlapping interests; Marxists focus upon dominant and dominated classes, originating in and unified by the relations of production.[2] In both views the state

3

is what the market makes it, whether the market (and therefore the state) reflects coercive relations or benign competition. Neither tradition, it is argued, accommodates the state as an independent rather than an intervening factor in social relations.

These perceived deficiencies prompted scholars to focus on the bureaucracy and to postulate the state itself as a central actor in the policy networks of industrial societies. Revisionist liberals see the motivation for state action arising from the pursuit of independent bureaucratic interests as much as from societal demands for a response to market failures.[3] The state is not the instrument that an undifferentiated society uses to achieve its goals. It is the instrument of a coalition of private and (often) bureaucratic interests acting authoritatively in the name of the general good.

Marxist scholars also propound a relatively autonomous capitalist state. Theorists have rejected the state as simply the instrumentality of a ruling class; they now recognize business-state conflict and divisions within the capitalist class.[4] State interests and capitalists' interests will collide in the near term, and the responsibility of the state is to act decisively and autonomously to maintain capitalism itself. The capitalist state exists to preserve relations of production and domination, even at the expense of parts of the capitalist class. These neo-Marxists reject the idea of a unitary, class-conscious, and sagacious ruling elite. They agree that state actors might constrain business and that business does not always act in or even fully appreciate its own best interests. Only the "relatively autonomous state" can transcend the narrow interests of capitalists in the broader interest of capitalism. State identity is not a matter of legitimacy, it is a matter of survival. In David Becker's words, the state is "the key institution through which political power is organized and social control exercised."[5]

A "statist" approach has challenged the capacity of these liberal and Marxist models to accommodate an autonomous role for the state.[6] This view defines the state by its unique ability to assign values, to define and pursue a "national interest" that might leave some parts of society better or worse off than others. The national interest is not reducible to the goals of any single group or coalition. This approach to state-society relations criticizes liberals for studying policy and bureaucracies without developing a historical or structural perspective; it criticizes Marxists for relying on circular, "functional" logics to account for state autonomy.

But whether they assign the state a coercive raison d'etre or merely a coercive monopoly, otherwise diverse approaches have converged on an understanding of state structures as identifiable and of state interests as autonomous. I also accept the state as a set of organizations endowed with authoritative power which can enforce solutions to social problems. I reserve judgment, however, on the extent to which an *autonomous* state can create those solutions and thereby dominate social relations. I prefer to evaluate the extent to which it can do so by tying my analysis to historical developments that shape both state and social structures. Instead of positing relationships that may exist only in the abstract, I frame this analysis with three important empirical questions.

To what extent and under what conditions are state structures identifiable as different from social structures?

To what extent and under what conditions are state preferences autonomous?

To what extent and under what conditions are state preferences unified?

The analytical pay-off of the statist perspective remains underrealized for several reasons. The first is straightforward and empirical. As proponents are quick to point out, there is not yet sufficient evidence to allow a priori attributions of state autonomy.[7] Consequently, this book asks these three questions and answers them with historically and comparatively informed cases. The second reason is that we cannot yet be confident about the consistency of state identity. The attribution of autonomy to bureaucrats and politicians has not contributed to a better specification of state structures themselves. These structures remain embedded in debates over state autonomy, and they need clarification on their own terms if the state is to serve as a coherent unit of analysis. Indeed, they may not represent distinct units of analysis; the entire statist perspective may be an analytical cul-de-sac. This possibility is central to this book and to the question of state capacity.

State Capacity

Comparative scholarship on state-society relations in the industrial democracies has turned toward systematic evaluation of the manner in which and effectiveness with which states intervene in their economies to restructure markets.[8] Sharing the premises that states can act autonomously and that their interventions will vary in predictable ways, many studies are concerned less with the relative *autonomy* of the state than with its relative *capacity*. This so-called strong state–weak state literature relates state capacity to the character of national policy networks as reflected in the historical balance of power between state and society. The strongest state can change the behavior of private actors as well as the economic structure itself, while a weaker state can resist private demands but is unable to transform private preferences. The weakest state cannot resist private demands and is colonized by pressure groups.[9] The state is, in any case, a coherent, identifiable, and autonomous institution.

This literature pairs France and Japan as the strongest of the mixed capitalist states. Both states, it is frequently argued, can influence markets because each has an administrative apparatus that is highly centralized, largely insulated, and staffed by a mandarin elite. The strength of these bureaucracies has been reinforced by stable, conservative political coalitions throughout most of the period since 1945. At the other extreme are such weak states as the United States and Italy, which suffer from highly fragmented structures of administration and interest. These states are said to be less able to diffuse political conflict and competition for state resources through corporatist intermediation. They therefore lack the capacity to transform society and to resist private pressure.

Acceptance of the premise that states can act autonomously invites empirical questions about state capacity: is it consistent across sectors and over time, and does state capacity predict policy choice? These questions have already been asked in other contexts, and the answers often frustrated unified characterizations of state capacity. On the one hand, even in a strong centralized France private actors have succeeded in effectively "colonizing" the state.[10] Many documented cases of intervention by weak states, meanwhile, most obviously the New Deal in the United States, have had significant implications for national economic development.[11] So there are important empirical exceptions to state strength and state weakness as ideal types, and evidence suggests that the actions of even the strongest states will reflect societal demands.[12]

No undifferentiated notion of state strength is sufficient, John Zysman argues, to predict the nature, extent, and effectiveness of state intervention in the industrial democracies. These will vary historically and sectorally; even "weak" states will intervene where market adjustments are required and where private actors have not yet sorted out their market or technological choices. Those choices, moreover, are established politically, and they depend in part upon the different ways in which different interests organize to relate to the state.[13] The observation implies more than that state action is a perfect reflection of balances of private power. It implies that bureaucrats and politicians can intervene to tip those balances. State capacity per se is thus likely to be less relevant than historically determined coalitions and conflicts for explaining the many ways in which states discriminate between firms and sectors. Neither attributions of past strength nor snapshots of current political coalitions can suffice to explain market change.

State Development

The final theoretical issue I address in this book concerns the development of the state. In particular, how can the relationship between past and present best be specified? There seem to be two choices. One holds that the historical accumulation of prior commitments and political struggles best defines what is and is not possible. Received political structures may well be systematically linked to particular phases of development in particular national settings. If so, then the clear implication is that the identity, autonomy, and capacity of states vary by patterns of national development. We are compelled to posit a current and future world dependent upon a past that either limits choice or provides freedom to choose. In either case the assumption is linear and perhaps historicist. The other choice is more impressed with the variety and diversity of paths from past to present and less concerned with how past shapes future than with the ways in which possibilities for the future are independent of constraints that limited the past. The assumptions are non- or multilinear and contingent.

Most of the extant literature chooses the former position, and there is broad agreement on the direction of national development.[14] There is a remarkable confluence in liberal and Marxist assumptions about the ways in which markets and technology drive political and social solutions to the problem of industrialization toward a common, centralizing, converging end. The opportunities and imperatives provided by industrialization ultimately produce similar institutions of work, governance, and family. I derive empirical questions for this book from these assumptions of convergence.

Do industrial democracies travel different roads toward a common end?

In which policy settings are discontinuities more relevant than continuities?

But theoretical problems remain unresolved. If, for example, we discover that more than one way to be successful exists,[15] how will we capture the diversity of paths to the present without ascribing everything to idiosyncratic residuals? This world of infinite possibilities is not unlike the one described by Stephen Jay Gould in his critique of misinterpretations of Darwinian theory: "Organisms are not billiard balls, propelled by simple and measurable external forces to predictable new positions on life's pool table. Sufficiently complex systems have greater richness. Organisms have a history that constrains their future in myriad, subtle ways."[16] So do political systems. But we must be confident that our concepts are sufficiently precise to explain these developments.

By bringing the state back in, debates over state identity, autonomy, capacity, and development have tried to fill this breach. Nevertheless I endorse Theda Skocpol's caution that "'bringing the state back in' to a central place in the analysis of policymaking and social change . . . does not mean that old theoretical emphases should simply be turned on their heads; studies of states alone are not to be substituted for concerns with classes or group. Nor are purely state-determinist arguments to be fashioned in the place of society-centered explanations."[17] In attempting to answer or refine important empirical questions, this book explores the strategies of public and private actors without assuming a priori the dominance of either. It will not "bring the state" so far "in" that politics is obscured and that the bureaucracy is all that matters.

THE POLITICS OF RECIPROCAL CONSENT

The political interdependence of states and markets is a matter of permanent negotiation, what I call the politics of reciprocal consent. The analysis of this politics begins not with the state but with the objective of those negotiations, control of the market itself. To explore the mutual accommodation of state and market, we must first ask whose market it is. Questions about identity, autonomy, capacity, and development (what is the state, whose is it, what can it do, and where is it going) often obscure explanation of market outcome by paying excessive attention to public policy and state structures. Our prior question compels us first to identify structural transformations in the market—alterations in relations among producers or between producers and consumers (and/or the state) which affect the ability of any or all of these actors to pursue the market strategies of their choice. Only then do we inquire about the role of states, firms, and other players, including labor. This approach assumes no barriers or permanent balances of power between state and society. Instead it uses compact and negotiation to explore how power and resources in shifting markets illuminate these other issues.

Reciprocal consent is the mutual accommodation of state and market. It is an iterative process of reassurance among market players and public officials, one that works better where the parties to these negotiations are stable and where the institutions that guarantee their compacts are enduring. I analyze these compacts with explicit regard for a subtle but critical distinction between jurisdiction and control. Jurisdiction is the territory within which authority can be exercised, and control is the exercise of that authority. By "consent" I imply that both public and private jurisdictions in markets are negotiated and draw attention to the interdependence of public and private power. Market jurisdiction is not monopolized by states or by private firms. Likewise control, defined in terms of leadership and authority, is something better discovered than attributed. Instead of assuming the leadership and autonomy of either state or private actors, therefore, I explore their mutual accommodations within particular markets and then explain the distribution of power.

By "reciprocity" I imply that jurisdiction can belong to private firms as well as to the state. Control is mutually constrained. In exchange for the use of public resources, private industry grants the state some jurisdiction over industrial structure in the "national interest." Business enjoys privilege, systematic inclusion in the policy process, access to public goods, and rights of self-regulation. It reciprocates by agreeing to state jurisdiction in the definition of market structure and by participating in the distribution of benefits.

The nature and extent of that jurisdiction is permanently being adjusted; private firms continuously seek to separate state aid from state control. Both business and government have jurisdiction; both lack exclusive control. Each, at different times, will surrender the one to retain the other. Businessmen are invited into the interior processes of government, and bureaucrats are invited into the interior processes of the market. In short, business in government is exchanged for government in business. A focus on market transformations rather than on state structures reveals how that exchange is consummated. It also reveals how each competing group defines its own vision of a national interest while trying to transfer the costs of pursuing that interest to others.[18]

The notion of reciprocal consent assumes that states, no less than markets, are a function of shifting compacts. The analysis of these compacts can accept structured relations between state and society, but it must not reify them. It must allow for state autonomy without ignoring private strategies. It assumes permanent negotiations for the distribution of public and private power without attributing a consistent monopoly of jurisdiction or control to particular groups or actors. It disaggregates states and markets to specify strategies of exchange. In sum, it recognizes there is no a priori way to sort out patron and client in most policy settings.[19] This book explores the market to reconstruct this compact and to explain how and to what extent private preferences and state preferences, when they diverge, are reconciled. It thereby provides a record of where preferences originate and how they are articulated.

METHOD: POINT OF COMPACT AND CRITICAL CASE

State Enterprise as the Point of Compact

I begin where public and private preferences are likely to diverge most sharply—where states have become competitors of commercial firms in the mixed capitalist economies. The public sector was the principal growth industry in most industrial democracies from the end of World War II until the privatization boom of the mid-1980s.[20] European states still own all or part of nineteen of the continent's fifty largest industrial firms. By one estimate, in the early 1980s public enterprises accounted for about one-quarter of all productive investments in Western Europe.[21] Levels of public employment and public investment had never been higher.

But levels of public employment and public investment do not tell us all we need to know about how, why, when, and to what extent states intervene in their economies. Nor do they tell us why intervention so often takes the form of state ownership, nor even whether state ownership means the same thing in different settings. Indeed, the pervasiveness of governments in business blurs the distinction between public and private sectors in most capitalist economies, so that it is often impossible to say where firms properly belong and to whom they are properly accountable. When we map the organizational loci of state power and private resources, therefore, we must distinguish ownership from control. The important distinction to make is not between ideal types but among the ways in which governments go directly or indirectly into business in the mixed capitalist economies. In most cases the difference between the public and the private economy is so seldom clear that state ownership is a reliable measure neither of state capacity nor of state autonomy. But because public ownership is one among many choices for both bureaucrats and businessmen, it is a revealing "point of compact" for the politics of reciprocal consent.

If states can intervene in markets without assuming ownership, then a conscious choice of state ownership suggests that the creation of a state-owned firm is a political event. The struggle for control of productive resources is important; the struggle for ownership is ancillary. To evaluate the role of the state in market transformation, therefore, we need to examine the origins of state ownership rather than its organizational form. Consequently, state intervention in the amorphous area between the ideal types of public and private economies is of most immediate interest. It is complicated by the ways in which governments, in Charles Lindblom's words, often "share their formal authority with corporate officials as a benefit offered to induce business performance."[22] It is also complicated by the ways in which private firms willingly surrender jurisdiction to retain control of markets. These are organizational loci of the permanent adjustments of reciprocal consent. Analysis of state intervention here should illuminate the political determinants of market structure and yield answers to the empirical questions posed above.[23]

There are three common explanations for why states become market players: the tactical, the strategic, and the historical. The first is associated with the literature on public law and administration.[24] Tactical and pragmatic, it centers upon issues of control and accountability, often reflecting contradictions between state enterprises as instruments designed to increase public control and enhance public welfare and those designed to enhance flexibility through the circumvention of legal regulations. "The single common objective in creating agencies outside the government structure," Harold Seidman argues, "is to evade some or all of the controls applicable to government agencies, funds, officers, and employees."[25] Specialists debate personnel ceilings, civil service regulations, ways to go "off budget," debt limitations, and legislative oversight.

Strategic explanation aims to redress the allocative inefficiencies and imperfections of unregulated markets; it is often (but not exclusively) associated with a social democratic ideology.[26] The state establishes a market presence for itself to fulfill socioeconomic objectives that private firms, acting on their own, find too risky or unprofitable. Sectoral stagnation, regional imbalance, protection of infant industries from predatory foreign competitors, employment maintenance, provision of collective goods, and the socialization of private risk are all viewed as legitimate goals for direct state intervention where markets fail.[27] By applying criteria associated with social justice instead of profit alone, the state can promote broad goals of national development, national security, and national integration without directly threatening private accumulation.

Taken together, these two rationales are prescriptive and pragmatic. The tactical approach pulls and tugs less upon the structure of the economy than does the strategic, but both share a basic assumption about political control of the economy and the ability of the state to intervene for a broad good beyond specific private interests. That choices are limited by such factors as timing of industrialization, market structure, distribution of power within the state, and position of the state in the international political economy is usually acknowledged but left underexplored.[28]

The third, or historical, explanation for state ownership is concerned with these matters. In sketching a coherent political economy of state intervention, it comes close to integrating political struggles and strategic choice. It also incorporates cultural and historical variables to explain when, why, and to what extent states intervene in economies. Andrew Shonfield, for example, argues that planning is a functional requisite for industrial states, and he looks to the state's role in the preindustrial economy for clues to the capability of modern states.[29] He identifies an etatist tradition in modern France as a natural extension of established French forms of business-state relations. Alexander Gerschenkron and his successors, arguing that patterns of national development and the role of the state vary by when the state started industrializing, seek to identify the political origins of economic institutions and the interests mobilized to support them.[30] Backward nations require different instruments of state power to industrialize. Only in the earliest cases could private savings sustain the investment necessary for industrial development, so state investment banks appeared in France and Germany where none appeared in Britain. For the same reason, the Japanese state took direct control of shipbuilding, munitions, railways, and mining in their early years. In the Third World today the state enters the breach ever more vigorously to counteract the influence of multinational corporations and to make new technologies available to its nationals.

Other explanations for state intervention are rooted less in historical opportunities and constraints than in functional necessity, in the inexorable logic of capitalism and its contradictions. States grow increasingly interventionist at the behest of private interests to save the system from itself. As the state shifts from indirect mechanisms of allocation to direct mechanisms of production to preserve conditions for private accumulation, it becomes the ideal collective capitalist. The very survival of capitalism obliges the state to enter the market place, sometimes in opposition to parts of the capitalist class, other times at their behest.[31]

The former view (opposition to some capitalists) allows for the emergence of an autonomous state interest, even if that interest is no significant challenge to private accumulation. The latter view adheres to Marxian notions of the state as a captive instrument of private interests, summarized by Ralph Miliband: "Business predominance over other economic groups is to be found in the financial and credit institutions of the state and in the nationalized sector. The creation of that sector has often been thought of as removing an important activity from capitalist control and influence. But ... business has carved out an extremely strong place for itself in the directing organs of that sector."[32] Capitalists often support the nationalization of infrastructure and support services to socialize risk.

Clearly there are several ways to explain why states participate in markets. Most presuppose that a state, or some part of it, can act upon a determination of the general public interest. Some address only tactical concerns about organizational form. Others posit strategic motives, which they also premise upon state leadership. Historical explanation splits on this point but directs us to examine the broader context of reciprocal consent. Politics is implicit in each explanation, but none explains the ways in which control of productive resources is derived from political choice, and none is explicit about the ways in which competition and conflict among organized political interests determine the final organizational form of state intervention.[33]

Conflict over the control of productive resources, the pulling and

Extent of State Intervention	Nature of State Intervention	
	Producer	Banker
Market-Displacing	Rival	Creditor
Market-Conforming	Partner	Guarantor

Figure 1.1. The state in domestic markets

hauling of reciprocal consent, defines the nature and extent of direct state intervention in the industrial democracies. Private interests everywhere have struggled to separate state aid from state control; the extent of their success helps explain jurisdiction in structuring domestic markets. Two political choices are important. The first concerns the nature of state intervention: What is the state to do? Is the state a commercial or a financial player in the market? The state may produce goods or it may provide banking services (obviously it sometimes does both). The second choice concerns the extent of state intervention: How much can the state intervene? What is the state's role vis-à-vis competitive sectors, both commercial and financial, in the economy? The state may displace private banks or firms by competing with them, or it may conform to the existing market and enhance private competitiveness by supplying factors. Thus states can be rivals, partners, creditors, or guarantors of private firms in particular sectors of the economy.[34]

The choice among these options, sharpened by the politics of reciprocal consent, results in quite different forms of state intervention. In the United States, for example, the state virtually never competes with private firms in commercial markets. Yet public financial guarantees for mortgages, college tuition, small businesses, and failing multinational corporations are a large part of the federal budget.[35] The allocative powers of Japanese state credit institutions are even more extensive, in part because they are more extensively negotiated with private commercial firms and put more to commercial ends. In most of Western Europe, by contrast, the state is often the largest rival of private firms in specific markets such as steel, automobiles, coal, and shipbuilding.

Historical evidence adduced in this book suggests that the choices between commercial and financial instruments are related. In many cases, as in the United States and Japan, the state employs financial intervention when and where it fails to establish a direct market presence or is blocked by foreign or domestic groups following their own market strategies. Although credit allocation is an effective tool of the strong state,[36] the creditor or guarantor state may well be the least threatening, and hence the most acceptable, to private interests.

I propose that the politics of reciprocal consent is conditioned by six factors: market structure, centralization, developmental timing, openness, ruling coalitions, and administrative tradition.

Market Structure

The concentration of private power has been the staple of the analysis of business-government relations, which frequently posits the oligopolistic position of interest organizations vis-à-vis the state as the crucial variable determining the capacity of private interests to achieve their goals.[37] The presence and political significance of oligopoly, like state unity, is a matter of empirical inquiry. State capacity and private power both depend upon the centralization of resources and the concentration of interests, a simple indicator of which is the number of firms in a given sector and the nature of their organization—in short, market structure.

Let us begin with the simple proposition that unified actors will prevail over divided ones. We can expect cartelized or otherwise allied private interests to prevail over fragmented ones, which suggests the first of several hypotheses concerning the relative capacity of states vis-à-vis their energy industries. Oil firms, characterized by a high degree of vertical integration, and electric power firms, usually structured as natural monopolies, should be more influential than coal producers, who operate in a more fragmented environment.[38]

The diversification of interests may invite state intervention. When market players are divided or unorganized, we expect the state to be able to displace commercial or financial markets and to act as a rival or creditor of private firms. Direct state intervention is even more likely where no private interests exist.[39] State intervention is more likely to conform to markets, with the state a partner or a guarantor of private firms, in highly integrated, politically unified sectors of the economy.

Centralization

Centralization, the public-sector analogue of concentration, has two different meanings. As an antonym of fragmentation, it involves horizontal concentration of authority within a national bureaucracy. This centralization obtains when differences across bureaus are minimized by extensive coordination and by executive leadership. As an antonym of decentralization or local autonomy, centralization refers to the vertical concentration of responsibility for national administration.

Either way, the centralization of state power should enhance the capacity of the state to intervene in markets. Well-coordinated national executive power is often associated with mercantilist behavior. In strong states a highly professional bureaucratic apparatus enjoys jurisdiction in coordinating economic and industrial policies. States that speak with a single voice should displace private firms more often and more easily than should fragmented ones. Likewise, local and regional officials who defer to and depend upon central power should more readily respond to central officials' tutelage than to private actors seeking protection from state intervention.

In short, the centralized state should be better able to coordinate the politics of reciprocal consent and thereby control its intervention in markets. Such states are likely to enjoy a broad commercial presence as rivals or creditors when they seek such a presence in markets. Two related sets of propositions can help explain both sectoral concentration and state centralization, and thereby the nature and extent of state intervention. The first addresses the timing of industrial development, the second the openness of the economy.

Developmental Timing

The demands of late industrialization, Gerschenkron argues, lead to the development of large investment banks and often to an explicit role for the state. The proposition commonly derived from this thesis is that states will gain control in sectors where investment needs are large and "lumpy," usually where production is highly standardized. For this proposition, of course, energy is an archetype, especially in the early years of energy industries and in late-developing nations. More generally, any late-developing economy that turns to state intervention does so first by enhancing the capacity of the state. Functions and powers in a developing state are apt to become more centralized. Early interventions should be market-displacing when they are not market-creating. The state, when not directly engaged in production, acts as a creditor in financial markets.

At the same time, where capital becomes concentrated for developmental purposes, banks and states alike find it desirable to cartelize industry to control their investments. This complex of cartelized industry and industrial banks should, as James Kurth argues, be especially well-positioned to shape industrial structure and, in turn, state intervention.[40] We should therefore expect financial institutions to play a significant role in the determination of industrial structure and of the nature and extent of state intervention, especially early in industrialization. Timing should affect the politics of reciprocal consent through the intervening variables of centralization and concentration.

Openness

The notion that exposure to world markets and foreign investment explains differential capacities of states and societal groups in various nations is central to much research on the political economy of advanced industrial states. Peter Katzenstein, for example, argues that openness stimulates democratic corporatism in the small states of Western Europe. As economies become more open, their capacity to direct structural change diminishes. David Cameron suggests that the degree of openness as measured by dependence upon trade predicts the growth of the public economy.[41] Openness generates structural changes, including industrial concentration and unionization, that are conducive to the expansion of the public sector.

When a state, for whatever reason, cannot protect its domestic producers, it may perceive the need to own or regulate part or all of certain strategic sectors of the domestic economy. Prospects for direct (and market-displacing) intervention thus increase where foreign firms dominate the private sector. Political coalitions that advocate state intervention and even public ownership are likely to coalesce around sectors dominated by foreign interests. Under these circumstances we should expect a competitive state presence as a producer in the market. Openness should stimulate concentration and centralization, and it should spur state intervention in strategic sectors.

Ruling Coalitions

State intervention in the economy will also depend, regardless of other conditions, upon the nature of the ruling coalition. Coalitions of bureaucrats and politicians will vary in breadth of constituency and in stability of authority. The balance of power between groups of policy elites will also vary over time and across nations. State intervention will probably be market-conforming and the state will play a financial role where governing coalitions are broadly constituted and the politics of reciprocal consent is stable. Breadth and stability should enhance trust among coalition members, providing opportunities for reciprocity and compacts that are precluded in unstable, rapidly shifting regimes. Ruling coalitions that break sharply with the past and are narrowly constituted are apt to be associated with a more competitive state presence in the economy. Such regimes will be associated with market-displacing industrial policies because their constituents cannot afford protracted negotiations over state intervention. These ruling coalitions cannot guarantee that jurisdictions negotiated today will be accepted tomorrow.

Administrative Tradition

The composition of a ruling coalition depends ultimately upon its inheritance from the past. French industrial policies express the nation's etatist tradition; in America, however, business came of age before the state, and a weakly institutionalized state responds to its weakness through regulation, one of the few options open to it.[42] This regulatory presence has become part of an administrative tradition identified with the weak state and with self-regulation by market players.

Surely historical precedents shape elite estimates of possible policy. States with interventionist pasts can be expected to pursue interventionist futures. This unexceptionable proposition has a counterintuitive corollary, however, what G. John Ikenberry calls the irony of state strength: policy planners unconstrained by an interventionist tradition may enjoy greater flexibility than their counterparts in countries where state intervention is more fully institutionalized.[43] Inherited, institutional commitments to particular forms of state action may be less efficacious than inherited commitments to market conformity.

In sum, I suggest six propositions that should help explain the nature and extent of state intervention. State intervention should be market-displacing when:

the targeted industry is fragmented vertically or isolated horizontally from other sectors;

the state is highly centralized either vertically, vis-à-vis local and regional governments, or horizontally, with a consolidated national bureaucracy;

the economy is undergoing late development or reconstruction, especially when this involves a concentration of financial resources;

the targeted industry is vulnerable in world markets;

the ruling coalition is narrow and unstable; and

there is an "administrative tradition" of state intervention.

The interdependence of these propositions and their causal hierarchy are not developed in this chapter. The cases of Chapters 2–6 refine their interactive effects, and the concluding chapter develops an empirically informed set of multivariate explanations for state intervention in the industrial democracies.

Japanese Energy as the Critical Case

Relations between state and society and between business and government, I believe, can be illuminated by a critical case study.[44] The purpose is to either support or refute propositions by applying them to the most difficult case one can find. Japanese energy policy is just such an analytically strategic case. Japan and the energy industries are each critical in different ways. Each offers a "most likely" scenario for state strength, state autonomy, and convergence. Taken together they represent a rare opportunity for the analysis of business-government relations in the industrial democracies.

Energy

Nowhere is there a less ambiguous test of state strength and state autonomy than in the energy sector. Energy policy, especially after 1973, should least reflect societal influences on states struggling to cope with fiscal and industrial adjustment. Strategic concerns, specifically those associated with the acquisition of stable supplies of petroleum, should a priori be less hospitable to societal demands than other sectors where society, polity, and economy seem less vulnerable. Moreover, the energy sector is an obvious candidate for state intervention if only because the state enjoys a comparative advantage over private interests in foreign policy.[45] The dependence of many industrial economies upon foreign energy supplies invites the intervention of the state.

The state should be especially strong in energy industries for another reason: energy markets are among the most standardized of markets. Because energy trade in gas, coal, and oil is commodity-based, policy planners need concern themselves only with production and distribution. They need not worry about market niches and product development as they might in electronics, automobiles, or machine tools. As state planners and private manufacturers alike see energy industries as upstream prerequisites for industrial development, we should expect these sectors to be early targets for state intervention.

Both points are easily asserted in an era of oil crises, Middle Eastern political instability, and interfuel substitution, but a similar argument holds for the interwar period and the wartime that interwar energy choices helped create. States have seldom been more assertive than they were in the 1920s, when they sought protection from foreign control through state ownership in the various energy industries, particularly oil.[46] If there is state autonomy to be discovered and state leadership to be evaluated, we are likely to find them in the energy industries.

Japan

Japan contributes even more unambiguously to a critical case for the analysis of business-state relations in the industrial democracies. Theories about state and society in Japan have long been at odds with central theoretical drifts elsewhere. In the West liberal and Marxist approaches to state and society share the fundamental assumption that societal preferences prevail when they diverge from state preferences.[47] Japan, on the other hand, has a long tradition of explicitly including the state in the explanation of economic development. One description of Meiji Japan gives the flavor of that interpretative tradition: "The Japanese state's awesome ability to extract unlimited compliance from its subjects and to mobilize all of the economy's resources for specific goals of the state indicates a perfect synchronization of polity, society, and economy."[48] The analytical notion of "bringing the state back in" is thus ipso facto curious to generations of Japan scholars who have assumed a pervasive state in the economy. Put simply, Japan is the most unambiguous case of state autonomy and strength.

Analyses of business-state relations in Japan rest on four often contradictory assumptions. In identifying the Japanese state, many analysts have posited harmony among interests in society. This book explores conflict. In assessing the relative autonomy of the Japanese state, most observers posit state independence and state control. This book separates independence from interdependence and control from jurisdiction. In evaluations of state capacity, the dominant view of Japan has been one of strength and, often, prescience. This book explores constraints and fortuity, occasionally discovering weakness. Finally, accounts of Japanese development have stressed inexorability. I examine choices and contingencies in an effort to restore bounded indeterminacy to models of the Japanese political economy. I explore each of these points briefly.

Views of a harmonious, consensual, monolithic "Japan, Inc." have fallen on hard times in recent years, and for good reason. A useful notion has been unfairly exaggerated.[49] It identified an interlocking directorate of competing elites from big business, the Liberal Democratic party, and the bureaucracy who, through institutionalized and exhaustive consultation and negotiation, reached consensus. Agreements could be enforced because of the stability of the Japanese elite. State and society were difficult to untangle. In its original formulation Japan, Inc. remains a valuable description of how the system works; no more elegant formulation has yet been developed. Unfortunately, popularizers chose to ignore competition within the ruling triangle, opting instead to explain Japanese competitiveness—and indeed the very identity of the competitor—as a monolithic, consensual, machinelike organism bent upon national aggrandizement.[50]

Two groups of scholars reject this simplified and teleological view of the Japanese political economy. Liberal economists deny that markets can be so orderly or even that the state could have played so determinant a role in Japanese development.[51] Political scientists point to the political significance of groups outside the triangle, demonstrating how important decisions are made through political conflict.[52] This book builds upon these efforts, looking to reconcile notions of conflict and consensus in the Japanese policy process without doing violence to the one by overstating the other. The identity of the Japanese state may, in the final evaluation, look very much like the interpenetrated, collusive Japan, Inc. of days past. But we need to identify the mechanisms of collusion and interpenetration. We also need to recognize that consensus, even where we find it, is the product of conflict rather than the alternative to it.

Questions of autonomy and development are closely connected to this point, and scholars have entertained a curious ambivalence on the issue. Bernard Silberman assumes the most extreme position. He speaks of a period of bureaucratic absolutism (1868–1900), followed by a limited pluralism under which the state was *primus inter pares* with private interests (1900–1936). In his view the Japanese state ultimately emerges as the organizer of all interests during a period of state corporatism (1936–45). He insists that "from the very beginning of the Restoration, the state played a dominant role in the organization of interests and the determination of public policy" and that during the 1930s "the state foreclosed on all concepts of interests." His Japanese state is an autonomous actor driving to depoliticize interests and substitute administration for politics to solve the central problem of the era—the governability of society. T. J. Pempel and K. Tsunekawa seem to concur. They argue that Japan between 1938 and 1945 was an "almost perfectly congruent example of state corporatism. . . . [By 1940] all autonomous interest associations were replaced by a monolithic organ of totalistic state control."[53] In political histories, then, the Japanese state looms large.

Economic histories have always cast the state as the central actor in Japanese economic development, but they have been more careful to incorporate a role for private interests. Jerome Cohen, for example, sees early Japanese development as "nurtured in a virtual state incubator," but he also sees how industrial interests unwilling to bow to the demands of the military and the economic bureaucracy compromised state efforts to separate management from capital.[54] Other students of the development of capitalism in Japan concur. Some Japanese scholars stress the role of political merchants (*seishō*) who learned early in the Meiji era how to use the state to protect themselves from excessive risk.[55] Others focus upon the state-sanctioned cartels and industry-specific legislation of mid-century Japan.[56] The consensus among economic historians is that, as Barrington Moore put it, "Japanese big business successfully resisted attempts to subordinate profits to patriotism."[57]

This point is too often overlooked because the confusion of jurisdiction with control is accompanied by a confusion of state autonomy with state capacity. The developmental state is often confused with the strong state. Chalmers Johnson suggests, for example, that most of the ideas for postwar reconstruction "came from the bureaucracy and the business community responded with . . . responsive dependence."[58] Ironically, this confusion has been more pronounced recently than it was even during wartime mobilization. Pempel and Tsunekawa argue, for example, that MITI's power to intervene "was much more institutionalized and corporatized than anything big business had encountered during the prewar period."[59] Analysts have groped for explanations, stressing the state's capacity to intervene in the Japanese economy at the expense of clear explanations for the ways in which markets and market players help shape that intervention. All analysts acknowledge the role of the private sector, but most stress the power of the state.

Most available descriptions of the Japanese political economy exaggerate state power at the expense of private power, as if the two were mutually exclusive; they use such terms as guided free enterprise, state-led capitalism, administered competition, quasi-capitalism, and bureaucratic inclusionary pluralism.[60] In contrast, when the Japanese are asked who governs, in public opinion surveys, they uniformly ascribe far greater power to the politicians, bosses, and big businessmen than to the bureaucrats.[61] But the bureaucracy gets the credit from scholars and, certainly, from elite bureaucrats themselves. Johnson's observation that "the elite bureaucracy of Japan makes most major decisions, drafts virtually all legislation, controls the national budget, and is the source of all major policy innovations in the system" is now widely quoted, ignoring the author's own caveats and more balanced observations about pressure groups and the private sector.[62]

Because so much recent scholarship has been concerned with comparative evaluations of how and how effectively states are able to intervene in their economies, the overstatement of the importance of key actors, particularly the state, in the Japanese policy process has important implications. Few studies of Japanese economic policy by Japan specialists are overtly comparative, and many overtly comparative studies of Japan are not by specialists; perhaps as a result, most work on contemporary Japan stresses the strength of the state rather than the constraints upon it. But the developmental state need not be the archetypical strong state; the comprehensive visions and role of the Japanese state do not necessarily resemble those of France more than those of the United States.

These distinctions have a significance beyond a better understanding of business-state relations in Japan. Japan's late industrialization and economic success have reinforced the idea that there is only one economic rationality, that of a standardized, efficient, and centralized productive machine. Japan has been portrayed as the very embodiment of economic modernity.[63] If this is so, it should nowhere be easier to demonstrate than when the Japanese state intervenes directly in the energy market place.

By examining energy and Japan as a critical case, and by subjecting market transformations to comparative and historical analysis, this book demonstrates that considerable diversity survives in state-market relationships. We ought not to assume state leadership a priori—not even in late-developing, homogeneous nations where conditions for decisive state leadership are most propitious. The book thereby illuminates the broader issues of state identity, autonomy, capacity, and development associated with the political economy of industrial democracies.

CHAPTER TWO

State-owned Energy Corporations in the Industrial Democracies

STATE OWNERSHIP OF ENERGY RESOURCES

Most industrial democracies are mixed economies in which the state is predominantly a producer, either as a rival or as a partner of private energy firms (see Figure 1.1). Despite its rich entrepreneurial history, the Japanese state is neither. Although nineteenth-century reformers quickly assumed the commanding heights of the economy through state ownership, that ownership was just as quickly transferred to private investors.[1] Public and private actors have been engaged ever since in a perpetual adjustment of jurisdiction and control over markets. Their negotiations over state intervention have been at the fulcrum of business-government relationships, and their mutual accommodations have resulted uniformly in market-conforming state intervention. The Japanese state, unlike most European ones, has assumed the role of banker, usually as a guarantor of private investment in energy businesses.

In this chapter I develop two perspectives on these contrasting configurations. The first is cross-sectional. I systematically review institutional differences as they currently obtain in the oil, coal, and electric power sectors in the industrial democracies. State ownership in each sector is associated with specific strategic concerns that shape the negotiations between state and business over the jurisdiction of each in the economy. The second perspective is historical. I explore the origins of state ownership, the "points of compact" between business and the state, in important European cases. I select these cases to illustrate patterns of conflict over the nature and extent of state intervention and to illuminate through empirical detail the propositions presented in Chapter 1. This chapter thereby provides comparative referents for the analyses of Japan which follow.

Public ownership of energy resources in the industrial states is greater today than ever before. Of the nearly one-hundred OECD state-owned energy firms whose founding I have been able to date, half were established after 1965.[2] Eleven of Europe's fifty largest firms are public energy corporations, among them two of the three largest corporate entities in France (CFP and SNEA), the single largest enterprise in West Germany (VEBA), and the second largest corporation in Italy (ENI). One-hundred percent publicly owned enterprises enjoy nearly 100 percent market shares for gas in Switzerland, the United Kingdom, France, and Ireland; for coal in France, and the United Kingdom; and for electric power in Austria, France, Greece, Ireland, Italy, and the United Kingdom. National oil firms in which the state is the largest shareholder dominate the domestic markets of Italy, France, Austria, Portugal, Spain, and Finland.

In France the ratio of public investment to total investment in energy is thirty times greater than for the economy as a whole excluding energy. In Italy it is three times greater.[3] Rare is the energy sector in an advanced industrial nation without a major public enterprise. Usually, moreover, the state-owned energy corporation is a commercial leader, and energy is the leading sector for public investment.[4]

Broadly speaking, there are three rationales offered for state participation in energy markets through the acquisition of equity in commercial firms: salvage, scale, and security. Each is related directly to strategic concerns of national states seeking to enhance their competitiveness in the international economy. Each is also linked to one energy business more closely than to others; in reviewing these links I map the variety of public-corporate solutions to the politics of energy security in the industrial democracies. I begin with coal, where state intervention has the richest history.

KING COAL—WHOSE SOVEREIGN?

In many industrial states, political demands for preventing the collapse of whole industries and regions have combined with the successful interventions of organized labor and affiliated political parties to establish the public management of coal. Interventions have been closely related to the strategic justification for public enterprise in capitalist economies reviewed in Chapter 1: the pursuit of social goals that existing markets cannot and will not serve. One key to the nationalization of coal has been the need for industrial states to respond effectively to dramatic reductions in the consumption of domestically produced primary energy. In West Germany, Belgium, Britain, and Spain the coal industries were completely or partly salvaged by the state when they faced imminent collapse.

Between the two world wars coal suffered from the challenge of cheaper oil amid deeply depressed industrial activity. Governments, under pressure from producers, often intervened to prop up domestic coal prices. Many coal industries were nationalized, and in marked contrast to the profitability of oil, most publicly managed coal companies have faced perpetual deficits and dependence upon state subsidy.

The identification of state coal corporations with the salvage of domestic industry and labor maintenance masks some of the diversity among forms of direct state participation, however. Each of the state-owned mining firms in the industrial democracies is engaged in predominantly commercial activities, as Table 2.1 indicates.

The state produces most frequently for the domestic market, but some coal-rich OECD states are actively engaged in the export business. Ruhr-kohle, for example, exports nearly one-quarter of its production. Of the five states best endowed with coal—Australia, Canada, West Germany, Britain, and the United States—only the United States leaves coal production and marketing entirely to the private sector. Yet even in the United States most western coal reserves are owned by the federal government and leased to mining companies.[5]

Coal-importing industrial states rely almost uniformly upon state-owned firms. France, Greece, Italy, Portugal, and Spain have all created government corporations to handle steam coal imports for their electric utilities (all of which, except for Spain's, are state-owned monopolies). In Italy, in addition, the state oil firm is active in overseas coal mining ventures. France's CDF, founded in 1946, monopolizes the domestic market while ATIC, a nonprofit association of coal importers (mostly nationalized industries) acts as a buyers' cooperative under the Ministry of Industry to monopolize coal imports.[6] In Finland, Canada, and New Zealand the state participates directly in coal mining at the provincial level. In Austria coal production is the responsibility of public managers of electric utilities. As coal-derived liquids and gases grew price-competitive with petroleum in the late 1970s, moreover, states without a commercial presence, such as the United States and Japan, created public corporations to develop new applications for coal-derived synthetic fuels.

This snapshot of current ownership reveals the ubiquity of the state in coal markets and suggests the relationship between this sector and the broader strategic concerns of industrial democracies. Yet it reveals little about balances of public and private power; we cannot infer control from ownership. To understand how and why the state attained its role

Table 2.1. State-owned coal corporations, 1986

	Year founded	% public	Domestic market share	Comments
Australia				
State government electricity authorities	Varies	100%	12% bituminous extraction 100% lignite extraction	Australia is a net coal exporter, but private sector controls exports.
Austria				
Oesterreichische Verbundgesell-schaft (OV)	1947	100%	95% extraction and sales	O.V. is also an electricity utility.
Belgium				
Kempense Steen-kolenmijnen N.V.	Pre-WWII	77%	33%	Government holds only active mine. Last private mine shut down 1984
Canada				
Regional authorities	Varies	—	more than 50% (extraction)	Provincial Crown Corporations.
Petro-Canada	1975	100%	0%	Petro-Canada acquired large coal holdings in 1978 and can extract it with government approval. Not currently producing coal.
Denmark				
Regional authorities	Varies	—	90% (sales)	Coal importing done by public power corporations.
Finland				
Vapo Oy	1984	100%	80%	Peat and wood pulp compete against coal. No coal produced in Finland.
France				
Charbonnages de France (CdF)	1946	100%	45% (sales)	CdF and region authorities together account for almost 100% of France's coal production. ATIC is responsible for coal importation.
Regional authorities	Varies	100%	—	
Association Technique de l'Importation Charbonnière (ATIC).	1945	100%	55% (sales)	

Table 2.1. (Continued)

	Year founded	% public	Domestic market share	Comments
Germany				
Ruhrkohle A.G.	1968	14%	70% (extraction)	
Saarbergwerke	—	75%	11% (extraction)	
Greece				
Public Electricity Undertaking	—	100%	100% (bituminous extraction)	Lignite extraction still in private hands.
Holland				
Dutch State Mines (DSM)	—	—	—	Coal production ended in 1960s. DSM still active in natural gas and chemicals.
Italy				
Ente Nazionale d'Idrocarburi (ENI)	1953	100%	—	Italy is a net coal importer.
Ente Nazionale per l'Energia Elettrica (ENEL)	1962	100%	—	ENI and ENEL together have monopoly on domestic extraction.
EN-Oxy	1981	59%	—	Joint venture with Occidental Petroleum.
Japan				
Japan Coal Development Co.	1980	30%	—	EPDC holds government share.
Electric Power Overseas Coal Corp.	1980	75%	—	EPDC holds government share.
Coal Mine Damage Corp.	1963	100%	—	MITI Affiliate. Financial instrument.
New Zealand				
State Mines	Varies	100%	—	Public entities together account for two-thirds of coal production.
Regional authorities	Varies	100%	—	
Spain				
Empresa Nacional Hulleras del Norte (HUNOSA)	1967	100%	—	HUNOSA runs coal mines in Asturia.
Empresa Nacional Carbonera del Sur	1961	83%	—	

(continued)

Table 2.1. (Continued)

	Year founded	% public	Domestic market share	Comments
Minas de Figaredo S.A.	1932	100%	—	Runs coal mines; became 100% public capital in 1980.
Empresa Nacional Adaro de Investigaciones Mineras (ENADISMA)	1942	100%	—	Development of exploration, supply, and uses of raw materials.
Sweden Svensk Kolkon- sortium A.B.	—	50%	—	25% equity held by Vattenfall (State Electricity Board); 25% by Stratsforetag A.B. (publicly held).
United Kingdom National Coal Board	1946	100%	95% (sales) 98% (extraction)	Operates on deficit grant basis but government financial aid is geared toward achieving breakeven by Financial Year 1986–7. Since 1980 a ceiling on grants from Treasury.

as market player, we need to explore the political origins of state owner-ship of coal. The politics of reciprocal consent has involved struggles for control of markets which illuminate the ways in which the state lurches toward particular forms of domestic intervention.

Great Britain

Perhaps the most illuminating history, especially for its parallels to the Japanese case, is that of the British nationalization of coal mining.[7] His-torically, coal was Britain's greatest basic industry. It was also the first British industry to be nationalized by a Labour government. Nationaliza-tion came in 1946, three decades after it was first seriously discussed, but it came only after the industry had virtually exhausted itself and the mineowners' resistance to the idea had dissipated. The state displaced the market and became a producer after more than a generation of political struggle.

State intervention in the British mining industry began with child labor laws in the early nineteenth century. Many decades later came safety legislation and wage guarantees. Industrial labor unrest in Britain during the First World War centered in the coal mines, and in 1918 the Labour party, with its "gas and water socialists," endorsed nationalization. The program was opposed by the mineowners and defeated in the House of Commons in February 1920.

But the British coal industry was already in decline, and foreign producers were usurping British markets at home and abroad. A highly fragmented industry (more than two thousand separate firms) found it difficult to manage itself or its relation to the state. In 1925 the Samuel Commission called for full reorganization of the industry, and the British government agreed to provide £23 million in subsidies to private owners who might cooperate. But the following year the miners rejected reorganization in a week-long strike over wage cuts. Ultimately the strike was broken; so too, for the time being, were plans for nationalization of the industry.

By 1930 the industry had fallen into a wretched state. Owners had invested little in capital equipment, and they needed rescue as desperately as the miners needed justice, but they were not yet inclined to support outright nationalization. Instead, they negotiated with the government a cartel system: legislation in 1930 invested the Central Council of Mine Owners with the authority to limit and allocate production and to set minimum prices. Mineowners successfully opposed provisions in the initial draft to establish a state-led commission with the power to force consolidation. Backing away, the government urged "autonomous" consolidation with state control as the last resort.

In the end the reform failed under the weight of its own contradictions and changing political circumstances. So did the British mining industry. Once the full effect of the Depression was felt, cheating began on the cartel system, eroding minimum price levels. By 1932 the system was in disarray. There were still more than two thousand separate mines producing an average of just over one hundred thousand tons of coal per year. Although the number of mines would decline faster than output over the next decade, the number of miners would decline even faster. Those workers who remained in the pits would be among the most militant in the British trade union movement. Those owners who remained in the business would be among the most grasping in the private sector.

Mobilization for World War II gave the British government its first taste of mine management. In May 1941 it applied the Essential Work Order to the coal mining industry, thereby assuming the power to hire, fire, and discipline workers. The state guaranteed wages, but miners were prohibited from leaving for higher-paid jobs in the munitions industry. Britain thus instituted state control of the work force as well as state control of the mines. Coal miners, already among the lowest-paid industrial workers in the country, deeply resented what they viewed as the formal endorsement of their social inferiority.

By spring 1942 the maintenance of coal production had become a central issue. In April Sir John Anderson, the minister responsible for wartime economic policy, proposed to the War Cabinet that the state should assume ownership of the collieries. The lines were quickly drawn: industry representatives defended the status quo while the Miners' Federation pressed strongly for nationalization. Various compromise proposals were entertained, but Conservative ministers, under pressure from mineowners, forced the withdrawal of all plans for rationing, requisitioning, and nationalization. Ultimately the state opted for a "dual control," under which mineowners retained their property while management became the responsibility of the Board of Trade.

In October 1943 debate over the relative merits of dual control and nationalization again flared in the Commons. Conservatives wanted increased state powers to discipline miners, reduce absenteeism, and allow the use of soldiers in the pits. Labourites countered that if the situation was so bad, nationalization was the only solution. Churchill abruptly closed the debate by challenging Labour to an election that would center on the issue. Labour backed off, accepting Churchill's reminder of their coalition's basic principle: "All for war, even if controversial, but nothing controversial unless it serves the war effort."[8]

With the war won, the government examined the future of the coal-mining industry. The Reid Committee Report of March 1945 sought to explain national disparities in mine productivity. They found in Britain low or no investment in mechanization, the absence of standards, no economies of scale, hostile labor-management relations, and dispersed ownership that inhibited consolidation and the closing of inefficient pits. Public opinion was deeply hostile to the owners, and so were industrial leaders from other sectors (some of whom sat on the Reid Committee). Bills for compulsory reorganization had already been presented to the Commons with Conservative support.

The Labour party achieved its first parliamentary majority in July 1945. Workers as well as leaders of coal-consuming heavy industries supported nationalization—proposals for state control of the mines had never been a leftist monopoly in Britain. Conservative governments throughout the 1930s had modified the coal cartel system, circumscribing the autonomy of mineowners, and after all it was Churchill's coalition government that was prepared to implement the Reid Report. Moreover, a significant number of mineowners apparently saw profits in exiting this business. As M. W. Kirby writes,

> if the miners and the Labour Party were committed to nationalization on the grounds of political and social justice it would be fair to say that in economic terms the history of the coal mining industry in the twentieth century dictated that no great issue of principle would be involved for the Conservative party. . . . This is also confirmed by the attitude of the colliery owners themselves. There were obvious financial advantages in acquiescing in nationalization with generous compensation . . . [implemented with] almost indecent haste.[9]

Emanuel Shinwell, minister of fuel and power for the new Labour government, later reported that while "the miners expected [nationalization] almost as a wave of the ministerial wand, the owners were hardly less anxious to get out of the pits—on terms . . ."[10] And those terms were generous. Compensation to the owners amounted initially to £165 million, swelling ultimately to £388 million paid with interest to the year 2006. Benefits to coal-consuming industries were also significant. Steel, for example, received coking coal supplied from the Durham pits at a loss by the new state-run Coal Board. By 1957, moreover, mineworkers had become the highest-paid group in Great Britain. In the end, nationalization helped entrench interests that staved off the decline of domestic coal as Britain's primary industrial fuel longer than free access to world petroleum markets might have permitted; it also presented the state with what has been described as "a ruined and bankrupt industry with the most out-of-date equipment . . . in the whole of Western Europe."[11]

The extended political struggle over the nature and extent of state intervention in the British mining industry was partially replicated elsewhere in Europe. In France, for example, a more consolidated coal industry, in which twenty-three firms accounted for 90 percent of production, was also nationalized in 1946.[12] French Communists emerged from the war with an electoral plurality at a time of extreme miner unrest. They supported the creation of Charbonnages de France in 1946 and were joined by small mineowners who were exempted from nationalization and, tacitly, by industrialists who would benefit from subsidized factor costs.

Perhaps the most striking historical case is that of the Ruhr coal syndicate.[13] Founded in 1893, Ruhrkohle is often considered the world's first modern industrial cartel. Although its awesome concentration of resources did not protect it completely from the kaiser's regulation, it fared well under Hitler's program of "industrial self-administration." In fact, it fared well precisely because it so frustrated the economic policy of the Nazi regime. Throughout the Nazi period Ruhrkohle waged guerrilla warfare against state-led rationalization campaigns. It refused to accept state production targets or to participate in energy planning. Although they refused to cooperate actively with the Nazi synthetic fuels effort, the coal producers extracted from the state operating autonomy, labor discipline, and large subsidies. As in wartime Japan, wartime state controls in Germany which should have reflected a highly refined form of state intervention were actually less direct than those achieved in Britain.

These cases indicate the importance of several of the hypotheses presented in Chapter 1. The Ruhrkohle case is powerfully suggestive of the capacity of highly integrated capital to thwart the market interventions of even the most totalitarian state. The British and French nationalizations are related to market structure and openness; there interfuel competition on open international markets crippled domestic coal industries and invited state intervention. The most directly relevant variable, however, is shifts in the ruling coalition. State ownership in Britain and France, in particular, was facilitated by the election of left-labor governments. Japan differed on the breadth and stability of the ruling coalition, which will be central to our explanation for observed institutional differences between market-conforming and market-displacing intervention. But the Japanese modus vivendi of reciprocal consent is also related to the concentration of domestic energy markets. The political relevance of concentration is best illustrated by comparisons in the electric power sector.

ELECTRIC POWER AND POLITICAL POWER

No energy business has a more nearly ubiquitous state presence than electric power. Nowhere is electric power generated and sold entirely for private profit; even the U.S. government is in the electric power business in a significant way. The federal government operates large-scale, regionally based electric utilities such as the Tennessee Valley Authority and Bonneville Power; municipalities and counties own utilities as well. In Japan, all power delivered to end-users is sold by one of nine private regional monopolies; but the Electric Power Development Corporation is a MITI-affiliated joint public/private venture that generates some power for wholesale distribution to the electric utilities.

Eight of the world's fifteen largest electric power companies, all eight either American or Japanese, are privately owned. But state-owned monopolies are the usual form of organization for the industry. Often the management and ownership of public utilities are decentralized to subnational levels of government, as in Switzerland, Canada, Belgium, West Germany, and Australia. These public utilities nearly always dominate their domestic markets, and only infrequently (as in the West German case) do they generate electric power for export to neighboring states.

There is an important extension of public ownership in the area of nuclear power. The technological, financial, and safety risks associated with the development of nuclear power have compelled most states to establish public monopolies over nuclear R&D, including prototype and demonstration reactors. This tendency has been especially pronounced in more advanced nuclear power technology, such as breeders, where economic prospects are poorest.[14]

Seldom do national states or regional authorities participate in their electric power firms with less than full public ownership (see Table 2.2). In state-owned coal mines and national oil corporations there is greater diversity in patterns of ownership, and states are often rivals of private firms. Here, however, the state is less often a rival than a partner, supplying a basic factor of production at socialized cost.

Indeed, governments justify their direct involvement as a partner of consumers by invoking economies of scale and natural monopolies. The economic argument for treating electricity as a utility is straightforward. Electric power differs from petroleum in the economics of transportation. There are more ways to transport oil economically than to transport electricity, and this diversity provides oil with what economists call close substitutability, making it more suitable for competition in the market place. In the absence of easy substitution, and because the long-run average cost of electric power decreases in relation to the size of its total market (a necessary though not sufficient condition for natural monopoly), economists treat electric power differently from other commodities.

But why treat electric power as a *public* utility? There is no purely economic rationale for distinguishing between state participation through public management and through regulation. Advocates of publicly owned monopolies in this sector must provide the same sorts of political or social rationale which justify direct state participation in other sectors in which governments are in business. In Canada, for example, almost two-thirds of the total assets of provincial Crown Corporations are held by electric utilities; as Aidan Vining notes, public ownership "has arisen from . . . a fear that the particular controlling monopolist would be detrimental to other capitalist and sectarian groups, especially middle-class industrial and manufacturing inter-

Table 2.2. State-owned electric utilities, 1986

	Year founded	% public	Domestic market share	Comments
Australia				
Regional authorities	1920s	100%	92%	Produce coal for their own use.
Austria				
Oesterreichische Verbunde- gesellschaft (OV)	1947	100%	95%	
Belgium				
Public corporations	Varies	100%	12% (distribution) 2% (generation)	3% state capital in nuclear plants,
Mixed corporations	Varies	1–50%	47% (distribution)	97% private.
ONDRAF/NIRAS	1981	100%	—	Nuclear waste management. Nonprofit.
SYNATOM	1981	50%	—	Aspects of fuel cycle not covered by ONDRAF/ NIRAS. 50% of capital held by three private electric companies: EBES 20%, INTERCOM 20%, UNERG 10%
BELGOPROCESS	1984	99%	—	Subsidiary of SYNATOM. Fuel- cycle processes.
CEN/SCK	—	—	—	Nuclear research agency.
BELGONUCLEAIRE	1957	50%	—	Nuclear reactor design, fuel development, and treatment. Private sector holdings: 16.9% EBES; 16.9% INTERCOM; 8.8% Soc. Gen. de Belgique.
Canada				
Ten regional authorities	Varies	100%	—	Nine of these supply 80–99% of electricity used in their regions.
Atomic Energy of Canada, Ltd.	1952	100%	—	R&D, engineering, and marketing of CANDU reactor.

Table 2.2. (*Continued*)

	Year founded	% public	Domestic market share	Comments
Denmark				
Regional authorities	Varies	100%	99.9%	Three regional authorities: Elkraft, Elsam, and Oestkraft. Some electricity imported from Sweden and Norway.
Finland				
Imatran Vaima Oy	1932	100%	40–45%	
Kemi jdki Oy	1954	96%	8%	
France				
Electricité de France (EdF)	1946	100%	89% (generation) 96% (sales)	5% of national electricity produced by CdF).
Commissariat de l'Energie Atomique (CEA)	1945	100%	—	Nuclear R&D.
Compagnie Générale des Matières Nucleaires (COGEMA)	1945	100%	100% (extraction)	Nuclear fuel production, mining.
Germany				
Vereinigte Industrie Unternehmungen A.G. (VIAG)	1923	100%	5%	Originally formed to salvage German aluminum production. VIAG holds interests in regional utilities, including Bayer Werke. One thousand firms supply electric power, 2/3 are publicly owned.
Regional and mixed authorities	Varies	—	—	
Greece				
Public Electricity Undertaking	1950	100%	100%	
Ireland				
Electricity Supply Board	1927	100%	100% (sales and generation)	

(*continued*)

Table 2.2. (Continued)

	Year founded	% public	Domestic market share	Comments
Italy				
Ente Nazionale per l'Energia Elettrica (ENEL)	1962	100%	90% (sales)	A few municipalities also sell electricity.
AGIP Nuclear	—	11.3%	100%	ENI subsidiary, imports uranium.
Nuclear and Alternative Energy Co. (ENEA)	1982	100%	—	
SIGEN	1979	over 50%	—	IRI subsidiary, operates nuclear power plants.
SOPREN	1979	over 50%	—	IRI subsidiary operates nuclear power plants.
Japan				
Electric Power Development Co. (EPDC)	1952	72%	0%	MITI affiliate, electricity wholesaler. Relatively diversified holdings.
Power Reactor and Nuclear Fuel Corp. (PNC)	1967	95%	0%	STA affiliate. Power reactor demonstration projects.
Japan Atomic Energy Research Institute	1956	98%	0%	STA affiliate. Nuclear R&D.
Luxemburg				
Cie. Grand-Ducale d'Electricité du Luxembourg (CEGEDEL)	1928	41%	59%	Distribution
Ste. Electrique de l'Our (SEO)	1951	40%	20%	Generation.
Ste. Luxembourgeoise d'energie nucleaire (SENU)	1974	50%	0%	Company to plan a nuclear power plant; finance for plant is private.
Netherlands				
Regional authorities	Varies	100%	—	

Table 2.2. (*Continued*)

	Year founded	% public	Domestic market share	Comments
Ultracentrifuge Nederland (UCN)	—	10%	—	Nuclear fuel processing Dutch State Mines holds a 10% share.
New Zealand				
Regional authorities	1925	100%	—	These together account for 100%
New Zealand electricity	1914	—	—	of electricity production and sales.
Norway				
Norwegian Water Resources and Electricity Board	1880s	100%	38%	
Regional authorities			47%	
Spain				
Empresa Nacional de Electricidad (ENDESA)	1944	97.9%	—	Production and distribution of electricity. Capital held by Instituto Nacional de Industria. Majority stockholder in three other power companies and one coal company.
Empresa Nacional de Uranio, S.A.	1972	100%	—	Supervises privately operated nuclear power plants.
Sweden				
Statens Vatten-fallsverk (Swedish State Power Board, SSPB).	1909	100%	35%	Operates nuclear, hydro, and fossil fueled power plants of main electric grid in about 70% of country.
Sydkraft A.B. (SKAB)	1910	60%	30%	Operates same types of plants as SSPB. Public capital is from local communities. Grid covers about 25% of country.

(*continued*)

Table 2.2. (Continued)

	Year founded	% public	Domestic market share	Comments
Oskarshamns Kraftgrupp A.B. (OKG)	1963	50%	10%	Operates nuclear power plants. OKG is owned 15% by local communities, 35% by SKAB, 50% by private capital.
Forsmarks Kraftgrupp A.B. (FKA).	1973	75%	15%	Operates nuclear power plants. Owned 75% by SSPB, 25% by private capital.
Studsvik Energiteknik A.B.	1947	100%		R&D nuclear power, and alternative fuels.
Svensk Karn-bransle-hantering A.B. (SKB)	1972	70%	100%	Nuclear fuel supply and waste disposal. Owned 25% each by SSPB, SKAB, OKG, and FKA.
United Kingdom				
Electricity Council	1945	100%	100%	
National Nuclear Corporation (NNC)	1973	35%	100%	Constructs nuclear power plants.
U.K. Atomic Energy Authority	1940s	100%	—	R&D.
British Nuclear Fuels Ltd.	—	100%	—	Produces nuclear fuel elements, reprocessing.
United States				
Several federally owned regional authorities	1933	100%	100% (in regions)	Tennessee Valley Authority (TVA) the first. Also Bonneville Power, Southeastern Power, etc.

ests."[15] Exploring the origins of state intervention helps us understand the current distribution of public and private (electric) power.

Electric utilities originated in most industrial states as private enterprises, and so arrangements with private entrepreneurs had to be made before ownership could be transferred to the state. These struggles and compromises first appeared during the Age of Illumination, when electricity was generated by numerous, uncoordinated small producers, chiefly as an alternative to gas lighting. By the time most governments had regulated or came to own their electric utilities, electric power rivaled coal as a primary energy source. Political struggles involving electric utilities, industrial consumers, and the state in Britain, France, and Italy reveal evolving balances of power and the ways in which industrial structure can affect the nature and extent of state intervention.

Great Britain

The British government first became involved in the electric power sector in 1881, when Parliament awarded franchises to private generating firms. Although the Liberal government authorized localities to purchase these franchises at favorable terms after twenty-one years, an 1889 Act of Parliament written by Conservatives precluded public acquisition by doubling the life of the private franchises.[16] Demand soared, and the number of generating firms rapidly expanded without national standards of public direction.

Economic mobilization for World War I made clear the urgent need for reorganization and, as electric railways were major consumers of power, an electricity commission was established under the Ministry of Transport. The House of Lords, under pressure from the power firms, struck a provision of the legislation authorizing the new commissioners to compel the consolidation of the industry. The commissioners would be mere supervisors, able only to encourage amalgamation.[17]

Despite calls for nationalization, there was no progress toward standardization or consolidation until the 1926 Electricity Supply Act. The Baldwin government thus created the Central Electricity Board and Britain's first national power grid. By then 491 power stations in Britain were operating without accepted standard frequencies and without coordinated interconnections. There was no transfer of ownership under the new Act, but the board itself took charge of building and maintaining the grid. Stations would remain privately held (or, increasingly, held by local government), and the board would purchase their full supply of power and sell it back at favorable rates for private distribution.

These rights of private distribution were not challenged until 1936, by which time there were 562 different suppliers of various currents and voltages. The McGowan Committee on Electric Distribution then recommended compulsory amalgamation and financial controls with the ultimate goal of nationalization. No action was taken on the report because private distributors pressed the Chamberlain government to maintain the status quo. Although two-thirds of generating firms were by then owned by municipalities, the largest power stations were privately held, and these entrepreneurs successfully protected their interests until 1945. By then the story was the same as in coal. Private entrepreneurs had invested little in new capital equipment; they faced a coalition of Labour party government officials, trade unions, and electric-power-consuming industrialists. They were bought out, compensated by gilt-edged stock and Treasury guarantees in what was arguably the most generous of all British nationalizations. The British state was finally the sole producer of electric power.

France

In postwar France the point of compact involved different players, even though the private utilities enjoyed similar benefits.[18] The nationalization of electric utilities attracted broad popular support, for it was directed against a discredited fascist legacy. The Vichy regime had soldered its relationship to the trusts through state guarantees of profits in electric power and other heavy industrial sectors. The French right, purged after the war, had little strength to bloc the impending nationalizations. Nevertheless, it was able to minimize the damage. The concessions made to private power firms including, according to Robert Frost, "the most lucrative set of financial bonds ever issued in France."[19]

The nationalization of the French electric power industry through the creation of Electricité de France (EDF) had first been proposed in May 1943 by the National Council of the Resistance. The council's initial postwar program squarely opposed capital and corporatism. It adopted syndicalist doctrine by conferring authority on a board broadly representative of collective interests: bureaucrats, consumers, and labor would manage a unified electric utility. But the French electric power industry, with more than seventeen hundred private firms exclusively engaged in generation, transmission, and/or distribution and another thousand firms partially involved, was even more fragmented than the British. Opposition to the initial program came from several quarters.

First there was frontal opposition from leading industrialists such as Edmund Giscard d'Estaing, who sought to limit nationalization to particular sectors of the electric power industry. These industrialists combined direct pressure with dilatory tactics to blunt the initiative and ensure generous indemnification. They were joined by the smallest producers, who demanded recognition of their commercial rights. In addition, foreign shareholders, mostly Swiss investors, who held nearly 10 percent of outstanding equity in the French utilities, demanded consideration. Finally, and perhaps most significantly, the autogenerators of electric power, the electrometallurgical and electrochemical heavy industries and the railways, insisted (with the support of the Ministry of Finance) that they not be disadvantaged by nationalization.

All were accommodated. Efforts by the Communists in the government to claim two-thirds of the seats on the syndicalist board were turned back; the socialist cabinet of Léon Blum redefined the rules for representation; and syndicalism, already compromised as an operating principle, was ultimately abandoned. The smallest generating firms (less than 12 megawatts) were exempted from nationalization, and this lower limit was raised as capacity grew. Autogeneration facilities, accounting for one-third of all power capacity in France, were formally nationalized, but the final compromise guaranteed electric power rates "corresponding to those which such firms would have been able to obtain had they continued to own and operate the facilities themselves."[20] In effect, these firms would get electric power at a discount. Indeed, the nationalization law specifically prevented uniform rates and honored all existing contracts. Rate adjustments were made only after current contracts expired.

The terms of compensation deserve special attention for their generosity. Shareholders of private utility firms received EdF equity in exchange for their private holdings. If a utility had been traded on the bourse, where at the time prices were depressed, then its shares were assigned a value 50 percent higher than current yield. If holdings were in privately held firms, committees of financial experts and government officials made a special evaluation before the exchange was made. Such firms were indemnified at nearly twice the rate of the others. These handsome adjustments enabled investors to recycle their compensation into other businesses. EdF bonds were the largest part of the venture capital for the Compagnie Générale de l'Electricité, France's largest electric equipment firm. One leftist summed up the electric power nationalization as a "monstrous giveaway to the electricity trust . . . [that] forced the ratepayers to pay for the enormous investments . . . that the electricity trust had avoided making before the war."[21]

Italy

In Italy nationalization of the electric power sector came later than in Britain or France. Like Britain, Italy made a series of false starts toward nationalization. Like France, it was faced with a massive bill for compensation. It is often pointed out that the creation of Italy's national electric utility, ENEL, was one of only two instances in Italian history where nationalization was undertaken for ideological reasons.[22] But the ENEL case was much more than this characterization implies.

In the Fascist period leaders of the electric power industry were among the closest allies of the Italian state. There is no record of state plans to assume ownership of the sector until after World War II. Immediately after the war the Communist (PCI) and the Socialist (PSI) parties began advocating the nationalization of industry on philosophical grounds, justifying it in antimonopolistic terms acceptable to non-Marxists and invoking the nationalizations in France and Britain. At the same time parts of the media attacked the private utilities, complaining that they were not investing in new facilities at rates necessary to meet forecasted economic growth. Indeed, investment in capital equipment in nonhydro technologies was rare.[23]

The first official discussion of nationalization took place when the Constituent Assembly, elected on June 2, 1946 to frame the postwar constitution, established a commission to study its feasibility. The Assembly began by polling elite opinion in both government and the private sector, which revealed wide support for public management of public services and monopolistic sectors, especially electricity. But divisions among private interests vis-à-vis state participation in the economy delayed further consideration of energy nationalization.

Legislation to nationalize the electric utilities was subsequently introduced four times before its final approval in Italy in 1962.[24] Writing in 1955, between the first two formal proposals for nationalization, Ernesto Rossi suggested that private industry still retained too great an influence upon the Christian Democrats (DC) to permit state ownership:

> as long as the present political situation prevails, no government will succeed in exercising an effective control because of the low efficiency of the bureaucracy and the influence of the business-controlled public utilities. The latter will continue to subsidize political parties and newspapers in order to influence political decisions and public opinion.[25]

The DC did not yet need Socialist coalition partners, nor did it yet fully appreciate the partisan advantages of state ownership.

By the early 1960s, however, the political and economic landscape was rapidly changing. Italy's ruling coalition was anything but broad and stable: twelve cabinets had come and gone in the decade between Alcide DeGasperi's first centrist coalition and the early signs in 1962 of the end of the economic miracle. Italy was beginning to appear dangerously ungovernable; its political architects were groping for a new grand design.[26] The successes (and profits) of its Ente Nazionale Idrocarburi (ENI) in the Po Valley convinced the DC of potential opportunities for patronage and independence from business. The DC also began to understand how to reproduce among city-bound migrants in the north those clientele structures which had long been a source of its power in the south. Consequently, the DC moved to attract part of the leftist electorate by drawing the PSI into the ruling coalition. It looked to isolate the Communists and fortify itself at the same time. This famous opening to the left was supposed to ensure DC preeminence for another generation.

The nationalization of electric utilities was the political price exacted by the left wing of the Socialist party as its condition for joining the rest of the PSI in coalition with the DC. In the words of Pasquale Saraceno, the most influential economic adviser to the DC, "if the nationalization is judged politically wise, neither its cost nor its financial consequences should render it inadvisable."[27] Indeed, the fundamentally political nature of the DC shift toward support for nationalization was widely reported in the press and was publicly acknowledged by the DC chairman of the parliamentary commission for industry, Dosi: "naturally, this rendezvous with the PSI carries a political price, and undoubtedly the nationalization of the electric power sector can be one of the elements of the deal."[28]

On January 25, 1962, Social Democratic party (PSDI) representative Guido Ceccharini submitted the final bill for nationalization. Modeled explicitly upon the French and British utilities, the bill was not much different from previous PSI or PCI drafts. It was not the concept but the constellation of political interests which had changed. The PSDI, as well as the Republican party (PRI), the DC's other major coalition partner, supported the opening to the left but exacted their own price for compliance: DC support for pet construction projects. Although minorities in the DC and PRI opposed nationalization, party discipline was never seriously challenged. In September 1962 the Parliament formally approved the creation of the state-owned electric utility, ENEL. Supporting the DC, PRI, and PSDI were the Socialists and the Communists; voting against the measure were the business-supported Liberals and the neofascists.

Party discipline was never seriously challenged because the private utilities had been isolated. Confindustria, the peak business interest association, which officially supported the utilities, was divided between industries willing to battle nationalization to the end and those such as the powerful Fiat which saw benefit in a rationalized electric power sector. It is important to note that some of the most influential firms in the ENEL debate generated a large proportion of their own electric power. The nationalization bill specifically exempted autogeneration from state ownership, and at its creation ENEL controlled only 70 percent of national production. As Alan R. Posner and S. J. Woolf point out, "it seems probable that figure would have been higher had not the private industries converted a proportion of their plants to internal uses during the lengthy discussions [over ten years] preceding nationalization."[29] By protecting part of private industry from the measure, the government bill mollified more potential opposition. The best the private utility owners could do was what their grandparents had done when faced by the railway nationalization of 1905. They extracted an exceedingly generous cash settlement from the state.

At the time of the creation of ENEL there were some 321 electric utilities, most of which were affiliated with five major groups. Moreover, publicly owned utilities accounted for over one-third of the nation's electric-power-generating capacity. The industry was fragmented in number but concentrated in control.

Handsome cash settlements to public and private utilities alike provided these firms with unprecedented liquidity. Shareholders could have claimed this cash but generally did not, providing management with an extraordinary opportunity for diversification. Edison, which had been the largest single electric power company and the most strident opponent of nationalization, diversified into textiles, metals, engineering, and chemicals; most of its investments were so poorly conceived that within three years it merged with Montecatini, another ailing industrial giant. Their union, Montedison, has never overcome its initial handicaps. Smaller, family-held utilities such as the SADE in Veneto and the Centrale altogether disappeared as productive forces in the Italian economy.

The DC strategy has paid off handsomely—for the DC. The PSI has been an on-again, off-again coalition partner in DC-led governments for twenty years. Never again, however, did the Socialists hold the DC at bay with demands for the nationalization of industry. Instead, it learned quickly and well how to enlarge and use the public sector for partisan advantage. Not until 1983 did a Socialist, Bettino Craxi, become prime minister, and then after an election in which the PSI received less than 12 percent of the popular vote. Each of the coalition partners (even the Communists) has representatives on a ruling board at ENEL which is thoroughly colonized by political interests and highly restricted in its managerial autonomy. It is free neither to set prices (which is done by the Ministry of Industry in close collaboration with labor) nor to sell shares to raise capital. It has become less an instrument of the state than an instrument of a broadened if still imperfectly stable ruling coalition— to the detriment of electricity consumers in a resource-poor industrial democracy.

ENEL richly illustrates how the instability of a ruling coalition can facilitate state intervention. But taken together with the British and French cases of electric power nationalization, it also suggests the political relevance of market structure in shaping the role of the state in the economy. In France and Great Britain it appears that the fragmentation of the electric power business impeded state intervention. In Italy what appeared to be a fragmented utility sector was in fact highly consolidated. When the political time was right, however, consolidation could not prevent a determined ruling party from making a deal with the opposition for its own survival.

When we compare these experiences to Japan's we see, as in coal nationalization, a striking resemblance to Japan's own incompleted lurch toward state control of electric power. The abandonment of a highly fragmented utility sector by better organized and well-consolidated industrial consumers seems to have been a factor in the Japanese solution. But the structural fragmentation of the Japanese electric power sector was more complicated. In addition to the split between producers and consumers of electric power, Japanese utilities were split vertically and horizontally. The Japanese case therefore provides the opportunity for a more nuanced evaluation of the ways in which market structure affects choices between market displacement and market conformity. Moreover, this same truncated industrial structure also characterizes the Japanese oil industry in ways that make for interesting comparisons to European experience.

Oil for the Lamps of Politicians

The political conflicts over state intervention which produced state enterprises in coal and electric power revolved about two of the three broader strategic concerns of states in the world economy identified earlier. Coal was associated with the salvage of a noncompetitive industry and the need to maintain employment, the electric utilities with rationales of scale and efficiency. In both sectors the industrial state usually acts as supplier of an important factor of industrial production. States are typically business partners of manufacturers. Intervention is linked to shifts in the ruling coalition and to market structure. For historical reasons usually associated with the third strategic rationale, however, oil is different.

Atop any list of the strategic concerns of states in the world economy is the security of energy supplies. Security has been a major objective of policy ever since states first recognized that domestic demand for energy in most industrial states vastly exceeded domestic energy supplies. This recognition is, of course, historically recent and has followed the emergence of petroleum as a critical industrial fuel. After all, the world consumes more oil in ten minutes today than it did in all of the year 1900.

Petroleum became a strategic energy source only after the British Admiralty converted its fleet from coal to fuel oil at the turn of the

century. The first motorized world war confirmed the strategic significance of oil. With the exception of newcomers created by oil-rich industrial states, such as Norway's Statoil, Britain's BNOC (now private), and
Petro-Canada, the state-owned oil firms in the mixed economies of the
OECD were created to ensure a stable supply of *foreign* energy. But even
in Norway, Britain, and Canada nationalist sentiment and the fear of
foreign control of this most strategic resource were central in the decision to nationalize production.[30] Propositions related to openness and to
the vulnerability of national economies find a ready test in the history of
oil.

Today the number of state-owned oil companies is greater, their scale
larger, their geography more dispersed, and their economic activities
more vertically integrated than any other type of state enterprise.
Three-quarters of the OECD states have nationally held oil firms. The
United States is the only major oil-importing or oil-exporting nation
without a national oil corporation, and Japan is the only such nation with
a national corporation that is not commercially active. By 1985 state-
owned oil firms outside the centrally planned economies were producing nearly two-thirds of the crude oil traded on world markets. They
were also responsible for nearly half of the world's refinery capacity.[31]
Joel Bell's observation is quite correct: "The private sector no longer
determines how much oil is produced, how much exported, at what
price, and increasingly, to whom it is sold."[32]

As the data in Table 2.3 show, the modal form of state participation is
complete equity shareholding, as in Austria, Canada, Denmark, Ireland,
Italy, Norway, Portugal, Spain, and Sweden. In West Germany's Demi-
nex and France's Elf-Aquitaine the state is the majority shareholder. A
less than controlling state interest is rare, but in France's CFP (35 percent)
and Britain's BP (reduced to 32 percent in 1984) the state nonetheless
retains the single largest shareholding.

In many of these national oil corporations, profitability dramatically
underlines the importance of separating state ownership and state control in analyses of governments in business. The petroleum business is
simply the single most profitable business in which governments directly
participate. Created for strategic purposes to counter the market domination of private multinational oil firms, these entities look far more like
multinationals than government bureaucracies. With the sole exception
of some smaller national oil firms, such as Turkey's Petrocorp and Denmark's DONG, these enterprises are nearly as fully integrated upstream
and downstream as the most powerful private multinationals with which
they compete at home and abroad. And with the exception of Japan's
JNOC, none are primarily financial instruments; most are deeply involved
in the exploration, production, and importation of crude oil as well as in

Table 2.3. State-owned oil corporations, 1986

	Year founded	% public	Domestic market share	Comments
Australia				
Geothermal Corp. of Victoria	—	—	—	Geothermal and s.a. Oil are govt. companies for exploration only. Pipeline Authority is a federal agency in charge of pipeline construction and operation.
South Australian Oil	—	99.98%	—	
Pipeline Authority	—	—	—	
Austria				
Oesterreichische Mineralver- waltung (OMV)	1955	100%	81% (sales)	Vertically integrated. Holding of Oesterreichische Industriever- waltungs.
Belgium				
Distrigaz	1978	50%	—	Empowered to negotiate state-to- state crude sales. No tankers or refineries.
Canada				
Petro-Canada	1975	100%	15% (sales) 8% (reserves)	Largest landowner in Canada.
Denmark				
Dansk Olie os Naturgas (DONG)	1972	100%	5% (sales)	Some oil imports: much oil received as payment-in- kind of taxes and royalties from indigenous producers. Participates in exploration since 1984.
Finland				
Neste Oy	1948	98%	23% (sales)	No exploration, but otherwise integrated and diversified.
France				
Compagnie Française des Pétroles (CFP)	1924	35%	25% (sales) 26% (refining)	Govt. has 40% voting rights. Took formerly

(*continued*)

47

Table 2.3. (Continued)

	Year founded	% public	Domestic market share	Comments
Societé Nationale Elf-Aquitaine (SNEA)	1976	70%	21% (sales) 21% (refining)	German equity in Turkish Petroleum Co. awarded France at San Remo Conference, 1920. Merger of Societé Nationale des Petroles d'Aquitaine, formed 1941 (mixed ownership), and Entreprise des Recherches et d'Activités Petrolières (100 percent public).
Germany Deminex	1966	54%	25% (extraction) 16% (refining) 11% (sales)	Consortium of German oil companies. German Electric Utility Holding Co. (Vereinigte Electrizitäts und Bergwerke AG, VEBA) holds 54 percent of equity. Wintershall AG (private) holds 18.5 percent.
Veba Oel A.G.	1978	40%	—	Wholly owned subsidiary of VEBA, founded in 1935. In 1973 VEBA brought 51 percent controlling interest in Gelsenberg AG. Two hundred subsidiaries up- and downstream, as well as nonpetroleum activities. VEBA privatized in 1987.

Table 2.3. (*Continued*)

	Year founded	% public	Domestic market share	Comments
Greece				
Public Petroleum Corp. of Greece	1975	100%	30% (sales)	Exploration for oil and gas.
Aspropyrgos Greek Refinery	—	100%	22% (refining)	
Ireland				
Irish National Petroleum Corp.	1979	100%	35% (petroleum) 35% (gas oil)	Importing and refining only.
Italy				
AGIP	1953	100%	39.5%	Subsidiary of Ente Nazionale d'Idrocarburi (ENI) with responsibility for integrated oil and gas operations.
Japan				
Japan National Oil Corp. (JNOC)	1967	100%	8% (extraction)	Finances private exploration, stockpiling. MITI affiliate. Limited production by subsidiaries.
New Zealand				
Petrocorp	1978	100%	10% (crude sales)	
New Zealand Refining Co.	1961	31%	70% (refining)	
Norway				
Den Norske Oljeselskap AS (Statoil)	1972	100%	—	Govt. company producing and exporting oil and gas.
Rafinor AS og. Co.	1971	85.3%	—	Owned 70 percent by Statoil/Noroland, 30 percent by Norsk Hydro Refining Company.
Norsk Olje AS	1976	100%	28% (sales)	Owned 74 percent by Statoil, 26 percent by government. Marketing company.
Norsk Hydro AS	1905	51%	—	51 percent govt., 49 percent private.

(*continued*)

Table 2.3. (Continued)

	Year founded	% public	Domestic market share	Comments
				Producer and exporter of oil and gas. Marketing.
Portugal				
Petroleos de Portugal (Petrogal)	1976	100%	74.7%	
Spain				
Instituto Nacional de Industria	1941	100%	—	Govt. holding company in coal, electricity, nuclear fuels, and oil; significant participation in all sectors.
Compania Arrendatoria del Monopolio de Petroleos SA (CAMPSA)	1928	100%	100% (extraction) 100% (sales)	CAMPSA will lose monopoly market when Spain joins EEC. A new group, in collaboration with four private-sector firms, will then take its place, and will adopt a new name.
Compania Espanola de Petroleos (CEPSA)	1923	100%	—	Refining.
Empressa Nacionale de Investigaciones y Exploraci-ones Petrolifa SA (ENIEPSA)	1975	—	—	Refining.
Hispanoil	1965	55%	—	Foreign exploration.
Compania de Invesitigaciones y Exploracion Petroliferas SA (Petroliber)	—	72%	—	Refining.

Table 2.3. (Continued)

	Year founded	% public	Domestic market share	Comments
Sweden				
Svenska Petroleum	1975	100%	15% (sales)	Owned 50 percent by Vattenfall (electric utility), 50 percent by Stratsforetag AB, a holding company. Obtained Petrosvede in 1975.
OPAB	1969	62%	—	Consortium of domestic companies for domestic exploration.
Turkey				
Turkish Petroleum Corp.	1954	51%	—	Not to be confused with pre-1939 Turkish Petroleum Co., which became the Iraq Petroleum Co.
United Kingdom				
British Petroleum (BP)	1909	32%	40% (extraction) 21% (refining) 20% (sales)	Public holdings divided between Bank of England and British govt. Total reduced from 51 percent in 1984.
British National Oil Corp. (BNOC)	1975	100%	—	Company abolished in 1985 and producing assets given to Britoil, created in 1982, as part of denationalization.
Oil Pipelines Agency	1985	100%	—	Following abolition of BNOC, OPA is agent for disposal of govt. oil and managing govt. oil pipelines and storage system.

the refining and marketing of petroleum products. All produce natural gas also and tend to be diversified into other energy fields—coal, uranium, and geothermal development—and nonenergy but petroleum-related industries such as petrochemicals and synthetic textiles. The largest are best characterized as state-owned holding companies; they have diversified into more distant activities such as glass manufacture and computer software. State control of these firms seems to decrease with their profitability.[33] Whether they operate as just another competitor in a free market in Britain and West Germany, as competitors in highly regulated markets in France and Italy, or as virtual monopolies in controlled markets in Austria, Finland, and Spain, they seem to move away from state control as they mature and expand.

British Petroleum, with 85 percent of its sales overseas and with 75 percent of its profits derived from foreign business, is a (perhaps extreme) case in point. It is the giant among publicly held petroleum enterprises. Its sales are five times those of France's CFP, the next largest such firm. In fact, most analysts exclude BP from lists of national oil firms because it has always operated as a private enterprise.[34] Its great profitability, product diversification, and international character make BP more likely to be included on lists of the Seven Sisters than on lists of state enterprises. In times of crisis, moreover, it has not acted as an instrument of the British state. During the OAPEC embargo in 1973, for example, BP informed the British government that it could expect no special treatment in the allocation of oil. The British government has never exercised its veto powers vis-à-vis BP and has accepted BP's own definition of its obligation to the state as financial rather than as an instrument of policy. Similar relationships are found with Petro-Canada, despite a mandate expressly designed to prevent the firm from adopting commercial practices that conflict with public goals, and with France's CFP and Italy's ENI.[35]

State-owned oil companies in industrial states other than Japan thus seem to share certain characteristics that distinguish them from other public energy corporations and from state enterprises more generally. To understand what makes oil so different, we must explore beyond profitability to the political origins of these firms and their special position in the global political economy.

Although there is diversity in their size (state-owned refining capacity in Italy is twenty times that in Denmark), age (sixty-one years and two world wars separate the oldest and the youngest), and degrees of public accountability, all state-owned oil companies were formed as commercial ventures justified by strategic national goals in the face of initial market domination by a small number of privately held, usually foreign multinationals. Labor parties and leftist programs were largely irrelevant as states pursued their goals. The state seldom had many domestic producers to be concerned with; electric power and coal industries were far more fragmented than oil in most industrial states when nationalization was carried out.

Great Britain

The first documented case of direct state intervention in petroleum came in 1908, when Emperor Franz Josef of Austria-Hungary approved a government-owned and operated refinery in Drohobycz (100,000 tons per year capacity).[36] But the history of significant state ownership in oil began further upstream the following year, when the forerunner of today's British Petroleum was created. The ostensible reason for British government participation in the Anglo-Persian Oil Company (APOC) was security of fuel oil supplies for the Royal Navy. The actual history is somewhat more complicated, indicating not only conflicting state goals but the need for significant private support to achieve them.

As early as 1903 the British Admiralty was investigating fuel oil as one of several means to modernize the Royal Navy.[37] At this time the world's largest oil producers were non-British, and so were Britain's largest oil firms. The British domestic market was divided between the Standard Oil Company, Royal Dutch Shell interests, and a consortium of anti-Standard oil companies and allied financial interests comprising the Nobels, the Rothschilds, and the Deutsche Bank, known as the Europäische Petroleum Union.[38] Although there were British investments in overseas producing regions, notably Russia, their presence in British markets was negligible. So Britain, like the rest of Europe, depended upon foreign sources of oil.

One of the few domestically capitalized oil firms in Britain was Burmah Oil. The company had begun in 1886 as a producer and refiner of Scottish shale oil; by the end of the nineteenth century it had diversified into subterranean oil extraction.[39] It obtained significant holdings in Burma and concentrated its marketing in India. With this company the Admiralty signed a fuel oil contract in 1905 for 50,000 tons a year, the navy's first efforts in what would become a major drive to fuel oil conversion. Uncertain about meeting requirements of this scale, and at the suggestion of Admiralty representatives, Burmah Oil approached William Knox D'Arcy, who had obtained a concessionary zone in Persia but was short of funds for prospecting.

Burmah Oil formed an exploration syndicate including D'Arcy, provided funds, and oil was struck in Persia in May 1908. D'Arcy was bought out, and in 1910 Charles D. Greenway became managing director of the company, now no longer an exploration syndicate but in effect a subsidiary of Burmah Oil. Aware of the perils of competing in a world industry dominated by Standard Oil and the burgeoning Shell interests, Greenway sought a means to preserve APOC's independence.

He faced two related problems. First, APOC refining technology, copied from successful Burmah Oil operations, was inappropriate for Persian crude, which had a high sulphur content; APOC was forced to conclude unfavorable crude supply agreements with the Shell-controlled Asiatic Petroleum, which had more appropriate refining facilities. Second, the combination of refining problems, large investments without immediate prospects of profitable return, and the desire not to upset marketing arrangements in profitable markets such as India led some directors of Burmah Oil to favor selling the APOC concession to Asiatic Petroleum. In 1911 Greenway put the matter bluntly: the "Royal Dutch have already made overtures of one kind and another to us, and in connection with these have indicated that if we do invade [their] markets they are going for us and will do their best to smash us."[40]

Greenway's ensuing moves expressed a genius born of desperation. APOC oil was suitable only for use as fuel, but oil companies had hitherto considered refined fuel oil a secondary product; the primary market was for the lighter, more highly distilled lamp oil. (This, of course, was the origin of the term "residual," still used today to refer to fuel oils.) Circumstances forced Greenway to conclude that he had to develop transportation fuel as his primary market. The largest potential customer in the world for fuel oil was the Royal Navy. For its part, the navy was grappling with another characteristic of oil as a transportation fuel: inelasticity of demand once the fleet was converted—in military terms, security of supplies. The navy would not consider conversion to oil unless it could find reliable, long-term sources.

Greenway exploited these concerns adroitly. He refused to fix fuel supply prices with Shell on contract bids for the Royal Navy. Shell, which was 60 percent Dutch-owned, was in any case of dubious loyalty in the eyes of the British Admiralty, for, as Marian Kent notes, "Holland, and therefore its international companies, were subject to strong German influence. Shell was consequently viewed with suspicion in its dealings with the British government."[41] Greenway argued before the Foreign Office and the Admiralty that some government assistance, in the form of direct capital investment and guaranteed purchases of fuel oil, was necessary if he was not to lose his "independence"—a polite way to refer to his selling out to Shell.

In parliamentary debate Winston Churchill advocated government equity participation. He argued that the Admiralty had the right to refine oil for its own use. Moreover, "on no one route and on no one field must we be dependent. Safety and certainty in oil lie in variety and variety alone."[42] There was little organized opposition to Churchill's attack on Shell, and by 254-18 Parliament approved the British government's buying 51 percent of APOC equity.

With government participation assured, Greenway next sought to secure the commercial character of his company. Minority private shareholding could have made the company a kind of public utility operated by the Admiralty. Greenway now reversed the earlier logic that had led him to fuel oil as his primary market. Manufacture of fuel oil as a primary product, he argued, left certain "residuals," such as lamp oils, whose marketing would enhance the solvency of the enterprise and help keep Admiralty fuel costs down. The government was induced by growing demand during World War I to advance significant amounts of capital for refining, in which it had an immediate and practical interest, in Persia and at Swansea. Although the government did not meet all of Greenway's calls for capital, it did lend an ear to recurrent pleas about insufficient capital to meet growth needs.

Greenway's actions were not entirely in the service of the Admiralty. During World War I the British Petroleum Company, a German-owned corporation that had marketed products for Shell, was confiscated as enemy property. In spite of chronic cash shortages, Greenway found the money to buy British Petroleum, in March 1917. The war saw APOC's vertical integration even though, in the words of one government official, it was not "what was intended when the government went into Persian oil. The object was to secure Navy supplies."[43]

The origin of government equity in the Anglo-Persian Oil Company, it seems, was owed at least in part to skillful manipulation of national interests by the company itself. In addition to fending off Shell, APOC had to contend with internal conflicts between the Admiralty and the Foreign Office. As early as 1916 some in the Foreign Office were accusing APOC of bad management and the Admiralty of excessive favor to the company. This bureaucratic dispute paved the way for Shell's retention of concession rights in Mesopotamia.

Oil histories focus upon commercial rivalries and government policies that were closely linked to the strategic and international politics of the postwar era, but our analysis directs us toward the coal industry's reaction to the adoption of oil as fuel in the Royal Navy. Although the technological and strategic reasons for oil were compelling, the British coal industry made a counterargument: coal was more reliable because it was domestic. During World War I the loss of Russian oil supplies, at first to the German-Turkish closure of the Dardanelles and then to the effects of the Bolshevik Revolution, underscored this vulnerability, but the enhanced effectiveness of the fleet brought oil supplies to England nonetheless. Domestic coal interests were unable to mobilize support for retention of their special relationship to the Admiralty. Although both Admiral Sir John Fisher and Winston Churchill agreed there were advantages in "home oil," the government ignored coal industry calls to create a domestic coal–based synthetic fuel industry as in Germany and Japan.[44] Proponents of coal liquefaction contended that what the Admiralty was investing in refining capacities at Swansea and Abadan, in combination with Scottish shale oil, could meet half of the nation's liquid fuel requirements.[45]

Why was the coal industry, despite its size and long-standing role in the British political economy, unable to mobilize more significant opposition to the intervention of the British state in the oil market?[46] Its failure is to be explained not just by technical or cost considerations but also by the political influence enjoyed by a coalition of military and oil interests. The relationship between Admiralty and APOC gave the latter a decisive advantage, one that was essential in its competition against Shell and that complemented its cost advantages in the competition against coal. Government equity participation ensured survival against a major multinational with only partial claims to British nationality. That openness in oil meant strategic insecurity was clearly part of the calculus for intervention, marking a significant departure for the British state.

France

The French modeled a state petroleum enterprise directly upon APOC in 1924.[47] Although established as a joint venture with private capital, the enterprise reflected more a failure of state bureaucrats to secure a commercial monopoly than a triumph of military/commercial coalition. In part the French oil industry found itself opposing an entrenched coal industry even more influential than England's. Coal's power was reinforced by the recovery of Alsace-Lorraine, with its large coal reserves. The industry hoped to participate in the developing liquid fuel market, through the marketing of by-products such as benzol from the gaslight and steel industries and, more speculatively, through the production of synthetic fuels such as methyl alcohol and oil-from-coal. Benzol mixed well with distilled ethyl alcohol and gasoline to form a "trinary" fuel suitable for high-performance auto engines. Thus the coal industry found a powerful ally in the French viticulture lobby, which sought to develop a distilled alcohol fuel market as a price support in the face of recurrent overproduction.[48]

For their part, and for a short time, French oil firms enjoyed a state-sanctioned oligopoly. From the middle of the nineteenth century until World War I, ten private firms were tightly organized as a refiners' cartel that indirectly included their chief supplier, Standard Oil.[49] The stability of this cartel was shaken immediately after the war by dramatic changes in the world oil market. Standard Oil acquired the Compagnie Générale des Pétroles, and Shell acquired two firms, the Raffinerie du Midi and Alexandre Deutsch and Sons, to integrate downstream in the French market. In addition, APOC opened a subsidiary, the Société Générale des Huiles de Pétrole, and bought out the Paix and Lesieur companies. Other French firms, such as Desmarais Brothers, made tentative efforts to expand into Rumanian production; still others were attracted to Poland. After the Treaty of San Remo stripped Germany of its oil investments in Rumania and awarded them to Britain and France in 1920, Rumanian investment drew financial support from French banks. One creation of the postwar period was the Omnium International des Pétroles, whose capital was divided between British, Rumanian, and French investors.

These and other shifts in world energy markets affected domestic oil and coal firms alike, but from 1921 to 1925 the French government did nothing. There were no cries for intervention in the name of national security. Instead, a free energy market generated fratricidal price wars. French firms that had not sold out to the majors were forced to acquiesce to a market-sharing agreement in 1925 assigning Standard Oil, Shell, and Anglo Persian 73 percent of the French market.[50] Further Russian exports to France began in 1927, and massive low-cost imports from Mesopotamia were in prospect. These low-cost fuels were opposed by higher-cost producers in Rumania and by the domestic coal industry. French oil and banking interests with experience in Rumania were well aware that access to the oil of Mesopotamia could prove a boon for them—if they could develop it without being wiped out by the majors, and if they could bring the oil to market without ruining their investments in Rumania.

The principal interventions of the French state in the interwar oil market admirably resolved this complex crisis of competition. By 1924 it was clear that French interests would acquire 20–25 percent of production rights in the Turkish Petroleum Company (the final figure was 23.75 percent)—additional spoils of Germany's defeat. The British asked the French government to designate a commercial entity to participate in this Mesopotamian oil development; that company was the Compagnie Française des Pétroles (CFP), which in 1924 was conceived as a joint venture of private investors, including the majors, French banks, and French oil interests but without state equity participation. For turning over its holdings in the Mesopotamian concession, the government was awarded representation on the CFP board of directors and a percentage of profits which rose as the ratio of profits to invested capital rose.[51]

French premier Raymond Poincaré's desire for balanced budgets and fiscal austerity neatly complemented the desire of entrepreneurs to participate in Mesopotamian oil.[52] Poincaré designated Ernest Mercier, then president of the Omnium International des Pétroles, to assemble the unlikely collage of competing multinational and national interests that would form the CFP.[53] A company that now appears to Leslie Grayson as "the embodiment of the contradictions and successes of French oil policy" thus owed its origins less to state leadership than to a confluence of private interests, belated mercantilist trade policies, and foreign threat. As Harvey Feigenbaum notes, "the formation of the CFP in 1924 was hardly testimony to the state's strength, but rather bore witness to the powerful influence of the private sector. The state was only able to weld the company into a potential mercantile instrument with the help of external pressure . . . [viz.] menacing competition from the international majors."[54]

In 1928–29 the CFP faced its first crisis: the development plans for Mesopotamia increased the capital investment required for participation there. Some of the international majors in the CFP, who opposed plans for the CFP to refine and market its own products, took the opportunity to squeeze their French partners. Mercier, threatened by an investment strike, sought Poincaré's support. The French state made up the capital deficiency by taking 25 percent government participation in equity. Had the CFP been unable to raise the capital, it might have been forced to sell out to its partners: Anglo-Persian, Shell, and the group led by Standard Oil. The Poincaré government's decision brought the CFP charter for the first time into Parliament, where the Socialists sought complete nationalization. Poincaré and his business supporters staved that off until 1931 when, faced with depression and the threat of dumping by the majors, they reversed course and supported a state bailout.[55] State participation was raised to 35 percent of equity, with 40 percent voting rights.

In 1929 the CFP, the French government, and domestic oil firms established an important joint venture, the Compagnie Française de Raffinage (CFR), a refining company whose business was reserved for six French companies that had survived the free-market carnage of 1921–25.[56] (These were the national companies that in 1925 had collectively shared at most 27 percent of the French market.) The state's entry into refining by means of a subsidiary of the CFP was a significant change, an aggressive move through which private interests and bureaucrats mobilized state protection from the marketing strategies of the majors.

The coal industry did not respond directly to the creation of CFP. After all, Mesopotamian oil did not come on stream until 1934. But a countermove of no small consequence against the general growth of the oil industry was the creation of the National Liquid Fuels Office (ONCL) in

1925. This office was designed to ensure a place for coal and viticulture in the expanding liquid oil market and, significantly, would become (along with the Finance Ministry) the government stockholder in the CFP. In the 1930s it became the center of struggles by the coal industry to restrict importation of fuel oils. One French author believes that ONCL was formed to "control" oil interests on behalf of steel and coal interests; though this is no doubt an exaggeration, regulatory struggles between nascent oil and declining coal did often center in ONCL.[57]

In 1928 an oil import law offered an omnibus solution to the disorder in French energy markets. Importers of refined products were given three-year licenses; twenty-year permits were given to importers of crude who built refineries in France. The immediate spur to the growth of the refining industry in France was perhaps the most significant achievement of state policy of that time. As we shall see in Chapter 5, the law was the model for Japanese legislation as well. It reduced the outflow of currency on oil purchases and thus helped stabilize the franc and the economy generally. It also brought the majors into France as refiners, freezing out independent producers from the United States and curtailing the threat of imports of refined products by retailers.

Domestic interests had long favored some sort of protective legislation, but what precipitated passage of the 1928 law was a division among the majors combined with two additional developments. First, commercially viable reserves were found in Mesopotamia in 1927, facilitating closure of protracted negotiations over development of the area. Second, the Soviet Union, recovering from its own revolution, was threatening again to become a premier oil exporter, and some private firms were uncomfortable with accommodating the Soviets (by no means all private interests held such reservations). This regulatory intervention continues to define the contours of French and, indirectly, Japanese oil policy to the present day.

Italy

State intervention in oil was occasioned by foreign domination and problems of scarcity in Italy as in Britain and France. But the Italian case is instructive about the state intervention where private interests are weak, unorganized, disinterested.

The first tentative step by the Italian state to enhance petroleum production was a March 1911 law that gave private entrepreneurs 30 lire for each meter drilled in new exploration. Discovery of oil was not required for receipt of the subsidy. By this time the Italian petroleum market was already dominated by foreign firms: a majority of supplies were delivered by the Società Italo-Americana per il Petrolio (SIAP), an affiliate of

Standard Oil of New Jersey founded in 1905. Fourteen percent was supplied from Russia by the Società Importazione Olii, an affiliate of a German firm which supplied another 12 percent of the Italian market with refined products from Rumanian wells. In 1912 Shell entered the Italian market where, under oligopolistic control, prices rose rapidly. Domestic exploration and production remained negligible.[58]

Italy was outmaneuvered at the postwar petroleum conference in San Remo in 1920.[59] Two years later, at The Hague, the young Fascist government had its first confrontation with the Western powers. A month earlier the Italian government had reached an oil supply agreement with the Soviet Union in what amounted to the first formal recognition by a Western state of the Bolshevik regime. At The Hague the Western powers sought an agreement to boycott Russian oil, but the Italians refused to comply. Benito Mussolini used this issue to demonstrate the consolidation of his power and his ability to do battle with the "international trusts."[60] By 1925, 17 percent of Italian oil imports came from the Soviet Union, the rest from U.S. and Anglo-Dutch sources.[61]

State subsidies for drilling did not produce greater private exploration, and in 1924 a report to Parliament called for more direct forms of state action. Private capital was criticized for its excessive aversion to unsecured investment and for exploring more extensively abroad (Poland, Rumania, Mexico) than at home.[62] Citing the dangers of oil supply interruptions, the report called for a more autarkic energy development program.

At the same time the liberal minister of the national economy, Corbino, was quietly initiating an agreement with the Sinclair Exploration Company. The pact would provide Sinclair with exclusive rights to explore for oil, gas, and related minerals in Emilia and Sicily for fifty years; the state would receive dividends and two seats on the Board of Directors as a 40 percent partner in the new venture. But when news of the agreement became public, accompanied by stories of pay-offs and other excesses, the Fascists forced its cancelation by Parliament. The Italian state then took two years to sort through the issue of exploration and its relationship to the Fascist program for autarkic development. The answer to the "petroleum question" was the Azienda Generale Italiana Petroli (AGIP).[63]

The story is confused, but we know that when AGIP was created in May 1926, Standard's SIAP and Shell's Nafta were together capitalized at 450 million lire, fifteen times greater than the next largest firms.[64] They accounted for 75 percent of Italian petroleum production in 1926 and a somewhat higher proportion of the market for refined products.[65] This domination was widely acknowledged, but it was not to be challenged at once. In one of his first speeches to Parliament, on November 15, 1922,

Mussolini promised that "the government will focus its energy for greater development of our mines, but without renouncing secure supplies from abroad to satisfy national needs."[66] In fact, Mussolini himself chaired the first interministerial committee for oil, established in February 1923. The committee's first act was to transfer to Italian firms the drilling equipment taken as reparations from Germany.

Domestic capital was unwilling to invest at home, a matter of concern equal to that of foreign domination. Before the Fascist period neither the state nor private entrepreneurs had pursued a strategy of domestic refining; virtually all private petroleum investments were abroad.[67] Total domestic production involved no more than 8,000 tons of crude oil in any year during the 1920s.[68] Low domestic production, justified by geological surveys to be sure, provided the state with relatively easy direct entry to the market. Italy lacked private enterprise that could organize to oppose, to stimulate, or to direct government action in the petroleum sector. This was not a fragmented but a prenatal industry. The Fascist state enjoyed a nearly free hand in this, its first major direct intervention in the economy.

AGIP was formally established as a parastatal body to assist domestic industry and commerce, to control the Italian oil market, and to end market domination by foreign trusts.[69] AGIP received wide discretion. It was formally required to secure ministerial approval of only its five-year plans. The breadth of its mandate is suggested in Article 1 of its establishment decree, which provided AGIP the responsibility for "the development of any activity related to industry and commerce of oil products." The first action plan called for procurement, refining, storage, and sales. To carry out these activities, Article 6 directly provided for all "necessary funds" as appropriations from the Ministry of the National Economy. Quite apart from these annual budgetary outlays, AGIP was capitalized with 100 million lire, 60 percent from the national treasury and 40 percent in two equal shares from the national insurance funds.[70] At its creation AGIP acquired two existing firms, over the opposition of many who felt the prices were too generous.[71] The Società Nazionale Olii Minerale was an unsuccessful naphtha producer; and the Raffineria Olii Minerali was a Fiume (Rijeka) refinery with Dutch ownership. Their combined purchase price exhausted AGIP's initial capital stocks, requiring the state to provide AGIP with its first capital increment and the first of its annual contributions of 7 million lire early in 1927.

In 1928 AGIP had a 90 percent interest in Prahova, a Rumanian oil field, and in Petrolul Bucharest, a Rumanian refinery. In 1930 it became a participant in the British Oil Development Company in Iran. In 1935 it took an important initiative in Iraq, acquiring a major shareholding in the Mosul oil fields. But because of the lack of investment capital it had to sell those shares in 1936, losing Italy's opportunity in the Persian Gulf. Clearly AGIP, unlike the private firms, was emphasizing exploration over production. Private firms invested only 9 percent of their capital in exploration between 1926 and 1944, whereas AGIP invested over half.[72] Equally clearly, the state, through AGIP, was following an established course in exploring abroad rather than developing at home.

AGIP never performed well, and it hardly contributed to Italian energy independence. As late as 1933 Standard Oil of New Jersey, through its SIAP affiliate, controlled nearly three-fourths of the Italian market. Although AGIP had by then acquired a 10 percent share in that market, it posed little threat to foreign suppliers, and Italian investors were showing no enthusiasm for the oil business.

By the end of World War II it was clear even to Italian capitalists that oil was profitable. The government decided to dissolve AGIP. But for the prescience and determination of Enrico Mattei, a Resistance leader and head of AGIP, the Italian oil market would have been completely privatized (and probably foreign-dominated). Mattei pressed ahead with exploration for oil and gas in the Po River valley. His geologists' successes, combined with his own considerable political skills, resulted in the 1953 re-formation of AGIP as the Ente Nazionale Idrocarburi (ENI), which Parliament granted monopoly rights to Po gas reserves and to the nationwide distribution of methane. Within one year ENI was producing 90 per of the nation's natural gas and marketing 25 percent of its oil products.[73]

The political battle surrounding the creation of ENI is among the most frequently told in postwar Italian political history, and numerous accounts have documented the exploits and daring of Enrico Mattei.[74] The story typically takes on a hagiographic tone, recounting how this uneducated partisan hero confronted private capital at home and abroad to win for his nation (and his political allies in the DC) control of Italy's energy market place. The facts are all true, but Mattei's daring was also bolstered by industrial support that helped him confront foreign oil interests.

In early 1949 at least one dozen private firms, many capitalized abroad, were competing among themselves and with AGIP for exploration concessions in Italy.[75] Standard and Gulf were supposed to have reached an agreement to divide the Italian market, thereby reducing competition for concessions.[76] Mattei, recognizing the strategic importance of national control, refused to sell AGIP to private firms, domestic or foreign. He set out instead to secure AGIP's privileged access to Italy's then unproven energy reserves.

His jingoistic slogans ("ENI is an antimonopolistic force"; "The Po Valley is an open safe") spoke both to a widespread popular disaffection with collaborationist Italian private enterprise and to Italian fears of foreign domination. As a result, in Dow Votaw's summary, "the most influential argument in the battle of the Po was that of keeping foreigners out of Italian resources, but it should be noted that Italian private enterprise was excluded also."[77]

An active campaign by some private firms also resulted, to block Mattei's designs for a state monopoly.[78] Private electric utilities wanted access to methane to generate electricity, but foreign oil and gas firms were Mattei's most determined opponents. Their opposition served only to arouse nationalist sentiment in Italy. Confindustria was widely perceived as a tool of foreign interests; its oil industry representative, for example, the Unione Petrolifera, was dominated by the foreign majors. Mattei secured support from DC leaders Amintore Fanfani and Ezio Vanoni, the finance minister. Acting as his political spokesmen, Vanoni and Fanfani repeatedly intervened on behalf of ENI against private oil firms. (For its part, Esso seems to have secured the support of Alcide DeGasperi and the right wing of the DC.)

There is evidence that other private interests encouraged the DC to support Mattei's plan. Fiat, for example, avoided any public involvement in the dispute, rightly expecting that plentiful supplies of inexpensive gasoline would stimulate demand for automobiles. The large northern industrial consumers of the natural gas that ENI would produce and supply supported the program more openly.[79] But most important was the absence of organized, domestically capitalized petroleum firms to oppose Mattei. In spite of ENI's appeal as an antimonopolistic force, there were no oil trusts to bust and no domestic producers to buy off. In 1953 the DC could take against private enterprise in the petroleum and gas sector a popular position that it could not (and did not have to) take until 1962 in electric power. There is little direct evidence that private industry united to oppose expansion of the Italian state. On the contrary, disunity, combined with the discredited foreign leadership of Confindustria and the absence of domestic interests, helps explain how the DC could move with such vigor to fortify a market-displacing state presence in energy.

The irony is, of course, that the resulting dominance of ENI extended far beyond the energy market place. Under Mattei, ENI was the legal instrument of a state unable to control it. Later, under Eugenio Cefis, after it accepted its first financial assistance from the national treasury, it became the instrument of the fragmented political interests that are the Italian state. Ownership was divorced from control as oil was diverted from the lamps of Italy to the lamps of politicians.

A comparison to Japan reveals many similarities with these three European experiences with oil nationalization. As noted, French legislation

of 1928 remains the centerpiece of Japanese oil policy today. Coal industry opposition to state support for oil firms (as in Britain and France);
naval expansion (as in Britain); and above all else the consuming fear of
foreign domination (as in France, Britain, and Italy)—all were important factors in Japanese oil policy. Yet in oil, as in electric power and coal,
Japan's state firm closely conforms to the market. The Japan National
Oil Corporation is a guarantor of private debt and a partner of private
investors. It competes with no producers, refiners, or sales firms. We are
left to surmise that in Japan the politics of openness was mitigated by
additional constraints on state intervention in the economy.

CONCLUSION

At the point of compact between business and the state each of these
historical cases reveals complex interactions among market structure,
centralized state power, developmental timing, openness, and shifts in
the ruling coalition, which result in a commercial and competitive presence for the industrial state in the energy market place. Different energy
businesses illuminate the impact of some of these variables better than
others. In particular, coal suggests the relevance of broad and stable
ruling coalitions; electric power stresses the structure of domestic markets; and oil is tied to vulnerability in international markets.

The pairing of oil and openness is obvious. In each of the cases a
vulnerability in volatile world oil markets is associated with the decisions
by states to become market players. This association obtains whether the
state is highly dependent upon oil imports, as in Britain, France, and
Italy before World War II, or had its own crude reserves, as in Norway
and Britain after 1970. These state interventions have been market-
displacing because they were intended to displace *foreign* market participants.

But the obvious is not always very revealing. Although a determination to establish state ownership of petroleum resources is uniformly
linked to security issues, the definition of national interest and the vulnerability of domestic markets to foreign control do not seem related to
state intervention in a consistent way. Japan, where vulnerability to foreign disruptions of supply has been greatest, relies on market-conforming intervention; so does the United States, where supply vulnerability is
mitigated by domestic production.

We need to consider how market structure and openness are related.
In France before 1914, for example, a refiners' cartel was overwhelmed
by vertically integrated majors. French capital responded by integrating

upstream into Poland, Rumania, and the greatest prize of all, Meso-potamia. This response encouraged private support for state interven-tion, for downstream integration, and for the 1928 legislation protecting French markets. In Britain, where private entrepreneurs also took ini-tiatives to help the military define the national interest, opposition from coal producers was unsuccessful against a determined coalition of navy and oil firms. In the AGIP case, however, the Italian state encountered neither support nor opposition on the domestic front. It was free to define the national interest and its own role in the market. Later, with the support of industrial consumers, AGIP was broadened into ENI and was able to displace foreign firms and overrule other private interests.

In short, it seems that the structure of domestic markets can mitigate the impact of vulnerability and openness upon state intervention. In Japan, we shall discover, oil markets are exceptionally fragmented. They are vertically truncated (refiners and producers are not the same) and have faced consolidated, politically influential competition from coal producers. Vulnerability and openness predict a commercially active Japanese state; the prediction is incorrect. State intervention depends not only on vulnerability but on *who* is vulnerable and *where* that vulnera-ble sector is in a particular political economy. We must examine the interactions among openness, market structure, and the breadth and stability of the ruling coalition.

The importance of this last variable is highlighted by the coal case, particularly by a comparison between Britain and Japan. Both nations were, in William Lockwood's phrase, "built on coal and surrounded by fish."[80] In both countries the history of state intervention in coal pre-dates and rivals in extent that of any other sector of the economy. More-over, the political history of state intervention in both coal industries is one of experimentation with statutory cartels, production schemes, col-lective marketing agreements, subsidies to marginal mines not to pro-duce, rationalization programs, and numerous false starts toward ulti-mately different experiences with state ownership. An observation offered by the 1930 Coal Mines Act, in Great Britain, applies to Japan at any time between 1930 and 1970: "In view of the unacceptability of the free market as a means of dealing with surplus capacity . . . government action [was] designed to expedite structural adjustment. . . . The most obvious form of government intervention, short of complete nationaliza-tion of the mines, was the promotion of amalgamation as a direct means of eliminating redundant units of production."[81] In both countries crises in coal production after the war raised the issue of whether there could be any resolution short of fundamental changes in ownership and the structure of control in the industry.[82] It is clear that public policy in both countries derived from similar constraints on state action; yet in Japan, unlike Britain, neither compulsory reorganization nor direct state ownership was ever legislated.

For all these parallels, the single most immediate difference was the Labour government that took power in Britain in 1945. Two years later an equivalent Japanese experiment with a Socialist cabinet lasted only eight months. This temporary instability in the Japanese coalition helps explain why the bureaucracy came so close to achieving state control, but subsequently Japan's "iron and rice" coalition consolidated itself and expanded, ending discussions of state ownership. State planners in both countries faced similar political constraints, but the limited prospects for alternation in power seemed to make market-displacing intervention in Japan ill-advised just as the better prospects for Labour government made market displacement an option in Britain. The stability and the breadth of the Japanese ruling coalition across war, depression, occupation, and reconstruction overwhelmed the opportunity for market-displacing change in Japan.

The significance of shifts in ruling coalition seems even better illustrated by the case of ENEL. In Italy a recalcitrant state met recalcitrant business in an artful negotiation of reciprocal consent that transformed the ownership and control of an entire industry. But ENEL and the other electric power nationalizations explored in this chapter also suggest that my initial hypotheses about the relationship between market structure and state intervention were incomplete. Although I proposed in Chapter 1 that states will intervene to displace fragmented markets sooner than consolidated ones, electric power indicates different possibilities.

In Britain and France industrial fragmentation may actually have impeded progress toward state control of electric power; consolidation in Italy may have facilitated it. The highly fragmented sector in Britain and France was divided into several politically relevant groupings, each of whose demands had to be satisfied before the state could become a market player. In France, there were 2,700 firms immediately after the war; they were divided among autogenerators, small, vertically integrated generating firms, and foreign-owned utilities; in addition, equipment manufacturers exacted a price for compliance. ENEL was different: although the political accommodations involved the same groups of utilities and industrial consumers, and though autogenerators abandoned alliance with commercial power firms to gain exemptions, in Italy the utilities were only nominally fragmented. Several hundred producers of electric power were controlled by five major holding companies.

Thus the evidence on fragmentation is mixed. All three cases resulted in a commercial presence for the state, a situation considerably different from what obtains in Japan. But it is not at all clear that market structure provides a clear window on explanations for the difference. We have to look at other sectors and incorporate Japanese cases more directly to understand how market structure may affect state intervention.

Without detailed explorations of politics at the equivalent points of compact in Japan, in short, we cannot explain these differences or even judge their significance. The next four chapters therefore provide historical analyses of Japanese struggles over the nature and extent of state intervention in four critical energy sectors. They trace how the Japanese state became a partner and guarantor instead of a competitor for private industry. The policy record of Japanese state interventions goes beyond single points of compact during nationalization debates. It provides a comprehensive history of market transformations in coal, oil, electric power and alternative energies. That history allows us to map the politics of reciprocal consent and to trace the negotiation of jurisdiction and control where states and markets intersect.

CHAPTER THREE

A Political History of
the Japanese Coal Industry

This chapter reconstructs several hundred years of transformation of the Japanese coal market. It is neither a business history nor a policy review. Instead, it outlines the role of the Japanese state in the coal market against the strategies of private firms and, in turn, the strategies of private firms against the capabilities of the Japanese state. This interaction illuminates the ways in which Japan's politics of reciprocal consent result in market-conforming interventions that contrast sharply with the European experiences explored in Chapter 2.

ORIGINS OF THE INDUSTRY

Coal was the primary industrial fuel and feedstock for the first half-century of Japan's industrial transformation. Long before the industrial revolution started, however, the coal mines had attracted state intervention. In fact, coal was the first business of the Japanese state. Mining commenced more than two hundred years ago, when coal from Kyushu's Chikuhō region was privately traded along the Inland Sea.[1] At first coal was only a personal fuel, produced by peasants as a sideline in primitive mines relying entirely upon human and animal labor. Later, a commodity market began to take shape, and a limited trade emerged for the use of coal in the manufacture of gunpowder and roofing tiles.

By the early nineteenth century Japan had, by the standards of the day, an advanced mining industry. Coal demand was increasing as the financial condition of many *han* governments was deteriorating. Feudal governments in coal-mining regions responded to their fiscal crisis by assuming direct ownership and management of coal mines.[2] Feudal managers instituted the *shikumihō*, an innovative technique for public control of production and trade. An annual forecast of production volume formed the basis for production allocations to each mine. Advance payments (*maegashi*) were proffered to cover salaries and rice for the workers before mining started. Each mine was compelled to deliver its product to *han*-managed control centers, where the coal was allocated to wholesalers (*tonya*), who sold it on behalf of the *han*. The system proved so successful that it was applied to poultry and egg production as well.[3]

The Meiji Restoration changed all this—several times over. Because *han* management filled the coffers of the daimyo with independent revenues, it was judged a threat to the new central government. In February 1869, months after the restoration, the new government proclaimed the release of all mines to the private sector. This "miniprivatization" was undertaken to consolidate the new regime; it did not represent a commitment to private mine development, nor was it a response to demands from private entrepreneurs. The young state had problems far more pressing than philosophical choices between private- and public-led economic development.

Indeed, the release of public mines proved quite short-lived. In October 1870 the Ministry of Engineering (Kōbushō) was established with jurisdiction over mining, railways, construction, and steel, and it immediately began a study of state management of the mines. Its first subsequent act, again to protect its new authority, was to remove the coal mine licensing system from local control in April 1871. Three months later the *han* were formally abolished and replaced by prefectures (*ken*) under central government control.

The Meiji state was confronting past and potential administrative rivals rather than an established private sector. In March 1872 the government promulgated its first mining regulations, the *kokoroegatasho*, providing that all mined substances belong to the emperor. This act formally separated land ownership from mining rights, and foreigners were prohibited from owning or managing mines. Four months later the charcoal offices, formerly *han*-managed, were abolished, and sales of coal were deregulated. The final act establishing the Japanese state as the central participant in the coal market was the promulgation on September 21, 1873, of the first coal mining industry law (Nippon Kōhō), which provided for public ownership and management and delivered "arbitrary powers" to the state (*kokka senken shugi*).

With this authority, the Meiji state assumed ownership and control of the Miike and Takashima collieries, which, like many other newly nationalized industries, had initially been developed by *han* governments. These were to become the most productive collieries in Japan. Their future owners and managers, the Mitsui and Mitsubishi *zaibatsu* respectively, are therefore central characters in the political history of the Japanese coal industry.

The Meiji government was nevertheless committed no more to state ownership than to private economic development.[4] High capital, technology, and transport costs and the need to exclude foreign capital or to produce munitions coalesce in a rationale for state ownership which is at best retrospective. In fact, the state initially showed little interest in direct management of the nation's coal mines. The problem was that private investors showed even less. Finding other investments more attractive, entrepreneurs were not prepared to risk the large-scale capital investments associated with technology importation and mining development. This conservatism extended to virtually all heavy industrial sectors; the state tried and repeatedly failed to entice private subscriptions.

We have no unambiguous record of the Meiji decision to assume control of the mines, but we do know that the business elite of the day initially welcomed the state initiative as protection from foreign merchants.[5] We know also that as soon as demands for privatization of the mines were voiced and private capital was prepared to shoulder the (by then reduced) investment burdens, the mines were quickly turned over to them. It seems reasonable, therefore, to consider the nationalization of Japan's mining industry in the context of business strategy as well as in the context of state leadership and vision. "It seemed almost inevitable," Raymond Vernon writes, "that Japanese business should summon up the help of government in overcoming its latecomer status."[6] Inevitable or not, this reciprocity has characterized relations between Japanese business and the state throughout Japan's subsequent and better documented industrial history.

An immediate problem facing state managers was a steady supply of labor. As government officials, they had access to a unique labor pool—the criminal population. In July 1873, fifty convicts were released from the Mitsuma jails and "employed" on an experimental basis. Subsequently more than one-hundred-fifty prisoners from Fukuoka jails joined the Miike mine labor force, and by 1880 fully 40 percent of the workers at Miike were prisoners from various Kyushu prisons.[7] In Hokkaido, where the government assumed control of the Horonai Mines in 1882 as part of its Hokkaido development program, prison authorities formally supervised some of the mines. Convict rebellions erupted on occasion, but negligible labor costs and technological gains resulted in exceptionally high profits, as much as 50 percent by 1886–87.[8]

Those profits were already being shared with the Mitsui *zaibatsu*. In July 1876 Mitsui Bussan, the general trading arm of the nascent commercial empire, was established. It was immediately granted a monopoly on sales of Miike coal, secured by a personal relationship between Masuda Takashi, the president of Bussan, and Itō Hirobumi, the minister of industry. An exclusive sales contract during this period of state ownership provided a 2.5 percent brokerage fee on all sales and 50 percent of net profits from all overseas trade. Moreover, the state supplied coal to Bussan at cost (2 yen/ton).[9] Bussan's profits soared. The capital accumulated through this special relationship was central to the development of the Mitsui *zaibatsu*.

The government had already sold the Takashima mines. Only fifteen months after the state had assumed control of Takashima, and although the colliery was operating smoothly and production had increased, it turned the mine over to Gotō Shōjirō in 1874.[10] Gotō was a Tosa *han* restoration activist, an early adviser to the new Foreign Ministry, and an intimate of the Meiji leadership. Two years earlier in 1872, he had used his influence to purchase other mines in Iwaki, an experience that seems to have helped him evaluate the potential at Takashima. The terms of the deal in 1874 were favorable: Gotō paid a bit over half a million yen, only 40 percent up front, for what were at the time the only mechanized mines in Japan. But if Gotō was a clever forecaster, he was an inept manager. Having borrowed operating capital from a British firm, he was unable to assume control of his own mines. To extricate himself from a lawsuit filed by his British creditors, and to raise capital to cover other debts, Gotō sold the Takashima mines to Mitsubishi in March 1881.

The wholesale privatization of state-owned factories had begun in November 1880, but with the exception of Takashima the coal mines remained under government management until 1888. In the interim the first major conflict between public and private mining firms erupted. The state had to compete in the market place to sell its coal, which occasionally resulted in what Sumiya Mikio calls "strong pressure and opposition from the privately owned mining companies." In 1885, for example, publicly owned Miike was advancing on the China market with the assistance of Mitsui Bussan. Mitsubishi's Takashima complained of unfair competition, and the Ministry of Industry responded by halving Miike's coal production for one year over vigorous objections from Mitsui.[11]

For the Japanese coal industry, 1888–89 was a year of epochal change. Eight years after the Government Factory Disposition Law had proclaimed that "various factories established by the government for the purpose of encouraging private industries having served their original purposes . . . should now be relinquished to private ownership," and after public funds had been used to modernize them through the importation of foreign technology, the two remaining state-run coal mines were sold.[12] In August 1888 the Miike mines were sold to Sasaki Hachirō, acting as proxy (*kagemusha*, or shadow warrior) for Mitsui Bussan's president.[13] Sasaki paid just 4.56 million yen and formally transferred the mining rights to the Mitsui Mining Company (Mitsui Kōzan) within five months. In December 1889 the government sold the mining rights to its Horonai fields and to its railway in Hokkaido, creating the Hokkaido Tankō Tetsudō Kaisha (Hokutan), which continued its close relationship with the state by cooperating in the development of the Hokkaido frontier. Clearly there was favoritism in the Horonai sale, but the Horonai collieries were sold not to a merchant with strong ties to politicians but to the former administrator of Hokkaido for the Meiji government, a Satsuman with close ties to Prime Minister Kuroda and other Restoration leaders.[14]

By 1889 the three most important government-run mines had become the three most modern and productive private mines. We know that there had been no competitors for mining rights when the state first assumed responsibility for developing these mines; no private entrepreneurs had come forward to share the risks and expenses of these projects.[15] How can we explain privatization? Was the Meiji state so completely the instrument of private interests that it delivered a massively profitable factor of production upon demand? Was the state already so deeply committed to free enterprise that it embraced its first opportunity to give control of Japan's economic future to a dynamic private sector?

The answers are not simple. This was surely the most extensive non-coerced privatization in economic history. Many Japanese scholars posit a Meiji bureaucracy eager to win the favor of the capitalist classes.[16] In this view, privatization was implemented to establish an alliance between the state and private industry which would ensure concentration and thereby facilitate control of the economy. As Sumiya puts it, by 1876 "the existence of private capital could no longer be ignored."[17]

Though no doubt true, this fails to explain why the Miike and Horonai coal mines were privatized eight years *after* government factories were first sold to private investors, in 1880. According to one account, Finance Minister Matsukata Masayoshi, the architect of these sales, opposed the sale of Miike because, unlike other government enterprises, it was turning a profit.[18]

Yet Matsukata was "compelled" (for reasons unspecified) to make the sale.[19] One reason may have been the desperate financial condition of the Meiji government in the early 1880s. Military outlays, the assumption of clan debts, and the issuance of bonds to buy off the aristocracy all drained the public treasury. Beyond that were the expenses of creating a modern economic machine, one that was far from profitable in its early years. Corruption and inflation, caused by a Meiji government living beyond its means, led to imminent financial collapse, and it is not unlikely that the state welcomed the chance to bail itself out. Coal prices had meanwhile recovered after a three-year recession, setting off active competition for mining rights in 1888. The ambiguity in this reconstruction of events is reflected in Sumiya's account:

> While there is no denying that [these sales] were related to political and fiscal considerations by the government, the coincidental timing of these events was by no means an accident. . . . The capitalist economic system that was coming firmly to establish its ground no longer welcomed large-scale publicly managed coal mines, and even the government no longer necessarily saw them as essential.[20]

What is clear is how the future structure of the Japanese coal industry was being shaped through this privatization. There were two varieties of Meiji-era mining firms. The larger ones, such as Miike, Takashima, and Horonai, had been state-managed and were the first to introduce Western mining technologies and geological survey techniques.[21] The three largest mines accounted for nearly half of Japan's total coal production, one-third to one-half of which was exported between 1874 and 1886.[22] In contrast, hundreds of smaller mines clustered in separate mining districts such as Jōban, Chikuhō, and Karatsu. These collieries produced exclusively for a domestic market that consumed coal chiefly in the manufacture of salt (50 percent), shipbuilding (30 percent), and factory use (20 percent).[23] Many of these mines had come into private hands after their release from the control of *han* governments. Often they depended entirely upon capital provided by their jobber/ wholesalers (*tonya*), who controlled much of the market for domestic coal, and some local families amassed great fortunes.[24] The bifurcation between *zaibatsu* mines, centered on formerly state-owned enterprises, and the remaining large mining firms, often referred to as local capital, became characteristic of the Japanese coal-mining industry.[25]

The domestic market for coal now exploded. In 1887 Tokyo Dentō, the progenitor of today's Tokyo Electric Power Company, began operation of Japan's first coal-fired thermal power plant. Shipbuilding, steel, munitions, and other heavy industries consumed an increasing volume of domestic coal. Although exports would continue to take around one-fifth of total domestic coal production as late as 1910, they would never again exceed the nearly 50 percent of 1886. By 1891 production exceeded three million tons for the first time, and by 1896 it was more than five million tons.[26] By 1903 it had reached ten million tons, by 1912 it neared twenty. In 1919 Japanese coal mines disgorged thirty-one million tons of

73

coal, a record that stood until military preparations after the Manchurian Incident in 1931 set off a new expansion in demand. By this time, of course, Japan was a major industrial power, and its profitable coal industry had made distinctive contributions to the consolidation of each of the *zaibatsu* empires.[27]

But explosive growth was accompanied by market volatility. Demand for coal expanded in fits and starts, shaken by occasional market crashes that sent producers and consumers (but, significantly, seldom the state) searching for a formula to stabilize coal supplies. The period 1889–1921 is best seen as an extended groping for collusion, one that failed to overcome the exigencies of both the domestic and the international market places. There were at least five different stock market crashes in Japan before the October 1929 New York crash sent the global economy spinning. Coal prices peaked four times between 1899 and 1939 in perfect correspondence to preparations for war. Each boom was preceded by coal price crashes from which they never fully recovered.[28]

Prosperity came and went, and so did labor unrest. Mine workers in Japan, as in Europe and the United States, were among the most exploited in the work force. They worked under ghastly conditions for the wages of poverty. Japan's first major mine accident, in Toyokuni in June 1899, claimed 210 lives, and miners' strikes disrupted production throughout the early years of the twentieth century. The industry went into depression in 1908, emerging nearly one thousand miner-deaths later with the nation's first coal labor organization, the Yūaikai, founded in August 1912 by fifteen Christian workers as a mutual aid society for miners in the Chikuhō region. It was broken up within five months by Mitsui Mining, which, fearing it might lose control of the work force, created a company union. Mitsui threatened to fire its miners unless they joined the company union.[29]

It was not until two gas explosions killed over one thousand miners in 1914 that the government finally issued its first Coal Mine Explosion Supervisory Regulations, effective September 1916. Numerous safety regulations followed, most in response to the International Labor Organization's 1919 Washington accord. But mining firms, particularly the labor-intensive small and medium-sized firms, lobbied successfully to delay the implementation of these regulations (including the eight-hour day and restrictions on nighttime labor for women and children) until 1928–29. Kiso Shigeyoshi, a leader of small mineowners and a Fukuoka prefectural assemblyman, had led the movement to delay the implementation of the 1919 ILO agreement on women and child labor.[30] Many small mines depended upon labor contractors; the backbone of a system not much changed since the Meiji era was the "double harness" system in which husband and wife worked as a team. One coal industry official, looking back at the early Japanese mines, remarked that "this was before we Japanese considered miners people."[31] Rice riots and coal mine disturbances were frequent until 1919, when the "shed system" (*naya seido*) was finally abolished; some labor organization followed, but it was never enough to alleviate the brutality of miners' lives.

Throughout this period the producers weathered market panics and labor unrest, fumbling for a stable instrument of collusion. During the recessions of 1890, 1907, 1909, and 1911 the large mines of Kyushu repeatedly tried and failed to support prices by limiting production. In January 1912 the Mitsui, Kaijima, and Aso mining firms agreed to pool accounts and create a joint sales system. Matsushima Mining joined in 1915, but the boom of World War I led to internal disagreements over coal prices. The arrangement was dissolved in November 1917, but not before it had succeeded in instituting Japan's first successful agreement to limit production, a 5 percent cutback in May 1914.

This cartel faced a competing cartel of Mitsubishi, Yasukawa, and Furukawa, also based in Chikuhō and established in 1913. But industry leaders had no success in making these agreements stick. In Hokkaido, where Mitsui was already predominant, a sales cartel was more easily established. In 1914 the sales divisions of Hokutan, Mitsui, and Bussan were joined and accounts pooled. In Jōban a cartel was established with the participation of Mitsui, Furukawa, Iriyama, and others. Although these regional cartels initially slowed the erosion of coal prices in their areas, violations of agreements were frequent enough to destroy each of them. The war boom and internal dissent temporarily ended overt collusion. When collusion reappeared in 1921, it was in different form and on an enlarged scale. But it would still not bear the stamp of state intervention, nor would its agreements prove much more lasting.[32]

COLLUSION AND SELF-CONTROL

As the twentieth century unfolded, the Japanese coal industry became even more pyramidal and oligopolistic; ten large, modern mining firms came to account for more than three-quarters of total production through the interwar period. These firms included five *zaibatsu* and five non-*zaibatsu* enterprises that found it convenient to organize themselves in a variety of producer and sales cartels to prop up prices. Yet the numerous failures of these associations betray the conflicts that simmered within them. Imputation of common interests among these largest firms also ignores conflict with the hundreds of surviving small producers, conflict that often served to shape both the structure of the coal industry and state intervention within it. Indeed, the persistence of

Husbands and wives worked together in the mines in the "double harness" system well into the twentieth century. Often shafts were narrower than 1.5 meters, forcing miners to crawl. No dynamite was used.

This "double harness" team emerges from one of the many "badger burrows" (*tanuki bori*) that dotted the landscape in Japan's mining regions.

Many thousands of Japanese miners lost their lives in accidents caused in part by the lack of safety regulations and in part by the inaccessibility of the coal deposits.

命切羽の水分の多い石炭は竹製代の（バラ）スラで曳きあげていた百斤も住積込んであるが足がかりとコロも無くツル鑑に伝度、網に充を寄えつた

唐津デザイ人がスる姿婆江戸絵からも摘々やさらねゴット！

Women miners were protected by the ILO Washington Accord signed in 1919, but Japanese mineowners delayed its implementation for a decade. This basket weighed 220 pounds when filled and had no wheels. Miners crawled through these narrow shafts, using small depressions in the floor for footholds.

Many Japanese miners were recruited from (and lived within) the margins of Japanese society. They included convicts in the nineteenth century and Korean and Chinese corvée laborers in the mid-twentieth century.

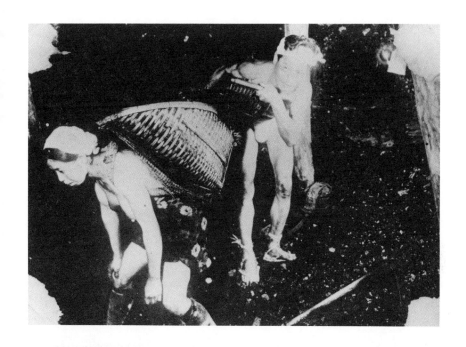

Men and women worked together half-naked in the pits until the late 1920s.

Table 3.1. Market shares in the Japanese coal industry by firm size,
1910–1950 (in percentages)

Year	*Zaibatsu* Firms	All Large Firms	Small/Medium
1910	44.9%	72.9%	27.1%
1914	45.3	76.2	23.8
1921	37.3	77.7	22.3
1929	40.6	87.1	12.9
1933	40.5	83.2	16.8
1938	46.1	85.5	14.5
1941	46.5	79.2	20.8
1943	45.9	77.3	22.7
1945	52.5	80.9	19.1
1947	43.7	73.2	26.8
1950	42.3	72.2	27.8

SOURCE: Ōki 1961: 252.

these small firms was, as we shall see, as much a political as an economic triumph. The five *zaibatsu* collieries did not extend their dominance at all between 1910 and the Pacific War (see Table 3.1). The stability of their share is more striking than is the expansion of the large firms as a whole.

Producers were too numerous and markets were too volatile to sustain collusive behavior for very long. That behavior—what the Japanese call self-control—formally began in May 1921 when producers agreed to limitations on coal transportation. In October a permanent, nationwide body to regulate private coal production, the Sekitan Kōgyō Rengōkai (SKR), was formally established with Aso Takichi as chairman. The state played no role in this agreement. The SKR was a production cartel designed to fix market shares through adjustment of coal shipments. All the large mining companies, both *zaibatsu* and non-*zaibatsu* affiliates, were party to it.[33] The collieries were organized into six regional groups, within which separate sales cartels could be administered. Members agreed to limit shipments to the market place by providing incentives to stockpile excess production at mine sites. But most of these cartel shipment limitations became meaningless almost as soon as they came into effect. The difference between agreed limitations and actual shipments was usually sufficient to keep prices suppressed and the market disorderly. The SKR established a system of levies or penalties for production in excess of agreed limits, but these agreements were renegotiated at least six times between 1921 and 1932, when a more formal sales cartel, Shōwa Sekitan, was established—clear evidence of failure.

The crisis in the coal industry finally erupted as a public policy issue in 1930. Stock prices plummeted again in March. By August the depression had bought stockpiles to their highest level in history, 3.2 million tons. Nearly five hundred of the nation's smallest mines, the so-called badger burrows (*tanuki bori*) shut down, resulting in widespread unemployment in mining districts. Small mineowners, who depended upon the large mining firms for sales and upon their wholesalers for finance, found themselves in desperate trouble. Their share of the market had declined precipitously through the 1920s, from 22.3 percent in 1921 to 12.9 percent in 1929, while the share of the *zaibatsu* firms had remained constant. Serving as a buffer, then, the smallest firms suffered first and worst with the global depression.[34]

If small mineowners suffered in the market, they were not without considerable political resources. They felled their first major target in April 1930, when they successfully protested prejudicial supply contracts with the national railways. Encouraged by this success, and facing literally a life and death struggle (*shikatsu mondai*), small and medium-sized firms organized in September 1930 as the Sekitan Kōgyō Gojokai (hereafter *gojokai*). They next demanded, in December 1930, that the private electric railway companies reduce their transport rates and ultimately won a 10 percent reduction.[35]

These limited victories were merely preludes to two separate political struggles that would firmly secure the commercial rights of these firms and frustrate state planners and large mineowners alike. In October 1931 Kiso Shigeyoshi and other *gojokai* leaders decided that the real threat to their existence was not the ILO labor accord but competition from cheap Manchurian imports, known as Bujun coal.[36] After the Manchurian Incident of September 1931, the Bujun Coal Company, a joint venture established in 1923 which combined the South Manchurian Railway Company (Mantetsu), Mitsui Bussan, and Mitsubishi Shōji, lost its access to the Shanghai market. It contracted to sell 1.85 million tons of coal to the Japanese National Railways at a delivered price 7–8 yen per ton below cost. Most coal imports from Manchuria involved coking coal for the steel industry, but this dumping of steam coal directly threatened the *gojokai* firms. Mantetsu summarily dismissed protests of a *gojokai* delegation accompanied by several Fukuoka Diet representatives. The army, in turn, sternly informed the delegates that the importation of Bujun coal was a matter of national policy and could not be challenged.

Kiso and his associates tried a different tack. They decided to make this a social issue. The *gojokai* organized a chain of mine closures, giving miners advance notice and informing them that Bujun coal imports were the cause. In June 1932, fanning tensions in the miners' camps, the *gojokai* then organized two thousand miners for an assembly at Hakata Station and a march upon the Fukuoka prefectural offices. The besieged governor of Fukuoka appealed the case to Tokyo, where the national press made it a *cause célèbre*. Within two weeks formal negotiations involving the SKR, the *gojokai*, and Mantetsu yielded an agreement: large mining firms would cut back their sales by 800,000 tons, and Bujun coal shipments would be reduced by more than half. Bujun coal would find a Japanese market, but not entirely at the expense of the small mining firms—the *zaibatsu*-affiliated firms, which had a financial stake in Manchuria, would assume a large share of the burden. Takeuchi Reizō, leading *gojokai* figure, announced the victory to miners assembled at Fukuoka, who thereupon queued up to receive 50 yen per day for their time. Soon thereafter, in February 1933, the *gojokai* split from formal association with the large mining firms, refusing to continue limitations on coal shipments.[37]

Small and medium firms, while far from dominating the coal market place, had nevertheless demonstrated a substantial independence and political power. And as we shall see, the *gojokai* was far from finished with defending its interests against encroachments of the state or the large coal firms.

In the early thirties militarism and state control were threatening small and large firms alike, in coal as in other sectors of the economy. In August 1931 the Important Industries Control Law was promulgated.[38] On March 1, 1932, the government declared the establishment of the Manchurian State. Four days later Baron Dan Takuma, the MIT-educated mining engineer who led the Mitsui holding company, was killed by militant rightists. Junior naval and army officers assassinated Prime Minister Inukai Tsuyoshi in May. In the face of these developments, and in what may be viewed as a protective reaction to the rise of interventionist bureaucrats and militarists, the large mining firms agreed in November to expand their cooperation beyond the SKR production system. They created Japan's first nationwide sales cartel, the Shōwa Coal Company (Shōwa Sekitan). As noted, virtually all previous efforts to limit competition in the coal industry had collapsed once recovery was under way. Now, for the first time, the threat of market volatility was joined by the threat of state control.

The model for Shōwa Sekitan was Ruhrkohle, the German syndicate.[39] The ten largest mining firms, joined by Mitsui Bussan, agreed to allocate market shares and fix prices. Most important, they strengthened penalties for violations of cartel agreements. Market prices, which had deteriorated badly, began to recover by the second half of 1932, though more because of increased military demand than stricter cartel enforcement.

By 1934 the industry was setting new production records; oil was still playing a minor role in the energy economy, an ambitious and ultimately unsuccessful coal-based synthetic fuels program was initiated (another importation from Nazi Germany), and import controls were in place. Mining company profits rebounded from under 3 percent in 1931 to almost 14 percent by 1934. In May the government issued its program to rationalize coal production and distribution under the Important Industries Control Law, but even the hint of state controls raised immediate and vocal opposition from the large firms. Furuta Keizō, the managing director of Shōwa Sekitan, was among the first publicly to condemn state intervention.[40] Production continued to expand. In 1936 Japan became the third largest coal producer in the world when domestic mines produced more than 40 million tons of coal for the first time. State planners backed off. They took no further initiatives until prodded in 1937 by representatives of coal-consuming industries, who complained about high coal prices and demanded intervention.

In May 1937 Matsumoto Kenjirō, the chairman of Shōwa Sekitan, was summoned to a meeting with Minister of Commerce and Industry Godō.[41] Godō presented Matsumoto with a draft five-year plan for continued production increases to meet projected demand from the military and related industries. Matsumoto used the occasion to denounce state control. He demanded continued self-control under the existing cartel arrangements and sought additional measures for public finance and labor supply. As late as June 1937 the government seemed unwilling to confront the cartel. A secret army plan dated June 10 stated that "whatever the final shape of the industry, we are not planning for it to be state-owned and state-run. To the best of our ability we should achieve national goals through self-control based upon private management."[42]

But industrial consumers were growing impatient. Between May 1932 and May 1937 Shōwa Sekitan raised coal prices eight times. "Progressive" (*kakushin*) bureaucrats at the Ministry of Commerce and Industry (MCI) issued a program in November 1937 in the name of new MCI minister Yoshino Shinji, calling for the state to control coal production and distribution.[43] This Yoshino Plan, formally presented to the Diet in February 1938, would have given the state sweeping powers to exploit idle coal fields. consolidate mining districts, and establish a unified sales organ with administered prices. Had this program been accepted, state powers in militarist Japan would have closely resembled those established under a Labour government in Britain.

The Yoshino Plan was tabled, however, because of opposition from the large mining firms. The firms made it clear that such controls, in the absence of fiscal measures and compensation, would discourage new capital investment. In addition, they argued, a licensing system should be created to regulate all new small-scale mining ventures. Instead of a comprehensive measure to ensure state control of the coal industry, "because the time was not yet ripe," the Diet passed a production incentive program for all mined substances in March 1938.[44] No further action was taken to implement direct state controls for almost two years.

In the meantime, in June 1938, the MCI queried the major coal-consuming industries about coal prices and distribution. With the full support of electric utilities and steel firms, and in response to their demands for more effective coal allocation, distribution, and pricing, the MCI established committees to control coal production and distribution (*tōsei kyōgikai*) under its supervision in early July.[45] By the end of the month coal prices reached historic highs on the Tokyo market, as large producers withheld shipments in protest. After a chaotic summer of negotiations the first direct price controls were finally imposed on September 1. Coal was designated as central to military planning; Shōwa Sekitan agreed to reduce prices, but only by 10 percent, and in October distribution controls were to be introduced. These negotiated agreements and controls notwithstanding, prices to end-users remained volatile. Black marketeering, substitutions of lower grades of coal, and steam coal shortages gripped the economy. The new controls had the iatrogenic effect of dampening production by the large mining firms. Worse, while Shōwa Sekitan coal production declined in 1939, production by "outsiders" was growing.[46] Prices, distribution, and production were all breaking down at a critical time. Self-control had failed.

"STATE CONTROL" OF COAL

As the Japanese nation prepared for war, the Japanese state sought more direct control of the economy. After the outbreak of hostilities in China in 1937, the military government began actively to invest in the nation's heavy industry. One after another, several dozen national policy companies (*kokusaku gaisha*) were created "to expand the productive capacity of the Empire, particularly in war essentials," and by 1939 the Finance Ministry was a leading shareholder in many of Japan's major firms, including Nippon Steel, a national electric utility, a synthetic fuels corporation, and various metals, fabricating, and trading firms. In addition, legislation targeting particular industries, beginning with the general Important Industries Control Law and including the Petroleum Industry Law, gave the government what appeared to be sweeping control over private industry and a productive role in the economy. Nonetheless, the politics of the Japanese policy process, even at this critical wartime juncture, severely circumscribed state power. Private coal interests repeatedly and successfully intervened in state deliberations, redirecting state controls toward more congenial mechanisms. This substitution of jurisdiction for control obtained in the petroleum and electric power sectors as well, but nowhere was it clearer than in coal.

In the summer of 1939 the wartime economy was desperately strained by problems in the distribution of strategic materials. Coal for electric power was in short supply or unavailable in western Japan. Nippatsu, the national electric utility established in April, was depending upon "outsiders" for 60 percent of its steam coal, whose quality had deteriorated because of simultaneous orders for price reductions and production increases.[47] Self-control, according to Tomoyoshi Nezu, had already fallen into "great disarray."[48]

The Yoshino Plan was resurrected, this time with the active support of Nippatsu, the steel industry, and the army. A report (Sekitan Taisaku Yōmō) issued by the MCI's Central Commodity Price Council on August 30, 1939 called for: unified prices and centralized distribution, administered by a monopolistic state corporation according to publicly established production and allocation targets.

Predictably this radical plan brought sustained political opposition. The "great uproar" (*ōsawagi*) of opposition was led by sales and distribution firms, which feared the loss of their commercial rights. To these wholesalers (and indeed to their affiliated small and medium-sized mining firms) a state monopoly over direct sales threatened their survival. In mid-September the Wakamatsu Commercial Association in Fukuoka sponsored a conference that resolved absolute opposition to state controls. The resolutions received nationwide attention and were repeated at meetings of local and regional associations throughout Japan. Within a month the National Association of Coal Sales Firms was demanding the preservation of the existing system and created a new and separate national federation (Zenkoku Sekitan Hanbai Gyōsha Renmei) to press these demands upon bureaucrats and politicians. These sectoral opposition voices were joined on October 26 by the more broadly constituted Japan Chamber of Commerce, which publicly endorsed the coal merchants' demands.

Meanwhile the *zaibatsu* firms, equally resistant to the state plan but with better access to state planners, were working behind the scenes to extract concessions directly from MCI. In October MCI minister Godō formally sought the support of the large mining interests at a meeting of the influential and restricted Public/Private Cooperation Council (Kanmin Gōdō Kyōgikai). Shōwa Coal chairman Matsumoto promised full cooperation in exchange for private control of, or at least private influence over, prices, production, and industrial structure.[49] The *zaibatsu* firms agreed to cooperate, in other words, but not according to MCI rules. *Zaibatsu* coal demanded representation on the establishment committee for the national policy company, the Japan Coal Corporation (Nippon Sekitan, hereafter Nittan). Matsumoto himself was nominated, and the *zaibatsu* were on board.

The committee never had the chance to convene. Active opposition from wholesalers and smaller mine operators forced delays of several months in formal presentation of a Nittan establishment bill to Diet. By mid-December representatives of these wholesalers were meeting with MCI officials further to revise the government's program for coal. On December 28, 1939, the Special Subcommittee on Coal Prices of the Central Price Committee announced it would formally reconsider plans for a national policy company to expropriate private sales and distribution.

Politicization continued. During January and February 1940 MCI found itself in protracted negotiations with highly agitated non-*zaibatsu* private interests. On January 12 the Central Price Committee announced a new program. It omitted the expropriation of sales functions by a state enterprise, relying instead upon the existing distribution system. It continued, however, to seek the rationalization of prices and allocation through guidance by the proposed Nittan.

Although this revision may have placated the distribution and sales firms that had led initial political opposition, it served only to intensify the strident opposition from small and medium-sized mining firms, which anticipated a strengthening of *zaibatsu* coal at their expense. Indeed, preparations for the submission of the revised bill now proceeded with the cooperation and support of the *zaibatsu* firms. On Janaury 23, four separate groups of small and medium-sized coal producers joined in coalition against the government program. They made three demands: 1) reconsideration of plans for any state monopoly; 2) immediate revision of any state controls on coal distribution; and 3) increased financial assistance for increased production. On February 17 the Osaka Chamber of Commerce demanded that the MCI raise its coal price ceilings, provide new production subsidies, and allow for a purely private coal market place. Two days later the small miners' *gojokai* convened a two-day conference in Fukuoka. Over two hundred businessmen cut out of the initial deal pledged to intensify their political efforts to eviscerate what remained of state control.

These firms now faced a formidable coalition: the state, *zaibatsu* interests, and the wholesalers upon whose goodwill and "paternal kindness" (*onjō*) they often depended for financial services. The small owners carried on through March 1940, but were ultimately unsuccessful. The ministry held that the state had already conceded enough to private interests; after all, the commercial rights of these smaller firms would now to be guaranteed.

On March 3, 1940, the Coal Distribution Control Bill was ratified by the cabinet, and Diet passed the measure before the end of the month. Large mining interests and wholesale distributors applied political pressures separately, resulting in major alterations in the MCI program for state control of coal. Matsumoto recalls in his memoirs that the plan was to establish a single national policy company that would purchase all coal and act as a single sales agency, but because this would eliminate the management rights of existing firms . . . and because the industry responded with great opposition, the plan resulted in a stalemate. . . . The government, after all, gave in.[50]

Kiso, the *gojokai* leader, recalls that the army was more difficult to convince than the MCI but that "in our negotiations with the military concerning the creation of Nittan, we made them revise their coal distribution control legislation and we made them establish a coal resale system."[51]

Nittan, considerably transformed through political debate, began operations in October 1940. Shōwa Sekitan was formally dissolved. The new coal control organ was an effort to "bundle up" coal brand names and administer prices according to a target price (*hyōjunka*) system. In fact, however, the state was not a producer; actual production and resale were conducted by existing firms. Nittan, lacking the authority to mine or distribute products, was metaphorically labeled a "tunnel company" (*tonneru gaisha*); it was an enterprise with holes at both ends linking producers upstream with consumers downstream (see Figure 3.1). Its pricing system, one observer claims, "bore absolutely no relationship" to the market place.[52] The low selling price of delivered coal had to be secured by heavy subsidies to producers; Nittan's ability to act as an instrument of state control had been seriously eroded. "As far as the system of direct coal distribution to consumers is concerned," Nezu argues, "the original proposal for a direct state monopoly was watered down, revised to allow a role for existing firms. For this reason, wartime controls were not complete and problems in the basic program later served to complicate matters quite severely."[53]

Controls were at best indirect; they were tied ultimately to the Coal Control Association (Sekitan Tōseikai), formed in November 1941 with responsibility for distribution but dominated by the large mining firms.[54] The inaugural meeting of the association was held twelve days after the Japanese attack on Pearl Harbor had introduced a new urgency to measures for industrywide coordination. This control organ and its local subsidiaries established under the Important Industrial Group Law (Jūyō Sangyō Dantai Hō) were charged with supply and demand planning, production plans, materiel allocation, capital acquisition, and labor procurement.

Some have argued that this system was established completely at the initiative of the state, and that with its creation self-control by private industry ended.[55] But although the association formally absorbed existing producers' organs such as the *gojokai* and the SKR, large capital retained much room to maneuver.[56] At no point did the large mining

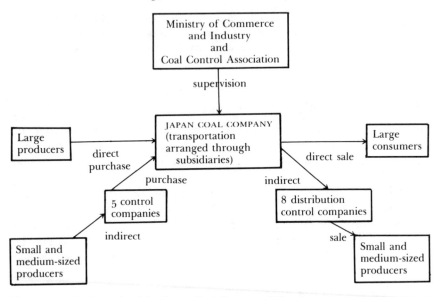

Figure 3.1. Wartime role of the Japan Coal Company (Nittan)

firms lose their independence, and while some leaders, such as Matsumoto, shed crocodile tears over bureaucratic controls, special allocations of labor and materiel to more efficient mines, and fiscal measures to boost coal production, all served (and to a large extent were directed by) the largest firms that dominated the control association's planning.[57] According to one of Matsumoto's assistants, recruited to the control association from Mitsubishi Mining, "while the government had general supervisory responsibilities, the largest mining firms were at the core of the planning process, making most allocative decisions both at the central and the district levels."[58] Others have observed that "controls meant [the pursuit of a coal policy] without damaging the interests of the large mining firms, especially the *zaibatsu,* or rather, the carrying out of a coal policy consistent with their wishes."[59]

The evidence supports this interpretation. The year Nittan was established, 1940, was also the year that Japanese coal production reached a historic peak, nearly 57 million tons. Production held relatively steady until the end of the war, and what increases were achieved were in the small and medium-sized coal mines that the larger firms progressively absorbed and paid for through state subsidies.[60] Public premiums were being paid for new coal, not new investments, guaranteeing profits no matter how inefficient the mine. Between 1943 and 1945 over a dozen different categories of new subsidies were created, often to defuse the complaints of the large mining firms.[61]

Between 1940 and 1942 Nittan merely paid for the coal it purchased and resold. But in the autumn of 1943 the resale or tunnel function was replaced for the first time by an independent sales function (*jibansei*). The government, through the association, moved very cautiously to implement this change ("to avoid confusion and obstacles" Kunisaki Shinsui noted at the time).[62] Now Nittan had the authority to sell coal from mine to consumer, and the prefecture-based control companies would be consolidated into regional blocs based upon wartime regional councils.[63] Mitsui Mining supported the program. These expanded functions were accompanied by expanded subsidies to the mining firms.[64]

Nittan was responsible for increasing coal production while maintaining stable prices for consumers. At the same time it promoted the consolidation of the coal industry in favor of the largest firms. On the production side Nittan paid the mine either the standard price or a price computed on the basis of costs plus profit, whichever was higher. On the consumption side Nittan held prices constant throughout the war. Between 1940 and 1945, while production costs skyrocketed (and were frequently padded), the price of coal to end-users was held steady at 20.13 yen per ton. The difference between production cost and sales price changed from 0.03 yen per ton in 1940 to 48.11 yen per ton by mid-1945. Subsidies from Nittan went from 11.6 million to 2.56 billion yen.[65] To maintain dividends toward the end of the war, moreover, profit margins on production costs were increased and separate production subsidies were introduced.

Those dividends were not trivial. The six major coal-mining firms in Japan maintained an average 7.2 percent dividend throughout the war, not once failing to provide a semiannual return to their shareholders.[66] From the establishment of Nittan until the cessation of hostilities, coal producers received a total increase of more than 400 percent for their coal while end-users enjoyed fixed prices. Only a combination of guaranteed dividends paid to shareholders, the full range of subsidies paid to mining firms, and taxes unpaid by an exempt state enterprise begins to approximate the public costs as well as the private benefits of what were exceedingly incomplete wartime controls.

There were other, human costs as well. Dramatic increases in coal production (200 percent between 1931 and 1945), stimulated in part by government subsidies, did not result from technological innovation. They resulted instead from a huge influx of new miners.[67] In 1932 there were 140,000; by 1944 there were 420,000, many of them women, children, and the elderly sent to replace military conscripts shipped off to Asian battlefields over the objections of mine owners. The number of full-time salaried miners fell dramatically. They were replaced by convicts, prisoners of war, and forced laborers from Korea and China. At the war's end 36 percent of all mine laburers were from this corvée.[68] Mine productivity plummeted; output fell by about 60 percent, from 13.9 to 5.6 tons per person per month. The rush to produce also and predictably produced tragedies of monumental proportions. In April 1942 an explosion in Manchuria killed over 1,500 Chinese workers in what may have been the worst mine disaster in history. At home there were five major mine explosions between March and May 1945 alone. For the miners, to whom the issue was not state control or self-control but survival, the war could not end soon enough.

THE OCCUPATION: TRANSWAR CONTROLS

In terms of labor policy and citizen participation, Japan's defeat in the Pacific War was a watershed in the nation's political development. From the perspective of Japan's industrial development and business-government relations, however, the continuity is as striking as the discontinuity. For one thing, state controls were enhanced by the American-led occupation forces (Supreme Commander for the Allied Powers, hereafter SCAP). In coal, as in oil and other industrial sectors, these postwar controls marked the high point of state intervention in Japanese economic history. Before the occupation ended, the Japanese state experimented and failed with an instrument of coal mine management more direct than any tried during wartime mobilization. That failure was due to the sustained opposition of private opponents to state participation in the economy and has served ever since as a reminder that no British- or French-style nationalization of the mines could succeed in Japan, even under a Socialist prime minister. From the perspective of industry, moreover, it suggests a deeper continuity with the patterns of business-government relations which obtained in the first seven decades of Japanese industrial development. Ōki Yōichi sees these continuities clearly:

> The coal mining industry directly faced two crises in the period of wartime and postwar controls. Those were the wartime demands for increased production of the Yoshino Plan and the postwar state management of the mines. Yet these crises were neutralized without changing the historical character of the coal-mining companies. Indeed, from time to time, using these economic policies, the industry was able to prosper all the more.[69]

SCAP was confronted by important choices and conflicting exigencies. Most important for economic reconstruction was the problem of coal production. By the end of the war shortages of steel and coal were combining in a downward spiral of production shortfalls. One of SCAP's earliest directives (September 15, 1945) ordered maximum coal production, and in October the cabinet adopted new emergency measures for coal production. Coal production was most immediately a matter of labor policy. By early October, even before SCAP's December 1945 Trade Union Law led to an explosion of organizational activity among coal miners, workers had begun organizing in Mitsui's Hokkaido mines. In October alone there were six work stoppages. The first organizers were the underfed and underclothed foreign corvée laborers who had suffered so much during the wartime mobilizations. Their liberation from forced labor released a pent-up hostility toward Japanese mineowners which American troops were required to quell. Riots and anarchy in several mining districts paralyzed production.[70]

Here SCAP's conflicting exigencies came most clearly into focus. The first significant postwar coal policy program was SCAP's November 1945 order to repatriate all foreign miners. In the short run, of course, the move would cripple production and compound the problems of reconstruction which stemmed from the loss of colonial sources for raw materials, lack of mine maintenance, and other materiel shortages. But liberated foreign workers posed too great a threat to Japanese political stability. Indeed, the majority of Korean and Chinese mine laborers had already fled the mining camps. Within five months of war's end the number of foreign miners in Japan dropped by 130,000. By the time of the SCAP order fewer than 20,000 foreign miners were left in the collieries; in December there were fewer than a thousand. In reality, SCAP was ordering the repatriation of *former* miners.[71]

Repatriation did not end labor unrest in the mines or the need for a coherent mine labor policy. Coal Production Emergency Measures after the repatriation order made the distribution of clothing, food, and shelter to miners a priority. Yet mine conditions remained most difficult. Although the number of miners was restored to wartime levels by 1947, over half the miners had less than two years' experience. Productivity barely increased. Japan in 1945 had fewer than one hundred coal unions; SCAP's progressive labor program encouraged growth to more than a thousand by 1948. Numbers of unionized miners grew from 75,000 to half a million within three years, and coal proved both an early and an intractable labor problem for economic planners. Though the labor movement was deeply divided, strikes, such as the March 1946 Miike shutdown by 18,000 workers, frustrated planning schedules. Workers also employed strategies such as "production control," under which miners would take over operations from management. The first official act of the Yoshida Cabinet, two days after its formation in May 1946, was to issue an injunction blocking such tactics.[72]

These difficulties notwithstanding, it is easy to overstate the degree to which labor impeded the recovery of coal production. During the war extraordinary demands for coal production led to undermaintenance and underinvestment. In the postwar transition cost-based remuneration schedules provided mineowners with little incentive to be efficient. Losses were heavily subsidized. If labor costs increased, so did mine subsidies. Firms therefore pursued the eminently rational strategy of preserving their best fields (leaving them idle), granting most labor demands, and witholding investment in new capital equipment. The use of modern mining technologies actually decreased between 1941 and 1947.[73]

The umbrella for this coal program, and a chief instrument for the reconstruction of the Japanese economy, was the Priority Production program (keisha seisan) authored in late 1946 by Professor Arisawa Hiromi of Tokyo University and a group of Yoshida braintrusters known as the Coal Committee.[74] These economists believed that coal and steel were the main bottlenecks impeding economic recovery. The dilemma was by now familiar: steel was needed to modernize the coal mines, but there was not enough steel because there was not enough coal. SCAP allowed the first postwar imports of crude oil to stimulate steel production, to provide for the reconstruction of the mines, to supply the mills.[75] Industrial development would be stimulated by the concentration, inflationary effects notwithstanding, of all the economy's assets in a few strategic sectors.[76] The two main pillars of priority production were allocation and finance: the Economic Stabilization Board (ESB) was created in August 1946, charged with economic planning and distribution, the Reconstruction Finance Bank (RFB) was established in January 1947 as its financial instrument. Both deserve closer scrutiny.

Before creating the ESB, in May 1946 SCAP had ordered the dissolution of the Coal Control Association. Anticipating this development, the association had already reconstituted itself, in SCAP's reported view, "along more democratic lines." Nevertheless, the new Japan Coal Mining Industry Association remained dominated by the large mining firms. Mitsui Mining president Komura Sentarō was its chairman. SCAP and the MCI had had no choice but to depend upon the "democratic" successor to the association and Nittan. The official SCAP history of the early occupation offers the following retrospective:

> By December 1946 no substantial changes had been effected in the distribution system, although the subordinate control companies had been reorganized as ordinary companies. Indeed, the Diet had reaffirmed the exclusive authority of the Japan Coal Company (Nittan). . . . Although black-marketing of coal was widespread and control company monopoly was manifestly undesirable, the delicate position of coal in the economy

made precipitate changes in the existing distribution system both unwise and unfeasible.[77]

The Temporary Demand and Supply Adjustment Law of 1946 authorized the ESB to use "democratically organized" trade associations and "temporary stabilization devices" in allocating materials. Thus private industry, through the designation of the Japan Coal Mining Industry Association as an auxiliary allocating organization, held great power in the reconstruction of the mining industry. But SCAP was doing what it could to enhance state control. Arguing that regulation of the private sector *by* the private sector would promote excessive concentration, and linking this concentration to Japan's war-making potential, SCAP required the three largest mining firms to divest their metal-mining enterprises.

In April 1947 nominal state control of Japanese coal reached new heights when Nittan was dissolved and replaced by the Solid Fuels Distribution Public Corporation (Haitan Kōdan). The Haitan Kōdan, capitalized at 300 million yen, was only one of several 100 percent state-owned corporations created to purchase, sell, and distribute specified strategic goods under the direction of the ESB. In spite of the existence of the coal *kōdan*, there was less than 7 million tons of coal to distribute after utilities and steel firms had received their priority allocations. Many smaller manufacturing firms were reduced to barter arrangements with the coal producers.

The *kōdan* differed from wartime national policy companies in several important ways. First, they were explicitly temporary. Official accounts portray them as steps toward a privatization of the Japanese economy which would ensure a *de*concentrated market place.[78] The implicit goal was consistent with that of *zaibatsu* dissolution. Second, they were 100 percent publicly owned. Most prewar national policy companies were joint public-private ventures, often because private firms opposed state competition in the market place. In the case of the *kōdan* no stock was issued on the capital markets. The government bore all administrative expenses, and all earnings were returned to the Treasury. Finally, these firms were denied ownership of fixed assets that could be divested for a profit. *Kōdan* officials, moreover, were denied financial interests in private firms dealing in the specified commodities.

In at least one and perhaps the most important respect, however, there was direct continuity between the Haitan Kōdan and Nittan. One unintended consequence of the priority production program was that, as before, the public treasury, not the industrial consumer or the producer, absorbed the difference between price and cost.[79] In buying coal, the *kōdan* relied upon a somewhat more uniform system than Nittan's.

Ten mining districts were established, as were standard prices for each variety of coal. But the subsidies offered to mineowners were still cost-based. As Sonoda Minoru argues, "under this kind of a purchasing system, the mining firms' main concern was how to embellish cost figures for the control organ's assessment. It is no mystery, therefore, why they had no desire to rationalize through cost reductions."[80]

The Reconstruction Finance Bank, forerunner of today's Japan Development Bank (JDB), was the main financial instrument of priority production. The top expense for the government of Japan during the occupation was the support of SCAP; the second-largest was the coal-mining industry.[81] In its first year of operation alone the RFB provided 33.6 billion yen, fully one-third of all RFB financial assistance, for coal mine redevelopment. By 1948 the RFB accounted for 98 percent of all mine financing and nearly half of all coal mine operating funds. While coal prices remained controlled, between 1946 and 1949, the subsidized difference between production costs and sales prices amounted to more than 100 billion yen. Indeed, state support may have been three or four times greater in the early years of reconstruction than during the war. Yet less than half of those funds were used for new equipment. Most built housing for miners and stockpiled equipment in anticipation of an end to price controls and cost subsidies. Often the subsidies found their way into the pockets of mine operators who preferred to build homes for themselves.

These misallocations make the success of the priority production program all the more extraordinary. Targets were met (nearly 30 million tons were produced in 1947), coal began to flow to consumers, and the economy began to rouse itself from its lethargy. Indeed, success, at what were enormously high real and nominal costs, was achieved in spite of government programs. To be more precise, if we are to credit the government with smashing the bottlenecks in coal and steel production, we should share that credit with the private firms that reinterpreted, thwarted, and transformed government programs every step of the way.

The best example is the failure to establish state control of the coal mines. This failure stemmed from intrabureaucratic, interest group, and party conflicts that shaped economic policy and party alignments for much of the postwar era. No case could be more instructive for an understanding of business-government relations in early postwar Japan. Nor could there be a better illustration of the ways in which private interests temper state control in mixed economies, even when state control is most likely to be achieved. This recurrent pattern illustrates a central theme of this book. A complete understanding of the role of the state in structuring the domestic market place in industrial democracies depends upon an understanding of how participants in that market place initiate, shape, and respond, both individually and collectively, to state initiatives.

THE BATTLE FOR "DEMOCRATIC" STATE CONTROL

The Priority Production Program, with its *kōdan* and public financial instruments, was unprecedented. Never before had state intervention in the Japanese economy been so direct. Although the mines were still privately owned, the state had not enjoyed so broad, so firm, and so independent a commercial presence in the coal market since the nationalizations of the Meiji period. Foreign occupation was not the only cause. Equally unprecedented, in May 1947 a cabinet was formed in which a right-wing Socialist, Katayama Tetsu, presided as prime minister. It is of no little significance for this book, or for Japanese political history, that the central plank of the Socialist campaign had been the nationalization of Japan's coal mines. This new government presented a unique opportunity for an occupation bent at the time on destroying *zaibatsu* control.

In its eight months the short-lived Katayama Cabinet grappled with more epochal policy issues than any of its successors. As the conservative camp reorganized, SCAP and the Socialists found themselves cooperating in such fundamental economic policy matters as fighting inflation, food distribution, and *zaibatsu* dissolution (through the implementation of the Excessive Concentration Law). Together they inaugurated major institutional reforms, including dissolution of the powerful Home Ministry, introduction of new police and court systems, establishment of the Fair Trade Commission, and new legal codes.

Chalmers Johnson describes the SCAP-Katayama relationship as a marriage of convenience which had great significance for state control: "The coming to power in 1947 of Japan's only Socialist government, something SCAP was very enthusiastic about, was a godsend for MCI—not because MCI advocated socialism but because socialism afforded it a plausible cover for its own industrial policies and because the Socialist government put Yoshida out of power for eighteen months."[82] In fact the relationship varied with SCAP preoccupations. It ultimately depended upon the structured caprice of the coalition itself; for one thing, the Katayama Cabinet contained as many Democrats as Socialists. Moreover, business interests were split in the extent of their opposition to state ownership and over the defense of private commercial rights. State control of Japan's coal mines became the greatest test and most conspicuous failure of the Katayama Cabinet.[83]

The issue of coal nationalization had first appeared on the postwar political stage months before the formation of the Katayama Cabinet. In early September 1946 General Douglas MacArthur asked for a detailed study of state control for economic rehabilitation. On September 4 SCAP formally proposed that the Allies' Advisory Council give serious consideration to nationalizing the coal mines as one method to produce coal and induce recovery. Within days Socialists in the Diet embraced the idea, while conservatives (both Liberal and Democratic party representatives) were sharply divided. Within two weeks the Socialists introduced their coal mine nationalization bill, but before the end of September compromise proposals submitted by Liberal party politicians, including Tanaka Genzō, deflected the measure.[84]

On June 3, 1947, less than two weeks after the formation of the new government, the Socialists announced their intention to present a state control bill to Diet. Responding to earlier signals from SCAP, the economic bureaucracy had already developed such a program—or, more precisely, competing parts of the bureaucracy had prepared two different plans. The evisceration of the formal government bill both before and during a physically violent Diet session in the autumn of 1947 fatally compromised state control and served to realign Japan's party system, but even the bill that had emerged from the bureaucracy was a compromise document.

The two competing bureaucracies were the MCI and the ESB. The former was the direct descendent of the wartime Munitions Ministry, the latter the stepchild of Priority Production.[85] Although the ESB was populated largely by seconded MCI officials, it also contained a large number from private industry, including such future business elites as Nagano Shigeo, the steel industry leader who would become chairman of the influential Japan Chamber of Commerce and Industry. Businessmen inside the ESB was the first obstacle to nationalization of the coal mines in Japan.

MCI established a study group in late 1946 to advise its Coal Bureau and to review every conceivable variety of control programs.[86] The MCI seems to have distrusted large mining firms. Its planners felt that unless mining came under the supervision of the state, either through direct ownership or through public management, private firms would set aside the best districts, preserving them for future profits. The initial MCI plan issued in early June 1947 called for direct government controls administered through a public coal corporation (at this point referred to as a *sekitan eidan*) that would take responsibility for coal production planning directly under the MCI Coal Bureau and directly above administrative committees at the mine level.

The ESB opposed the plan. It preferred to retain direct private management of mine sites and opposed what it considered the introduction of multiple lines of authority. In the MCI program it saw a resurrection of wartime coal control. In place of the MCI-designed public corporation, the *eidan*, ESB proposed one with greater independence from the state which would functionally resemble the wartime Industrial Reconstruction Corporation (Sangyō Fukkō Kōdan). This organ would be responsible for assembling materiel and repairing equipment. The supply of capital would remain the responsibility of the RFB.

On June 28 the ESB's Wada Hirō and Mizutani Chosaburō of MCI emerged with a compromise draft. Their compromise called for 1) state control of the largest mines; 2) the separation of mine management from management of the parent firm through the creation of separate financial structures; 3) the establishment of an ESB supervisory position at each mine site; and 4) the creation of a decentralized advisory committee, including labor representatives, at each mine. But the ESB also managed to ensure that 5) a *majority* of MCI Coal Bureau officials be selected from the private sector, in both the central and the district offices. Moreover, the top central administrative officer of the Coal Bureau (*sekitanchō chōkan*) and the top regional officers (*sekitan kyokuchō*) could not be chosen from the ranks of career bureaucrats.[87]

The advisory committees were included to placate organized labor. In fact, coal labor initially opposed bureaucratic control of the mines, despite its support of the Katayama Cabinet. Representatives of Zentan, a coal labor federation representing more than a hundred thousand workers, met with the prime minister and with Mizutani twice in the first weeks of June. They had objected to the emphasis on bureaucratic controls (which they saw as little different from wartime controls) at the expense of long-term socialist effects. With the cooperation of Tankyō, another federation representing 340,000 miners, they forced the government to accept the syndicalist fourth item. Labor thereupon seemed satisfied with the program and with conscious government efforts to publicize its solidarity with the workers. Mizutani, for example, entered a Fukushima mine clad only in a miner's loincloth on June 29, the day after the government program was announced.

The issue, however, was far from decided. On July 3 Yoshida's Liberal party strongly renounced the plan. Later that month industry groups formally joined the fray. The Japan Coal Mining Association (Nihon Sekitan Kōgyōkai), the re-formed wartime control association, and the Japan Industrial Association (Nihon Sangyō Kyōkai) both proclaimed strong opposition to state control. Industry money was spread liberally across the political spectrum, and Yoshida's Liberals, with ties to the mining districts of Hokkaido and Kyushu, were particularly receptive. One conspicuous tie was the marriage of Yoshida's daughter to Aso Tagagishi, the Kyushu mine owner and leading Yoshida financier.

Yoshida, the Liberal party's secretary general Ōno Bamboku, and other party officials met frequently with mining firm officials, often at Yoshida's home. Kiso Shigeyoshi, leader of small mining companies, who first came to prominence in the Bujun coal crisis, recalls visiting Yoshida's home, where he found Aso "at Yoshida's side." Yoshida patiently explained to the mine owners that they were preaching to the converted; he was firmly committed to free market principles. He told them to visit the opponents of the nationalization and sent them away with a polite request for help with his campaign war chest. According to Kiso, "we gave him the support he wanted, and our campaign succeeded—state management of coal was destroyed."[88]

But there was much politicking ahead. Kiso helped organize small and medium-sized firms in opposition to the program. They joined formally in the Popular Alliance against State Control of the Mines, unfurling banners at their Ochanomizu headquarters which warned that under state control "black coal would turn red" (*kuroi sekitan o akaku suru mono da*). Small mining interests, and Kiso in particular, were better known for extralegal tactics. It was widely rumored that cautious large mining interests used smaller firms to distribute funds to politicians. Men like Kiso and Takeuchi, according to one insider, "had no elite pedigrees" and could "get caught without embarrassing big finance."[89] The difference between large mining capital, associated with various *zaibatsu* families, and small mining leaders is often expressed as the difference between bankers and loan sharks. In any event it is a matter of record that Kiso and a dozen Dietmen, including future prime minister Tanaka Kakuei, were arrested in the Coal Control Incident (Sekitan Kokkan Jiken), the first of several major postwar bribery scandals.[90]

As the largest political party outside the ruling coalition, one with impeccable conservative credentials, the Liberal party could ally itself with industry and openly oppose state control. Indeed, it made much political hay by threatening no confidence votes and by proclaiming itself, unlike the Democratic party, the only uncompromised conservative opposition party. The lesson was not lost on the coal industry, which lined up behind Yoshida. In the 1952 general election, for example, the Liberal party received nearly nine times as much in contributions from coal interests as the other leading conservative party did.[91]

The problem for Ashida's internally divided Democrats was severe. Party leaders chose not to withdraw from the government (which would have forced its collapse) but to use their influence to make the coal control program as ineffective as possible. Democratic party representatives had already had a hand in the drafts that resulted in the June 28 compromise. They requested additional revisions in August. The MCI, for its part, temporarily reneged on its deal with the ESB. On July 19,

1947, it issued a draft bill providing for a mining industry public corporation (Tangyō Kōdan) that would give the state the authority to "manage the production of coal and the development of coal resources."[92] This draft most nearly resembled the European nationalizations of the period.

The Democrats had their work cut out for them if they were going to block their own government's programs and hold the cabinet and their party together at the same time. The faction within the party which opposed state control was led by two Fukuoka-based Dietmen, Nagao Tetsuo, formerly president of his own mining firm, and Nishida Takashi, a former mining company president and a managing director of the Coal Industry Association. These two led a group of Democratic party Dietmen estimated at upward of two-thirds of the party's strength in the Lower House.[93] The group drew heavily from Oita, Fukuoka, and Fukushima legislators; it opposed labor participation in management and, in particular, the provision of decision-making power to localized "production councils." Throughout the summer Ashida and the Socialist MCI minister Mizutani met frequently with this group to allay their fears. But Nagao, Nishida, and their group remained firmly opposed to any form of state control, bureaucratic or democratic. What is more, both Nishida and Nagao served on the Mining Industry Committee of the Lower House.[94]

The best that can be said for this uneasy alliance is that the cabinet was held together as long as possible by common interests in governing Japan and by the commitment among some in the Democratic party and their business supporters to a "revised capitalism," something close to European planning.[95] By now the bureaucracy, the cabinet, and even the private sector were all divided over state control of the mines. SCAP, growing as Cohen says "impatient (with) the Japanese government's fumbling of the coal situation," intervened with tacit support for a compromise.[96] While Katayama defended the government's left flank and Ashida did what he could to defend the right from pressures that might topple the coalition, General MacArthur wrote directly to Prime Minister Katayama on September 18 stressing that dramatic production increases to wartime levels would justify state control of the coal mines. Citing Japan's experience with fifty-million-ton production levels, he returned the government draft bill and wrote "There is no objection to its presentation to the Diet for consideration on its merits without prejudice of any kind from this Headquarters."[97]

With SCAP breathing down its neck, the cabinet ventured one final, eviscerating government revision just after formally submitting a bill for state control of the coal mines (Sekitan Kokka Kanri An) to the Diet on September 25. The ESB, prevailing over the Commerce Ministry, had the cabinet formally approve a "plan to substitute a production increase program for the MCI Mining Industry Public Corporation (*tangyō kōdan*)" on September 30.[98] Under the final government draft, the large mines would be closely supervised, entailing an elaborate machinery for state control. The MCI minister would be empowered to appoint as an advisory group a national control committee composed of mineowners, labor, consumers, and scholars. He would establish regional bureaus to supervise mine site committees. Corporate plans would be submitted quarterly to the MCI for review, giving the ministry formidable nominal controls over corporate planning and policies for capital allocation. Transfers of major capital assets would require formal MCI approval, and, to make state control even more complete, MCI could order such transfers itself. Finally, divestiture without authorization was to be prohibited.

There would be no state ownership. Nonetheless, even though the bill had already been transformed from state ownership (*kokuyū*) to state control (*kokka kanri*), under which private ownership was left intact, Diet deliberations would further enfeeble it. The transformation fractured Ashida's Democrats and led to the introduction by probusiness Liberals of some of the dilatory parliamentary tactics later associated exclusively with left-wing parties. The bill was presented as a temporary, emergency measure before priority production had achieved results and when coal production had declined precipitously. In fact Japanese mines had not produced so little coal since 1916.

Production and politicians stalled. Dissident Democrats on the House Mining Industry Committee held up the bill for two full months. The committee met twenty-seven times between September 25 and November 25 to hear testimony from related government officials, cabinet members, and industry representatives. In particular, Socialist MCI minister Mizutani braved withering attacks centered on the allegedly socialist character of the government program. Exasperated, he averred in testimony on October 11 that "this is not a socialist production program." He defended state control as a step toward "so-called democratic revised capitalism." Some representatives of industry, particularly from steel, electric power, and steamship transportation, testified in favor of increased coal production and did not rule out state control as a means toward that end.[99]

It required direct intervention from the speaker of the House to move an interim report and force a committee vote. Finally, on November 25, the committee voted to *defeat* the bill. Fueled by animus against the Socialist government, only the Communists, seeking popular control, and the Liberals, seeking private control, maintained party unity against the measure. Despite the Democrats' formal endorsement, not a single Democratic party committee member voted to support it. Indeed, three of them (Nagao included) bolted the party. Party leaders responded by expelling all members who had voted against the measure.[100] Delay in committee was critical to the opposition, for under the new parliamentary rules committees could only report bills to the floor for a plenary vote. Although the bill was reported negatively out of committee, it *was* reported out: it reached the plenary session the same day—"while," according to Kiso, "we were busy congratulating ourselves"[101]—and it passed the plenary with amendment. Three days later seventeen Democratic party representatives, including Tanaka Kakuei, also left the party. Subsequently the same scene was acted out in the House of Councillors, and a badly weakened bill, much transformed in the year since nationalization was first formally debated, became law. Barely half of the coalition's Democratic representatives supported the measure. Many formally defected to Yoshida, in the following March forming the Democratic Liberal party that returned him to power even before the next general election.

State control of the coal mines had been, in a historian's resonant phrase, "officially established and fatally compromised."[102] Years later Katayama reflected wistfully that "when all was said and done, it was a pretty tepid piece of socialist industrial policy."[103] Formally the new law gave the Coal Bureau Chief sweeping supervisory and control powers. He could change production plans, move materiel among mines, supervise budgets, authorize mine closings, and order consolidations. Modeled in part upon early postwar France, the state control program established mine committees involving management, labor, consumers, and technical experts. Over 60 percent of all mines, including all the largest ones, became objects of state control.

There was less to state control than meets the eye, however. Implementation was delayed until early 1949, by which time even the officials responsible for it had become fed up.[104] The source of their frustration was that the law actually gave the state precious little control. Most significant, the private sector had retained its authority over personnel decisions (*jinjiken*). The much revised plan had required that all bureau chiefs and their principal section chiefs be recruited from the private sector. By December 1948 nearly half of all Coal Bureau officials were not career bureaucrats, but career private managers. From day one until the bureau's dissolution, they came from Mitsui, Mitsubishi, Sumitomo, and other firms to help direct the purported state control.[105]

A leading MCI Coal Bureau official, one of the architects of state control, explains the bureau's failure as the pursuit of too many objectives at the same time. The state had tried to satisfy too many interests:

> It was truly a miracle that such a measure ever became law. . . . The Diet process was excruciating. Even the small mine operators would come to my office and bang their sandals on my desk—they didn't want their property

taken away. . . . Private-sector leaders participated with us, but the perspective of private enterprise and the perspective of state control reflected our completely different upbringings. There was no way to achieve consensus. We built a structure [of state control], but its insides rattled all around.[106]

A leading coal company official who participated in the wartime control association, and who helped design the private sector's response to state control, put matters succinctly: "Of course, we didn't like state control, but we saw it as a tool for recovery. We could not publicly oppose it due to our dependence on the RFB. . . . So, at our Presidents' meetings it was agreed that state control was a 'necessary evil' . . . we needed the materials and the cash. We used it to build ourselves up. Then we let it crumble."[107]

Freeing the Market

Although production hovered at less than two-thirds of wartime levels, output did increase, as noted, during the years of priority production and state control. But production increased most rapidly in the small and medium-sized mines that were not under state control. The number of these small independent and "satellite" mines increased from 628 to 803 between 1948 and 1949, while the large mines' share of national coal production was declining from 74 percent to 70 percent.[108] This growth can be explained by the nature of incentives offered under state controls: profits were fixed, based upon costs, and so only the expensive, low-quality fields were exploited. No care was taken for quality. Rock and gravel increased the volume of coal shipments. Larger firms claimed to be preparing better fields and accepted shipments of material—cables, girders, shafts—which they promptly stored in warehouses to await the lifting of controls.

By 1949 the supply of basic commodities was finally stabilizing, but inflation raged. SCAP began to question the need to continue priority production. By this time the occupation planners had begun to review their economic concentration program and labor policies. SCAP made the reintegration of Japan into the international economy a priority and to that end introduced a Draconian deflationary program reminiscent of the Matsukata initiatives of the 1880s.[109] The Dodge Line, named after the banker who was dispatched to make it work, was above all else an effort to get Japan off the U.S. Treasury "aid dole." Continued American underwriting of Japanese trade deficits, it was argued, could not stabilize Japan's currency (nor, one might suppose, could it be defended in Congress). Dodge introduced a program of balanced budgets and industrial rationalization achieved in part through eliminating priority production and all RFB subsidies. These measures touched off a recession that continued until the Korean War boom.

The first Dodge Line measure to affect the coal industry was also the first official step toward liberalizing the industry. In June 1949 the government revised the Haitan Kōdan law, eliminating controls on anthracite, natural coke, coal powder, and other products and permitting licenced private dealers to distribute them to end-users. In July controls on most inferior grades of coal were lifted. On August 25 SCAP ordered the dissolution of the Haitan Kōdan, an order carried out on August 30. A cabinet resolution of September 15 declared an end to state controls. Subsidies and RFB financing were cut off in October. Japan's short-lived experiment with state control was ending, and it was followed by an even shorter-lived experiment with a free market. Soon interfuel competition would make state intervention attractive again, to producers and consumers alike.

The mining industry used the period of controls to accumulate capital and equipment at little or no expense to itself. It also anticipated the end to price controls. Coal stockpiles, which had held constant at about 1.5 million tons throughout 1948 and the first half of 1949, began a sudden and vertiginous three-month climb in June, when the announcement was made that coal controls would be lifted. Stocks peaked in October, just as production allocations were abolished and controls eliminated.[110] Production held nearly constant. In the month that controls were formally eliminated, stockpiles plummeted. Middlemen and mineowners had used the three months between the partial return of their commercial rights and the elimination of controls to maximize the value of subsidized production, building their stockpiles while they could still obtain subsidies.[111]

The first battles between the coal-mining firms and the steel industry were fought in the spring of 1949. About to lose the protection of the state, specifically subsidies for the purchase of domestic coal, the steel producers began lobbying for reduced coal prices.[112] They squared off with the coal industry for over a year, while price increases for higher-grade coal further aggravated relations. Finally, in what would become a common role, MITI's good offices (in particular the Industrial Rationalization Advisory Council) were used to strike a bargain: a three-year plan for the rationalization of the coal and steel industries. The program was announced on June 24, 1950. The Korean War broke out the following day. New demand, based largely upon special procurements for the American forces, put a temporary end to these disputes. Profits reduced steel industry concern with price and increased concern over access to coal. For the time being, however, foreign currency allocations for imported coal were disallowed; although frustrated, the steel producers had no alternative but to make their peace with the coal industry.

In the meantime the coal producers were getting their own house in order. The first order of business was to reorganize into a coherent association. As in the prewar period the state played no direct role as the industry groped toward a formula for collusion. The Japan Coal Association (Nihon Sekitan Kyōkai) was formed in March 1948 as the direct successor to the wartime Coal Control Association and the temporary Nippon Sekitan Kōgyōkai. At first all mining firms, large and small, were included. The new association, it was hoped, would help reconstitute the control of large mining interests by "unifying the position of the mine owners vis-à-vis the government."[113] But a common front was maintained only as long as controls remained in place. Once controls were lifted, in the autumn of 1949, the differences between large and small firms came into focus.

History was not merely repeated, it was reconfirmed. In March 1951 there was a wholesale defection of the small and medium-sized mines from the association. Five regional associations of small firms formed a loose association, the Nihon Sekitan Kōgyō Rengōkai (NSKR) with an office in Tokyo, in what amounted to a postwar reincarnation of the *gojokai*. Large mining interests may actually have paid the small firms "alimony" (*sōbetsukin*) to leave the new association, in part to avert the unionization of these less mechanized, labor-intensive mines.[114] One industry leaders confirms that the split was indeed welcomed by the larger firms: "Our management positions were different. Even though the democratic reforms had rendered us nominal equals, we were not. We wanted a split, preferring to deal on our own in labor negotiations."[115]

Here, however, history changes course. Never again would small mineowners prevail over large ones as they had in the Bujun coal case of 1932. Important struggles now would be those between producer and consumer, as coal made a desperate and ultimately unsuccessful bid to maintain a competitive advantage in a rapidly changing international energy market. Indeed, beneath these realignments was a development far more ominous for the Japanese coal industry. In January 1950 SCAP permitted the reopening of Japan's Pacific Coast refineries, planting the seeds of interfuel competition that would dominate debates over energy policy, and much of national politics, for the next thirty-five years.

MARKET POLITICS

The Korean War so stimulated demand for Japanese coal that the industry suspended its plans for rationalization. Stockpiles virtually disappeared; the number of workers increased to 370,000 in 1951, a figure never again equaled. Production rose to 46 million tons, 84 percent of wartime levels, and the number of mines increased. This boom lasted two years. By late 1952 coal prices were 160–170 percent higher than they had been under the *kōdan*-controlled system.[116]

The political behavior and market strategies of the mining firms, particularly the eighteen large firms that dominated the Japan Coal Association, shaped state coal programs. In March 1952, for example, the Coal Subcommittee of MITI's Industrial Rationalization Advisory Committee (Sangyō Gōrika Shingikai) issued a three-year plan for coal mine rationalization between 1952 and 1954. The largest eighteen firms would have received more than 55 billion yen in rationalization funds, to raise production by 42 percent and lower prices by 15 percent. But the mining firms, having helped design the program, decided ultimately to reject the idea. Their debt had grown in the rush to produce, and they were unwilling to assume new financial burdens. MITI dropped the program. So the industry gave the first indication that it recognized limits to its future. It was going to concentrate on reducing debt and accumulating capital for other enterprises. Profit taking rather than investment began as early as 1952. Investments by the industry *outside* its own firms doubled as a percentage of total investments between 1952 and 1953, doubled again the following year, and rose to near parity by 1955. The Japanese coal-mining industry had a clear market strategy, and, at least equally important, as long as oil remained less competitive it had the political resources to pursue that strategy. It would take state help when it wanted it and demand state help when it needed it.

Once price controls and subsidies had been removed, coal prices rose to reflect the real costs of production. As demand slackened with the end of the Korean War boom, industrial consumers renewed demands for price reductions. Coal producers responded in the autumn of 1952. They tried to maintain prices, defer wage increases, and demand increased productivity, which set off enormously complex and protracted labor disputes. These combined with price demands from manufacturers to produce three long-term effects. First, it ensured the adjudicatory role for MITI which would later form the basis for a claim to state leadership. Second, it accelerated the exit of the mining companies from the mining business. Third, it introduced significant interfuel competition into Japan's energy market place for the first time.

On October 13, 1952, wage negotiations broke down, and Tanrō-affiliated miners struck the large collieries to protest the "labor-centered rationalizations" announced by the industry. Although small, non-unionized mines continued to produce, the effect on the general economy was considerable. Production was down nearly 6 million tons, coinciding with walkouts in the electric utilities. The pressure to intervene was great, and the government did so after sixty-three days, in mid-December, in favor of the owners. But by then industrial consumers had lost confidence in domestic coal as a stable source of supply. Petroleum's share of primary energy supply jumped from an insignificant 5.2 percent in 1950 to 17.7 percent in 1953.[117]

The recession of 1953–54 confirmed that these market changes were structural and that political solutions were required. At a New Year's Day press conference in 1953 Bank of Japan president Ichimanda Naoto linked lower coal prices to lower commodity prices, and declared this the most pressing economic policy problem for 1953. He also acknowledged that a political price would have to be paid, though he seriously underestimated the ultimate public costs:

> It is politically necessary to implement every sort of possible subsidy program. The benefits of these subsidies will be restored to the nation, for even if it means recognizing rationalized profits for the mine operators, we simply must control coal prices. This is not a matter of ideology. It is an economic necessity ... that will disappear when our nation's economy grows stronger.[118]

MITI minister Ogasawara Sankurō and Finance minister Mukai Tadaharu agreed; so did heavy industry. Leading the charge for lower coal prices, the steel industry claimed that it needed a one-third price reduction (almost 2,500 yen per ton) if it was to compete effectively in international markets.[119] On January 17 Prime Minister Yoshida instructed MITI to find a way to bring coal prices down for end-users.

Intervention, it turned out, would have been superfluous, for slack demand and competition from oil sufficed to force coal prices down. Between 1952 and 1954 more than 140 mines were closed and 90,000 workers lost their jobs. Strikes continued, escalating with each new "labor-centered rationalization" announcement. One million tons of coal were lost, for example, when Miike workers struck for 113 days in mid-1953. The problem was not one of production but of demand: stockpiles in early 1953 had reached the highest levels since sales rights were returned to the firms. The Coal Association responded with a production limitation agreement that almost immediately collapsed when members dumped coal on the market and leased their commercial mining rights to nonmember firms.[120] Prices dropped by as much as 25 percent.

At this point, the coal industry invoked two concurrent strategies, exit and voice (loyalty, at least to one another, was already a lost cause).[121] The government found out that owners preferred exit in January 1953, when MITI's Coal Bureau issued a five-year plan for mine development.

Table 3.2. Capital investments by Japanese coal firms, 1950–58

Year	Total Investment (billion yen)	Investment outside the firm as ratio to Total Equipment Investments
1950	8.8	.07
1951	12.1	.15
1952	16.9	.17
1953	16.8	.34
1954	11.2	.63
1955	9.3	.94
1956	15.3	.90
1957	24.3	.75
1958	27.2	.88

SOURCE: Sonoda 1970: 31.

The scheme would have provided 49 billion yen to 22 firms for coal mine investment.[122] But just as in the previous March the large mineowners, whose RFB debts still totaled 48 billion yen, refused the extra assistance. Instead they obtained a cabinet resolution to make some RFB loans interest-free retroactively; the Yoshida Cabinet also allowed mineowners a discount on the balance owed to the public treasury by arranging to have some repayments forgiven, considering them redeemed through price reductions.[123] Investment data from the period confirm that mineowners were concerned more with profit-taking than with investing in coal's future (see Table 3.2).

Except for the very largest firms, such as Mitsui, Mitsubishi, and Sumitomo, the industry was very passive about new capital investments. Equipment investment did increase, but mostly in the maintenance of existing machinery. What is striking is the rapid growth of investment *outside* the parent firm. The data do not allow us to differentiate clearly among these external investments, but, though investments seem to have varied considerably by firm, most took three forms. First, there was much continued investment in the so-called satellite fields (*eisei tankō*) that ensured quick profits at low cost but had no future. Second, many firms began buying stock in their customers' companies. Coal-mining firms became minor shareholders in many electric utilities and steel firms. Third, the group-affiliated mining firms (the former *zaibatsu*) accelerated their purchase of shares in other firms in the same group. As of March 1957, for example, 69 percent of the outside investments of Mitsui Mining were in other Mitsui group firms. The corresponding figure for Mitsubishi Mining was 52 percent. Some of these investments were in affiliates that had a relationship with coal, such as cement, salt, briquet, and transportation firms. Others, however, were only distantly related: real estate speculation, land development, tourism. Later supermarkets, oil exploration firms, and amusement parks became significant business activities for former coal-mining firms.[124]

COAL MINE RATIONALIZATION

There was also "voice." It was loud, and it was heard. Throughout the recession, even as they were positioning themselves to exit the coal business, mineowners demanded that MITI restrict oil and coal imports, that it directly finance purchases of new equipment, and that it subsidize sales. According to one former Coal Bureau chief, the industry even demanded the resurrection of the *haitan kōdan* to purchase all coal stockpiles.[125] The small mineowners' association demanded that the state purchase the mines, urging MITI to adopt a mine-scrapping policy.[126]

MITI was divided. It had to pay careful attention to these demands, because coal interests were enormously influential in both major conservative parties, Hatoyama's Democrats and Yoshida's Liberals. Moreover, unemployed miners were a social problem that could not be ignored. In addition to the need to conserve still scarce foreign exchange, the fear was emerging that foreign oil majors could dominate the Japanese market unless an alternative supply of energy could be secured. In fact, in March 1954, under heavy pressure from the coal lobby, MITI reversed the program it had begun in 1952 of promoting heavy oil use.[127]

On the other hand, MITI was disenchanted with the coal-mining industry. Many in the Coal Bureau lost sympathy after the owners rejected three separate programs between June 1950 and October 1952.[128] Also it was quite clear to MITI planners and to much of heavy industry that petroleum had overwhelming cost advantages.[129] Some argued that a switch to cheaper oil might generate more competitive finished goods, leading to higher exports and a net gain on foreign exchange. Cautious bureaucrats were concerned with the drain on the treasury that a mine buy-out would involve; others, pointing to the labor problems plaguing the industry, denied that coal was a stable source simply because it was a domestic source.[130] Although neither faction within MITI ultimately prevailed, their compromises produced the first significant coal legislation in postwar Japan.

These internal compromises took two forms. First, in June 1954 Coal Bureau chief Sahashi Shigeru assembled an "unofficial" coal policy plan and circulated it among mineowners.[131] The Sahashi Plan proposed a considerable strengthening of MITI control over the coal industry, calling for: 1) MITI-directed elimination of marginal mines, based upon long-term demand forecasts; 2) mine rationalization with state financial support accompanying government supervision of mining firms' management and the establishment of maximum dividends for shareholders; 3) creation of a public corporation to purchase coal stockpiles; and 4) creation of a public agency to mediate labor disputes in the coal-mining industry. At the same time others in MITI were promoting a second, even more direct instrument for state control. Their internal plan called for a coal production public corporation (Sekitan Seisan Kōdan) that would give the state direct responsibility for selecting premium mining areas and for building technologically advanced "model mines."[132]

A united and still influential mining industry punctured both "trial balloons," and MITI was instructed by the cabinet to draft a market-conforming proposal. Responding to recession in the industry, the demands of mineowners, and clearly articulated limits to state intervention, MITI formally proposed a new coal industry assistance package in November 1954. The package called for: 1) a five-year plan of mine rationalizations, envisioning cost reductions of 20 percent and production of 42.5 million tons by 1959; 2) creation of a public agency (Sekitan Kōgyō Seibi Jigyōdan) to purchase inefficient mines (a total capacity of three million tons,) and to restrict the opening of new ones; 3) restriction on new installations of fuel-oil boilers, to prop up demand for domestic coal, and at the same time the resurrection of oil tariffs; 4) a standard price system to stabilize the market; and 5) establishment of a coal mining industry council (Sekitan Kōgyō Shingikai) as an advisory organ to the minister.

It still took eight months and seven revisions for the Coal Mining Rationalization Special Measures (Sekitan Kōgyō Gōrika Rinji Setchi Hō) to become law. Although the coal industry had no reason to object to boiler restrictions or heavy oil tariffs,[133] the large firms demanded even more generous terms for state intervention, including the transfer of responsibility for mine damage indemnities to the state; relaxation of cost-reduction targets; exclusion from the Anti-Monopoly Law for price and production cartels; additional rationalization funds; and elimination of the standard price (*hyōjun tanka*) program.

It was the battle over standard prices which was joined most vigorously. The Ministry of Finance insisted upon regulated standard prices as its condition for accepting costs associated with the MITI program. The state would agree to supply funds if it could control prices, but it wanted to prevent renewed profiteering with state funds. Neither producers nor consumers were anxious for this state intervention, which they labeled a revival of bureaucratic controls.[134] Consumers were enjoying exceptionally low coal prices and wanted no part of state-imposed prices. Producers, in an age of competition from oil, could not be confident that the state would consistently intervene to maximize coal prices and refused to cooperate.

MITI gave in, excluding coal price and production agreements from the Anti-Monopoly Law according to Sonoda "because industrial demands were particularly strong."[135] MITI also changed the way of determining standard price. Instead of a "regulated/controlled" (*kisei*) market price, there would be "indicated" (*shihyō*) market prices, giving greater flexibility to the producers and consumers. These changes decisively compromised the ability of the state to intervene in pricing decisions. As a result of industry opposition, therefore, one editor wrote, "although the system itself remained, its method of computation and application were eviscerated. . . . The 'standard price' had no meaning, no function. It merely existed."[136]

Then there was the issue of mine consolidation. In March 1955 the small mineowners' association, NSKR, issued its response to the MITI plan. Supporting the scrapping of inefficient mines but seeking to maximize their take from it, small owners demanded that the government also purchase mine roads and other physical assets. They suggested alternative methods of assessing their property as well, methods that would yield them greater returns. Their leader, Takeuchi, demanded that the government assume the full burden of dismantling mines, claiming that many of the mines had been created in response to government demands for increased production.[137]

There was also labor to placate. The Coal Bureau did not present the program to the unions until May. Naturally the unions opposed rationalization programs that would eliminate jobs. They demanded the creation of a public coal sales corporation (Sekitan Hanbai Kōsha), punctuating their demands with four waves of hour-long nationwide strikes. Local governments lobbied not to be responsible for the financial support of unemployed miners. MITI responded by expanding subsidies to include "mine damage" grants to local governments and with emergency programs to put former miners to work on public works projects.

Even the large mining firms were split over the final compromise on the MITI program, and this split forced substantial delays in Diet deliberations. Although most large group-affiliated mines supported the measures, Aso, Nittetsu, and Ube remained opposed to the very end, convinced that state and market could mix only on their terms. Sumitomo, which was fully integrated downstream in sales and distribution, feared the rationalization program would threaten their franchise dealers.[138] The Coal Association split fourteen to four in favor of the program.

The bill went to the Diet on May 31. In the February 1955 general election the Democratic party had captured 185 seats (up from 124), and Hatoyama formed his cabinet in mid-March. The Liberals were reduced to 112 seats, and throughout the summer, in the midst of the coal debate, talks of party unification proceeded in fits and starts. Although the

Liberals were more united in support of the measure once they had wrung major concessions from MITI, some in the party, presumably those associated with Aso, were moving behind the scenes to destroy the legislation.[139] Unlike in the 1947 Diet debates on state control, the parties maintained formal discipline, but pronouncements of support were at best reserved. Hatoyama needed help from Ōno Bamboku and others in the opposition to bring the Liberal party around. He even had to deliver the Labor Ministry portfolio of his second cabinet to Nishida Takao, the northern Kyushu mineowner who had once led the fight against state control.[140] The Diet session had to be extended a full month before the bill passed, on July 30. To the measure were attached thirteen separate resolutions, the most important of which, from industry's perspective, called for flexibility in setting standard prices.

No sooner had rationalization been legislated than prosperity returned to the Japanese economy. This second postwar boom, the so-called *jimmu keiki* or divine prosperity, combined with the autumn 1956 Suez crisis to stimulate demand for domestic coal. The collieries were soon selling all the coal they could produce. Domestic coal temporarily enjoyed price advantages over imported fuels and seemed a more stable source for Japanese industry.

Indeed, the mineowners had double good fortune. On the one hand the 1955 legislation ensured state funds to buy out superannuated mines, 137 of which were scrapped between 1955 and 1958. On the other, the renewed demand for coal led not to the reduction in number of mines envisioned by MITI but the *creation* of 253 new mines in two years, an expansion of almost 40 percent.[141]

In the three years after the rationalization law 4.2 million tons per year of productive capacity were *added*. Most new mines were affiliated with large firms, growing in clusters around the main shafts but as separate entities. The large mining firms, projecting a short-lived recovery, opted to open cheaper, smaller facilities rather than modernize their larger mines. Although the new mines met the minimum efficiency standards of the 1955 legislation, they were not intended to remain efficient for long. In 1958 the large mines accounted for 18 percent of added productive capacity, while mines "leased" from large firms accounted for 32 percent and small and medium-sized mines accounted for 49 percent. In fact the large mines' share of production continued to decline, from 71.9 percent in 1950 to 64.2 percent in 1958, as owners accelerated the shift toward production from leased mines to protect themselves in a volatile market. One result of this strategy was that large mines grew dependent upon small mines for a significant share of their own supply.

As in 1952–53, and like American steel firms twenty-five years later, the large coal owners were actively reinvesting in new businesses. The irony seems quite clear. As Sonoda says, "there can be no mistake that this was the most effective policy to increase profits . . . but it represented a complete divergence from the basic policy of rationalizing the industry through the nurturance of the best mines and the consolidation of the inefficient ones."[142]

Between 1956 and 1958 times were good once more for the coal firms. Direct negotiations between large mineowners and large coal consumers were the basis for computation of standard prices. Individual transaction prices were not coordinated with standard prices. A rare sellers' market allowed producers to announce price hikes before the standard price could be established. In fact, standard price levels for 1955 were set in early 1956, and those for 1956 were set in November, *after* the transactions were completed.[143]

The consuming industries and MITI were not entirely without influence. During negotiations in the second half of 1957 the coal industry, citing wage increases and debt burdens, insisted upon price increases of 550 yen per ton for large consumers and 800–1,000 yen per ton for small consumers. Heavy industry called upon MITI to admonish producers to show better self-control, and in June the producers announced an exceptional 50 yen per ton price reduction. It was the first time that MITI, intervening on behalf of heavy industry, succeeded in disciplining the coal industry.

Divine prosperity soon proved anything but providential for the coal industry. Government planners, who had failed completely to anticipate the recovery, now projected continued increases in demand for coal. They were off by 9 million tons—coal began a steep decline in 1958. Many new hydroelectric plants had come on line, and petroleum had a new 13 percent price advantage. Coal prices were forced down, stockpiles rose, mines closed. The industry turned again to collusion. Agreeing that stockpiling, though expensive, was better than fratricide, the large mining companies reached into their prewar history to create the New Shōwa Coal Company (Shin Shōwa Sekitan) as a joint stockpiling instrument. This cartel, permissible under antimonopoly law exclusions added to the 1955 rationalization law, was to purchase and store coal to clear the market. It also bought the excess output of small and medium-sized mines to lessen downward pressures on price. In July 1959 stockpiles peaked at nearly 6 million tons. Prices nonetheless dropped significantly. More ominously, banks began to refuse to finance the stockpiles. Their confidence in the future of coal was dissolving. The new cartel was, like the old one, largely a failure, and predictably the small mining firms suffered most. Layoffs followed bankruptcies. The public agency created in 1955 to buy out inefficient mines exhausted its budget in

August 1958, and again in January 1959. Oil had become fully competitive. The energy revolution was under way, abetted by foreign pressures to open the Japanese market.[144]

The First Coal Program

The use of heavy oil for electric power generation increased 16.3 times between 1955 and 1965. Coal consumption, propped up by policy demand (*seisaku juyō*), increased by less than three times in the same period, a shrinking portion of the needs of the electric power industry. Fuel-oil boiler restrictions might not have existed (see Table 3.3).

The change was more a function of cost than of policy, more a matter of market than of state. The electric power industry had not strongly objected to the boiler restrictions in 1955 because coal then was still cheaper as a thermal power source. By 1958, however, a 5 yen per calorie cost advantage for coal had become an 11 yen advantage for oil. Despite nominal restrictions, the electric power industry had been able to convert to oil quite freely, because MITI did not actually supervise the implementation of the boiler conversion restrictions. MITI had appointed the Keidanren Fuel Committee chairman to head his own oversight committee. The fox was inside the henhouse. The result, as Martha Coldwell notes, "was that under Keidanren leadership a series of exceptions were made for big industrial users, and the regulations were applied only to the smaller users."[145] The law, slated to expire in August 1960, was extended for three years only after the utilities received price concessions from the coal industry. Such intramural agreements between producers and consumers, usually reached under the aegis of

Table 3.3. Fuel composition for thermal electric power generators, 1955–65 (in percentages)

Year	Coal	Heavy Oil	Nuclear
1955	92.5%	7.5%	—
1956	86.4	13.6	—
1957	80.3	29.7	—
1958	82.4	17.6	—
1959	81.8	18.2	—
1960	62.5	37.5	—
1961	58.5	31.5	—
1962	55.7	44.3	1.0%
1963	56.9	41.4	1.7
1964	47.8	49.9	2.9
1965	44.9	52.1	3.0

SOURCE: Denki Jigyō Kōza Henshū Iinkai 1969: 29.

Keidanren in response to the competitive pressures of petroleum, set the policy agenda for MITI.

MITI planners would have preferred better control. Throughout 1961, for example, as MITI and industry grappled with problems of liberalization and coal mine rescue, MITI proposed a basic energy law (Enerugī Kihon Hō) to give it authority to stabilize energy supply and demand. The energy industries would not support the measure, and in the end MITI had to settle for separate laws for electric power, coal industry rationalization, and the petroleum industry.[146]

The First Coal Program, issued in May 1962, was therefore only the first in a series of authoritative ratifications of privately negotiated agreements. These negotiations included labor as well as industry and confirmed the mutual dependence of MITI, private elites, and politicians in the design and implementation of Japanese energy programs. The negotiations that denied MITI the control it wanted, giving it jurisdiction instead, cannot be understood without reference to mine labor unrest that had reached crisis proportions.

The longest and largest strike in the history of Japanese labor relations began in mid-Janaury 1959, when the Mitsui Miike Mines announced a work force rationalization. By this time coal workers were facing massive layoffs throughout the industry; unemployed miners were the object of charity campaigns in all the big cities. In late 1959 Diet responded with public assistance to former miners. When Mitsui locked out the Miike strikers, however, the miners responded with violence that culminated in a famous "naval battle" in which 150 miners and 50 police were wounded.[147] Ultimately Mitsui broke the strike and rationalized its work force. One after another, the large mines followed suit.

In late 1961 the coal mine unions changed their tactics, shifting the protest from firms to government. Thousands of workers went to Tokyo to camp out before the Diet building and to march upon the ministries and the prime minister's residence.[148] The press was sympathetic, and in a meeting with Prime Minister Ikeda Hayato union representatives made quite clear the social effects (and political costs) of an unconstrained shift to oil. Under great pressure the cabinet responded by forming the first coal industry task force (Sekitan Kōgyō Chōsadan) to develop a policy response to rationalization and unemployment. That response is now known as the First Coal Program. It subsidized production to maintain an annual production level of 55 million tons by guaranteeing long-term, large-volume consumption by heavy industry.

It did so by ratifying one set of agreements already reached within Keidanren and by securing another with public funds. The first were supply agreements between coal producers and their major industrial customers, the second price agreements that coincided with the Miike unrest. In early 1959 Uemura Kōgorō, then vice-chairman of Keidanren, and Kobayashi Naka, formerly governor of the Japan Development Bank, created the Comprehensive Energy Council (Sōgō Enerugii Kondankai) to bring together high officials from energy-producing and -consuming industries.[149] Coal producers were asked to lower prices to meet the competitive challenge of oil. They promised to reduce prices by 1,000 yen per ton if they were to produce 72 million tons. So preposterous a scenario provoked ridicule.[150] In July the Coal Association issued a more realistic program, which envisioned 55 million tons of annual production and an 800 yen per ton price reduction by 1963. Steel and electric power demanded more: they wanted a 1,500 yen price cut by 1960.

MITI was invited to intervene. The council understood that state subsidies would be required to guarantee price reductions. The debate shifted to the Coal Industry Advisory Council (Sekitan Kōgyō Shingikai), chaired by Uemura himself. He turned the matter over to Arisawa Hiromi, an architect of the postwar Priority Production Program, and Arisawa's final report, in December, called for a 1,200 yen price reduction with government assistance. The coal firms had convinced the council that most of the 400 yen per ton difference between their offer and industry's demand should come from special rationalization subsidies and tax revenues. The 1960 MITI budget included 2.14 billion yen in interest-free modernization loans, 40 percent earmarked for equipment to rationalize the coal transport system. Differences between cost and price would be made up through state subsidy.

Keidanren had yet to work out its agreement on supply. In June 1961 Uemura brought together the leaders of Keidanren to forge an agreement on long-term stability in coal transactions which essentially exchanged coal purchases for price reductions. The electric utilities agreed to purchase up to 20 million tons of domestic coal by 1967 if price reductions continued below the agreed 1,200 yen per ton. The steel industry, would conclude long-term supply contracts for 13 million tons of coking coal for similar considerations. The gas and cement industries also participated in the agreement. In sum, the large consumers agreed to purchase domestic coal at specified levels if prices continued to fall. The initiative for this agreement was private industry's, and the state played no apparent role in its development. As Sonoda writes, "this agreement was not guaranteed by law, but was a gentlemen's agreement that became the authority for the subsequent establishment of a coal demand and supply policy."[151]

Before the agreement was made public the electric power industry used it with MITI to gain additional exemptions from the Boiler Law so as to build new oil-fired thermal plants. Having promised to buy an agreed minimum of domestic coal (but only if that coal was price-competitive), it secured permission for new oil plants even before the ineffective Boiler Law expired. Meanwhile the utilities finessed the coal supply agreement and significantly reduced their risk by volunteering a MITI-industry joint venture, the Electric Power Development Corporation (EPDC), to assume the bulk of the compulsory coal purchases and to build most of the coal-fired plants.

The first Coal Industry Task Force, created by cabinet order and chaired by Arisawa, got under way in May 1962. Its final report, issued in October, recognized that coal could not compete with oil, even with price reductions of 1,200 yen per ton, and it sought a way to ameliorate the social dislocations of mine closings. The task force proposed that coal consumption be increased to 55 million tons by 1967 through encouraging the construction of coal power plants and increasing mine subsidies to preserve the price reduction targets. Thus it not only ratified the Keidanren agreement on long-term coal supply but also designed a mechanism by which the government would assume much of the financial burden. The task force proposed that the state pay for the difference between the Keidanren's negotiated agreement and its own, slightly higher targets.[152]

The government's First Coal Program closely followed the contours set by the task force. The centerpiece of its mine modernization program was the scrapping of inefficient mines and the building and consolidation of competitive ones. The Coal Mining Facilities Corporation (Sekitan Kōgyō Seibi Jigyōdan) was reorganized as the Coal Industry Rationalization Corporation (Sekitan Kōgyō Gōrika Jigyōdan). MITI sought progressively to raise coal purchase targets for coal-burning electric utilities and for steel and gas, all to be achieved by state guarantees that would shoulder the burden of increased fuel costs. The government, through its Electric Power Development Corporation, would construct new coal-fired generating plants. On the labor side, firms would receive subsidies for hiring displaced miners, and public funds would supplement private pensions. Public housing would also be added in mining districts.[153]

Within two years oil had nonetheless replaced coal as the top source of thermal power for Japan's electric utilities. Of government efforts in the 1950s to retard the switch from coal to oil, Nakamura muses that it was "like trying to empty the ocean with a bucket."[154]

The Second Coal Program

Official accounts of the energy revolution that swept the Japanese economy between 1955 and 1965 often suggest the skill with which government planners, collaborating with industry, managed a dramatic and difficult transition from coal to petroleum. One such account points to the reduction of mines from over 800 to just over 300, the reduction from nearly 300,000 mines to just over 110,000, and the increase in mine productivity from 14 to 38 tons per person per year as evidence of the "success of 'scrap and build.'"[155] But the facts tell a different tale about the efficacy of public policy. The First Task Force had planned to scrap seven mines with 1.5 million tons of capacity in 1963; the actual figures were twelve mines and 4.5 million tons. The next year MITI anticipated three times more scrapping than industry actually undertook. "Build" funds consistently lagged two to three years behind actual levels of investment, which suggests they were more a political response to production declines than an anticipation of industry's needs.[156]

Those needs, in fact, were rapidly changing. No sooner had the First Coal Program gone into effect than a "setting sun" mood gripped the mines. Workers confounded plans for a smooth transition as they sensed the futility of employment in a dying industry. Their flight from the mines to industrial jobs in the cities accelerated. By 1964 the number of miners had already fallen below targets for 1967. It became difficult to maintain employment even in priority mines; retirement and severance benefits became the principal expense for mineowners. Production plummeted, and the problem was soon transformed into how to keep miners in the collieries. Major strikes in late 1962, and a horrible mine explosion in Miike which claimed 458 lives a year later, underlined the urgency of the situation. The compulsory purchase targets for the electric utilities were revised downward. No MITI plan had anticipated supply falling faster than demand.

Production plummeted also because of a lack of capital. Healthy mines were unable to use what machinery was salvaged from scrapped mines, and because profitability projections were negative, even those firms which wanted to modernize facilities found it difficult to raise capital. Between 1959 and 1964 the mining firms sold property, recalled mortgages, and took other measures to raise over 120 billion yen in cash, a figure greater than the industry's accumulated deficits at the end of 1964.[157] Yet in that period dozens of firms introduced rationalization programs, and many others went bankrupt. There was not a single year of black ink between 1959 and 1964, and operating deficits increased from 15.4 billion yen in 1958 to 82 billion yen in 1964.

It now seems clear that neither banks nor mineowners were determined to save the industry. Instead, public debt was used to replace private debt just as that debt was skyrocketing (see Table 3.4).

In 1963, when government financing exceeded private financing for the first time, the government took an unprecedented step. The large

Table 3.4. Changes in coal industry borrowing, 1958–64 (in percentages)

Source	1958	1959	1960	1961	1962	1963	1964
Government loans	38.9%	37.0%	35.7%	38.3%	46.2%	54.7%	58.2%
City bank loans	61.1	63.0	64.3	61.7	53.8	45.3	41.8
Total (in billion yen)	64	77	91	103	125	156	171

SOURCES: Sonoda 1970:130; Noguchi 1965.

Kaijima mines in Kyushu were about to fail, and the Coal Advisory Council, in pursuit of its 55 million tons, deemed it necessary to rescue the firm. The government revised the rationalization law to authorize funds to the private sector not just for equipment purchases but also for operating funds. Under this Kaijima Formula the firm was placed in receivership (designated a *saiken kaisha*).[158] The testing of the fiscal resources of the state, and its political will, was only just beginning.

Under renewed political pressure from the Liberal Democratic party, MITI resolved again to plan. The Second Coal Industry Task Force in August 1964, Arisawa Hiromi again its chair, openly acknowledged the failures and contradictions of the previous program. Arisawa nevertheless remained committed to finding a politically assured level of demand for domestic coal. It would not be easy.

The second task force's report was made public in December 1964, the month that shareholders of Taishō Kōgyō voted to dissolve one of Japan's largest and one of Chikuhō's most famous mining firms. The premise of the report was clearly stated: national dependence upon foreign energy was rapidly growing, and foreign exchange as well as supply security required that coal be promoted with hydroelectric power as Japan's only domestic alternatives. A target of 50 million tons per year was set, at least until 1967, and coal prices would be raised by 300 yen per ton for general use coal and 200 yen per ton for metallurgical coal.[159] With state leadership and guidance the fiscal condition of the Japanese coal industry would improve by 1967.

Who would pay how much for more expensive domestic coal? The report proposed an extension of the existing oil tariff restitution system (*kanpu seido*) and provided for other (unspecified) measures to reduce the burden on heavy industrial consumers. The total sum returned to the utilities in 1964 had been 1.5 billion yen. The 300 yen per ton price increase would add 6 billion yen in costs if the utilities accepted the targeted 20 million tons of domestic coal. The report did not provide a mechanism for full restitution. Private industry, refusing "to take the blame for the mistakes of the coal industry," Sonoda writes, "was not necessarily going to be faithful and move in the direction of (this kind of) policy."[160]

Protracted negotiations with MITI minister Sakurauchi Yoshio in March 1965 and a compromise plan subsequently submitted by Coal Advisory Council chairman (and Keidanren vice-chairman) Uemura were necessary before coal consumers agreed. The total volume of "policy coal" was lowered, accounting procedures were revised to increase the restitution, lower-grade coal was left untouched by state intervention, the government committed itself to a fuller burden of extra coal costs after 1966, and the starting date of the program for the steel industry was delayed until June 1965. Moreover, electric utilities in the coal-producing regions of Hokkaido and Kyushu could continue to pay the 1964 price for coal, and utilities located further from the coal fields could substitute the inferior grades of coal excluded from the increase. A joint sales agency envisioned by the task force was limited to steam coal for the electric power industry. State leadership and guidance had once again been negotiated to the point of being almost negligible.

The instrument designated for this compromised state administration of prices and supply was an upgraded version of the Steam Coal Payment Liquidation Company. On June 1, 1965, the Coal for Electric Power Distribution Company (Denryoku Yōtan Hanbai K. K.) began operations, capitalized at 400 million yen. One-third of the capital was supplied by the government, the rest was divided among forty-five coal-mining firms. The president was Aso Tagakichi, now chair of the Japan Coal Association. The company's new activities included the purchase and delivery of steaming coal for the eight utilities with coal-fired plants at prices agreed between the coal and electric power industry associations supervised by MITI.[161] The electric utilities proceeded to increase their dependence upon oil and nuclear generation. Compulsory purchases and administrative guidance notwithstanding, coal, which had produced 56 percent of Japan's steam-generated electric power in 1965, when the joint sales firm was established, was a trivial source (5.1 percent) by 1975. Oil's share expanded to 60.1 percent in the same period.

On the left, Tanrō chairman Koga Sadashi expressed his dissatisfaction with the second task force report. It was, he claimed, designed only "to protect the capitalists."[162] The unions and the socialists presented their own plan to nationalize the mines, which avoided such terms as state control (*kokka kanri*) and stressed syndicalist solutions and the consolidation of mining districts. The leading academic spokesman for this program argued for a "nationalization from below," instead of the de facto "nationalization from above" being carried out by MITI through its receivership system.[163] However lively the media debate, by 1964 Tanrō spoke for fewer than 63,000 workers, a two-thirds' reduction in five years. It did not have to be taken seriously any longer.

Someone who did have to be taken seriously, however, was Hokutan president Hagiwara. The other owners had long mistrusted Hagiwara, criticizing him for planning to abandon the mines as early as 1955. Yet they respected his connections with conservative politicians. He served as chairman of the Coal Association for many years through the late 1950s and early 1960s. He claims to have first advocated the complete nationalization (*kokuyū kokuei*) of Japan's coal, steel, and electric power industries in 1957, during discussions with his closest LDP ally, Kōno Ichirō.[164]

His colleagues were unreceptive to the idea at the time, nor was there much support in 1959 when he privately demanded that the government buy out the coal mines.[165] In late 1965 he began once again to agitate publicly for his own brand of nationalization. As he was accelerating his company's investments outside the coal business, he produced pamphlets advocating state ownership in the form of a One Company Plan (Issha An). But he still had no support within the industry:

> The workers were all in favor of it. The problem was the mining company presidents. It is just like the amalgamation of local governments—local assemblymen lose their jobs. Their biggest problem with my plan was the loss of directorships for their senior managers. So I said to them: "Hey, didn't you guys lay off tens of thousands of miners? You don't think that laying yourselves off will be as painful as all that, do you?" They all got pretty offended by that.[166]

It would be several more years before any other major mining firm would grasp at the idea of nationalization. By then it would be too late.

The Third Coal Program

The crisis in the Japanese coal industry intensified, and once again the market confounded the planners. Operating deficits doubled within a year; debt exceeded 200 billion yen.[167] The coal industry temporized, delayed major investments, and negotiated for financial intervention by the government. The banks, for their part, continued to extend operating funds to the coal industry in the expectation of a government bailout. The crisis persisted for two reasons. First, oil prices dropped faster than anticipated, and the state lacked either the will or the capacity to slow interfuel substitution. Second, mine reconstruction and labor costs had increased faster than anticipated, and firms were accelerating their (by now not terribly graceful) exit from the industry. They needed help with existing debt, not new obligations.

Again the coal industry turned to the LDP for help. In August 1965 Coal Association chairman Aso appealed directly and in person to the Policy Affairs Research Council (PARC) of the LDP and to MITI minister Miki Takeo. He urged the government to assume 100 billion yen in pension payments for workers from scrapped mines and the full operating expenses of all mines slated to be scrapped in the future. He requested an additional 500 yen per ton price increase and state subsidies for interest payments on "build" funds due to city banks. (Earlier loan subsidies had been limited to public loans.) He also sought 70–80 percent interest-free capital for equipment; and, invoking the Meiji formula, he proposed that if this were not possible, the state should develop mines and sell them to the firms. The public reaction was a widespread disbelief at the selfishness of the mineowners, but conservative politicians judged that they had no choice but to respond. That month the coal policy committees of both houses of Diet reaffirmed the need for drastic action. Familiar themes now took on a newly urgent tone.

At the minister's direction MITI created an energy policy roundtable (Enerugī Seisaku Kondankai), largely from the now familiar cast of Arisawa, Inaba, Tsuchiya, Enjōji, and other intellectuals and former economic planners. A report, issued in mid-October 1965, proposed that the Rationalization of the Coal Industry Public Corporation be authorized to assume 100 billion yen of coal industry debts (the term used was *katagawari*, a metaphorical reference to the bearing of another's palanquin). Also proposed was a further 200 yen per ton subsidy. But the central issue from that moment on was the *katagawari*.[168] Would the state bail out the mineowners?

The industry intensified its lobbying with the LDP. Pressure and past favors paid off. Some in the LDP proposed 120 billion yen in public bonds to underwrite coal mine debts and various new subsidies financed by a new petroleum consumption tax.[169] After all, they reasoned, the previous May the Bank of Japan had intervened to bail out Yamaichi Securities from a near collapse. Coal, it seemed, was going to be simply a more expensive repetition. The obvious comparison was drawn to rice subsidies that had enabled the LDP to buy electoral peace with the farmers.

LDP leaders were split on the bailout plan as they had been on rice price supports. Tanaka Kakuei, then secretary general of the party, was disposed to support his friends (including some former cellmates) in the coal industry, but PARC head Akagi Muneyori and Finance minister Fukuda Takeo blocked any hasty decision.[170] The Finance Ministry and a part of Uemura's Coal Industry Advisory Council supported the delay, insisting that the role of coal in future energy demand was not yet clear. They insisted that budgetary commitments wait until the new Advisory Committee for Energy (Sōgō Enerugii Chōsakai) set a firm course for coal. Parts of the LDP, MITI, the Coal Association, and parts of the Coal Advisory Council squared off against the Finance Ministry, heavy industry, and others in the Advisory Council and the LDP.[171] It became less likely than ever that a politically acceptable solution to the coal crisis could be fashioned in time for the 1966 budget.

It was not. The best Uemura could deliver was an interim report of his Advisory Commission in early December. Commission members were barely able to agree on more of the same subsidies and interest-free loans; they wanted to test public opinion about massive public expenditures to rescue the industry. Although it took an additional year and a half of negotiation and debate, a third coal program was finally announced in July 1966 which included a 50 million ton production target and a new special coal account to treble public funds for coal-mining firms. A 100 billion yen *katagawari* for the mine owners was also included, despite a minority view on the Coal Advisory Commission that the government was throwing good money after bad in a futile attempt to salvage a dying sector. MITI's public premise was that the coal industry could be salvaged. The council projected an end to its deficits by 1970.

The public refinancing of coal industry debts brought MITI and the Ministry of Finance once again into direct confrontation. The proposed *katagawari* amounted to 60 percent of the industry's outstanding debt. MITI and the banks had preferred that the Coal Industry Public Corporation assume the industry's city bank debts, thus cutting ties between the city banks and the mines. Finance, whose control of the pace of coal recovery would be tied to its influence over the city banks, opted to subsidize the mining firms directly on an annual basis; firms would pay the banks directly. This way the coal industry's debt would not be paid off all at once, and if a firm were to fail, its banks would share the losses. The Finance Ministry never spoke of *katagawari;* it attached what it considered strict conditions on the dispersal of funds, limiting them to mines with a "competitive future" (i.e., with the prospect of stable production for ten years) and requiring annual audits to ensure that the funds were not being distributed to shareholders as dividends.[172]

Negotiations between MITI and the coal consumers were equally difficult. The issue of policy demand again provoked extended debate, for consumers were no more willing now than they had been earlier to pay for coal they did not want or need. Once again they forced the government to find a way to indemnify them at acceptable levels for their compulsory purchases. But it was not easy. Initially the roundtable had sought a 1970 target of 29.5 million tons for steam coal demand, of which the private utilities would be expected to accept 23–24 million tons. It had also sought 12 million tons in metallurgical coal purchases by the steel industry. The electric utilities agreed to accept the 23 million tons for which they had earlier contracted, but they attached price conditions:

> We agreed to long term purchases of 23 million tons premised upon price reductions of 1,200 yen per ton. However, since there had been a "policy price" increase of 300 yen per ton since 1965, that promise has been broken. We will therefore agree to purchase 23 million tons if we can return to conditions before last year's 300 yen per ton price increase by receiving full indemnification for the increase in price.[173]

The utilities' plan was accepted nearly in its entirety. The state-owned Electric Power Development Corporation was required to absorb all additional "policy coal" by adding two entirely new coal-fired generators to the three already under construction.

The steel industry likewise set full indemnification as the condition for their acceptance of compulsory coal deliveries. Even then it agreed to accept only 10.5 million tons of domestic coking coal. In the meantime the Japanese steel industry moved aggressively to procure long-term supplies from overseas, particularly Canada and Australia. The steel industry had little interest in the shrinking of domestic coal; it needed only the reassurance that domestic supplies would not disappear all at once. As it turned out, the steel industry grew and the coal industry shrank so fast that there were shortages, especially in 1968–69, just before new Canadian and Australian supplies came on line. MITI and the Finance Ministry agreed to provide the steel firms in the meantime with nearly 53 billion yen (based upon an agreed 700 yen per ton price differential between domestic and imported coal) as indemnification for accepting even this low volume of domestic coking coal. These indemnities were based upon the steel industry's calculations and proposals; the targets ultimately agreed upon by MITI and the coal consumers were those privately negotiated by Keidanren and accepted by the First Task Force a decade earlier.

The Third Coal Program was no more successful than its predecessors. Indeed, its provision for the public assumption of mine debts, the *katagawari,* proved most embarrassing. No sooner had these funds been dispersed than one of the nation's largest mining firms failed. Dai Nippon Tankō, whose creditors had received 160 million yen in September 1967, declared bankruptcy in mid-October. Two smaller firms followed suit almost immediately, and the reaction in official circles, was one of "mute amazement."[174] The coal industry and its banks were supposed to have used the relief to become competitive by 1970. MITI Coal Bureau chief Inoue announced sternly that "the banks that will be receiving this favor had better from here on invest in the coal industry. Those who do not will have the *katagawari* terminated." But the banks, like the coal-mining firms themselves, had other ideas. As one newspaper account said, "they had already prepared to flee."[175]

Ninety-five percent of the initial government acceptance of coal indus-try debt went to the thirteen largest mines.[176] To qualify, firms had to demonstrate that their rehabilitation was possible; they did a great deal of embellishment, as accelerating failures clearly demonstrated. The largest portion of the funds went to the creditors of mines with the largest debt burdens, such as Mitsui, which had invested in the develop-ment of world-class mines. Kiso Shigeyoshi, still active as a leader of small mining interests, was sharply critical of this arrangement: "Of course the small mines had small debts—the big mines had group-affili-ated banks behind them. We had no [such ready] creditors. . . . It was as if the government was telling us "you fellows are free to die at your own convenience."[177]

By 1967 a large number of mine firms was on the verge of collapse. Five of the most famous (Kaijima, Meiji, Nittan, Aso, and Kishima), unable to attract funds from city banks, had already fallen into receiv-ership. Production had fallen to the lowest levels since 1955. State lead-ership had been victimized once again by the market and by the interests operating within it. But there still remained one final, climactic effort to restructure the Japanese coal industry. It would come closer to na-tionalization than any other in the postwar period and, ironically, it would be subverted by MITI.

The Final Debate: The Uemura Plan and the Fourth Coal Program

For a time MITI and its Advisory Commission seemed uncharac-teristically inclined to do nothing. After the first shock of the Dai Nip-pon Tankō failure some wanted to let matters take their course, to permit a natural weeding out of uncompetitive mines through "non-policy" (*musaku*). But a combination of uncoordinated demands from mineowners and bankers for action, the impatience of heavy industry with excessive coddling of the coal industry, and MITI's own proclivities not to leave the market alone led to a final, concerted effort to restruc-ture the Japanese coal industry. Intractible political differences made the Fourth Coal Program, finally issued in December 1968, look more like the Third Coal Program than like any of the many radical proposals being debated at the time.

Those proposals came from all quarters. Most, even those from the coal industry itself, entailed some degree of national ownership. The industry offered at least five schemes, including the revived One Company Plan of Hokutan's Hagiwara, the Three Company Plan proposed by Hokkaido Sekitan Kōgyō chairman Funabashi, the Joint Sales Company Plan of Mitsui Mining, and the Coal Mine Purchase Plan of Kiso Shigeyoshi.[178] In addition, labor unions and the Socialists endorsed two different plans to nationalize the mines and the coal transport system (Sekitan Kōsha).[179] Most influential of all was the program submitted by Coal Industry Advisory Commission chairman Uemura Kōgorō. The so-called Uemura Plan dominated business-government coal negotiations for almost a year.

The most important early debates took place within a hopelessly (and, one might correctly suppose, fatally) divided Coal Association. Hagiwara's One Company Plan served as the lightning rod for disputes. He invoked foreign solutions to crises in coal management, including public ownership in France and Britain, as well as the German Ruhrkohle consolidation then taking shape. But it was the Belgian district consolidation program and single firm reorganization that served as a convenient model. He proposed that a single new company purchase all shares of existing firms and take over the management of all mines nationwide, starting in Hokkaido and Kyushu. Purchase price for these shares would be determined by averaging their price over the previous three years. The new entity would be a special legal entity (*tokushu hōjin*), 50 percent public and 50 percent private, and public funds for its investment and operation would come from the special coal account generated by petroleum taxes.

Hagiwara claims he received broad political support for his scheme and that it failed because of the recalcitrance and narrow-mindedness of his fellow mineowners. He also maintains that the banks, understanding that failed firms cannot repay loans, supported the idea.[180] He claims further to have secured the support of many shareholders who would have welcomed being bought out at prices higher than those then being quoted: stockholders "would incur no losses. The one holding the bag would be the government."[181] Hagiwara has said that he also secured the support of the LDP and of Prime Minister Satō Eisaku and Secretary General Fukuda Takeo, who made him alter the program to differentiate it from the Socialist proposal for nationalization. He claims they invited him to develop it with the Special Coal Committee of PARC as an LDP plan.[182]

Opposition to Hagiwara within the coal industry and throughout the business world was widespread however. I therefore discount his claims of strong LDP support. Kiso apparently spoke for a majority of mineowners when he said that Hagiwara could not be trusted with the future of the Japanese coal industry.[183] For one thing, Hagiwara was by then deeply involved in developing the tourist industry. Second, the One Company Plan, based upon regional consolidation, would make him king of Hokkaido coal and potentially leader of the nation's mines. Hagiwara acknowledges that other mineowners, led by Mitsui Mining president Kurada, launched a vigorous campaign to discredit him and to kill the plan.[184]

Hagiwara inflamed this opposition when he gave the press internal Coal Association documents detailing the positions of each of the fifteen member firm presidents on the issue of industry reorganization. The document, appearing in *Hokkaido Shimbun* for December 12, 1967, publicly revealed the positions of each firm on the critical questions of the 50 million ton production level, joint sales, use of fiscal resources, industrial restructuring, and "supplemental policies." Clearly Hagiwara had very little internal support. Sumitomo supported the One Company Plan; Kishima supported only regional consolidation. Mitsui, Taibeiyō, and Matsushima directly opposed Hagiwara.

Although the firms were nearly unanimous about the desirability of a balanced reduction of productive capacity, the two firms pressing hardest for a sales cartel, Nittan and Mishima, also wanted to preserve the 50 millon ton capacity. A sales cartel was strongly supported by Mitsui, Matsushima, Taibeiyō, and Furukawa, but Hokutan strongly opposed it. Mitsubishi remained silent on the sales cartel and took the position that the coal business was no longer tenable as a private enterprise. This leading voice of Japanese private industry took the extraordinary position that any future consolidation of the coal industry should be "based on law and should be state-owned and privately managed." The Japanese bureaucracy, so often credited since with leadership and vision, had no program of its own. Caught in the cross fire between labor and capital, producers and consumers, large and small firms, and (most significant) between Mitsui and Mitsubishi, it deserves credit for inertial rather than for administrative guidance.

Its most critical test came when, with the major coal firms unable to agree, Coal Advisory Council chairman Uemura submitted his own "informal" proposal on February 27, 1968. Two things about this proposal are of particular significance. First, Uemura, having informed the MITI Coal Bureau chief of this initiative, privately submitted it, in his nongovernmental capacity as vice-chairman of Keidanren, to Japan Coal Association chairman Aso and four other mining company presidents. The plan was not made public until several weeks later. Second, this plan was actually written by a close associate of Uemura's from Mitsubishi Mining Industries.[185] Mitsubishi had interests in the Uemura Plan very different from those of Mitsui and some of the other large companies. Mitsubishi was the strongest supporter of the Uemura Plan until the very end, Mitsui its strongest opponent. Thus the Uemura Plan was no simple confrontation between private sector and state; it involved complex subgovernmental patterns of supporting and opposing coalitions, whose analysis requires that we "unbundle" Japan, Inc.

The Uemura Plan invoked West Germany's Ruhrkohle as a model, providing incentives for private firms to come together independently and establish a special semigovernmental corporation to manage the coal mines, control production, and coordinate sales. This joint public/private control organ (*kanri gaisha*) would be capitalized by state funds from the Special Coal Account and shareholdings by the mining firms, steel firms, electric utilities, and private banks. This "trust organization" would consolidate coal-mining divisions voluntarily divested by each of the mining firms. Uemura proposed that the coal mining of the major conglomerates be separated from the rest of their businesses; the incentive to do so would be guarantees that the new trust would refund the debts of the parent companies up to the level of transferred assets. Divested mining divisions would be free of encumbrance; debts returned to the parent companies would be partially offset by assets delivered to the new special legal entity. Debts not offset might be reduced by means of profits generated by the new business activities of the parent firms or a new *katagawari*.[186]

Two kinds of coal-mining firm strongly favored such a solution. The first were Aso, Kaijima, Meiji, and Kishima, those already under the de facto receivership of the Japan Development Bank. They had no competitive future on their own, and this plan provided them with tenable prospects for reconstruction. The second were Mitsubishi and Hokutan, firms that were already divorcing themselves from the coal-mining business.[187]

With Mitsui in the lead, the remaining, healthy coal-mining firms, including Taibeiyō and Matsushima, responded with an energetic campaign to block the Uemura Plan and the "peeling off" of their coal businesses. They proposed instead a tertiary organ (*daisan kikō*) that could include financial and consumer institutions to adjust price, production, and distribution. In this way they would pursue a target of 35 million tons—near capacity production by their own mines.[188] Their group within the Coal Association helped develop an official response to the Uemura Plan in March. That response accepted the need for a collaborative management organ to anchor the industry's reorganization but cautioned against the organ's "falling into bureaucratic control." The management of the coal industry should be based "to the utmost" upon private competition, and in the process of reorganization no harm should be done to employees, financial institutions, other creditors, or stockholders. No mention was made of the second company portion of the Uemura Plan.

The Uemura Plan ran into similar problems with MITI in Uemura's own council. At the end of April 1968 MITI minister Shiina Etsusaburō formally charged Uemura's Coal Industry Advisory Council to produce a comprehensive program for reorganization of the coal industry. Eight months of deliberations followed. Chairman Uemura seems to have controlled the pace of deliberations until July. During these first several months the council dismissed as too costly the Hagiwara and Socialist party nationalization plans. A majority of committee members felt that these plans portended sprawling bureaucratic controls that past experiences with "state control" made unattractive. But the Uemura Plan proposal for a *kanri gaisha* seemed little different.

Clearly, also, MITI itself was no longer anxious to administer the nation's coal mines. Dramatically reversing a long history of thwarted efforts to achieve a direct commercial presence in the nation's coal market, MITI was now actively avoiding such an intervention. In June the council, with MITI's blessing, discarded the *kanri gaisha* plan. Overruling its own chairman, the council's Policy Deliberation Subcommittee proposed to scrap the idea that the state should hold equity in a public corporation. Instead, firms could be amalgamated on a districtwide basis, production targets could be reduced to 35 million tons, and subsidies for closure could be raised.[189] No state agency would manage mines, but one would be authorized to accelerate scrapping with funds from the Coal Mining Special Account, extended for another three years. For the time being the notion of transferring debts from parent firm to subsidiary remained intact. Discussions through the rest of the summer remained inconclusive.

It is possible that MITI no longer wanted state control because it no longer thought that state control was viable. MITI may finally have abandoned aspirations to bureaucratic control in the face of widespread industry reservations.[190] Yet MITI had to be extremely cautious in taking on Uemura, who, to make the politics all the more complex, had become chairman of Keidanren in May.[191] Internal documents reveal the respect government officials had for Uemura and his power, as well as the distance the economic bureaucracy had come since it first designed programs for state control of coal.

One such document, apparently prepared that summer, strongly criticized the Uemura Plan as "idealistic and textbookish" and suggested the need for a more concrete solution. It was a thoughtful, detached analysis of the future of the Japanese coal industry, which referred to the Uemura Plan as "U-Boat." Perhaps the most interesting reason suggested for why

"U-Boat" was a bad idea was the expressed doubt that Uemura's plan for an industrial trust would be politically effective. This doubt took the form of a revealing lamentation by the author:

> When one looks at the history of trusts, what is called a "trust" (in the Uemura Plan) is really little more than a federation. . . . No decisive, effective policy can emerge from this sort of pluralism. It would be one thing if the state could have a mechanism with the capacity to realize its aims, but this would mean national ownership and a public corporation, so it would prove difficult . . . given the current political circumstances.[192]

The pluralism that precluded effective, centralized authority clearly extended beyond the confines of the coal industry itself. In addition to Mitsui's objections, "U-Boat" faced the opposition of the Finance Ministry, the banks, and the coal-consuming industries.[193] Finance, as guardian of the public purse, feared that the separate company formula would provide disincentives for diversification; consequently the burden on the treasury would grow. At this point the banks turned away from the coal industry.[194]

Private banks had reluctantly "yielded to political pressure" to extend loans to mining firms, and the bulk of their loans were conditioned upon state debt guarantees.[195] But while indebtedness to the public Japan Development Bank was increasing by over 14 billion yen that year, city bank debt actually decreased by more than 6 billion yen. There were more attractive outlets for city banks, and pressures on them finally had abated. As one magazine noted, "not only were the city banks now refusing to advance new loans to the coal industry, they were actually using their power to collect outstanding debt."[196]

By autumn several deadlines for the council's recommendations had passed. The press was now characterizing coal policy as a debate between MITI and Uemura, both brought front and center on the policy stage by protracted conflict among and within each sector of the economy. The final month of debate in the Advisory Council involved how to pay for more of the same, because the status quo ante was the only program that all parties to the issue could agree to disagree about. As one energy economist sums matters up, "it was these differences of opinion that . . . not only prolonged (the deliberations) . . . but also . . . reduced [the program's] conclusion to a mere expedient for compromise. The final conclusion of the Council proposes only to strengthen the past measures."[197]

The council sought an extension of the Special Coal Account until 1973 to help pay indemnification for expected bancruptcies. But the electric utilities, the Ministry of Finance, parts of MITI, and the petroleum industry opposed the idea. The refining firms, heretofore powerless to resist having to pay to prop up the coal industry, finally began demanding that some of the finance derived from oil tariffs be freed to finance overseas petroleum exploration. The utilities wanted some of the funds earmarked for research and development on nuclear power.

In the end, political opposition from both within and without the bureaucracy swept aside all drastic proposals for the restructuring of the domestic coal industry. In Sonoda's words, "the Fourth Coal Policy was truly unexpected, emerging as it did from the vortex of debate over numerous radical plans for restructuring the industry. . . . What came to the surface represented no change from previous policy ideas, premised as they were on support for the existing private enterprise structure."[198] The Fourth Coal Program, endorsed by Diet in April 1969, was thus quite familiar, filled with reconstruction subsidies, mine closure subsidies, and stabilization subsidies (all at higher levels of expenditure) and including an 85 billion yen "second *katagawari*." The program abandoned high levels of production, opting instead to encourage mine closings by setting maximum limits for subsidies. Resolute withdrawals from the coal business were to also be encouraged by administrative guidance when firms could not sustain profitability. The Special Coal Policy Account was extended until 1973 to help pay for these subsidies, but the utilities and the petroleum firms succeeded in their claim to entitlement to part of these funds.[199] After the December 1968 Council Report was announced, Chairman Uemura, who had been overruled in his own Advisory Council as well as within Keidanren, offered a blunt but accurate evaluation: "I lost."[200] So did Mitsubishi and many others, for a final solution to the crisis of the Japanese coal industry was as elusive as ever.

The Final Shaft

Irresolution persisted, and the industry deteriorated. Once the new program was in place, three of Japan's oldest, largest, and proudest mining firms closed down.[201] This was just the beginning of an avalanche. In 1969 the MITI program had projected 3.9 million tons of scrapped capacity; actual totals came to more than twice that amount. Government targets and forecasts were obsolete as soon as they were developed. The new policy, like the Third Program, stimulated a rush for subsidies. On the "build" side, final contracts were signed between coal firms and government for the second *katagawari* (in the form of reconstruction subsidies) in late September 1969. Ten large firms were named to receive 80.2 billion yen, six smaller ones to get 4.8 billion yen. But by year's end nearly 20 billion additional yen had been allocated.[202]

Between 1961 and 1971 coal's share of primary energy supply in Japan declined from 31.3 percent to 8.1 percent. Production declined from 55 to 31 million tons. Five hundred seventy mines had become 68, and the mine work force was reduced from 210,000 to 40,000 workers. By 1975 production was less than 19 million tons, and only 35 mines and 20,000 miners remained in all of Japan. Under these circumstances, it is no surprise that the state continued to grasp for a lasting solution as the mines grasped for survival.

This time, however, labor and management grasped together. In late 1971 the Coal Association, with the support of labor representatives on the Coal Council, unveiled a new proposal for a control organ (*kanri kikō*) that might, it claimed, "resuscitate the private enterprise system."[203] But labor realistically acknowledged that renewed discussions of national consolidation would go nowhere. "It would be one thing if the LDP government would consider a state-owned public coal corporation, but while questions of industry structure have been with us for some time, decisions on how to dispose of currently pressing problems have to take precedence for now."[204]

The most pressing of these problems was the maintenance of demand. Steel firms and electric utilities claimed that, for any of several reasons, further domestic coal purchases were impossible. Countercharges came from the unions and the mineowners: consuming industries had forgotten that it was domestic coal that had made them powerful economic forces.[205]

The steel industry refused to purchase additional domestic coal, claiming that its growth was slowing, that new steel-making technologies had reduced its need for coke, that foreign suppliers were pressing for long-term sales contracts, and that the strengthening of the yen had made overseas coal even cheaper. It refused to make further sacrifices for the sake of national policy and in fact resolved to reduce domestic coal purchases unless it received full reimbursement.[206]

By the early 1970s the utilities had a new reason to fight policy purchases of coal. Japan had legislated stringent antipollution regulations, and the utilities could legitimately claim that these ordinances and citizen protest compelled them to reject domestic coal, with its high sulphur content, in favor of clean-burning natural gas, nuclear power, and other fuels. Moreover, the utilities could still divert a large share of policy demand coal to the state-owned Electric Power Development Corporation.

By this time Nippon Steel president Inayama Yoshihiro, another future chairman of Keidanren, had succeeded Uemura as Coal Industry Advisory Council chairman. Throughout the spring of 1972 this steel company executive presided over deliberations among producers, consumers, labor, and MITI which resulted in adoption of the Fifth Coal

Program. Coal producers began by demanding support for 28 million tons of production in 1975, and consumers began by resisting any more than 15.5 million tons of consumption. Compromise plans for 20 million tons submitted by MITI, with promises that consumers would not be expected to carry the full burden of these purchases, were greeted with tepid enthusiasm by council members representing steel and electric power. In late March, Tanaka Kakuei, the MITI minister, through his Coal Bureau chief demanded that maximum efforts be made to prevent 1975 production from falling below 20 million tons. Chairman Inayama, allowing that 15 million tons was more likely, nevertheless agreed to guide the 20 million target through the council if MITI would find rebates and subsidies to make it up to consumers. Although consumers agreed to accept 20 million tons of domestic coal in 1975, they met proposals by MITI for a public pricing agency with blunt refusals to cooperate.[207]

The Fifth Coal Program was announced on June 29, 1972. We may link Minister Tanaka's success in establishing this 20 million ton target to the declining importance of domestic coal for the consuming industries. The Fifth Program included expanded policies to prop up domestic demand, a third *katagawari* of 70 billion yen, and higher rates for every variety of subsidy. New private mechanisms were created within the coal industry to adjust coal prices in a timely fashion with the cost of fuel substitution.[208] The private utilities agreed to accept 3.5 million tons of domestic coal (EPDC was assigned 4.95 million tons), and the steel firms took 8 million tons.

Not even the OAPEC embargo and two oil crises could revive the domestic coal industry. A sixth coal program was issued in 1975, a seventh followed in 1981, and the eighth was announced in 1986. None had any impact upon the structure of the coal industry other than to prop it up. All the while, domestic coal firms recorded staggering losses, for which subsidies were paid.[209] Even Mitsubishi's once great Takashima mine was closed permanently in 1987. Although official targets for domestic coal production were finally reduced to 10 million tons, industrial consumers still dug in their heels. Inayama was still chairman of the MITI Coal Industry Advisory Council when steel firms announced in early 1986 that they would not accept delivery of domestic coking coal after 1992.[210] But the final shaft had been sunk long before—and, as usual, directly through the heart of the Japanese taxpayer.

CONCLUSION

The lengthy debates and incomplete solutions to the crises of coal chronicled in this chapter reveal striking historical continuities. The Japanese state has been pervasive across centuries of uncertain and volatile coal markets. But it has had a commercial market presence only when domestic producers were weak and disinterested, as in the Edo and early Meiji periods; when there was a military government (and even then state participation was limited to nonproductive, "tunnel" functions); or when a foreign occupation force advocated state control. The coal mines in Japan were never permanently nationalized, nor even effectively consolidated by the Japanese state. Prices were never set by state agencies, except when costs were subsidized and profits were guaranteed to producers. Instead, the Japanese state has served as guarantor to private firms whose own commitment to coal mining ultimately (and rationally) evaporated.

The failure to nationalize the mines in Japan is due neither to lack of effort nor to a bureaucratic commitment to free market principles and efficiency. It is directly attributable to the politics of reciprocal consent and to the several factors that have shaped these negotiations about the nature and extent of state intervention.

Consider first how market structure has constrained the state. Coal-mining firms were divided in several politically relevant ways. Large mining firms were split between *zaibatsu* and local capital. These producers assembled and disassembled collusive mechanisms, only occasionally with the state's help, and their collusive history is riven with exceptions and violations. Add to this mixture the politically savvy and influential small mining firms and industrial consumers. In the absence of a well-coordinated, highly centralized, and markedly determined state, we are left with all the ingredients for an exceedingly messy policy process.

This is precisely what the policy record reveals; it is related to state centralization, the second variable that seems to shape the capacity of states to intervene in markets. Characterizations of "clear state visions" in Japan and "conflated" private interest notwithstanding,[211] the policy record shows fragmented but individually powerful private interests laboring with a divided economic bureaucracy to assure state intervention that was extensive but market-conforming. Neither business nor state was consistently unified. It was conflict among subgovernmental coalitions that set the policy agenda on coal.

Third, the breadth and stability of Japan's ruling coalition was critically important in ensuring that intervention would remain market-conforming. The impermanence of Japan's Socialist coalition in 1947 was matched by the impermanence of state control of the coal mines. Although the Katayama Cabinet made nationalization thinkable for economic bureaucrats who had long coveted such a role in the economy, the opportunity proved only fleeting. The experiment with state control was eviscerated even before its enactment and was responsible for the collapse of the only "progressive" cabinet Japan has ever had. The bureaucracy put forward other proposals for nationalization, but as one former MITI Mining Bureau chief put it, MITI finally abandoned the idea of nationalization because "once the LDP had consolidated its power, there was no chance such a program could seriously be considered."[212]

Timing also mattered. It is no coincidence that the state enjoyed its most direct role in the management and ownership of Japan's coal mines when the Meiji oligarchs were starting their forced march toward industrialization. The observation conforms nicely with Alexander Gerschenkron's hypothesis about state intervention being likely where private capital is underdeveloped and where investment requirements are large and lumpy. Once private capital, particularly *zaibatsu* capital, became concentrated, the state forever relinquished ownership of the mines.

The state's lingering temptation to become mineowner and manager is linked to the displacement of coal by oil as the energy of choice. Interfuel substitution, derived from import dependence, resulted in an energy revolution that overwhelmed domestic coal. As Japan's industrial economy slowly opened foreign oil, the public treasury bore the escalating costs of the state's acting as guarantor. The political benefits of providing unlimited state subsidies to coal producers seemed always to outweigh the staggering economic costs. Johnson has noted the inefficiencies of "the policy of extensively subsidizing the coal industry in lieu of nationalizing it."[213] A former Coal Bureau chief, who tried and failed on at least three separate occasions to establish precisely that presence, concurs in a blunt retrospective: "All things considered, it would have been cheaper to nationalize the mines."[214]

In short, despite its repeated efforts to control domestic coal production, prices, and distribution, the Japanese state has participated in the market only on terms negotiated with and acceptable to other market players. Coal policy was doomed to be inconclusive because market volatility clashed with the political stability of policy choices. It seems clear that no government policy, no known technological innovation, no industry strategy could have produced a competitive Japanese coal industry in the late twentieth century. Mining firms seem to have appreciated the fact sooner and more clearly than state planners did. These firms consistently shaped and used public policy to ease market transitions, and they did so in ways that frustrated the very state programs for which they had lobbied before circumstances changed.

Coal, then, is a case of negotiated jurisdiction and reciprocal consent. But coal was not exceptional. Similarly negotiated constraints on state power obtained, as we shall see, in other energy sectors.

CHAPTER FOUR

A Political History of the Japanese Electric Power Industry

No sector of the Japanese political economy offers more sustained evidence of private resistance to state intervention than electric power. At every turn and in every era, as Chalmers Johnson notes, "electrical entrepreneurs have been among the strongest and most outspoken opponents of government controls."[1]

Negotiations over Japanese state intervention have always entailed great public costs and significant private benefits. Although national or regional management of electric utilities is usual in the industrial democracies, in Japan the state has majority holdings in only one national utility, the Electric Power Development Corporation (EPDC). But the EPDC was established to supply the private utilities; it is prohibited from selling to end-users. Local governments hold an average of only 5 percent equity in just four of Japan's nine private electric utilities. The only wholly state-owned electric utility is the regional utility in Okinawa, established when Okinawa reverted to Japan in 1972; it is slated for privatization. Japan's private utilities are among the largest privately owned and operated utilities in the world. They account for fully 10 percent of total investment in Japanese industry.[2] In electric power, as in the case of coal, the Japanese politics of reciprocal consent has resulted in market-conforming interventions that contrast sharply with what has happened in the rest of the industrial democracies.

ORIGINS OF THE INDUSTRY

From the beginning, and for most of its hundred-year history, Japan's electric power industry has been completely private, making it distinctive not only among electric utilities in industrial democracies but among industrial sectors in Japan as well. Unlike mining, transportation, steel, or munitions, for example, the utilities were developed with private capital. Entrepreneurs, often daimyo and their retainers, flush with government bonds issued to promote private investment (and to coopt potential opposition to the Meiji revolution), invested without state guarantees in the private development of electric power as early as 1882. This was only three years after California Electric, the world's first commercial electric power firm, built a central electric arc lighting station in San Francisco, and only one year after the world's first hydroelectric plant was constructed in Wisconsin.[3] The Age of Illumination came no later to Japan than to the rest of the industrializing world.[4]

Japanese industrialists soon realized the advantages of electric power. The first Japanese electric light plant (100 hp), sold by Thomas A. Edison, was installed in the Imperial Palace in 1887. By 1890 Japan had its first electric street car (in Ueno Park) and its first electric elevator (in Asakusa).[5] Electric power rates were high in the early years, however, and apart from these conspicuous applications, most use was limited to industry and the bureaucracy.[6] Tokyo Dentō was established in 1886 as Japan's first electric utility; within a decade private utilities modeled after it provided electric power to every region of Japan. By 1891 there were eleven such firms, by 1897 forty-one, capitalized at 9.4 million yen. As in Europe, many industrial firms purchased their own generating capacity, because transmission facilities were unreliable. Tokyo Dentō became a supplier of finished plants to factories and mines that required highly localized, heavy-load capabilities. More than fifty companies established autogeneration facilities in Japan between 1887 and 1893.[7] For the time being, most of the capital was still being raised in Japan itself.[8] By the turn of the century, in Japan as elsewhere, the Age of Illumination had already become the Age of Energy.[9]

Government regulation began as industry adopted electric power, and interestingly it first emerged at the local level. By 1889, four different unregulated electric utilities were operating (and rapidly expanding) in Tokyo alone. The first documented instance of government intervention was actually a prefigurative form of administrative guidance in which Tokyo governor Takazaki Goroku prevailed upon two of these competitors to consolidate operations. Their merger lasted only a short time. In 1890 the Kyoto Municipal Assembly required a public license to use electric power within the city. Even after central government introduced nationwide utility regulations in 1891, prefectural authorities routinely granted the licenses that private utilities sought. The utilities, seeking to keep regulation at bay, began to pay local governments compensatory offerings (kenkin) in response to consumer complaints that rates were excessive. The first was from the Osaka Electric Light Company to the Osaka municipal government in 1906, and it was followed by similar agreements in Nagoya in 1908 and in Tokyo in 1911.[10]

The central government was prodded into action not out of concern for excessive competition or to serve clear goals of industrial policy but because an electrical fire in 1890 destroyed the Imperial Diet building. The following year the Ministry of Communications (Teishinshō) was made the supervisory agency responsible for electric power. It thereupon distributed police safety regulations to each prefectural administration. As the number of firms and consumers rapidly expanded, the ministry usurped from prefectural governors the ultimate authority to issue permits. Upon the advice of the Fujioka Commission, a group of private entrepreneurs, the ministry issued its first comprehensive supervisory regulations in 1896.[11] For the first time legislation required safety precautions for generators and electric railways, standardized transmission voltages, and centralized permit authority. These regulations were adopted verbatim from the commission's report. Although the entrepreneurs were drafting statutes with the bureaucrats, they had not yet formed an industry association.[12] As in coal, that would wait until the private sector itself had had enough of excessive competition.

The Japanese victory over China brought indemnity payments of 360 million yen. With investment capital again plentiful, the electric power industry expanded rapidly to meet industrial demand for electricity. The number of utilities trebled in the next decade, accelerating further with the defeat of Russia in 1905. Between 1903 and 1914 the number of mechanized factories in Japan increased from fewer than four thousand to more than ten thousand, with the fastest increase in chemicals and machinery. At the same time safety problems were largely solved, and the pace of technological development quickened with the introduction of long-distance transmission facilities and the shift from small steam generators to larger hydroelectric facilities. The electric railway system extended throughout the nation, further stimulating demand for electric power.

The bureaucracy first looked at the prospects for state control of the electric power industry during this period of rapid and relatively undisciplined expansion. It did not get far. In 1909–10 Gotō Shimpei, minister of communications in the Katsura Cabinet, sought a state monopoly on hydropower generation. Arguing that the rivers were a public resource, and responding to demands from industrial consumers for rationalized electricity tariffs, Gotō pressed for state control. He was opposed not only by the utilities but by the Home Ministry as well. He abandoned his efforts.[13]

Gotō settled instead for the weaker Electric Power Industry Law of 1911. Government and consumers were concerned about monopolistic pricing practices, which the utilities claimed were a reflection of high capital costs, and so in 1909 the Ministry of Communications had sought more general state controls and for authorization to set rates. The rate-setting provisions were excised in committee in the Lower House of Diet. Representatives objected to a state role in the setting of prices in a free market. Even the revised bill had difficulty in the House of Peers, and Japan's first electric power law finally took effect in September 1911. State leadership for recentralization and for rate setting was rejected.[14] The new law replaced the Supervisory Regulations of 1896 and remained in effect until 1932.

In 1918 Minister of Communications Noda Utarō invoked foreign models in Diet testimony proposing the nationalization of the utilities.[15] This initiative failed too, and throughout the Taishō period the general legal status of the industry did not change. The Ministry of Communications licensed and regulated private firms as public utilities, but these firms were never threatened by direct state intervention.

Under minimal regulation, and stimulated by World War I, the Japanese electric power industry experienced turbulent, uncontrolled, and fratricidal expansion. As late as 1914 light industry still accounted for 80 percent of mechanized factories and 80 percent of the factory work force. In the next four years investments in Japanese chemicals, shipbuilding, metals, and machinery production expanded twenty-two-fold. To meet the demands of these heavy industries, the utilities increased investment in new power generation by 500 percent. By this time five electricity wholesalers accounted for one-quarter of all power generated in Japan.

Although these five firms had succeeded in consolidating their positions vis-à-vis smaller competitors, their competition with one another for the emerging markets of Japan's major industrial centers was chaotic. In the capital region Tokyo Dentō and Daidō Electric Power duplicated each other's distribution systems. In certain areas other competitors triplicated them. In Nagoya, Tōhō Electric, Japan Electric Power, and Tokyo Electric Light did likewise. In the Kansai area battle was joined by Japan Electric Power and Ujigawa Electric.[16] (The October 1921 creation of a nationwide industry association, the Nihon Denki Kyōkai, did not help.) The government contributed to redundancy by granting several licenses in the same district.[17] Duplication and inefficiencies meant, as in the early years of the British electric power industry, reduced returns to investors. Nonetheless it took more than a decade for market participants, government officials, and financial interests to recognize the desirability of regulation and to negotiate an end to the Electricity Wars.[18]

The first calls for regulation came neither from government nor from the utilities, but from the two leading political parties, the Minseitō and the Seiyūkai. The relationship of the parties to the utilities, the larger financial community, the state, and the expanding electorate during this period was extremely complex. The parties often became involved in the electric power issue as advocates for utilities seeking water rights and district licenses. In some cases one party influenced the bureaucracy to reverse decisions that favored the other party's utility. The utilities' political influence was not insignificant. President Wakao Shōhachi of Tokyo Electric Light, for example, was at the same time secretary general of the Seiyūkai in the mid-1920s. Indeed, some historians see the competition between the Seiyūkai and the Minseitō as a proxy for the competition between Tokyo Electric Light and Tōhō Electric.[19]

But the parties had other constituencies as well. For one thing, universal manhood suffrage was introduced in 1925. The utilities could no longer merely placate local political bosses.[20] Politicians had to promise lower electric rates, and failure to deliver resulted in citizens' protests. Industrial consumers also had a claim on the parties and made their demands for rate reduction clear.

The prosperity, moreover, was finished. With reduced demand, duplicated facilities exacerbated the problems of excess capacity. Suddenly the utilities wanted some form of relief. In June 1926 a special committee in the House of Peers debated the future of the industry. Reflecting its conflicting constituencies, the Seiyūkai proposed two separate plans. The first called for a joint public-private enterprise capitalized by state-guaranteed bonds; it would integrate and manage the nation's generation and transmission facilities. The second called for state purchase and management of all but the smallest hydroelectric and thermal plants. Neither plan addressed the commercial rights of distribution firms. Both proposals would make the state the wholesale supplier of electric power, and private industry would continue to sell to end-users. The Minseitō lost no time in responding with its own cluster of programs—a range of possibilities from state management to mere regulation.[21]

The following spring the utilities' industry association formally concluded that public intervention might be welcome to secure water rights and land for new plants. Yet the majority preferred no state buyout and formally recommended regulation and more effective self-control.[22] There are two important points to be stressed. First, whatever industry leaders might say in the future, there is no evidence that all opposed a state presence in electricity as a matter of principle. Private entrepreneurs were more than willing to negotiate an acceptable form of state intervention; as one observer has put it, there was always "a part of the electric power industry that saw state control as a profitable chance to unload its facilities onto the state."[23] Second, and as a result, proposals for heightened state intervention came first from private interests, not from the economic bureaucrats who would ultimately take credit for rationalizing the Japanese electric power industry.

That rationalization took its first official step forward with the creation in March 1927 of the Special Electric Power Investigation Bureau (Rinji Denki Jigyō Chōsabu) within the Ministry of Communications. The bureau was instructed to formulate a program for the regulation and control (*tōsei*) of the industry. Its head was a Ministry of Communications bureau chief, but leading representatives of the electric power industry also participated. A survey concerning the coordination of transmission facilities, water rights, rate structures, and other matters was distributed to more than eighty industry officials. In September a report was issued which centered on public versus private management. Agreement was reached on the desirability of legal revisions to permit the state to give long-term financial assistance to the utilities and to arbitrate in rate setting and other areas, but the bureau was unable to reach consensus on the basic character of the industry. There were at least seven different views of what constituted acceptable state intervention in the sector.[24]

One view belonged to Matsunaga Yasuzaemon, the president of Tōhō Electric. In May 1928 Matsunaga proposed regional private monopolies and a public utility commission. He took the lead among private entrepreneurs in promoting a coherent formula for self-control, to keep the bureaucracy out of the management of the utilities. On May 19, 1928, the five largest utilities agreed to study cartelization and to end the competition that was inviting intervention by their creditors and the state. But another four years would pass before the situation became sufficiently critical to entice them to adopt "self-control."

The pace was quickening. The Ministry of Communications dissolved its Special Electric Power Investigation Bureau after the inconclusive report was issued. The replacement was a higher-level advisory body, the Special Electric Power Investigation Commission for State Control (Rinji Denki Jigyō Kansei Chōsakai). Thirty commissioners, including the top bureaucrats from the Ministries of Finance, Agriculture, and Commerce and Industry, along with industry officials, began deliberations in January 1929. Debate over the character of the industry was narrowed from seven to three alternatives: public management, private management, and joint management. The political influence of the utilities, according to a leading history of the period, made "a shift to public management . . . close to impossible,"[25] however, and a revision of the Electric Power Industry Law was finally agreed upon as a compromise solution. Existing firms agreed to cooperate with government programs, including unification of generation and transmission, as long as there was no tampering with private ownership. Two of the five large utilities, Daidō Electric and Ujigawa Electric Power, however, voiced support for the creation of a joint public-private utility.[26] The top five firms were not themselves agreed upon strategy.

BANKS AND SELF-CONTROL

Debate continued for several years, with some industry leaders seeking state intervention and the most powerful resisting intrusion. Negotiated revisions to the Electric Power Industry Law were submitted to Diet by the Ministry of Communications in March 1931. Although the legal character of the industry was formally changed to a "public utility" (*kōeki jigyō*) for the first time, there was still no threat to the premises of private ownership.[27] Regional monopolies were now recognized as embodied in an electric power self-control association, the Denryoku Renmei, which got under way in April 1932, eight months before the legal revisions took effect. The rules governing this self-control had been hammered out by the five large utilities (whose combined generating capacity now accounted for 61 percent of the nation's total) at the insistence of their creditors and the ministry.

The banks were critical in the creation of the control association because of the peculiar nature of the utilities' financial crisis. Electric power was the only industrial sector in Japan to rely heavily upon foreign capital. The first major foreign borrowing by a Japanese utility was in 1923, when Tokyo Electric Light issued a £3 million note on British capital markets. Within a few months the other four major utilities had followed suit.[28] Government action actually stimulated this dependence. In 1927 legal revisions helped the industry meet its capital requirements by waiving the legal limit on foreign borrowing and allowing utilities to issue corporate bonds equivalent to twice their existing debt. Another revision, in 1931, permitted the utilities to enter into completely unsecured borrowing. By then nearly two-thirds of Japanese corporate securities held abroad were bonds issued by the electric utilities.[29] Between one-quarter and one-half of the outstanding debt of the electric utilities was held by foreign investors.[30] To cope with the global economic crisis and to quiet the "dollar buying–yen selling" fever that gripped financial circles when Britain went off the gold standard, the Minseitō finance minister Inoue appealed to nationalist sentiment. He labeled sale of the Imperial yen an act of treason.

The large banks ignored his exhortations and continued to buy dollars, which compelled Finance minister Takahashi Korekiyo, Inoue's successor, to prohibit the export of capital. To the industry, already suffering from excess capacity and reeling from currency devaluations that engorged its foreign debt, this was the final blow.[31] The electric utilities were ready to settle their differences by suppressing competition and accepting the leadership of the banks and the jurisdiction of the state in the formation of a control association. One immediate reward from the government came in November 1932, after the control association was established but before further Electric Power Industry Law revisions took effect. The Finance Ministry approved the industry's request for a state buy-out of its foreign debt. By March 1934 virtually all of the industry's foreign debt had been cleared.

The control association was central to the accommodation reached in 1932 among state, utilities, and creditors.[32] Each of these actors had a deep interest in such an accommodation. The state, especially after the Manchurian Incident, was preparing for war and anticipated a new boom in demand for heavy machinery and plant construction which would require cheap and stable sources of electric power. The banks had underwritten enormous debts for the utilities. Whereas the dependence of the utilities upon debt financing had been less than 10 percent in 1903, it was 70 percent by 1929.[33] The banks had long been active in managing the affairs of the utilities. In prominent cases they had forced changes in top management, as in 1927, when Mitsui Bank leaders forced President Wakao of Tokyo Dentō to resign;[34] at other times they had forced the utilities to reduce dividend payments. Now their "self-defense policy"[35] was clear; one insider claims that "the competition among the firms had grown so severe that the banks had to intervene in order to protect their investments and to insure that these firms would survive to pay them back."[36]

Collusion seemed a reasonable self-defense to the utilities as well. In a late 1931 conference convened to promote control of the industry (Den-ki Jigyō Tōsei Sokushin Iinkai), each of the five large utilities presented a separate plan for restructuring the industry; the plans included several varieties of state ownership. Matsunaga of Tōhō Electric proposed a special corporation to pool generating equipment. Kobayashi Ichizō of Tokyo Dentō urged regional monopolies. Hayashi Yasushige of Ujigawa wanted national management of the wholesale electric power provided to private firms for distribution to end-users. Naitō Kumaki of Nihon Denryoku proposed a control association, with the active support of financial and government agencies.[37] In these fumblings toward collusion there was at long last a will thought not yet a way.

In February 1932 the utilities' major creditors, the Mitsui, Sumitomo, Mitsubishi, and Japan Industrial banks, met with Minister of Communication Mitsuchi Chūzō to consider a control system for the electric power industry. They agreed to a national electric power holding company (Denryoku Mochikabu Kaisha) that would eliminate duplicated facilities, increase profits, and hold the public stock of the large five firms. Capitalization of the new national utility would be 160 million yen; management would be the collective responsibility of the five firms, under the supervision of the banks.[38] But the plan did not survive the opposition of some of the power companies. Agreement was reached instead on the "self-control" formula, the Denryoku Renmei.

The banks retained substantial control of the utilities. The agreement to create the association included a provision that members would submit all unresolved problems to the bankers for final arbitration, and no major investments in new generating capacity could be made without consultations. Modeled on the self-control cartels of the period, the Denryoku Renmei would be responsible for the allocation of production, markets, and prices—closely supervised, of course, by the banks and the government. The charter of the control association reflected this ambiguity toward the free market:

> Insofar as the electric power industry provides a public service and is an essential element of culture and industry, and in order to provide convenient services to customers at reasonable rates, avoiding the duplication of facilities that results from competition, we plan the control of the industry and join in the reality of mutual dependence and mutual benefit. . . .[39]

Shortly after the association began operations in April 1932, fifteen more utilities joined. Until the establishment of a national electric utility in October 1938, the association coordinated the third-largest electric power industry in the world.[40]

STATE CONTROL

Once the 1932 accommodation had been ratified and the utilities' foreign debts cleared, little was heard of public management and state control for almost four years. In the meantime Japan and other nations were preparing militarist solutions to the global economic crisis. Following the Manchurian Incident a nationalist and largely anticapitalist economic bureaucracy, supported by the military, abandoned even the fiction of adherence to "free economic principles." As we shall see, the state was joined by banks and industrial consumers who wanted more than anything else the cheap and plentiful power the state was promising.

The first official bureaucratic step toward state control of the nation's utilities was taken in December 1935, when "progressive" (*kakushin*) bureaucrat Okamura Kiwao issued a blueprint for state management under the authority of the Cabinet Planning Bureau. Within two months a group of young army officers launched an abortive coup in the famous 2/26 incident. Using the consequent uncertainty as an opportunity to reintroduce proposals for state control and to justify them as being in the interest of national defense and mobilization for war, the Hirota Cabinet accepted a draft program (Denryoku Kokusaku Yōkō), similar to the Okamura Plan, prepared by a group of *kakushin* bureaucrats in the name of Communications minister Tanomogi Keikichi. News of the program caused utility stock prices to plummet. The Tanomogi Plan called for state management of generation and transmission facilities through a special corporation (*tokushu kaisha*) with joint public-private capital, leaving distribution to the private sector.[41] The state justified seeking the consolidation of electric power resources not on grounds of scale or natural monopoly but of national security. The electric power sector was considered a basic industry, not merely a utility.[42]

The plan completely ignored the intractable issue of the purchase of and compensation for the fixed capital assets of private firms. Okamura and his *kakushin* associates are often credited with a creative solution to the problem. The Japanese state was already facing major fiscal constraints. The 1936 budget was in deficit by 10 million yen, and military expenditures were expected to skyrocket. Outright nationalization of the utilities would require some 5 billion yen in compensation, under the circumstances an inconceivable public expenditure. Hence a special corporation under state management, separating ownership and control, seemed an inexpensive and efficient solution. Private firms would receive shares of stock in the new firm in exchange for their transferred assets.[43] Neither public bonds nor treasury funds would be required, and as Ōtani said, "the government could make millet with wet hands."[44] This view implies that it was fiscal rationality and the opportunity for state control without state expenditure which suggested the public management—private ownership formula (*kokuei minyū*).

There is another explanation, however, for state plans were diverted by the active opposition of private firms that feared for their commercial rights. Although neither the banks nor the utilities had much interest in the profitless rural electrification envisioned by military and economic planners, they seemed unconcerned at first with the state control plan. It was not until July 1936 that they began publicly to organize their opposition. As part of a larger effort by private industry to stop the state from assuming too direct a control of industry, they gathered the support of the Tokyo and Nagoya Chambers of Commerce, as well as the major national federations of commerce and industry. Ownership and management were first separated clearly by the bureaucracy only in June, months after the first drafts of the Tanomogi Plan had leaked to the press. Determined private opposition and difficult interbureaucratic negotiations followed throughout the summer and fall;[45] it is likely that Johnson's interpretation is correct: the bureaucrats who "had wanted to nationalize the electric power industry . . . had to settle for public management and private ownership in order to get any law at all."[46]

But they were not going to get that law for some time. The bill that went before Diet in January 1937 stimulated memorable and blistering attacks on the military/state control program. One fabled denunciation by representative Hamada Kunimatsu came on the eve of the fall of the Hirota Cabinet, in late January.[47] The following day Matsunaga made nationwide headlines by denouncing, at a meeting of the Nagasaki Chamber of Commerce, the state control bureaucrats as the "scum of the earth."[48] With the resignation of the Hirota Cabinet, the Okamura/Tanomogi state control bill died stillborn. The electric power industry, Ōtani says, "breathed a sigh of relief."[49] The program for state control that over a year later became what Johnson calls "one of the most impressive reforms of 'industrial structure' of the prewar period"[50] remained a casualty of unstable cabinet government and private opposition. G. C. Allen summarizes matters thus: "Business interests were sufficiently powerful to defeat this attempt until after the outbreak of war in 1937."[51]

It took the state almost a year to regroup and resubmit its program. The reform bureaucrats found their most responsive government in the Konoe Cabinet, formed in June 1937; Minseitō representative Nagai Ryūtarō was made minister of communications. On June 10, Nagai revealed his intention vigorously to pursue state control of electric power. His first task was to snuff out internal bureaucratic battles. The most direct confrontation was between the Electric Power Industry Bureau chief Ōwada Teiji, a member of the National Policy Study Group (*kokusaku kenkyūkai*) of reform bureaucrats, and the top ministry civil servant, Hirazawa Kaname, who believed that self-control and joint thermal generation would suffice as national policy. Minister Nagai approved the state-control "reform" program in August. When Hirazawa refused to cooperate, Nagai, siding with the military and the young radicals in the bureaucracy, took the extraordinary step of forcing the resignation of his most senior civil servant.[52] A formal ministry draft finally appeared on September 11, 1937.

At this point Nagai established a special electric power task force (Rinji Denryoku Chōsakai) as a formal consultative body on the legislation and implementation of state control. When presidents of utilities protested that a time of national crisis is no time to change the basic form of industry and issued their own proposals, including submission to comprehensive national planning, Nagai moved the discussions to a subcommittee he packed with supporters of state control. Only two of the twelve subcommittee members represented the utilities; the Nagai Plan was approved. Nagai dissolved the task force without bringing the program to a vote in plenary session.[53] His task force was apparently a red herring from the very beginning; Electric Power Industry Association president Ikeo Yoshizō said that "I became a committeeman thinking that the purpose of this body was to study the merits and demerits of state management of the electric power industry. But when I look at the substance of the debates, state management is already an accepted premise, and we are merely being asked about how to implement it. I will not cooperate with this."[54]

The Nagai Plan approved by the cabinet in December 1937 was very similar to the Tanomogi Bill of the previous year. It proposed the Japan Electric Power Generation and Transmission Company (Nippon Hassōden K. K., hereafter Nippatsu) in the form of a joint public-private national policy company supervised by both government officials and private leaders. Actual management, however, would reside with a newly created electricity agency within the Ministry of Communications responsible for electric power supply and demand, construction, rates, and planning. The state also reserved the right to appoint the chief executive officer of the firm. Whereas under the Tanomogi Plan the new Nippatsu would have been empowered to claim existing facilities, the Nagai Plan allowed the public utility to build new ones in addition.[55] Nippatsu would sell the electric power it generated to private distribution firms.

The Nagai Plan was submitted as the Electric Power State Control Law and three related bills to the 73d Diet in January 1938. It had the full support of Prime Minister Konoe. Interpellators expressed their doubts about the efficiency of state control, pointing to the railway and telephone companies. Others had more abstract concerns, such as the potential damage to national unity from private opposition to the measure and in particular the violation of private property rights. Professor Matsumoto Jōji, a peer formerly of Tokyo University, called the measure the Electric Utility Seizure Law.[56] Nagai responded that under the Imperial Constitution all property was merely being held for the emperor. He insisted that no Japanese could place individual interests above national interests and that the government had the right to exercise eminent domain to acquire the utilities' facilities in the public interest.[57]

The Seiyūkai and the Minseitō joined forces in Diet to press for revisions of the Nagai drafts on March 25, after more than two dozen debates in the Lower House committee.[58] Konoe himself had to appear in the Upper House and stake his cabinet on passage of the measures. For his part, Nagai was prepared to resign from the Minseitō. In the end the politicians made revisions reluctantly tolerated by the finance and communications ministries. These revisions included 1) specific exclusion of distribution facilities from central management; 2) the exclusion of auto-generation and autotransmission from state control; 3) enhancement of the formal power of the Electric Power Advisory Council that would be created to oversee Nippatsu and in which private-sector leaders would participate; and 4) assurances that all exchanges of shares would be accompanied by a state guarantee. Just to spite the Ministry of Communications, it seemed, they added a clause prohibiting employment by Nippatsu of any supervisory bureaucrat from the ministry within five years of his retirement. State guarantees of shareholder dividends were already a critical part of the legislation; as one well-placed businessman said, "without a government guarantee, state control would not have been possible. It was in this way that the industry's reluctance to cooperate was overcome and further investment could be attracted."[59] The Electric Power State Control Law was passed in April 1938 by the same Diet that approved the National Mobilization Law. Peter Duus has compared the paths to both laws, and he notes that "the electrical power generation bill was modified far more substantially than the National Mobilization bill. As a result of compromises between the Cabinet and Diet, the bill was amended so that . . . [there] were substantial concessions to private business interests."[60]

These concessions notwithstanding, the Japanese state was forcing the pace of social and industrial transformation. In the electric power sector this was made possible by divisions among firms. There was no longer a united opposition to the program (if indeed there ever had been). Support for nationalization of the utilities went well beyond young military officers and reform bureaucrats to include small businessmen and farmers.[61] More significant, however, was the support from heavy industry and financial circles. Industrial consumption of electric power had trebled between 1926 and 1936, and on the eve of the Pacific War industry was consuming two-thirds of all electric power generated in Japan. Some historians suggest that state control was more complete in electric power than in other sectors because of widespread support for state control among heavy industrial consumers.[62] Moreover, small and medium-sized power firms were receptive to a state buy-out; only the five large utilities strongly opposed state control to the very end—and even they seem to have protested too much.[63]

The large banks that had come to control much of the industry since the 1932 accord also warmed to the idea of state control.[64] Bankers understood that investment-to-sales ratios are substantially greater for utilities than for manufacturing firms; the same total sales volume might require nine or ten times the fixed capital investment. Military supply industries promised higher returns. Mitsui Bank, for example, had held one-fifth of all outstanding debt of the nation's utilities in 1933. By 1937 demands for increased capital investments in the sector were competing with the bank's plans to move vigorously into heavy industry and chemicals. Two historians argue that Mitsui "welcomed" the state's underwriting of the financial burden of the electric power sector.[65] So, apparently, did other private investors. The first public offering of the guaranteed shares was made in January 1939, and was scheduled to last for three days; but there were applications for more than seven times the number of available shares on the first day. With this strong show of support among private investors, sales were terminated.[66]

National management of the utilities eliminated risk for the financial community: the government guaranteed quarterly dividends for the first ten years of Nippatsu's existence. Outstanding debt could legally amount to three times paid up capital (three times the normal legal limit), with all debt fully guaranteed by the state, which helps explain why heavy industry and the banks did not oppose state control to the bitter end but instead made their well-known accommodation (tenkō) with the Nippatsu program.

Finally, how deep was opposition among the large utilities themselves? The previous decade had seen precious little consensus about industry consolidation. As in the railway industry, entrepreneurs were always willing to sell unprofitable facilities to the state. During the Depression, for instance, Daidō Electric and Nippon Electric, both with excess capacity, had petitioned the state to buy their underused generating facilities. In 1938 this same Daidō Electric was burdened by the largest outstanding debt among the five large utilities and, apparently because it welcomed financial relief, it became the most avid supporter of state control. Its president, Masuda Jirō, became the first president of Nippatsu. Even one of Matsunaga's most valued braintrusters, Ide Teijirō of Tōhō Electric, ultimately became an advocate for state control. He became Masuda's first presidential secretariat chief when Nippatsu began operations and the Denryoku Renmei was abolished.[67]

The Nippatsu establishment law was promulgated in April 1938, with the national utility slated to begin operations in April 1939. Private ownership was formally preserved, and the government was required to compensate utility companies for acquired facilities. Private firms could not sell their facilities to others once the government had notified them of its intent to purchase. Assets were transferred under a system of exchange (genbutsu shusshi) of Nippatsu shares for fixed capital assets. There were no cash payments. Assessments were based upon profits of the previous ten years and current book value. (Dual criteria were invoked because private firms preferred the former and the state the latter.) It may have amounted to little in reality, but an elaborate appeals system was included in the Nippatsu legislation for firms that felt that state evaluations were unfair. If the appeal succeeded, state funds (cash) would be used to make up the difference. Thus unlike Nittan, which was a national policy company (*kokusaku gaisha*) with joint capital from the state and the private sector, Nippatsu was a joint stock company in the form of a special corporation (*tokushu gaisha*). Foreigners were prohibited from holding shares. So the state gained control without massive investment. In return twenty-nine utilities (accounting for 83.3 percent of the equity) and other shareholders enjoyed guaranteed dividends, even if at a relatively low 5 percent. As if to reward the company's support, the corporate headquarters of Daidō Electric became corporate headquarters for Nippatsu.

As the state had sought to separate ownership and management, so private firms had sought to separate state funds from state control. These simultaneous struggles determined the nature and the extent of state intervention in the Japanese electric power sector. When private firms could not achieve the separation they preferred, most simply resigned themselves to state control and accepted state funds. Two presidents of leading firms became early chief executives of Nippatsu.[68] Some, however, refused to submit, and Matsunaga led a group of industry executives into self-imposed "exile" before the opening of the Pacific War.[69]

Those left to cooperate with the Communications Ministry had their work cut out for them. At the end of 1938 Japan had 407 commercial firms supplying electric power in addition to 147 electric railway companies and 110 other assorted generators of electric power. Some were municipal or prefectural public entities; some were joint stock companies, partnerships, or closely held family enterprises. Nippatsu started by acquiring the transmission facilities of thirty-three firms, 60 percent of the nation's thermal generating capacity, and some hydropower plants. The first problem facing management was organization. Ōwada Teiji, the "reform" bureaucrat who had struggled within the Communications Ministry for state control, was given responsibility for it. His office became the Electricity Agency (Denkichō), which invited confusion concerning the distribution of supervisory responsibilities between the agency and the new national utility, Nippatsu.[70] The entire program suffered from a lack of coordination, and in November 1943 the electric power administration was moved to the Munitions Ministry, forerunner of MITI.

The procurement of coal soon emerged as the most vexing problem for administrators. Private utilities had used the year between promulgation and implementation of the Nippatsu law to run down their coal stocks: Nippatsu acquired power plants but no fuel. Under wartime conditions, and for reasons I explored in the previous chapter, Nippatsu found it increasingly difficult to procure coal. Its planning was consistently too optimistic, assuming (incorrectly) that a national policy company in coal could smoothly supply a state-controlled electric utility. Nippatsu managers had to resort to the black market, as well as to purchases from Canada and India, in transactions through Mitsubishi that angered the military.[71]

In September 1940 the government unveiled plans for a second-stage consolidation of electric power management which would reach more deeply into hydropower and the distribution system. These plans came amid both the forced consolidation of political parties into the Imperial Rule Assistance Association (Taisei Yokusankai) and business community's struggle against the reform bureaucrats' Plan for a New Economic Order (Keizai Shintaisei Yōkō). Some private utilities, again led by Matsunaga, made another effort to block increased state controls. Because Daidō and Nippon Denryoku had collaborated with the state control program, Matsunaga now turned to the independent capitalists whose financial interests in hydropower were being threatened by state seizure.[72] After his impassioned speech in November, private-sector support began to spread. Even within the cabinet a former business leader, Kobayashi Ichizō, fiercely opposed the new proposal.

On December 7, under intense pressure, the cabinet approved a version of the New Economic Order different from what the bureaucracy had submitted. Private management and the status quo were preserved. The Communications Ministry then withdrew its draft bills for the second phase of state control of electric power, and instead, in January 1941, it merely submitted a revision sweetened by six rather than four guaranteed annual dividends. Business opposition dissipated.

The revision permitted Nippatsu to compel hydropower investments and to absorb the TVA-like Tohoku Development and Power Company (over local objections). It did so in December 1941, and Nippatsu thereby grew to account for 70 percent of national hydropower and 60 percent of thermal power generation. Once the National Mobilization Law was implemented in April 1942, several hundred electric power distribution firms (haiden) were merged into nine regional companies. The wartime system thus culminated in a giant, state-controlled electric utility, delivering power through nine regional firms. Ironically it was this state-led transformation which served as the structural basis for the postwar privatization of the industry.

Proponents of Nippatsu had promised that consolidation and state control would bring "abundant and cheap" (hōfu teiren) electric power to consumers. It did neither. Nippatsu failed to meet its targets for lack of resources, capital, and labor. Under a joint accounting procedure, Nip-

Table 4.1. Nippatsu: financial performance, 1940–45 (million yen)

Fiscal year	Presubsidized earnings	State subsidy	Total earnings
1940	7.0	21.2	28.2
1941	14.3	20.1	34.4
1942	81.1	7.4	88.5
1943	61.2	31.7	92.9
1944	36.6	71.1	107.7
1945	−60.3	160.0	99.2

SOURCE: Cohen 1949:176.

patsu would sell power to the nine distributing firms at a temporary rate, and then, upon reporting of costs and expenses, both would receive subsidies from the state if necessary. There were no incentives for cost reductions and efficiency, and corruption was reportedly widespread.[73] Guaranteed dividends ensured a drain on the treasury, and Nippatsu required state subsidies in all but four accounting periods between 1940 and 1945 (see Table 4.1).

By war's end Nippatsu subsidies and legislated dividends amounted to 300 million yen, nearly one-third of all wartime state support to Japan's public policy companies.[74] As had happened in the case of coal, wartime struggles among entrepreneurs and between entrepreneurs and the state ensured that private benefits were exceeded only by public costs.

THE OCCUPATION

At the end of the war the Supreme Commander, Allied Powers (SCAP), inherited a consolidated Japanese electric power system (see Figure 4.1). The problem of coal was pressing, and so the young Occupation administration did little at first to the electric power industry. Although SCAP created public agencies in other sectors, the existence of Nippatsu made such reorganization unnecessary in electric power. There were other exigencies also. Once workers' rights were returned in December 1945, for example, labor unrest emerged as an early and intransigent problem. In April 1946 the Nihon Denki Sangyō Rōdō Kumiai (Densan) was established to represent organized employees in electric power companies. Densan involved a group of workers more sophisticated than those in mining or other industries. Eighty percent of its members were involved in technical activities, and more than half had better than a middle-school education.[75] In August, Densan launched its first strike, demanding higher retirement allowances, lower tariffs, and "democratization" of the industry.

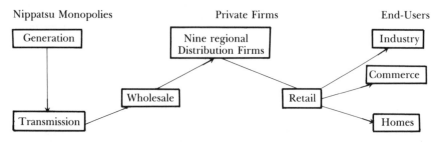

Figure 4.1. The wartime electric power system of Japan
SOURCE: Shinobu 1967:1202–1205.

In September, SCAP ordered the abolition of the National Mobilization Law, rendering moot many of the control regulations of the Electric Power Industry Law. Formal ministerial authority for utility regulation, supply/demand forecasting, financial authorization, and rate structuring was weakened. The distribution firms became subject only to the commercial codes regulating the activities of ordinary stock companies, and, to confiscate wartime profits, SCAP cut off subsidy and debt payments as well as government guarantees. On balance SCAP moved to dismantle Nippatsu much more deliberately than it did for the national policy companies for coal and petroleum. The authorities favored provisional bureaucratic control of the economy until the private sector could be "democratized." Where SCAP faced *zaibatsu* dominance and concentrated holdings, as in oil and coal, it dissolved the control associations and replaced them with temporary *kōdan*.

In the meantime, however, labor unrest intensified. Densan, like the mineworkers' union, Tanrō, demanded "democratic" state control. It turned off the nation's electric power for five minutes on October 19, 1946, as a reminder of its members' strength. Strikes and occasional violence continued throughout 1947, but apart from assorted programs to increase production, SCAP did little for several years. Nippatsu stayed in place. The Socialist Katayama Cabinet, busy with coal nationalization, could fight only one battle in the energy industries at a time.

In February 1948 SCAP took its first step toward breaking up the electric power monopoly. Nippatsu and the nine distribution firms were designated as "excessively concentrated companies" under the deconcentration law of December 1947. This law required 325 designated firms to file reorganization plans with SCAP. Distributors and Nippatsu opposed the measure; even before the order was issued, they had petitioned to be considered a "natural monopoly" exempt from economic reorganization, and on April 22 they jointly submitted a proposal to preserve the status quo. It may have been the last time that Nippatsu and the distributors agreed about industrial reorganization.

The plans for reorganization that resulted were uniformly self-serving. SCAP rejected them all and was coming to believe that removal of the utilities from bureaucratic control was necessary to restore a healthy electric power sector. In the official view "the bureaucratic semi-governmental monopolies controlling the generating and distributing of electricity were inefficient, curtailed incentive, and failed to fix responsibility in the administration of the industry."[76]

But there was still much debate ahead. Several reorganizations had already been proposed.[77] The left had been earliest, proposing a democratization of the industry. Densan, and later the Socialists, called for the unification of Nippatsu and the distributing companies into a single, national electric utility with management decisions to be made by committees composed of workers, capital owners, consumers, and scholars. Private capital would be accepted and limited dividends would be paid, but investors would have no voice in management. The Communist party added steel, cement, coal, paper, textiles, railroads, broadcasting, and shipping to its list for nationalization.

Local governments took a stand on the matter as early as February 1946, when the Tokyo Assembly called for the transfer of control of electric power generation and transmission to the localities. In April the National Association of Mayors began a nationwide campaign for municipal control. The Governors Association, at the initiative of Fukuoka Prefecture, quickly responded with a campaign for prefectural control.[78] Some conservative Diet members who relied heavily upon regional support groups took up the cause, arguing that utilities should be reconstituted as local public corporations. Their plan would preserve Nippatsu but change the character of the distribution firms; it was issued in May 1948.

Formal discussion started in the Electric Power Industry Democratization Committee (Denki Jigyō Minshuka Iinkai), established by Prime Minister Ashida Hitoshi soon after SCAP issued deconcentration orders. The committee was chaired by Tokyo University professor Ōyama Matsujirō and included representatives of heavy industry, local government, finance, and labor, as well as coal producers and Dietmen. This representation was unusually wide, even for a Japanese advisory committee, perhaps as Otake argues "reflecting the confusion of the times."[79] Despite this confusion, and despite the plethora of proposals debated, most Japanese opinion—industrial, ideological, and bureaucratic—seemed inclined toward some form of unified, national electric utility. Nippatsu was desperate enough to enter a peculiar marriage of convenience and offered a program similar to the one Densan had proposed. Manufacturing firms were divided, but the largest consumers of electric power opposed an unregulated breakup of Nippatsu, fearing regional inequities in rate structure and supply. With opinion favoring an integrated utility, Nippatsu was optimistic about its future as late as autumn 1948.[80] Only the nine *haiden* closed ranks in opposition. The one opinion that mattered most, however, was not represented on the committee. SCAP now wanted a private electric industry. The distribution firms had all the support they would ever need.

The Ōyama Commission deliberated until October 1948 before issuing a report. Opinion within the committee (with the obvious exception of the distributing firms) favored some form of national utility; but in anticipation of SCAP objections, the commission recommended a plan that left Honshu and Kyushu power systems unchanged while introducing financial measures for rate equalization. Essentially the plan consolidated generation and transmission in a single national joint stock company and did not affect the distribution firms. SCAP ignored the report. Reform had reached a stalemate; labor unrest intensified.

The next initiative was taken by a now exasperated SCAP. In May 1949 Roy S. Campbell, president of a New York shipbuilding firm, was brought to Japan to head a five-member study panel. This Deconcentration Review Board, three of whose members were American utility executives, was adamant about the privatization of electric power:

> Since the *Hassōden-Haiden* Monopoly had deep roots in the political life of Japan and since officials of the industry put bureaucratic loyalties above company loyalties, the Deconcentration Review Board recommended the abolishment of the Electric Power Bureau, the administrative link between the industry and government, and its replacement by a national public utility commission.[81]

One of the commissioners, Edward J. Berger, a senior executive from Cleveland Public Service Corporation, privately urged MITI officials to produce a plan for seven regional blocs. The idea confused the nine distribution firms, previously the only private-sector advocates of the dissolution of Nippatsu. If a seven-bloc plan were accepted, two firms would be legislated out of existence. The debate grew even more chaotic. Once the committee returned to the United States, General MacArthur's chief economist (and a former utility president), T. O. Kennedy, inherited responsibility for getting the Japanese to accept a breakup of Nippatsu. After a summer of Densan strikes Kennedy had a note secretly delivered to MITI on September 27 demanding 1) the dissolution of Nippatsu; 2) the unification of generation, transmission, and distribution on a regional basis; 3) the privatization of all state holdings in the electric power sector; 4) the creation of a new, independent regulatory agency (a public utilities commission) to replace MITI's Electricity Bureau; and 5) rate-setting autonomy for the new firms. SCAP's official history claims that "SCAP's objective was to remove inefficiency from the existing organization, free the industry from government control, and establish it as a privately owned free enterprise industry subject only to such regulation as was required by the public interest."[82] More critical histories suggest that these goals were "deeply related to the structural rebirth of Japanese capitalism" and were pursued to assist American capital gain control of Japan.[83]

Under pressure from Kennedy, the government created yet another new commission to develop a program that would please SCAP. In November 1949 Prime Minister Yoshida Shigeru established the Electric Industry Reorganization Council (Denki Jigyō Saihenseibi Shingikai), chaired by Matsunaga Yasuzaemon, whose clean wartime record (most of his political enemies were still in jail) and history of vocal opposition to bureaucratic controls made him the ideal choice for SCAP. From Yoshida's point of view, the suspicion with which Matsunaga viewed bureaucrats was an additional advantage. The Matsunaga Committee differed from the Ōyama Committee in two significant ways. First, fewer interests were formally represented; Nippatsu, Densan, and the political parties were excluded. Second, and more important, the committee had the confidence of SCAP. To Matsunaga, however, it was at best a marriage of convenience. He had sat out the Pacific War, refusing to cooperate with the state control bureaucracy, but he was realistic about what lay ahead. He would later interpret his role in industry reorganization as "the start of my war with the United States."[84]

His committee issued its report in February 1950. Matsunaga and the distribution firms were outnumbered by heavy industrial interests, led by Nippon Steel president Miki Takashi, which wanted low rates and a plentiful supply of electric power. Questions of ownership and control were secondary to them. They feared that privatization would lead to more expensive electricity, and they preferred subsidized power to keep their production costs low. Matsunaga found himself outgunned in his own committee. The majority, clearly understanding the risks it ran with SCAP if it overruled Matsunaga in a plenary vote, issued its report with Matsunaga's dissent attached.

The majority report, written by Miki, called for dissolution of Nippatsu and the *haiden*, and the creation of nine regional firms as well as the Public Utilities Commission sought by SCAP; but it included a tenth entity, a public agency responsible for power generation and transmission to equalize rates and supplies across the regions. This Electric Power Accommodation Corporation (Denryoku Yūzū K. K.) would take over 42 percent of Nippatsu's facilities, returning the rest to the *haiden*. It was a poorly disguised clone of Nippatsu.

Matsunaga's personal recommendations strongly opposed the tenth company, arguing instead for integrated regional power firms. He diverged slightly from SCAP, however, in advocating that the larger, urban-based utilities build and operate generating facilities outside their own districts. SCAP wanted firms with surplus power to sell to those which needed additional supplies. But Matsunaga feared that if the imbalance between generators and users grew too great, those in the producing districts might come together in a reincarnation of Nippatsu.

This confrontation between consumers and producers bore an ironic but not coincidental resemblance to the prewar struggles for control of the industry. If the Matsunaga Plan was reminiscent of the Denryoku Renmei cartel agreement of 1932, the Miki Plan looked suspiciously like the state control program of the Communications Ministry.

SCAP unceremoniously vetoed the majority report; Kennedy even had to be disabused of the notion that the Matsunaga Plan needed a major overhaul.[85] On March 11, 1950, Kennedy finally approved a slight revision of Matsunaga's program (he wanted a more independent public utilities commission), and the committee was authorized to plan the reorganization of the electric power industry. Two draft bills were submitted to the Seventh Diet in April of that year.

Industrial consumers organized regionally to lobby against the plan. Industrialists in western Japan, where hydropower was scarce, particularly opposed the reorganization. The Osaka Chamber of Commerce and Industry, the Kansai Economic Federation, and other groups issued joint statements of opposition. The Tokyo financial community remained silent.[86] The ruling Liberal party was divided. Ōno Banboku, chairman of the Lower House Commerce and Industry Committee, and his lieutenant Fukuda Hajime led a group of Liberal politicians in public opposition. (Ōno was widely known as leader of the antibureaucratic wing of the party, yet ironically he was arguing against privatization. One observer has explained his position in terms of his "close ties to contracting and engineering firms that build electric power plants.")[87] On the other hand were those loyal to Prime Minister Yoshida who could not openly defy SCAP. There was little support for the program from MITI, the rest of the government, or the press.[88] Johnson correctly points out that "industry wanted cheap power; company owners wanted to make a return on their capital; the bureaucracy was interested in keeping its sphere of influence intact—and all had political representatives in Diet."[89]

On April 20, the day that the Matsunaga Plan was submitted to Diet, Kennedy told MITI minister Takase Sōtarō that unless the measures passed the current Diet, U.S. funds for electric power development would cease. The Yoshida Cabinet supported reorganization, but with nationalist resentment about SCAP's heavy-handedness running high,

Diet defied SCAP. It failed to act on the measures before being prorogued on May 2, 1950. The bills were shelved, Nippatsu stayed alive, and reorganization was delayed.

On June 19 SCAP's General William F. Marquatt met with Yokō Shigemi, the fourth MITI minister of the year, to deliver a final warning: unless the reorganization measures were resubmitted to the Special Eighth Diet session due to convene on July 12, all SCAP Counterpart Aid funds would be cut off. On July 10 the government declined to submit the legislation, claiming local tax reform was more pressing and asking SCAP to "please understand the government's position and to act with restraint."[90] An angry SCAP froze all financial assistance to the electric industry on July 23. As "designated firms" under the deconcentration order, Nippatsu and the nine *haiden* were prohibited from issuing bonds, increasing capital, expanding capacity, or building new plants until a reorganization law acceptable to Occupation forces passed. These measures were particularly hard on Nippatsu, which had depended heavily upon debt financing. Also they adversely affected the construction, electronics, cement, and wire-manufacturing industries.

By midsummer the political deadlock over reorganization was being nudged by the Korean War–induced recovery. In September the government demanded that the two top Nippatsu executives resign for their outspoken opposition to reorganization. MITI began circulating plans for a return of autogeneration facilities that Nippatsu had confiscated more than a decade earlier. The Democratic party weighed in with a five-bloc proposal. Local government made yet another bid for municipal and prefectural management. By November 21, when the Ninth Special Diet opened without a formal government bill in the docket, control was clearly slipping away from SCAP. The following day a message was delivered from General MacArthur to Prime Minister Yoshida. The prime minister was formally instructed to abolish the existing regulatory structure for electric power and to implement the industry reorganization plan submitted to the Seventh Diet.

These instructions became the basis for two Cabinet Orders issued as "Potsdam Ordinances," carrying the full force of law as derived from the terms of Japan's unconditional surrender. Nippatsu and the nine *haiden* were placed in the receivership of a new public utilities commission. The media and industry were furious with Yoshida for submitting to such a violation of Japanese sovereignty so late in the Occupation, but as Japan was not yet sovereign, there was nothing the government could do.[91]

On December 15 the Public Utilities Commission began operations. Its chairman was Matsumoto Jōji, the former Tokyo University professor who had eloquently opposed the creation of Nippatsu from the floor of the House of Peers in 1938. He immediately turned over actual operations to Matsunaga Yasuzaemon. The remaining three commissioners were a banker (Kawakami Hiroichi, former president of the Kōgyō Ginkō), an industrialist (Miyahara Kiyoshi, president of Kamijima Chemical Company), and a commercial representative (Itō Chūbei, the chairman of Itō Shōten). Three days later SCAP released 9.4 billion yen in funds to Nippatsu.

Formally, of course, utility reorganization under the Potsdam orders entailed the dissolution of the *haiden* and Nippatsu, and their replacement by entirely new firms. In reality, as the *haiden* had desired and as Nippatsu had feared, it amounted to the absorption of Nippatsu facilities by the *haiden* reorganized as private regional monopolies. Matsunaga guided the entire program with the full assent of SCAP.

Predictably, the most difficult issue was the evaluation of Nippatsu assets. Nippatsu insisted on current prices, while the *haiden* preferred book values. Nippatsu president Kosaka Junzō, Yoshida's proxy in the battle for control of the utilities, cleverly tried to enlarge his staff and increase the firm's capital so as to have greater influence in the nine utilities after they absorbed Nippatsu facilities and personnel. Matsunaga blocked his attempts.[92] Kosaka also failed to arrange a ratio for the *haiden*-Nippatsu exchange of shares higher than what he ultimately obtained, but he did succeed in authorizing a special dividend of 600 million yen and a liquidation settlement of 745 million yen for his shareholders.[93]

Nippatsu was abolished, and the nine private utilities were inaugurated formally on May 1, 1951, amid new labor unrest.[94] No sooner had the new system started than the Public Utilities Commission proposed a 76 percent increase in utility rates. The uproar was loud and predictable. Matsunaga's most recent antagonists, Miki of Nippon Steel and Kosaka of Nippatsu, publicly called for his resignation.

With the Korean War simulating demand, coal shortages and labor unrest limiting supply, and industry leading public opinion against "selfish" rate increases, Matsunaga feared that the case for nationalization might be reopened. He therefore arranged for the creation of a central research institute to coordinate resource development by the nine utilities.[95] He was especially keen to promote programs separate from those under development by an Economic Stabilization Board (ESB) staff composed largely of former reform bureaucrats and leftist economists who would argue for state management. Government economists were promoting coal and projecting only a 3 percent annual increase in demand for electric power. The Matsunaga group projected 8 percent annual growth and prevailed upon key figures, such as Bank of Japan governor Ichimanda Naoto, to reflect higher projections in government investments.[96] Funds would have to come from somewhere, but public opinion firmly opposed the rate increases that Matsunaga was proposing.

Matsunaga encouraged the introduction of foreign capital, an idea anathema to more nationalistic MITI bureaucrats and Dietmen. Although legislation in May 1950 permitted capitalization on foreign money markets, no private utility ventured to raise funds in this way.[97] On August 12 SCAP approved only a 30 percent rate increase, but three days later it provided 6.2 billion yen in Counterpart Aid assistance to the nine firms, which fortified their one-billion-yen bond offering made on August 20. After some initial reluctance the Occupation had intervened forcefully and decisively to establish a privately owned, regionally consolidated electric power industry in Japan.

But while a state-controlled public policy company was transformed into nine private regional monopolies, political conflict about the state's role was by no means over even if SCAP's ability to determine its outcome was fast dissipating. Immediately after the San Francisco Peace Treaty was signed on September 8, 1951, but well before the formal transfer of authority seven months later, the Yoshida government started to reintroduce a direct state presence in electric power. Many of the industrial elites and politicians (including Yoshida) who had so vehemently opposed state participation in the coal industry now raised their voices for a limited public presence in the market to ensure cheap, stable supplies of electric power.

On October 1, 1951, Prime Minister Yoshida instructed the Liberal party Policy Affairs Research Council to prepare a bill to create a new national policy company for the development of electric power.[98] Yoshida's supporters, allied to local interests and big business seeking subsidized power, had led parliamentary opposition to the Matsunaga/ SCAP privatization program. Now, with the prospect of a SCAP-less (and therefore undefended) public utilities commission, they found a convenient opportunity to reignite the debate. On October 29, although the peace treaty had already been signed, SCAP publicly opposed a new public corporation, claiming that such an entity would be contrary to the goal of democratization of the economy (a goal already far from the top of the SCAP agenda). The House of Representatives, flexing its new muscles, passed a resolution favoring the idea over SCAP's objections.

Matsunaga, still presiding over the Public Utilities Commission, strongly opposed a special corporation as a reincarnation of Nippatsu. At the end of November he countered with a commission plan, calling for multiple private joint venture firms with foreign capital to promote development of electric power. Speaking to Mitsui Mining Company president Yamakawa Ryōichi about the government/industry plan, he argued:

> Your thinking is fundamentally wrong. It is just like Miki and the others on the reorganization committee, who believed that large industrial consumers

should get special treatment in access to electric power. But that sort of idea is little more than a reflection of their view of themselves as somehow specially privileged. It constitutes a slavish submission to power. Generating electricity with tax money to sell at special rates to privileged customers is a perverted form of capitalism that I cannot abide.[99]

Holding a different view, of course, were construction and engineering firms, former Nippatsu bureaucrats (particularly at MITI and the ESB), and large industrial consumers, all of whom wanted a centralized, coordinated, and subsidized power industry. They pushed the Liberal party plan ahead. In January 1952 the party completed a draft law for the creation of a public corporation to develop hydropower resources. SCAP and the nine private utilities demanded that the plan be made to conform to the Public Utilities Commission proposal of November. Meetings continued through the early spring, and by late March a compromise was reached allowing the nine private utilities to hold equity in the new company. On March 25 this draft, authored jointly by Tohoku Electric Power president Shirasu Jirō and Liberal party leaders with the cooperation of MITI, was submitted to Diet as a member's bill (giin teian) sponsored by the Ōno faction, which in the Seventh Diet had opposed the nine-bloc system. Submitted in this way, it did not need the prior approval of SCAP or the Public Utilities Commission.

The new plan had three components. First, it called for public financial assistance to the private utilities. Second, it established a new public enterprise to develop Japan's electric power resources through the acquisition of land and the construction of hydropower plants; these were eventually to be leased by or transferred to the private utilities. Third, an Electric Power Resources Development Coordinating Advisory Committee was to replace the Public Utility Commission.

Although most private utilities publicly opposed this legislation, they gained several important concessions in the process. The new Electric Power Development Corporation (EPDC) would not threaten their regional monopolies, and they would hold equity in the new company. Its functions would be limited to wholesale generation and transmission of electric power to the private firms; and the state would provide most of the capital required for large-scale construction projects that otherwise would strain the indebtedness of private firms. The law was not without its attractions.

Moreover, there was little support for the Public Utilities Commission. Under Matsunaga it had championed a private utility system, but a commission-like organ, independent of any formal affiliation to the ministries, was held to be alien to Japan. And many people in the industry, of course, felt an animus toward Matsunaga. The commission, much like the Securities and Exchange Commission and the Fair Trade Commission, was widely viewed as an excess of the Occupation. Adding fuel to his own pyre, Matsunaga proposed a 28.8 percent rate hike in March 1952 in the midst of the debate over a new public electric utility. Prime Minister Yoshida sardonically declared his a "*Private* Utility Commission," and Matsunaga, now a scapegoat for high electricity rates, was reviled in the press. On April 28 the Occupation formally ended. One month later Diet committees began formal debate of the EPDC package, which was enacted with minor revisions on July 31. The following day the nineteen-month-old Public Utilities Commission was replaced by a twenty-eight-member advisory commission reporting to the Public Utilities Bureau within MITI. The commission had been one of the most powerful, peculiar, and short-lived organs in the history of Japanese public administration.

THE FINAL SHAPE OF THINGS

On September 16, 1952, as if in symbolic confirmation of institutional continuity, the EPDC opened its offices in the old Nippatsu headquarters in Koishikawa, which (to complete the symbol) had been partially destroyed by American bombs in 1945. The EPDC, formally a special corporation (*tokushu gaisha*), thus became the only commercially active public energy firm in Japan. Unlike other special juridical entities, it has never been formally limited to finance, subsidy, and loan guarantee. But though it produces and sells a product, it is prohibited from selling directly to consumers. It cannot compete with private utilities. It is a mere shadow of Nippatsu, kept at arm's length by vigilant private utilities.[100] In the late 1980s it generates only 5 percent of the nation's electric power.[101] Its establishment in 1952 was the final significant structural transformation of electric power in Japan. Political debate over state ownership has emerged from time to time in the thirty-five years since, but never has the debate dominated the agendas of business or the state.

The EPDC was surrounded by scandal from the beginning. One of the first politicians accused of tampering with its public trust was the young Tanaka Kakuei. Tanaka, already tarred by coal bribery charges, was accused of accepting payoffs to influence the siting of Tadigawa Dam and an associated decision on water rights affecting neighboring Niigata and Fukushima prefectures.[102] Even worse, a scandal involved EPDC's first president, Takasaki Tatsunosuke, a former Manchurian Heavy Industries official. Takasaki ran into trouble for negotiating with foreign investors without political or bureaucratic consent. There was also a matter of illegal cement procurement. He was replaced within two years by Matsunaga's old nemesis, Kosaka Junzō, formerly president of Nippatsu.

EPDC's initial projects all involved construction of hydropower plants, beginning with the Sakuma Dam, an extraordinary national effort to bring 350,000 kw of new power on line within three years.[103] Water resources soon grew scarce as national demand for electric power was dramatically increasing. Within three years the EPDC sought to enter the thermal power generation business, though its first thermal plant did not come on line until 1962. EPDC thermal plants, predominantly coal-fired, increased in capacity and number with the blessing of the private utilities, which refused to cooperate with government policy and burn expensive domestic coal.[104] Today thermal power accounts for two-thirds of the firm's total power generation.[105]

This shift succeeded in large measure because private utilities supported it. Other initiatives were less successful. In October 1954, for example, EPDC president Kosaka, with the backing of MITI, asked that the EPDC law be revised to permit it to engage in electric power transfer (yūzū). MITI had been formally studying revisions since December 1952 and had already made its recommendations to the cabinet. Kosaka wanted the EPDC to be formally reconstituted as the Electric Power Transfer Public Corporation (Denryoku Yūzū Kōsha), which would balance the nationwide supply and demand for electric power among the nine private utilities. The proposal also seemed to authorize a reconstituted EPDC to sell electric power directly to consumers, which the private utilities opposed. No bill was ever presented to Diet.[106]

Adjustments were made in the rate structure instead. They held until April 1957, when the Tohoku and Hokuriku electric companies, seeking to cover the costs of new capacity, applied for rate increases. A new round of debates followed, as industrial consumers appealed to MITI and the LDP to coordinate utility financing, power sharing, and rate setting.[107] MITI suggested that amalgamation of the industry might reduce regional rate disparities and that the EPDC might become a central coordinating mechanism for regional management and planning. Instead, the private utilities devised and implemented a regional management system one year later. The nation's electric power system was divided into three regional blocs of three firms each plus the EPDC, under the umbrella of the nongovernmental Central Electric Power Conference (Chūō Denryoku Kyōgikai). For its part, MITI established its own advisory council on electric rates (Denki Ryōkin Seido Chōsakai) to promote tariff rationalization. In 1964 this council became the central MITI/industry policy organ for electric power, the Denki Jigyō Shingikai. But no industrial restructuring had been accomplished; never again would MITI formally challenge the private utilities this way.

On the contrary, the next abortive reform effort would aim to abolish the EPDC itself. In September 1964 Japan's first postwar administrative reform commission, chaired by Mitsui's Satō Kiichirō, recommended that the national railways be sold to the private sector and that electric power development be reformed. Anzai Masao, another business leader, chaired a government panel established to specify these recommendations. In March 1970 the panel formally proposed that the EPDC be eliminated.[108] Ironically, the first oil crisis saved the EPDC, for the nine private utilities found themselves needing EPDC's near monopoly of the few remaining coal thermal plants and technical personnel. Ōtani, observing this on again–off again relationship between private utilities and EPDC, notes that "when the nine electric utilities are healthy, the position of the EPDC declines. But when the private utilities are having troubles, the EPDC revives. The position of the EPDC is a barometer of the well-being of the nine private utility system."[109]

The same oil crisis also spawned a final effort to transform the industry. This time the impulse came neither from the utilities or private enterprise nor from MITI, nor was it directed at the EPDC. The electric industry was hit especially hard by the oil price shock of the mid-1970s, because 70 percent of its generating capacity was oil-fired. In April 1974 the utilities applied for a large rate increase to compensate them for the OPEC price increases; an average increase of 56.8 percent was approved in June. Consumer groups and opposition parties organized nationwide protests, and the utilities came under heavy criticism for their large political contributions. As public utilities they needed permission to raise tariffs, but as private firms they had strongly supported conservative politicians. Cleverly the opposition sought to legislate a subtraction (*sashihiku*) of political contributions from utility profits. They also sought a new rate structure based upon the costs of generation (*genkashugi*). In August, Tokyo Electric Power Company (TEPCO) chairman Kikawada Kazutaka ordered a halt to all overt political donations. The other private utilities followed suit.[110]

The issue came to a head in the summer of 1977, when the opposition parties, at the height of their influence in postwar Japan, made energy policy the centerpiece of their campaigns.[111] In 1976, apparently as compensation for earlier cooperation, MITI had approved another 21 percent rate hike for the utilities, bringing Japanese electric rates to the highest levels in the industrial world. The Socialists and the Communists, with the support of other opposition parties, called for the nationalization of the utilities and their reformation as a single electric power public corporation (Denryoku Kōsha). This firm was to be one part of a comprehensive energy public corporation (Sōgō Enerugī Kōsha).[112]

Public management, its proponents argued, was necessary to smooth out the lumpiness of major investment decisions, but the banks seemed content with the consultative mechanisms already in place and offered no support. Although industrial consumers of electric power expressed their unhappiness about high electric rates to LDP leaders, they were also political realists. In the mid-1970s the opposition parties had achieved numerical balance with the LDP in Diet, and private industry was not about to sacrifice LDP dominance for lower utility rates. The utilities themselves responded with political and public relations campaigns to demonstrate their efficiency and their high levels of service to customers.[113] The opposition campaign was not translated into votes; nothing came of the debate; and the system remains intact today.

A complex set of industry-government committees has evolved to regulate that system. The most important is the Electric Power Industry Advisory Council (Denki Jigyō Shingikai) established under the 1964 industry law. The Electric Power Industry Law itself was modeled on the 1932 legislation in a formal reversion to pre-Nippatsu government regulation of the utilities. Like most advisory councils, this balances representation of utility and consumer interests. Formally it studies issues assigned to it by the minister of MITI and makes recommendations for public policy. Also important is the Electric Power Resources Investigation Advisory Council (Dengen Kaihatsu Chōsei Shingikai), which plays a pivotal role in the siting of power plants. Here twelve related ministries attempt to reconcile their differences. At least three different advisory councils relate to the nuclear power industry alone, all of which report to the prime minister. MITI's Agency for Natural Resources and Energy supervises seven councils, among which it distributes authority for deliberation about rates, siting, forecasting, fuel choice, and so forth. In addition, as noted above, there are organs such as the Central Electric Power Council, made up chiefly of the utilities and the EPDC, which coordinate industry views before bringing them before formal government councils. The past decade's reports by the Electric Power Industry Advisory Council make it clear that the issues facing the Japanese electric power industry have long since become economic ones. Serious debate about the nature and extent of state intervention has not dominated the agenda for some time.

The same sort of agenda has obtained for council subcommittees, and the postwar system has evolved into a model of business-government collaboration. Conflict over the nature and extent of state intervention in the Japanese electric power sector has reproduced a status quo ante bellum in which private capital vigilantly and successfully stands guard against potential excesses of bureaucratic control.

The most likely instrument of those potential excesses, the EPDC, has always been profitable. Although its primary business has been the

Table 4.2. Major topics debated by the Electric Power Industry Advisory Council, 1974–81

Date of report	Major Topics
March 1974	Sliding rate structure, load factor, discount, cost accounting period, adjustment
October 1975	Expansion of debt limit
March 1976	Rate structure change for commercial users, expansion of special contract system
March 1979	Rate structure changes, public relations, depreciation allowances, recycling of spent nuclear fuel
December 1981	Cost allocation for recycling of spent nuclear fuel, nuclear waste disposal, reactor safety measures

SOURCE: Central Electric Power Research Institute, internal memorandum, October 14, 1983.

provision of wholesale power to the nine private utilities, it has diversified and now owns parts of two overseas coal development firms. It also owns a tourism firm, a fertilizer company, and EPDC International, a wholly owned subsidiary engaged in electric power development projects with Third World countries. Other moves to diversify have been politically nettlesome, however. MITI has consistently sought additional commercial responsibilities for the EPDC, and at virtually every turn it has been blocked (or at least severely constrained) by the private utilities. The most striking cases of public-private confrontation in the electric sector have come in the development of the nuclear industry, and most have been resolved in favor of the nine utilities (see Chapter 6).

CONCLUSION

In the one-hundred-year policy record of efforts by the state, financial institutions, industrial consumers, and utilities to negotiate the nature and extent of state intervention, we find that private control of Japan's electric power industry has mostly been preserved. The utilities repeatedly blunted state efforts to displace private markets. A review of market transformations in electric power, as in the case of coal, reveals sustained efforts by producers to effect a protective collusion. It also reveals a bureaucracy eager to force the pace of consolidation under its own control. Only during the Pacific War did the Japanese state and its allies in the private sector achieve even a significant part of its vision for comprehensive transformation of the sector. This incomplete nationalization came undone quickly after the war, and though the idea resurfaces from time to time, never since has nationalization been a matter for serious debate. Instead, MITI supervises the Electric Power Development Corporation, an anemic heir to Nippatsu which is prohibited by its private shareholders from displacing any but the most peripheral markets participants. Japan has the most fully private electric power sector in the world today.

Several factors help explain this outcome; the most convincing are related to market structure. The failure to nationalize electric power in Japan reveals much about the politics of reciprocal consent where private markets are well developed. State intervention in electric power, unlike in the case of coal, began after private capitalists had already established control over the generation, transmission, and sale of electric power. Meiji-era bonds to displaced samurai may have bought the new government time to restructure the national state, but they also provided partners for such entrepreneurs as Shibusawa and Fujioka. Unregulated electric businesses grew apace, immune from all state designs on private markets which private actors themselves did not help draft. Indeed, industry succor of young political parties during the Taishō parliamentary experiment helped preserve private control.

But "private control" has not always meant "self-control" by the utilities alone. This distinction, too, is related to the development of private capital markets in Japan. In 1932 the banks were a critical ally as the state forced a reorganization upon the industry which significantly and permanently altered the structure of competition. This bank intervention was occasioned by the 1932 currency crisis; it was related as much to the openess of the economy as to the plurality of interests operating within it.

The SCAP Occupation of Japan provides a caricature of openness as an explanation for market restructuring. The only unalloyed state initiative ever to succeed in restructuring Japanese electric markets occurred under the extraordinary circumstances of foreign occupation. Only a foreign power stood between state ownership and private control. When SCAP intervened with its Potsdam Ordinance to create the private, regional utility system, the economic bureaucracy had assembled the broadest subgovernmental coalition ever to favor nationalized electric power. But once again the state was discomfited, this time by American reformers. Whether SCAP intervened to prop up bureaucratic controls, as in coal, or to dismantle them, as in electric power, its rule was the apex of state control in Japanese economic history.

Patterns of business-state relations emerge, despite these extraordinary times, from the history of electric power markets in Japan to confirm those which we observed in the coal sector. It is the plurality of interests associated with the debates over state intervention which seems most important. This plurality obtained within both the state and the private sector. The Japanese state, despite widely accepted characterizations of its capacity, unity, and vision, was seldom well-coordinated, even during wartime. Although it has a pervasive presence, it consistently exchanges jurisdiction for private control. State initiatives succeed only when bolstered by considerable private support. Electric power provides a clear illustration of the ways in which state centralization, market structure, and openness combine to limit state jurisdiction in markets and to shape the politics of reciprocal consent. Like coal, however, it is not exceptional in this regard. We turn next to the oil sector for additional evidence about the negotiated limits to state intervention in private markets.

CHAPTER FIVE

A Political History of
the Japanese Oil Industry

For nearly sixty years the Japanese state has fought a losing battle to consolidate the petroleum industry on its own terms. Never has the government tried so hard, so often, so unsuccessfully to restructure an industry. Central to most of its efforts were plans for a national oil champion like those of France, Britain, and Italy. But despite every incentive the Japanese economic bureaucracy has never succeeded. Its interventions have always been limited to market-conforming guarantees for private firms. The story of Japanese oil is protracted variant of the political history of coal and electric power, adding another exceptionally clear view of the politics of reciprocal consent in Japan.

This politics has been more complicated in oil than in coal or electric power. First, oil is uniquely embedded in the international political economy. Many Japanese businesses depend upon foreign markets and resources, but none depends as oil does upon foreign capital. This unique foreign equity in Japan's domestic markets has rendered oil firms less influential vis-à-vis consumers and the state. Second, there are actually two "Japanese oil industries," explorers and producers upstream, refiners, wholesalers, and retailers downstream. An inability (or unwillingness) in the industry to integrate vertically has helped shape divergent and uncoordinated political strategies to influence the nature and extent of state intervention in the oil market.

ORIGINS OF THE INDUSTRY

Like electric power but unlike coal, the oil industry in Japan originated in private initiative. Unlike both, however, it did not become central to the national economy until after the Pacific War.

The modern history of Japanese oil begins soon after the world's first commercial well was sunk by Edwin Drake in Titusville, Pennsylvania, in 1859.[1] In 1869 the first American geologists arrived in Japan, at the invitation of local entrepreneurs and at the expense of the Meiji government. The Nagano Coal Oil Company was founded in 1871, barely one year after J. D. Rockefeller founded Ohio Standard. Its first effort failed when the owners neglected to import piping with their drilling apparatus. In 1888 the same group, led by Naitō Hisahiro, established Nippon Oil in Niigata. Its Amase field, Japan's first, began production in 1891.[2]

The early scramble and consequent shakeout of the industry are a model of unregulated market transformation. In 1888 Japan had five oil production firms with a total capitalization of under 150,000 yen. By 1891 there were 430 such firms, capitalized at more than 5.5 million yen (averaging less than 13,000 yen each). Total capitalization declined slightly over the next six years, as hundreds of small firms went bankrupt or were acquired by the two emerging domestic giants, Nippon Oil and Hōden Oil. By 1897 only fifty-eight survived.[3]

Petroleum product trading firms, mostly foreign, also grew in numbers. In 1893 Standard Oil of New York opened an office in Yokohama. Soon thereafter the Samuel Trading Company (later part of Shell) joined Standard to sell lamp oil. The government then met demands from Niigata field owners by introducing its first tariffs on imported petroleum products.

The foreigners reacted aggressively by establishing their own exploration, production, and refining firms in Japan. In 1900 Standard moved in next door to Nippon Oil in Niigata with its International Oil Company; by 1902 it was the most heavily capitalized oil firm in Japan. Samuel Trading followed suit in Fukuoka with its Rising Sun Oil Corporation. Because costs of production in Japan were high relative to other fields worldwide, both were short-lived. Yet the foreign challenge was permanent. *Genrō* leaders, including Matsukata Masayoshi and Gotō Shimpei, fearing that foreign capital might dominate Japan's domestic market, urged Hōden and Nippon Oil to merge in 1902. Their pleas were ignored.

Two years later Nippon Oil president Naitō Hisahiro visited the United States and returned convinced of the potential benefits of a merger with Hōden. In November 1904 the two firms established a domestic petroleum joint sales office (Kokuyū Kyōdō Hanbaisho). The young venture collapsed within two years, leading Naitō to observe, in words now ironic, that "the Japanese have the poorest spirit for cooperation, and that is why there have been so few successful cases of joint sales and joint ventures."[4]

In 1906 Standard abandoned domestic production in Japan and sold its facilities to Nippon Oil. Through the rest of the century the battle for the Japanese market would be fought by the international majors with extraordinarily cheap, often dumped, imported products. Larger domestic producers continued to consolidate their positions while resisting cooperation.[5]

There was no state leadership, no coordinated national fuels policy. Apart from nearly annual tariff increases, the only evidence of government intervention before World War I was geological surveys by the Ministry of Agriculture and Commerce and public funding for a Karuizawa-to-Yokogawa pipeline in 1905. Even the tariff revisions provoked domestic opposition. By 1908, for example, President Asano Sōichirō of Tōyō Kisen, a leading steamship company, sought to block new tariff legislation. A Finance Ministry evaluation of California versus domestic oil that Naitō initiated concluded that domestic fields were potentially competitive. Tariffs were again raised.

The collusive experiments that characterized coal and electric power in this period were apparent in petroleum as well. The arrangements defied simple distinctions between domestic and foreign firms. In 1910 Standard, Rising Sun, Hōden, and Nippon Oil reached a four-way sales agreement that crumbled within two years. In 1913, and again in 1914, the large domestic and foreign firms tried and failed to divide up the Japanese market. Stable collusion was especially elusive because demand was itself undergoing transformation. As in electric power the Age of Illumination was giving way to the Age of Energy. Lamp oil had surrendered to electric lighting, and factories, motor vehicles, and ships were beginning to consume residual fuel oil for power and other refined products for lubrication.[6]

The Imperial Navy played an important role in this transformation. It began research on converting its coal-fired boilers to heavy oil in 1898. In 1905 it built its first heavy oil tank (holding 6,000 tons) at its Yokosuka Yard. In 1919 the navy installed its first liquid fuel boiler, of British design, and all subsequent ships were powered by oil. Although oil was less than 10 percent of Japan's primary energy supply on the eve of World War II, it had long since become critically important to the navy.[7] Also in 1919 the navy signed a long-term agreement with Rising Sun Oil for one million barrels per year of residual fuel oil from Borneo.

Soon it went into production on its own. To meet projected demand, the navy built the Tokuyama Fuel Depot in 1921, placing the Japanese government in a productive oil enterprise for the first time. Existing producers mobilized political influence to protect their commercial rights. As Masuo Uehara notes, "even at that time the problem arose concerning public management's restriction of private industry. So, the principle was adopted that the production of the Navy's refineries would

In 668 A.D. "flammable soil and flammable water" were presented to the emperor.

not infringe upon the main product lines of private industry, namely, gasoline, lamp oil, and lubricants. . . ." The naval refinery's production was limited to fuel for naval vessels. All commercial by-products were distributed to selected private firms for resale.[8]

For their part, the private firms were still seeking a stable modus vivendi. Their most immediate concern was the poor performance of domestic wells. Domestic production peaked at just under 3 million barrels in 1915 and did not surpass this minimal level until long after World War I. As imports of refined products surged, they threatened completely to overwhelm Japanese producers. At long last the consolidation of Hōden and Nippon Oil, urged by Matsukata in 1902 and again by Gotō Shimpei in 1911, was carried out in October 1921.[9]

More significant than the merger was the recognition of the geological limits of domestic reserves. In merging, the two leading firms, centered originally around fields near the Sea of Japan, changed the character of the nation's industry. The new Nippon Oil Company, accounting for 80 percent of the nation's limited production, soon began importing and refining foreign crude itself. Nippon Oil built its first Pacific Coast refinery in 1923 to refine imported crude, and so the practice of "refining at the consumers' doorstep," official policy until 1986, originated in these

Oil lamps had become common in Japanese homes by the late nineteenth century.

酒を燗する法

Lamp oil had uses other than illumination. Here a Taishō-era artist reports an ingenious way to heat *sake*.

market shifts, not in public policy. Public petroleum policy for the civilian economy was passive, late, and largely ineffectual.

The first formal government study group for petroleum policy (Sekiyu Chōsakai) was established by the navy in July 1925. It concerned itself exclusively with military planning. One year later, in July 1926, the Ministry of Commerce and Industry established its Fuel Investigation Committee (Nenryō Chōsa Iinkai) in belated response to demands from Japanese oil company leaders, many of them Dietmen, for a national fuels policy.[10] The government finally started subsidizing the development of domestic fields in 1927, four years after Nippon Oil had decided to shift downstream.

The development program justified Nippon Oil's strategic shift. Although government subsidies stimulated great activity, ultimately including development of the productive Yabase field in Akita, Japan was simply not oil-rich. Even the moderate increase in domestic production of the early 1930s could not satisfy Japan's growing demand; it did not even top the production peak of 1915.

For the domestic oil industry, things would get much worse before they got better. Imported crude surpassed domestic production in 1924 and then trebled in volume between 1925 and 1928. Until the new subsidies began to stimulate activity, domestic production fell. Dramatic discoveries of petroleum reserves in Venezuela, Sumatra, Russia, Texas, California, Iran, Iraq, and elsewhere sparked epochal competition among the international oil companies and their governments in markets around the world. In Japan, Standard and Rising Sun fought price wars that nearly eliminated the Japanese industry. Imported crude was half the cost of domestic crude even with increased tariffs. Some Japanese firms, such as Mitsubishi Shōji in 1924, concluded long-term crude oil purchase agreements with foreign suppliers.[11] Between 1923 and 1934 domestic crude oil lost market share, declining from more than one-third to less than one-tenth of the refined products market.

The international oil firms also shipped refined products. While domestic refineries were increasing their output fourfold during this period, mostly by refining foreign crude, the importance of refined petroleum products expanded fivefold.[12] Between 1926 and 1931 the price of gasoline in Tokyo dropped by 40 percent, to the lowest level in any city anywhere. Nippon Oil and the few remaining domestic producers had begun repositioning themselves downstream, but their situation remained precarious. Double-digit oil company dividends, common until 1926, dipped under 5 percent by 1930, under 1 percent by 1932.[13]

With market conditions threatening their very existence the firms turned to the state for help. The Ministry of Commerce and Industry (MCI) was asked to enforce a price cartel that had failed several times already. In August 1928 Standard, Rising Sun, and Nippon Oil had jointly announced a rise in gasoline prices. They were joined by Ogura, Mitsubishi, and Mitsui in a six-firm *naigai* (joint domestic/foreign) price cartel. It lasted less than a month. A similar effort one year later, which allowed the two foreign firms 55.5 percent of the Japanese market, met a similar fate. The agreed price/volume controls to be enforced by MCI were identical to what had collapsed. Two foreign firms would be allotted 55.5 percent of the market, and four domestic firms would get 44.5 percent.[14] The cartel was established under the Important Industries Control Law in August 1932, and gasoline prices soon rose by 30 percent.[15]

This arrangement did not last long either. Its terms had to be revised when taxi firms and auto manufacturers protested. On September 25, 1932, eight-hundred vehicles surrounded the MCI offices in Tokyo; protests continued into November, when the ministry intervened to reduce gasoline prices slightly. Heavy industry took no interest in these matters as petroleum was not yet an important industrial fuel. Much more significant for the Japanese oil market were unexpected new supplies.

田油瀬浦

Japan's volcanic islands were never richly endowed with fossil fuels, especially crude oil. A domestic oil production record set in 1915 stood for more than forty years. Pictured here is the Urase field of northern Japan, one of the most active, in the early part of the twentieth century.

In August 1932, just as the MCI ratified the gasoline price cartel, Matsukata Kōjirō (the son of *genrō* Matsukata Masayoshi) secretly went to Moscow to negotiate an agreement to import 35,000 tons per year of Russian refined petroleum products.[16] The announcement of the agreement in September mentioned strategic concerns and the need to reduce Japanese naval dependence upon American petroleum, calling the accord "a sensation from both commercial and political perspectives."[17] It was nothing less. The American industry, press, and government were alarmed; Berlin welcomed the move.[18] At home, Matsukata's strongest supporters were domestic auto makers. Matsukata purchased transport and storage facilities upon his return, and his newly established commercial company accepted its first shipment one year later. He undercut the six-firm cartel by almost 40 percent.[19] The cartel briefly tried a price war, and within a year gasoline prices had fallen more than 50 percent. Over the strenuous objections of Standard and Rising Sun the four domestic firms offered Matsukata a peace plan, which he ignored, and only Nippon Oil was able to avoid suspension of dividend payments.[20] Matsukata's "red oil" significantly destabilized the Japanese domestic

Oil-drilling technology in Japan, originally imported from the United States in the 1880s, remained labor-intensive and small in scale for half a century.

market, indicating to many participants the desirability of more formal state intervention. The nature and extent of that intervention remained to be negotiated.

State Control: The Wartime Petroleum Industry

Business interests were by no means so anxious for state protection that they would accept intervention in any form or at any cost. In early 1933 the navy established the interministerial National Oil Policy Council (Sekiyu Kokusaku Shingikai), expressly charging it to examine disorder in the oil market, rising demand, and foreign domination of petroleum resources.[21] This group, affiliated with MCI's Mining Bureau, developed two alternative programs, announced formally by MCI in May.[22] The first was a plan for the nationalization of the Japanese petroleum industry (Sekiyu Kokka Kanri An). The state would have a monopoly on all crude oil production, refining, trade, and sales, which rights it would then delegate to a half-public–half-private corporation. All profits of this vertically integrated and fully consolidated firm, after dividends and operating expenses were paid, would accrue to the state treasury[23] and would be earmarked for domestic resources and synthetic fuels. Significantly this plan also provided for expropriation of all foreign petroleum holdings in Japan; these facilities would constitute the state's equity in the joint national oil corporation.

The more limited alternative, the Licensing Control Plan (Kyokashugi Tōsei An), was modeled on the French Petroleum Industry Law of 1928.[24] The draft gave MCI the right to license crude oil imports, refinery construction, stockpiling, and other up- and midstream commercial activities. It provided MCI with funds to subsidize oil supplies from fields outside the British and American spheres of influence, in Russia, Rumania, Borneo, Manchuria. The MCI was to organize a syndicate to handle overseas oil exploration and the development of alternative energy.

Both plans were debated throughout the summer by top ministerial officials and representatives of private industry. The Foreign Ministry, fearing reprisals by foreign governments for expropriation, opposed nationalization. Parts of the MCI and the army were concerned lest such a move result in an embargo on crude oil shipments to Japan when the military was unprepared for war.[25] Also important, Mitsubishi Oil, with strong capital ties to Associated Oil, led a private effort to block nationalization.[26]

The Petroleum Industry Law (PIL-I), based upon the second MCI plan, was implemented in March 1934. It was the first comprehensive sectoral measure implemented under the 1931 Important Industries Control Law. Private industry apparently sought the protection afforded by the legislation as much as state planners sought to enhance national security by controlling the industry. MCI was empowered to license production, refining, sales, and imports. It was also granted authority to establish quotas, fix prices, force compulsory purchases, allocate market shares, and require the stockpiling of six months of supplies by each refining and importing company. All firms under a minimum size became targets for consolidation, for from the perspective of military objectives, as Okamato Ryūzo notes, "oil policy was designed around the large firms." When PIL-I was promulgated there were 53 refining firms, 17 importing firms, and 20 production firms in Japan.[27] By 1945, as we shall see, the industry had been consolidated into eight privately controlled groups of refiners and one quasi-public producer.

PIL-I directly challenged Anglo-American suppliers and distributors. The stockpiling requirements were particularly onerous. Volumes were calculated on the basis of 50 percent of the previous year's imports, clearly discriminating against foreign firms that imported 100 percent of their crude. Moreover, only domestic firms qualified for public funding for the purchase of stocks.[28] When the MCI formally allocated smaller market shares to foreign affiliates in August, Standard-Vacuum and Rising Sun resorted to diplomatic intervention that included plans for embargo.[29] MCI capitulated, waiving the stockpiling requirement until 1936, when Mitsui Bussan was persuaded to act on behalf of the foreign firms by building and leasing back the necessary storage tanks.[30]

Not all foreign interests were adversely affected. Associated, for example, held 50 percent equity in Mitsubishi Oil, Japan's number-three refiner. It was refining in Japan, not shipping refined products to the Japanese market, so PIL-I actually stimulated its business and that of other crude oil suppliers to the Japanese refiners. Well over four-fifths of Japan's crude oil imports were from the United States in the mid-1930s, and, as Irvine Anderson says, about half of this volume "came from American companies that had absolutely nothing to gain from an embargo—notably Standard Oil of California, the Associated Oil Company, Union Oil, the Texas Company, and Richfield."[31] This division of interests may have been an advantage to Japanese oil firms, but oil was only one part of the U.S.-Japan commercial relationship. By 1936 total U.S. exports to Japan had already surpassed U.S. exports to all of Latin America. PIL-I and related "exclusionary" industrial policies seemed to threaten American interests and were interpreted as preliminaries to Pacific war.

As the nation mobilized for war after the Manchurian Incident, petroleum was made a priority sector; the state intervened in every part of

Table 5.1. Instruments of wartime control of oil

Business	Instrument Control Co./Cartel	Instrument Public Policy Co.	Year founded
Exploration/ Production		Imperial Oil Resources Development Co.	1940
		Imperial Oil	1941
Transportation		Tōa Oil	1940
Stockpile		Joint Enterprise Co.	1937
Synfuels		Imperial Fuels Co.	1937
Refining/		Tōa Nenryō	1939
Distribution	Kokusan Kihatsuyu Rengōkai		1934
	Sekiyu Rengo K. K.		1936
Sales	Zen Nippon Asufaruto		1934
	Seizō Rengōkai		1934
	Kōyū Seiseigyō Rengōkai		1934
	Jūyu Kyōgikai		1936
	Kokusan Tōyu Rengōkai		1936
	Sekiyu Kyōhan		1939
	Sekiyu Haikyū Tōsei K. K.		1942

the industry to enhance the availability of petroleum for military use.[32] Before long, exceptionally strict controls were placed on the civilian use of petroleum products. State intervention meant market restructuring in favor of domestic producers and the military, and the conflict over the nature and extent of this intervention is best explored by tracking the variety of instruments invoked for wartime control (see Table 5.1).

Downstream

The first restructuring occurred downstream. The protection that PIL-I afforded domestic firms emboldened them to make their peace with Matsukata and desert the six-firm cartel. In June, less than three months after PIL-I had been promulgated and for the first time since Russian imports had set off a price war, the firms came to a gentlemen's agreement on gasoline prices with Matsukata. In September, Nippon Oil, Ogura, and Mitsubishi established the Domestic Gasoline Association (Kokusan Kihatsuyu Rengōkai) as a price and sales cartel. In March 1936 the association was supplanted by the Petroleum Federation (Sekiyu Rengō K. K.), a joint firm capitalized at 300,000 yen with nine shareholders, to regulate and allocate crude and refined products. Press reports indicate that foreign firms were invited to participate but declined.[33] One of the firms that did participate, however, was a separate Japanese–Russian Oil venture established by these firms and Matsukata in November 1935. As a result Russian oil flowed into Japan until *1942* without disrupting prices. By 1937 prices had risen by nearly 60 percent, almost to 1926 levels.[34]

Similar arrangements were also made in transportation and storage. In May 1936 the firms asked for legal authority for a joint public/private oil storage firm.[35] Although the MCI welcomed the idea, the Foreign Ministry expressed concern about potential foreign reactions. Nonetheless, the Joint Enterprise Company (Kyōdō Kigyō) was established in October 1937 with 10 million yen of entirely private capital. Its members included all major importers, transport firms, and refiners. Yet because the company was a de facto public policy company, working closely with the three-month-old MCI Fuels Bureau, it received state support. Government indemnification covered oil price and oil supply losses, dividends were guaranteed at 6 percent, intermediation was offered for investment capital (the Industrial Bank of Japan, through MCI, supplied 91 percent of all investment capital), and grants were made available for tanker construction.[36] The chairman of the new venture was a familiar character, Hashimoto Keizaburō. By late 1939 the Joint Enterprise Company ran into bureaucratic problems, MCI lost a struggle for control to the army, and in 1940 the company was dissolved. The army assumed direct control of its own storage operations. In 1941, fourteen private firms established a second joint enterprise to acquire North and South American crude oil with government guarantees.[37]

Further downstream the army and MCI ran into more serious political difficulty on the eve of the Pacific War, when they took two initiatives that private interests rebuffed. The failure of the first initiative helped define the postwar petroleum industry. After hostilities commenced with China in 1937, military demands for aviation fuel became pressing. In the autumn of 1938 the army proposed to amalgamate all of the nation's refineries into a single company (*daidō danketsu*). When the navy objected, the MCI Fuels Bureau, with Nippon Oil's Hashimoto (who collaborated with the military throughout this period), agreed to champion the program among the refining firms.[38] Ogura Oil also strongly supported the plan, although it preferred to separate fields from refineries.

The rest of the industry opposed consolidation, sensing a threat to their existence. Leading the opposition was Mitsubishi Oil. Mitsubishi maintained that it could serve the state better as an independent firm and that its tradition of independence stood in the way of a merger. More truly, as top executives privately admitted, the company's ties to Tidewater made such a merger inconceivable.[39] In early 1939, according to an official history, at a directors' meeting of the Petroleum Federation, "there was no reaching agreement among these many firms; with their varied interests and histories their opposition was strong."[40]

To evade consolidation, the firms decided to invest separately in a new firm that would primarily produce aviation fuel. This new firm, Tōa Nenryō, was established with 50 million yen of private capital in July 1939. Its charter clearly limited foreign participation, and Mitsubishi was represented by three Mitsubishi Group companies but not Mitsubishi Oil. Tōa Nenryō was both a de facto national policy company and an illustration of the political power of the private sector, very different from the enterprise that the army had first proposed. One observer has noted that "even more time and more pressing conditions would have to arise to achieve the consolidation of the industry."[41] But what is the essence of relations between business and the state if wartime mobilization, military control, and the support of the dominant firm are not sufficient to transform industrial structure? It seems clear that the politics of the negotiated market economy did not stop even at the very threshold of war.

The point is underlined by the second state initiative downstream, which was also transformed after much struggle over the preservation of commercial rights. Believing that, for the distribution of refined products, one monopoly is more efficient than three cartels, the MCI brought together thirty-one firms in August 1939 to establish the Petroleum Joint Sales Company (Sekiyu Kyōhan K. K.), capitalized at 20 million yen. Hashimoto was again made chairman. Under this central organ, distribution and sales firms in each prefecture would be consolidated into a single, direct monopoly for all product sales.

The company was scheduled to begin operations on November 1 but was delayed by political conflict. Distributors protested strongly that they would be put out of business. There were two sorts of firms involved. On the one hand were the special contractors for large distributing firms, which were placated by absorption as shareholders into the new firms, designated for six dividends annually. But agricultural and maritime federations that had been storing and selling petroleum products for decades had major investments in storage facilities; they vowed not to let MCI take their facilities and commercial rights.[42] They directed their campaign at Godō Takuo, at the time both minister of commerce and industry and minister of agriculture and forestry. Feeling betrayed by Godō, they called for his impeachment; their cries about neglect of farming and fishing villages touched a chord in the nation. Among their leaders was the young Kōno Ichirō, then the director of the Central Storage Industries Association.[43]

On October 3 Godō's two ministries produced a revised program that would allow farmers and fishermen to store and distribute fuel acquired from central distribution organs. Petroleum distributors and shareholders in the new Petroleum Joint Sales Company immediately launched their own protests, arguing that a dual distribution system would divert up to one-third of the market away from the new company. Retail merchants, blocked by refining firms from organizing before PIL-I, consolidated politically for the first time. They created a national sales league (Zenkoku Sekiyu Hanbaigyō Rengōkai) to stop the dual system. Leading them was Idemitsu Sazō, the man who would become the most prominent oil entrepreneur and (with Matsunaga Yasuzaemon) the most prominent antibureaucrat in postwar Japan.

The retailers felt that the government had sold them out: "We have made great sacrifices to push on with national policy, but at present, a public promise has been betrayed and the unified distribution system has been subverted."[44] They demanded repeal of the concession to rural distributors and threatened to delay the consolidation of wholesale firms at the prefectural level. Shareholders of the (still precommercial) Joint Petroleum Sales Company went even further. On October 23 they voted to dissolve the fledgling venture, claiming that the government's concession destroyed the company's raison d'être.

Compounding these problems was the suspension of imports from Britain's Rising Sun because of tanker shortages in Europe. The November 1 starting date for the Joint Sales Company passed without resolution. A new minister of agriculture and forestry was appointed. Finally on November 27, Kishi Nobusuke of MCI announced a compromise that slightly lowered limits on sales volumes and blocked the construction of new storage facilities. From the perspective of the retailers, however, this was a defeat, for the initial concession to agricultural and maritime interests was preserved: there would be a dual distribution structure after all. Refiners and wholesalers were persuaded to carry on by being given the authority to negotiate separate sales volumes with their prefectural distributors and the farmers and fishermen.

Even the protests of Stanvac and Rising Sun had to be accommodated. They had been excluded from the joint sales company, but diplomatic protests forced the government to excuse them from having to sell their products to the central facility. They sold refined products directly to wholesalers until the beginning of the Pacific War. The final wartime incarnation of this politically negotiated and therefore far less than perfect monopoly was the Petroleum Distribution Control Company (Sekiyu Haikyū Tōsei Kaisha), established in June 1942.[45]

Upstream

Interwar oil exploration relied upon state-subsidized private drilling both at home and abroad, but state subsidies were never very large. Between 1927 and 1934 total subsidies amounted to less than 2 million yen.[46] On occasion the MCI would attempt to stimulate Japanese exploration ventures abroad by providing half the capital for specific ventures, as in 1935 in an effort to entice Nippon Oil to explore in Central and South America. More often than not, however, the Finance Ministry refused funds for these projects, and subsidies were suspended entirely in 1934's fiscal crisis. Only after war began in China were significant public funds made available. Until then entrepreneurs pressed for a national fuels policy to socialize risk and preserve profits. Hasegawa of Taiyō Oil articulated this combination of patriotism and self-interest:

> Private firms cannot undertake the risks involved. If private firms cannot join hands to do the drilling required to confront the urgent need for field development absolutely essential to the state, there will be no alternative but to make this a directly managed national project. But (given the shortages of trained personnel) it would be difficult for the state to manage this exploratory drilling directly. So from the perspective of convenience, the best method would be to leave it to the more experienced private sector . . . and the largest portion of financing must be borne by the state for these delegated tasks.[47]

Finally, with the exigencies of war overruling the prudence of Ministry of Finance officials, a petroleum resources development law was enacted in August 1938. Under its terms the state could bear up to two-thirds of expenses incurred by private firms for drilling equipment and half the costs for test-well construction. In return, the state got 2 percent of the value of any oil produced for five years.[48]

Soon it became clear that even this was not going to stimulate the desired level of exploration activity, and the subsidy program was reorganized in public corporate form. The Imperial Oil Resources Development Company (Teikoku Sekiyu Shigen Kaihatsu K. K.) was established in July 1940. All of the largest exploration firms joined the venture, which guaranteed 6 percent quarterly dividends for five years and assumed expenses not covered in the subsidy program. Their lack of success and the scarcity of public capital brought them together for joint exploration with state guarantees.[49] They were, however, still reluctant to agree to a formal consolidation of the industry.

Circumstances changed (many would argue, to the permanent detriment of the industry) in 1941, after MCI minister Kishi and Nippon Oil's Hasegawa reached an accommodation. Kishi implored Hasegawa "as a matter of the nation's life and death to offer to the nation all the technology, fields, and drilling materials" of Nippon Oil. He claimed that the state had nurtured the company for fifty-five years and that without Nippon Oil's cooperation, there could be no consolidation of oil field management, either domestically or in the South Pacific. Hashimoto replied that Nippon Oil had "never enlisted the help of the state," but he promised to consult with his Board of Directors about cooperation with national policy. He asked point blank for "something to deliver" (*mukui*) to his directors and shareholders, and he claims that Kishi promised to "do everything in his power to act at his discretion in favor of Nippon Oil."[50]

In September 1941, fewer than ninety days after the U.S.-U.K. embargo on Japan, the Imperial Oil Company (Teikoku Sekiyu K. K.) began operations. It was capitalized at 100 million yen, half of which the state supplied.[51] Nippon Oil held close to two-thirds of the remaining shares. The new firm absorbed the holdings of its predecessor, the Imperial Oil Resources Development Company, which had just trebled in size through the acquisition of fields in Borneo. Most significantly, the production departments of each major firm were separated from parent companies to form this new national policy company. Nippon Oil was allowed to dominate the new venture. With sources of crude cut off, many refining and sales firms were eager to gain access to fields they had not developed. Mitsubishi Oil, for example, firmly opposed downstream mergers but supported the new venture to replace the crude oil lost from its American parent firm. Once again dividends were guaranteed, corporate taxes were exempted, and all exploratory drilling and extraction became collaborative; risk was not simply reduced, it was eliminated. By the end of the war the company's capital had been increased to nearly 300 million yen, and Imperial Oil controlled 98 percent of all domestic fields and many of the overseas fields seized by the military. It did not own any refineries, however, for its parent firms had refused to consolidate downstream. Imperial Oil was thus the first institutional confirmation of separation between upstream and downstream activities—a separation that characterizes the Japanese petroleum industry today. (See Figure 5.1.)

By war's end eight major refining companies survived: Nippon Oil, Nippon Mining, Shōwa Oil, Maruzen Oil, Daikyō Oil, Tōa Nenryō, Kōa Oil, and Mitsubishi Oil. During the war these firms pooled profits and losses, selling products exclusively through the Petroleum Distribution Control Company.[52] PIL-I clearly accelerated the consolidation of the industry, even if in ways the military government and economic bureaucracy did not intend. Nippon Oil acquired four firms between 1940 and 1942, the most prominent being Ogura Oil in June 1941. Shōwa was itself created by three refiners in 1942. Maruzen was the product of a six-firm merger that same year. Daikyō was the most complex of all, an amalgam of more than two dozen smaller refining firms. The state was pervasive throughout the industry, but as in coal and oil, state control never challenged private profits; it guaranteed them at public expense.

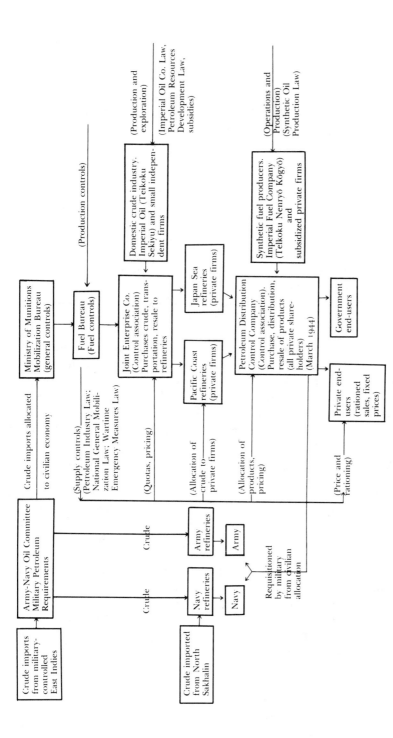

Figure 5.1. Wartime organization and control of the Japanese petroleum industry

SOURCE: GHQ-SCAP 1952b: 3–4.

After 1945 the introduction of foreign capital and heavy industrial demand for petroleum would create new alliances for the oil policy debate. But despite dramatic changes in the international market, the fundamental structure of the Japanese oil industry, as shaped by wartime compromises and opportunities, dominated public and private agendas for industrial transformation.

THE AMERICAN OCCUPATION

At war's end Japan's only remaining sources of petroleum were refineries on the Sea of Japan, producing less than 4,500 barrels daily, and synthetic fuels plants producing a negligible 500 barrels per day. South Pacific oil production, refining, and shipments to Japan had peaked in 1943, at only one-third of prewar imports from the United States. Domestic production had not been so low since 1902. Tanker sinkings had drastically reduced supplies, and by 1944 a desperate government was mobilizing the population to collect pine roots for distillation as aviation fuel under the slogan "Two hundred pine roots keeps a plane aloft for one hour."[53] By the spring of 1945 oil storage facilities ran dry and were scrapped. Eighty-five percent of Japan's total refining and storage capacity was destroyed by American bombs. Nationwide, fewer than nine hundred sales dealers were still in business by the end of the war. A long energy crisis was just beginning.[54]

It is difficult to characterize oil policy during the American occupation as coherent. SCAP prescribed over an extended sorting out of the market, both up- and downstream, which reflected changing priorities, conflicting signals, and at all times American leadership. State control in petroleum, as in coal and electric power was enhanced by directives aimed at the democratization of the economy. In October 1945 SCAP abolished controls regulating petroleum product sales and rationing. That same month it formally permitted oil production and refining in the few remaining domestic facilities. In December it abolished the Petroleum Industry Law. By January 1946 SCAP had dismantled most oil industry legislation, but because there were no ready alternatives, abolition of the distribution system was delayed for six months.

A chaotic and uncontrolled product market emerged. Black markets erupted everywhere; retail merchants, forced from their shops by final spasms of wartime mobilization, were unorganized, isolated, and unsupplied. SCAP dissolved the wartime control associations and made allocations first through the reconstituted Petroleum Distribution Control Company, followed in May 1946 by a state-owned petroleum distribution corporation (Haikyū Kōdan) that got under way in May 1947. The corporation served as a temporary state monopoly on distribution and sales.[55] It was enthusiastically supported by the Socialist cabinet of Katayama and by the MCI but was publicly opposed by Yoshida.[56]

In August 1947 the first conflict emerged, over licensed distributorships; agricultural and marine interests again faced opposition from retail merchants. This renewed conflict went unresolved until the end of state controls and the return of distribution to private markets in March 1949 (perhaps not coincidentally once Yoshida had again become prime minister). When the first allocations were made in 1949, three-quarters went to American firms. In the meantime, as we shall see, the downstream market had been radically restructured, largely under the direction of seconded U.S. oil executives who comprised SCAP's Petroleum Advisory Group.

Upstream

Occupation planners faced related problems upstream. In January 1946 SCAP banned crude oil imports to Japan. But the Occupation needed fuel, and after a great deal of internal debate it waived concerns about economic deconcentration to secure supplies. Many top oil industry executives were purged, including Hashimoto, and all but a handful of oil firms were designated under the December 1946 Excessive Concentration Order; but a decision was made to leave Imperial Oil alone.

> The Imperial Oil Company, producing more than ninety percent of the domestic crude, was the only organization capable of contributing effectively toward [the aim of maximizing domestic crude production] since it alone had comparatively large resources of funds, equipment, and technical personnel. Pending a later decision as to the necessity for the dissolution or reorganization of this semigovernmental company, it was given the responsibility for maximizing production of crude.[57]

Accordingly the Finance Ministry continued to hold half the equity in Imperial Oil. Capital was increased in March 1946 to 460 million yen, nearly doubling wartime operating capital.[58] In conjunction, a joint public/private advisory commission (Sekiyu Kaihatsu Sokushin Iinkai) was established within the MCI to begin planning oil field development. In September five foreign oil firms formed the Joint Oil Security Company to supply petroleum to the Allied Forces. They soon expanded downstream.

Imperial Oil had problems from the start. Most serious was its shortages of personnel. Some 4,500 petroleum engineers and technicians had been sent to the Dutch East Indies at the start of the war to reconstruct sabotaged wells and refineries, and repatriation was slow and incomplete.[59] Most activity centered on production, little attention was paid to exploration. American geologists and engineers boosted success rates from 7 percent in 1946 to 30 percent in 1948.[60] Nevertheless the repatriation of most of Imperial Oil's overseas staff in 1948 was a mixed blessing for the firm. Labor unrest erupted in March 1948; SCAP had to intervene, laying off nearly three thousand employees.

SCAP intervention was made easier by an earlier policy reversal: in February 1948 Imperial Oil had been designated an excessively concentrated firm. In April 1949 it was ordered to dispose of all holdings in other firms, present a plan for financial reorganization, and submit for disposal a full accounting of oil reserves not under active exploitation. Imperial released over 40 percent of its licensed exploration sites and reduced the state's shareholdings. In December 1949 the legislative requirement that the state hold half the outstanding shares of the firm was eliminated, opening the way for an infusion of private capital. Total equity increased to over one billion yen, with the Finance Ministry holding less than one-quarter of the total. The deconcentration of shareholding was very dramatic. Whereas during the war eighteen shareholders had controlled 80 percent of the firm's stock, by early 1950 the top one hundred shareholders held only 53 percent of total equity.[61] In June 1950 the Imperial Oil Company Law was repealed, and in August its designation as excessively concentrated was canceled.

Imperial Oil immediately began paying dividends, the first since the end of the war and, at 10 percent, the highest in the history of the firm.[62] Even higher dividends soon followed and, released from legal restrictions, the firm began to integrate downstream. It acquired transportation, refining, distribution, and sales facilities despite considerable opposition from domestic and foreign refining firms. In March 1951 these firms prevailed upon the government to refuse a formal distributor's license to Imperial Oil. While SCAP was pleased—the company had been "transform[ed] . . . from [a] government liability to a [taxpaying] national asset"[63]—Imperial would never achieve the integrated market presence it was seeking. The market downstream was too crowded.

Downstream

The downstream market grew congested by foreign capital, whose entry was made possible by a SCAP policy that followed a winding course of controls, reversals, and intimidation. The result was an unprecedented penetration by foreign capital. From the very beginning SCAP petroleum policy was dominated by private oil interests. For example,

SCAP banned crude oil imports in January 1946 in anticipation of the next month's report from Edwin Pauley, an American oilman, who urged the scrapping of Japan's Pacific Coast refineries and the use of Japan's industrial facilities for war reparations. Pauley recommended strict limits on Japanese refining and stockpiling to eliminate the country's military potential.

Beyond the first flush of victory lay confusion. General MacArthur ignored a recommendation from his Far East Commission and directed an about-face on petroleum refining, announcing in January 1948 that the Japanese petroleum industry would be revived. In February all eight major Japanese refining firms were designated excessively concentrated firms. The next month the "Report on Industrial Reparations Survey of Japan," the so-called Strike Report, was issued. Warning of the dangers of an economically weak Japan, it recommended that reparations payments halt. But it also singled out petroleum refining for special treatment: superannuated facilities should be scrapped, and firms should import refined petroleum products. Almost immediately the contrary Johnston Report was issued, arguing that scrapping was unnecessary.

These reversals may have reflected differences within SCAP's Petroleum Advisory Group and at General Headquarters, or they may have reflected changes in overall Occupation policy vis-à-vis America's most important Pacific ally. They certainly reflected shifts in the global strategies of the major multinational oil companies. Between 1945 and 1949, when no market existed for a full range of refined products, these firms invested little in Japan. Shell, Stanvac, and other firms were content to reconstruct prewar marketing channels, because it was cheaper to sell products refined abroad. After 1949, however, the calculus changed. For one thing, the United States became an importer of crude oil, forcing these firms to rely upon Middle Eastern oil for the Japanese market. For another, the Iranian nationalization led corporate planners to reconsider the wisdom of depending upon export refineries. Politically stable regions of potentially heavy demand, such as Japan, became attractive. At the same time the demand for petroleum products, especially for feedstocks, was rapidly expanding and growing more diversified. Currency shortages in Japan also made the construction of local refineries advisable.[64]

To many Japanese this convergent shift in corporate and Occupation policy smacked of conspiracy, one designed to demonstrate that capital ties with foreign oil firms were inevitable.[65] Idemitsu Sazō, the outspoken doyen of the domestic industry, claims that

the majors were out to create an international petroleum monopoly. . . . They were closely tied to GHQ and together they put the squeeze on MCI. . . .

189

It was the seconded officials from the five oil firms who were really making things happen. . . . [The Strike Report] shocked the Japanese refining industry. Foreign crude suppliers were telling us, "Don't worry, everything will be all right if you leave it all to us."[66]

The message that ties to foreign capital could ensure stability and security was not lost upon Japanese executives. Nineteen forty-nine was an epochal year for the Japanese petroleum industry. Tōa Nenryō, former stepchild of the army, moved first. In February the Haikyū Kōdan was abolished, allowing petroleum product distribution to return to private control; Tōa Nenryō sold Stanvac a controlling equity interest. The move touched off a rash of supply agreements and partnerships between Japanese refiners and American majors: between Nippon Oil and Caltex and between Mitsubishi and Tidewater in March (a reincarnation of prewar associations), between Shōwa and Shell in June, Tōa and Caltex in July, and Maruzen and Union Oil in October. These agreements usually exchanged equity participation for long-term crude oil supplies and development capital for new refinery and distribution facilities. As deals were consummated, so Japanese firms were removed one after another from the list of excessively concentrated companies, and the Pacific Coast refineries were reopened. In September the Noel Report provided official blessing for this market restructuring, urging priority in the reconstruction of refineries for those refiners which already had supply agreements with foreign firms. Additional tie-ups continued through 1951. The most notable exception was Idemitsu Kōsan, which, as in the prewar period, preferred to go it alone—and still does today.

Neither the Japanese petroleum industry nor the primary energy market would ever be the same again. These arrangements ratified the truncated structure that had emerged by the mid-1930s. Japan responded to its lack of oil resources by integrating downstream refining, wholesale, and distribution (*motourigyō*). The basic principle, referred to as "onshore refining," is often credited to MITI planners, who used it as a way to refine "locally conserved foreign exchange."[67] MITI policy would in the ensuing decades often confirm the principle, but the idea predates the war and reappears with a vengeance in Occupation reforms and foreign multinational strategy. It was the result of calculations by private firms whose options, while clearly limited, had long been clearly understood as well. As one wartime energy planner put it,

top *zaibatsu* leaders saw the war as short-term—an interlude during which they would have to shout "Banzai! Banzai!" but after which they would have to make their peace with American interests. They were therefore very cautious about outright confiscations of foreign assets.[68]

The foreign majors had a rare foothold in a growth market, and a captive one at that. They also had a place to divert Middle East oil when American import quotas were exhausted. The Japanese benefited from stable supplies of crude, capital for reconstruction of their refining industry, new technology, and the prospect of secure access to one of the cheapest factors of production ever available.

THE 1950S: AN INCONCLUSIVE DECADE

It was not immediately clear to most policy planners that petroleum would power Japan's economic transformation. Nor was it clear that a foreign-infiltrated oil industry could muster the political resources to rival the powerful coal industry. Energy policy throughout the 1950s therefore vacillated between the promotion of coal and the promotion of oil, usually leaning toward the former. The market seemed always to confound government programs. In 1950 coal accounted for more than half of Japan's primary energy supply; petroleum accounted for less than 7 percent, barely half the level of firewood and charcoal and a lower share than it had held in 1936. But by 1956 petroleum accounted for over 20 percent of Japan's primary energy supply, and coal had dropped to less than half. Soon after the end of the decade the mixture finally was clarified, and petroleum became the fuel of choice for the first time.

During this revolutionary shift MITI enjoyed an unusual degree of control of the market—a control it derived, ironically, not from energy industry laws but from the more general Foreign Exchange and Foreign Trade Control Law of December 1949. Until the liberalization of the early 1960s that accompanied Japan's entry into the OECD and the GATT, MITI enjoyed what Johnson terms "absolute control over the use of all 'foreign means of payment.' "[69] MITI used currency allocations to nurture domestic firms not tied to long-term supply contracts. Firms that secured cheap spot oil could in principle increase their currency allocations for the following year,[70] and so many firms struggled mightily with barter arrangements to increase volume without exhausting allocations. Preference also went to crude oil over refined products, at a 70-30 ratio, encouraging the expansion of domestic refinery capacity. Labor unrest in the mines abetted the shift to oil from coal. In late 1952, faced with coal shortages and price instability, MITI began actively promoting petroleum. By January 1954, however, under extreme political pressure from the coal industry and conservative politicians, MITI reversed itself, retiring draft legislation to provide added incentives for conversion to oil. In fact, as Chapter 3 showed, coal promotion programs were introduced to *limit* oil conversion.

Downstream

From the end of Occupation until the early 1960s, MITI took only two steps to enhance petroleum supply and establish a commercial presence in the market place. The first was downstream in 1952–53, when the government unveiled plans to nationalize the naval refinery at Yokkaichi.[71] Competition for this site was intense. Foreign-affiliated Mitsubishi and Shell seemed to have an inside track, but Maruzen and Nippon Oil appealed to politicians for intervention to keep the site under national control. MITI and several influential politicians tried to dissuade Shell/Mitsubishi from ownership; they suggested an annual lease instead, which was rejected. In the end Mitsubishi blocked a cabinet compromise, negotiations with the United States followed which seemed to have implications for the Mutual Security Treaty, and Yoshida vetoed further nationalization plans. In 1955 Shōwa Oil and its partner Shell, in collaboration with the Mitsubishi Group, was awarded the site, and the case was closed. The Yokkaichi debate was the first of several postwar debates about the need for nationally capitalized refineries. Although this effort to exclude foreign capital failed, it prefigured numerous attempts by MITI and the purely domestic firms to secure greater national control over the Japanese oil industry.

Upstream

Upstream, MITI and Imperial Oil still harbored hopes that commercial exploitation of oil in Japan could help circumvent the dominance of foreign capital. Imperial Oil had not had notable success. When labor unrest in 1952 led to the mass resignations of top management, Mitsui Mining president Tashiro Shūichi took control (at least some in the coal industry were preparing for the postcoal era). But Tashiro was replaced in 1954 when Ayukawa Yoshisuke, ally of the wartime bureaucracy and cofounder of the Nissan *zaibatsu*, purchased a controlling interest. According to one observer, this move was welcomed by those in MITI who wanted an oil-centered energy policy to give their petroleum resource development program political clout.[72] One of Ayukawa's first moves was to make Tanaka Kakuei an informal adviser (*komon*) to Imperial Oil. Tanaka was from Niigata, one of Japan's few oil-producing regions. He and Ayukawa organized a group of Niigata Dietmen and engineering firms whose support in Diet would be critical to the plans of Ayukawa and MITI for a new initiative in oil exploration modeled after the wartime

Imperial Oil. These plans for joint domestic exploration were first formally debated by MITI's Oil and Natural Gas Resource Development Advisory Commission in 1953.[73] A report issued in September 1953 became the basis of MITI's first Five-Year Petroleum Resources General Development Plan, issued one year later. Central to the plan was a new instrument for collaborative development of Japan's domestic petroleum resources. The new venture would be called the Japan Petroleum Exploration Company (JAPEX).

Before JAPEX could be established, however, responsibilities had to be divided between Imperial Oil and the new venture. Imperial, as noted, had already lost the formal protection of the state. Although the Ministry of Finance still had limited shareholding,[74] the firm did not enjoy the support of the refining firms (tied to foreign suppliers), nor did it have the capital necessary for major new projects. Ayukawa offered to accept a 50 percent state shareholding in a new public corporation but urged the state's presence be limited to exploration. He suggested that the new firm be required to divest its holdings to domestic production firms (his own Imperial Oil being the most prominent) upon the discovery and exploitation of deposits.[75] Other private investors, including the refiners, found his scheme unattractive. They argued that profit lay not in exploration but in production, so equity in a firm that produced neither oil nor profits would amount to little more than a subsidy program for Imperial Oil. Unless it made provisions for production and sale, MITI was unlikely to attract private participation in the new venture.

Private participation became all the more critical when a chary Finance Ministry raised a second problem. MITI had originally sought a public commitment of 1.2 billion yen for the new company.[76] Finance, in April 1955, initially offered only 100 million yen and refused to recognize the MITI plan for a new public entity. The ministry thought a new public corporation ill-advised because proposed programs were more ambitious than the public treasury could support and because, even if the corporation discovered new resources in Japan, output would amount to less than 1 percent of national consumption. Only after vigorous negotiations (and skillful manipulation of the remaining Ministry of Finance shareholding in Imperial Oil) did MITI win 300 million yen for its five-year plan to develop petroleum resources.

With the government bill in trouble, MITI began to bargain. JAPEX would be allowed to produce and sell oil, satisfying the objections of private investors, but its exploration would be limited to new fields, preventing it from competing directly with Ayukawa's Imperial Oil. Imperial would continue to exploit all existing fields and was also allocated those most likely to produce natural gas.[77] Moreover, Imperial could become the largest private shareholder in JAPEX, and Ayukawa would be the first chairman. Now satisfied, Ayukawa, Tanaka, and MITI minister Ishibashi Tanzan arranged for enabling legislation to be submitted on July 1, 1955 as a member's rather than a government bill, thereby precluding Finance alterations at the eleventh hour. The Finance Ministry, in turn, was partially placated when public guarantees for all corporate liabilities were shifted from law to a nonbinding resolution on July 9, 1955.[78]

Diet created JAPEX on July 28, 1955. The Finance Ministry paid in 56.2 percent of the initial 1.02 billion yen in capital, mainly through an accounting procedure by which remaining Finance shares in Imperial Oil were transferred to the new venture. On November 23 Imperial and thirteen other investors provided cash equity investments to join the government as partners. JAPEX began operations in December 1955. In the end it had been carefully crafted in extensive negotiations. Private demands gave it a commercial presence in the market place not initially intended. To satisfy Imperial, its activities were carefully circumscribed. JAPEX is most often compared to the wartime Imperial Oil, upon which it was clearly modeled as a national policy company, but in certain important respects, the negotiations produced something that more closely resemble the Electric Power Development Corporation. Like the EPDC, JAPEX was created as a limited public service corporation; state and industry created a joint public-private supplier of a basic factor of production for industry's benefit on terms designed to limit competition with existing market players. It displaced no existing firms.

JAPEX began production in 1958. Although it fell far short of its ambitious goals, it did achieve one dubious breakthrough: in 1960, the year after JAPEX made its first offshore discovery, domestic crude oil production exceeded 500,000 kl (3.1 million barrels) for the first time, breaking a production record set in 1915. But Japanese petroleum consumption had expanded by many orders of magnitude in the intervening forty-five years, and this achievement, less than 2 percent of total demand, hardly satisfied the refining firms. Indeed, the ten refining firms that had joined the venture at its inception with a combined 10 percent of equity began to chafe at JAPEX demands for capital. Other, more productive investments were available. In an era of assured supplies of crude at a dollar a barrel, the refineries wanted to invest only in capacity expansion, leaving exploration and production to their foreign partners. In the spring of 1960, anticipating liberalization of crude oil imports and apprehensive about costly JAPEX and MITI plans for overseas fields (particularly in North Sumatra), the ten refineries announced their intention to cease capital cooperation with JAPEX after 1961.[79]

State support was enlisted for several additional private initiatives upstream during this period. The most notable was the creation of the Arabian Oil Company, Japan's first successful overseas oil development firm.[80] The Suez crisis in 1956 highlighted Japanese vulnerability in the international oil market. An alert entrepreneur, Yamashita Tarō, followed the lead set by Enrico Mattei in Italy and with the cooperation of the Foreign Ministry and the Kishi Cabinet set out to secure independent crude oil for Japan from the Saudi government.[81] He offered the Saudis better terms than the majors would (57 percent of all profits plus infrastructural investments and rental fees). But the project immediately encountered problems at home. The Finance Ministry was alarmed by a cabinet resolution of June 11, 1957, which helped Yamashita obtain his lease; it refused to invest in such a risky venture or even to provide funding through Export-Import Bank loans. The electric power industry, poised for major new investments in oil-fired thermal capacity, eagerly supported Yamashita, as did virtually the entire Japanese financial community and industry, at the urging of Keidanren chairman Ishizaka.

The refiners, however, were reluctant to jeopardize relations with their foreign partners. When the field began producing in 1960, refineries at first would not accept its crude oil. Debates intensified during the 1960s, as Japanese energy markets lurched from coal to oil and on to new crises.

FROM ENERGY REVOLUTION TO ENERGY CRISIS

At the beginning of the 1960s Japan was poised on the brink of an energy revolution. MITI had already violated the spirit of the 1955 Boiler Law by granting permission for the electric power industry to build ten oil-fired thermal power plants by the end of 1960. Businessmen and bureaucrats recognized that demand for oil would grow faster than for any other energy source. MITI's long-term energy projections, issued in September 1960, forecast that coal demand would double between 1960 and 1980 where oil demand would more than quintuple (see Table 5.2). Relative shares in the nation's primary energy market would shift dramatically, and they did—but much more dramatically than any projections anticipated. Between 1961 and 1973 petroleum consumption nearly quadrupled, increasing over 11 percent annually. Gasoline sales increased 400 percent, and oil's share of the nation's primary energy supply increased from under 40 percent to almost 80 percent.

This epochal shift was no less significant for oil firms than for coal mines. At first, shareholders in refining firms enjoyed relatively high rates of return on investment. But the refineries, struggling to keep pace

Table 5.2. MITI's long-term energy
forecast, 1960 (percentages of primary
energy supply)

	1959 (actual)	1970	1980
Coal	38%	29%	22%
Oil	29	50	63
Other	33	21	15

Source: Tanaka 1983:9.

with exploding demand, added capacity throughout the decade; their financial structure weakened, and their numbers grew. The Japanese oil market soon became as fragmented as the American one. Between 1965 and 1970 demand expanded 20 percent annually. Equity/capital ratios were cut in half. At the same time the share of Middle Eastern oil in Japan's total import volume rose to 90 percent. The state took repeated initiatives to control these transformations and to use them to promote the competitiveness of Japanese industry.

Table 5.3 gives a complete list of MITI advisory commission initiatives from 1961 to 1986. Early efforts to achieve a market presence for the state in the form of an ENI-like "Japanese major" (*wasei mejā*) were sacrificed to political expediency. MITI settled for a second petroleum industry law (PIL-II) instead. Successive MITI visions of an integrated national oil champion were transformed into more limited proposals for a state presence in the oil market place which finally became little more than the state exhorting the private sector to consolidate. State policy never served to transform the market, as we shall see; it consistently served to ratify it.

LIBERALIZATION WITH PROTECTION—A SECOND PETROLEUM INDUSTRY LAW

In September 1960 the directors of the International Monetary Fund resolved that Japan had to liberalize its markets to be accepted as a full partner in the international trading regime. Japan's trade successes had eroded the need for currency restrictions. Foreign reserves had rapidly increased. Japan welcomed the opportunity to enter the GATT system but feared sudden liberalization in sectors such as oil, where foreign governments and corporations appeared to wield overwhelming power. Accordingly MITI began to search for a way to buffer the economy against the onslaught of foreign capital and the "excessive competition" that

Reporting body	Date	Integ. P.C.	Upstream P.C.	Downstream P.C.	Integ. Consol.	Downstream Consol.	Comments
Energy Roundtable	12/61	X	X				Wasei Major, ENI-like
Indus. Struc. Council	6/63		X	X			Antei Kikin
	12/63	X					Organic integration
	11/64					X	Kyōdō Oil
Advis. Com. for Energy	2/67			X		X	Overseas Kōdan
	12/71				X		Daidō Danketsu
	7/73				X		State leadership for integration
	7/74				X		Impatience with private sector (Morozumi Plan)
	12/75					X	Group-based consolidation (refining $ to JNOC)
	10/78					X	Promote mergers
Petrol. Council	12/81					X	Shūyakuka
	5/83					X	Promote joint use, cooperation

SOURCES: *Sekiyu Seisaku*, June 10, 1982, pp. 39–45; Petroleum Council Internal memorandum, "Sekiyu Sangyō Taisei ni Kansuru kore made no Seisaku no Kangaekata no Keifu" (A record of the thinking about the structure of the oil industry until the present) (October 1983).
NOTES: Integ. = vertically integrated; P.C. = Public Corporation; Consol. = private-sector consolidation.

would accompany new market entrants. Without some form of control, it was believed, the Japanese oil industry would be at risk; national security would be compromised.[82]

Seven scholars, led by Arisawa Hiromi, were appointed as an informal committee to advise MITI on policy alternatives. This Energy Roundtable (Enerugī Kondankai) began its deliberations in August 1961.[83] Although MITI showed some sympathy for industry wishes and the Petroleum Association was granted an audience from time to time, no industry official formally participated. The Petroleum Association has claimed that it was excluded "to keep out any background noise [because] it was judged that [we] would obstruct the deliberations of the council. . . . The deliberation process of the Roundtable was completely concealed . . . [while we] were restricted to seats in the upper gallery."[84]

In December 1961 the Energy Roundtable reported, offering two equal alternatives: 1) create a national oil corporation, and 2) invoke a new petroleum industry law. Speaking for MITI, the Roundtable predicted that liberalization without protection would unleash devastating consequences upon the weak Japanese oil industry. It consequently proposed two separate public oil corporations, both involving joint public–private investments with state control. Plan A would give the state a direct and comprehensive presence in the market. It sought to maximize access for Arabian and domestic crude by assigning a fixed portion of the Japanese market to a half-public–half-private special public corporation (tokushu kokusaku kaisha).[85] This firm, modeled upon Italy's ENI and France's CFP, would import crude oil and refine and sell petroleum products. The Roundtable expected electric utilities, steel firms, and other large private consumers to invest with the state in such a venture. Plan B recommended a different sort of public policy company, one that would act as a financial agency (tokushu tōshi kaisha) to invest in private refining and sales companies and that would establish subsidiaries "through which government intentions could be reflected."[86]

MITI lacked confidence in the competitiveness of the domestic industry and felt "it had no alternative but to intervene in the business activities of the oil industry."[87] Many in private industry felt otherwise. Although the Roundtable Report was as MITI claimed an "epochal document in the history of the Japanese oil industry,"[88] it lacked for neither precedent nor opposition. The precedent was unpleasant, especially to foreign-affiliated refining firms, for the proposed Petroleum Industry Law was modeled directly upon PIL-I. It would give the state the same licensing and regulatory powers as those granted in 1933 when the MCI nationalization plan had been rejected. Indeed, much in the Roundtable Report was reminiscent of prewar days, particularly what Ōi calls "the strong radiation of the color of private ownership with public management."[89] The report touched off a "seething debate among business elites and critics . . . who saw it as opening a road toward bureaucratic control."[90]

The most negative reaction came from those the program purported to assist. Even before the final report appeared, Japanese oil-producing firms had rejected a separate MITI plan for a domestic crude oil refining corporation (Kokusan Genyu Seisei Kaisha). MITI sought to convince Imperial Oil, JAPEX, and Arabian Oil to join it in a national policy company to refine domestic crude. But the plan was buried in August 1961, when Imperial decided to build its own refinery in Niigata and Arabian stated a preference to build its own refineries. This unwillingness upstream to join MITI in integrating a domestic oil industry meant that the Petroleum Association did not even have to voice its own objections. MITI's problem remained as difficult as ever, but contrary to most accounts, it was not entirely due to the opposition of foreign-controlled refineries.[91]

The Petroleum Association, representing the refining industry, labeled the Roundtable Report "merely the irrational arguments of people without any experience in the oil industry."[92] The association came together reluctantly in 1955, to counter the fishing industry. Politically weak from its inception, it is divided by size and by affiliation. Domestically capitalized firms, such as Idemitsu and Daikyō, and foreign affiliates, for example Nippon Oil and Shōwa, consistently split on issues of security and supply. At the same time, however, Nippon Oil and Idemitsu are giants compared to Shōwa and Daikyō, and so on other issues concerning market share and allocation, firm size is likely to be more salient. The only issue upon which association members regularly agree is consumption and import taxes. Although the association was publicly outraged by the heavy-handedness of MITI and its Roundtable, internal divisions left it unable formally to repudiate the report. It united to oppose a state oil corporation but remained undecided about the proposal for a second petroleum industry law.

MITI, however, was committed to some form of national oil corporation. The Roundtable had been impressed with the French and Italian national oil champions.[93] From European responses to domination by foreign majors MITI concluded that it is the responsibility of the state to secure cheap and stable supplies of petroleum. The European combination of regulatory legislation and state ownership was clearly contrary to the spirit of impending liberalization, but of the Europeans and even the Americans MITI noted that "Although in these countries there is a formal pretext of a relatively liberalized system, in reality general laws, tariffs, and other routine practices protect citizens' interests."[94]

MITI supplemented the Roundtable Report with four proposals.[95] The first sought a refining, sales, and investment corporation to refine and sell a fixed percentage of the natural increase of Japanese crude oil production (thereby avoiding the usurpation of existing arrangements). This firm would be awarded preferential treatment under PIL-II; it would hold shares in Japanese refining companies and provide low-interest loans to place one-third of the market under national control. The second was modeled after Plan B. It proposed a special investment corporation to facilitate the importation of untied crude oil. This firm would hold shares in refining companies and provide low-interest loans. It would also establish a subsidiary as a purchasing agent for "special crude." The third proposal, favored by JAPEX and much of the upstream industry, called for a petroleum supply stabilization fund that would make capital available for domestic oil and gas. MITI's final proposal called for a special crude oil purchasing agency as a state monopoly to acquire and distribute Japanese-developed crude oil. MITI argued strongly that "the establishment of a public policy company is no less important or fundamental vis-à-vis a stable supply structure than is the Petroleum Industry Law."[96]

State ownership of a commercial firm was the first casualty of the debate that ensued. When MITI submitted its final draft of PIL-II to Diet (on the same day the Roundtable Report was formally issued), it omitted plans for a state oil company. One Roundtable member now claims that MITI dropped the plans because it anticipated strong opposition from the majors: "There is no question that our first choice would have been to create a national oil corporation modeled upon the French or Italian one. But we were fully cognizant of political reality, the most important component of which was the power of the majors in the Japanese market. . . . We opted instead to promote the Petroleum Industry Law."[97]

Interestingly, a national oil champion had many supporters in Diet. During the summer of 1961 five committee directors (*riji*) of the House Commerce and Industry Committee and the parliamentary vice-minister for MITI embarked on a study tour of Europe and North America. Their report to MITI and the cabinet strongly supported legislation that would emphasize national security and stability of supply. They identified sectionalism and bureaucratic politics within MITI as obstacles to a national oil program and proposed a comprehensive national energy public corporation (Enerugī Kōdan) modeled upon the British Energy Ministry. They wanted a state agency to develop domestic resources, import crude oil, set prices, and fix volumes.[98] Nakasone Yasuhiro and a suprapartisan group of legislators also called for the creation of a national energy corporation to manage the energy revolution.[99] These legislators even succeeded in attaching nonbinding resolutions to PIL-II calling for a public oil firm "to secure stable oil supplies."

There was some support from the oil industry itself. Producing firms, which stood to lose everything if MITI's worst fears about liberalization came true, organized into the Japan Petroleum Development Association (Sekiyu Kōgyō Renmei, or JPDA) to push for the MITI program.[100] The JPDA actively campaigned for PIL-II and almost every variety of state corporation for oil finance to secure state-guaranteed market shares. The Petroleum Association was united in its opposition to competition from the state: "We were being pushed to the edge of the ring by all sorts of government plans to force us to buy the oil [that the proposed new public policy company] . . . would supply as well as by government plans to use this public policy company to march into the area of refined product sales."[101] But the association had at least three different factions. One was made up of six small, domestically capitalized refiners, which favored continued government assistance to firms unaffiliated with foreign capital. Like their upstream cousins, they feared for their survival after liberalization. A second group of large, foreign affiliates unalterably opposed the measure. The remaining nine firms were willing to accept PIL-II if it were made provisional and limited to stabilizing supplies after liberalization. Internal debate prevented the association from issuing its opinion. It was well after the MITI bill had been submitted to Diet that the Petroleum Association finally found common and uncontroversial ground. But it had to skirt the central issues entirely: its "majority opinion" called for "slight regulation" and "self-control," closely echoing earlier decades and different times.

Keidanren recognized these historical continuities, and equally vigilant, it was far more influential than the association. Facing clear and determined opposition from Keidanren, the LDP and MITI prudently deleted all proposals for a national oil corporation from PIL-II. Nonetheless, heavy industry continued to oppose the legislation, fearing it would impede conversion from coal to oil. Steel firms, electric utilities, and other large consumers had one overriding interest in this legislation— the preservation of their right to choose the cheapest source of fuel. Keidanren therefore joined the Petroleum Association in opposing PIL-II as initially drafted. Its delegation to MITI on December 25, 1961, argued that "wartime experiences taught us that controls in one sector lead to control in others." Disagreeing with "the bureaucrats' predisposition to control in order to protect," the business leaders expressed confidence that the majors could ensure stable and cheap supplies of petroleum to Japan.[102] It has been observed that they did not build their position entirely upon principle: "The positions adopted by industries affected by the proposed legislation more strongly reflected their own interests than they reflected a broader view of our general national energy and petroleum policy situation."[103] Ōi Ryūaki is largely right. The steel firms, for example, would accept PIL-II as long as they received oil price supports. The electric utilities agreed if the law exempted consumers who, like themselves, planned to refine their own supplies.[104]

Keidanren issued its formal position in late February 1962. It was willing to compromise with MITI but not to surrender to strong state control. It insisted that the responsibility for importing special crude be left in private hands, though it agreed that legal measures could be taken for a transitional period. Keidanren leaders insisted that relief from "excessive competition" be left to the market. Concessions were made especially to the utilities. There would be no national oil corporation, and the system would have a five-year limit. MITI excised vestiges of "excessive bureaucratic power." The licensing of facilities replaced the licensing of firms, and a petroleum council, to include formal representatives of the oil and consumer industries, would be established as a formal MITI advisory commission. When PIL-II was enacted in July 1962, "to control domestic petroleum supply and demand after the imports of crude oil were liberalized,"[105] it reflected a final compromise between MITI minister Satō Eisaku and top Keidanren leaders. As Ōi notes, "in response to Keidanren's effort to minimize restrictions on the free economy, [Satō] inserted the opinions of industry into the original draft. As a result there were in reality no major differences from industry's position [in the final legislation]."[106]

While it would be an overstatement to argue that PIL-II was completely eviscerated, private industry did succeed in negotiating its first formal role in oil policy. A significant element of the compromise was the creation of the Petroleum Council, for after the promulgation of PIL-II, all policy deliberations formally included industry representatives. As Raymond Vernon has rightly observed, "the willingness of industry to countenance a delegation of power to government depended in part, of course, on its expectation that it would have a hand in the exercise of that power."[107]

MITI was granted enlarged jurisdiction but denied extensive control. PIL-II, like its predecessor, gives the state licensing authority for new and expanded refinery installations. MITI also got authority to allocate shares in the retail market based on annual five-year supply/demand forecasts drawn up by the Petroleum Council. Mergers and acquisitions, crude oil import plans, production schedules, and (in extraordinary times) pricing require the approval of the MITI minister. Allocations, through "administrative guidance," are derived from an averaging of three factors: 1) the actual volume of crude oil imported and refined in the previous six months; 2) actual sales over the same period; and 3) total capacity. In practice, however, MITI has found control to be elusive, for reasons that deserve attention.

The Petroleum Association provides the data upon which MITI makes allocations and also enforces them. When objections to MITI guidelines are raised, as they frequently were in the early years of PIL-II, the guidelines are changed. The stiffest challenge to PIL-II controls came in the autumn of 1963, when Idemitsu Kōsan, feeling it was unfairly treated regarding allocations, resigned from the association. It took a full year of cajoling, and ultimately a higher allocation, to bring Idemitsu back into the fold. Two years later Idemitsu deliberately exceeded its quota, and to calm a rebellious, resentful industry, MITI had to grant an additional quota to all producers. The domestic refining firms, those which PIL-II was designed to nurture, turned out, in one bureaucrat's words to be "much tougher to deal with and much less cooperative than the foreign-affiliated companies."[108]

Although PIL-II was designed to strengthen domestically capitalized oil refiners and distributors, assistance has not come entirely at the expense of foreign affiliates. The expansion of domestic firms got priority, but before PIL-II was implemented, foreign affiliates expecting difficulties rushed to expand their capacity. Foreign capital shares in the Japanese petroleum industry doubled.[109] Once in place, however, PIL-II's encouragement of domestic expansion left domestic refiners vulnerable and overextended, especially in the era of high-priced oil (1973–1986). Foreign affiliates had less excess capacity and so were better positioned to withstand the first oil shock. In the meantime they shared profitably (if not equally) in the expansion of demand (see Table 5.4). Clearly domestic firms grew faster than foreign-affiliated firms, but in the first four years of the PIL-II system less than half of the new refinery capacity licensed by MITI was for domestic firms. As Martha Caldwell notes, "while some . . . would go so far as to argue that MITI policy strengthened the domestic companies, it is fairer to say that it protected the status quo."[110] The important fact for this period was that demand was rapidly expanding; policy could be positive-sum if the program could be artfully administered.

But bureaucratic struggles inside MITI, born of divisions within the

Table 5.4. Changes in licensed Japanese refinery capacity (unit = 10,000 barrels/day, number of firms in parentheses)

	Capacity		Growth rate
	Before PIL-II	1974	
Domestic firms	48.25 (8)	297.25 (15)	516.1%
Foreign affiliates	64.90 (9)	307.95 (13)	374.5%
Total refineries	113.15 (17)	605.20 (28)	434.9%

SOURCE: Petroleum Association of Japan, internal memorandum.

industry, have frustrated execution of the law. Divisions between upstream and downstream interests have proved even more frustrating than divisions between domestic and foreign firms.[111] No sooner had PIL-II been implemented than "negotiations between crude suppliers and refiners became deeply troubled."[112] At the very first meeting of the Petroleum Council, on July 17, 1962, the disposition of Arabian Oil's Khafji crude became the central problem. Refiners had only reluctantly agreed to accept 31 million barrels of Khafji crude for 1962. When MITI and Arabian Oil sought increased commitments from refiners, they ran into strong opposition. MITI wanted the refiners to accept three times the Khafji crude they were offering to accept. "Upstream" bureaucrats were growing impatient to place a significant portion of the nation's oil supplies under domestic control, and some officials advocated that the government secure a domestic sales network for Arabian Oil as a part of national policy.[113] Others, mostly the "downstream" bureaucrats in the Petroleum Division, blocked their efforts, refusing Arabian Oil a refining license lest it throw the industry into chaos. As a result the unintegrated status quo survived, frustrating MITI designs on coordinated oil policy and state control. Parts of MITI would make half a dozen additional false starts toward restructuring the industry under state control before the first oil shock hit in 1973.

RESTRUCTURING: FALSE STARTS AND LIMITED SUCCESS

Upstream

Efforts to bring the supply of crude oil under national control did not end with MITI's withholding proposals for a national oil champion from PIL-II. Despite the active support of exploration and production firms in the JPDA, three MITI plans for state corporations to promote crude oil development by Japanese firms—the Petroleum Supply Stabilization Fund (1963), the Overseas Crude Oil Promotion and Finance Agency (1964), and the Crude Oil Public Corporation (1965)—all failed to gain political support among refiners and consumers. Each met fatal opposition from industry and the Finance Ministry. Finance was willing to increase the JAPEX budget during the 1960s, but not to accept a new public agency. Private industry was likewise willing to accept new public funds but resisted new public controls.

Debate resumed as soon as PIL-II passed in Diet. Oil exploration and production firms were unhappy that MITI had sacrificed an upstream agency to political expediency. They argued that PIL-II alone was "exceedingly insufficient to satisfy . . . demands for the kind of special national instrument the Energy Roundtable had endorsed."[114] With their supporters in MITI they resolved almost immediately to try again. In August 1962, barely four months after PIL-II became law, the JPDA announced its "Demands Related to Crude Oil Liberalization Policy." These included calls to establish a sole agency for the import of special crude and for additional funds to develop new crude oil resources. These demands were reissued at budget time, four months later, enhanced with proposals for instruments to "preserve the independence of Japanese refiners." This controversial proposal merely rehashed the Roundtable programs: it aimed to place one-third of the Japanese market under Japanese control through state investment and equity holdings in refining firms as well as in resource development upstream.[115]

The refiners reacted with immediate opposition; so did the heavy industrial consumers and Keidanren. The Petroleum Association stressed free choice for consumers and the efficiency of refineries, opposing state interference with "commercially viable" development of petroleum resources. The refiners, Keidanren, and much of heavy industry argued that the collaboration of the foreign majors was necessary for stable petroleum supply. Opting for economy over security, they claimed that compulsory purchases and market allocation would be counterproductive. Their opposition conformed to the predisposition of MITI's Petroleum Division to avoid conflict with the majors who were, in fact, supplying an exceedingly cheap factor of production.[116] Arabian Oil, which had just lost its battle to establish a refinery, had used virtually all of its political capital in gaining access to the Japanese refineries. The JPDA and MITI were compelled to back off. The proposal was not reported out of the Comprehensive Energy Division of the Industrial Structure Council, where it had been debated.

Like the phoenix, this proposal would die many deaths. Within six months the same division of the Industrial Structure Council called for the stabilization of crude oil supplies through diversification of sources, construction of a Japanese tanker fleet, increased stockpiles, and further development of domestic fields. It sought to guarantee the industry's independence through state-funded overseas exploration and consolidation of the refining industry (*shūyakuka*) by active state investment. To accomplish these goals, the committee formally proposed that "the establishment of a public policy company that reflects government opinions and planning for the organic integration of crude oil development and refining should be debated."[117] Less than six months after vetoing plans for a state oil-finance company, therefore, the Industrial Structure Council formally approved proposals to consider a national oil champion "to integrate crude oil production and refining."[118] The goal was to create a consolidated, integrated petroleum industry under state control "just like in Europe."[119]

The debate was revived, it seems, by a shift in the position of industrial consumers. In October 1963 Keidanren issued a position paper on the future of the Japanese oil industry which argued for increased state assistance through fiscal and tax programs. It called for state funds for exploration and a risk-reduction system under which state loans for oil exploration would be repaid only when a well was successful. Keidanren stated that "if existing government agencies could not implement this, then the creation of some sort of special agency must be considered."[120] A new round of negotiations began between business and state: business wanted risk-free funds, the state asked for control. The state sought an integrated industry, business sought new market opportunities.

What should a new public oil corporation look like? MITI initially took up the cause of a public agency to promote and finance overseas crude oil (Kaigai Genyu Shinkō Yūshi Jigyōdan) for inclusion in the 1964 budget. This new public agency would have provided up to 80 percent of project financing for overseas petroleum exploration. When the Finance Ministry balked, MITI and the exploration firms settled for increased financial support through JAPEX and a special 500-million-yen rebate system for refiners who would accept Japanese crude. The JAPEX mandate was reinterpreted to permit overseas exploration, and an additional 200 million yen was made available to it for FY 1964. The following year its state funds for overseas exploration were increased to 700 million yen, and by 1966 it was receiving an extra 2 billion yen.

Although the Finance Ministry was willing to provide additional funds for overseas projects, it remained reluctant to authorize a new public agency to administer them. The refining firms, ever vigilant against MITI controls, shared that reluctance. MITI and the upstream industry, on the other hand, were still dissatisfied with overseas exploration by Japanese firms. In July 1965 Ōjimi Yoshihisa, then chief of MITI's Mining Bureau, proposed a new, comprehensive state presence upstream, the so-called Ōjimi Program.[121] A crude oil public corporation (Genyu Kōdan) would promote oil exploration through financial incentives both for exploration firms and for refiners who accepted their crude. The *kōdan* would become the sole agency for importation and sales of Japanese overseas crude; its funds would derive from tariffs on crude oil and would be incorporated in the FY 1966 budget; it would be completely state-owned. Ōjimi and the JPDA lobbied energetically for the plan, reminding everyone that influential Dietmen had attached resolutions to PIL-II calling for a national oil champion.

There was sufficient interest within the Petroleum Association and Keidanren to necessitate formal debate. The association's Planning Committee deliberated throughout the summer, ultimately opposing the *kōdan* for two reasons. First, the introduction of a state corporation enhanced the potential for state control and had to be resisted. Second, if the revenue source for this new body were linked to the crude oil tariff, that tariff would likely be permanently fixed at too high a level.[122] In its formal petition opposing the MITI initiative the association declared that "we fear the strengthening of controls and restrictions upon the business activities of refineries that are now free firms. . . . [We also fear] the general difficulties in importing crude oil that would result from a renewed presence in the oil market by an agency of the state."[123]

The refiners were joined by the electric power industry, by dissenters within MITI, and by parts of the Foreign Ministry.[124] Finance rejected the program in compiling the 1966 budget, and LDP leaders rejected it when MITI tried again during the revival negotiations.[125] In the end MITI again tabled the plans. A public agency to promote oil exploration was clearly in the offing, but its politically acceptable limits remained to be negotiated. One participant in the negotiations put it bluntly: "Ōjimi wanted an ENI/Elf-type organization for Japan, and this would have been a first step. But it was politically impossible. Private industrial leaders who later came to strongly support (a revised) *kōdan* proposal vetoed any sort of Italian- or French-style strong state corporation.[126]

Downstream

MITI also tried to restructure the downstream industry to enhance national control. In June 1964 three private refiners, Asia Oil, Nippon Mining, and Tōa Oil, initiated discussions to merge their sales and storage of refined products.[127] In this unprecedented opportunity MITI used a variety of fiscal incentives to assume leadership of these negotiations, and throughout the summer it helped plan for 7 billion yen in low-cost (6.5 percent) loans for the venture. It then tried to include other domestic refining firms in the consolidation. According to Mark Brown, "MITI tried to ensure the success of the new venture by enlisting the participation of more powerful non-affiliate oil firms, namely Daikyō Oil, Maruzen Oil, and Idemitsu Kōsan. However, these firms, in particular Idemitsu, were basically opposed to MITI's efforts to create a public policy company and refused to participate."[128] Nonetheless, in November the Comprehensive Energy Division of MITI's Industrial Structure Council directed oil policy toward "orderly marketing and production" and "scale" downstream for the first time. The declining financial and competitive strength of smaller, domestically capitalized oil firms was of particular concern to the committee. So was the negative effect that "excessive competition" and the "evils of a disorderly market" might have on the rest of the industry.[129]

The result was Kyōdō Oil, established in August 1965 as a joint sales firm with public financial assistance "to strengthen the sales activities of domestic capital." Initially Kyōdō Oil was created out of the merger of the sales divisions of Nippon Mining, Asia Oil, and Tōa Oil, with generous financial support from MITI. Between 1965 and 1973 the government provided more than 100 billion yen to nurture Japanese oil companies. Nearly half went to Kyōdō Oil directly; the rest went to the refining companies of the firms participating in the joint sales venture.[130] This was the first step toward an integrated Japanese national oil champion "that would play an active international role in the future in every stage from production through refining and marketing."[131] MITI hoped eventually to consolidate the upstream and downstream industries and bring them together as an instrument of national control. But despite administrative guidance and financial incentives, the firms refused to merge their refinery operations—the larger domestic refiners refused to participate at all. Furthermore, politicians intervened to include two noncompetitive refineries about to fail. The result was merely another weak company in the market place. In August 1969 MITI tried to salvage the situation by intervening strongly in the management of the firm. MITI issued directives for the distribution of profits and losses, rationalization of personnel and management, sales planning and coordination, assistance in transportation planning, and other reforms. It was all to no avail. Asia Oil and Tōa Oil abandoned the venture entirely. Professor Arisawa, the frustrated architect of a consolidated Japanese petroleum industry, put it this way:

> Although I was a proponent of 30 percent domestic control of the Japanese oil market, and although I proposed that a centralized firm be formed to achieve that control, I did not have anything like Kyōdō Oil in mind. We were thinking more of a vertically integrated firm, from refining on down to sales. Initially Maruzen Oil and Daikyō Oil would have been included, but in the end this did not happen and the result was a separated refining and sales sector. That is why the industry is still weak.[132]

A NATIONAL OIL CORPORATION IS BORN: FROM JAPANESE MAJOR TO JAPANESE MINOR

Upstream, MITI's prospects finally seemed brighter. After numerous false starts private industry and the Finance Ministry agreed to a new public corporation, though in a form more limited than MITI planners originally envisioned. In September 1966 MITI's Mining Bureau issued its plan for a Japan Petroleum Development Corporation (Seikiyu Kaihatsu Kōdan). The Keidanren accepted this version; indeed Industrial Bank of Japan president and Keidanren leader Nakayama Sohei was a leading advocate. Unlike previous plans this one, while it consciously invoked French and Italian models, did not provide a direct commercial role for the state either upstream or downstream. It established a non-competitive (and therefore more welcome) form of state assistance: the state would intervene as *banker*. Large industrial consumers and major steel and construction firms were now anxious to accept state-stimulated industrial expansion. The plan omitted any mention of direct state presence in the market place, explicitly calling for a "public policy company–*like* mother body."[133]

Unlike previously proposed state agencies, this *kōdan* could not import, sell, or allocate crude oil or refined products. Even its authority to hold equity in production firms was left purposefully ambiguous. Even among refining firms, as a result, although Petroleum Association chairman Fujioka admonished MITI to "respect free market principles," most were ready to live with the new agency.[134] At the same time, MITI at last reached internal consensus between its upstream and downstream sections. The latter finally were convinced that a national effort to secure independent sources of crude would not damage relations with the international majors. Japan would not have the integrated national oil champion many had sought, but this solution nonetheless was no minor political achievement. The principals in MITI and industry all understood the limits exacted by these many compromises; as one JNOC director recalls. "it took us four years to get an upstream state corporation. We had no chance of securing industrial support for a fully integrated public corporation."[135]

Significant opposition came from only two quarters. First, the Administrative Management Agency and the Finance Ministry remained adamant that the number of public agencies not increase. Second, JAPEX, which had already begun overseas exploration with additional funding procured after the 1964 budget compromise, was not anxious to share its special privileges with other firms or to surrender its prerogatives to a new public body. But because Imperial Oil was certain to object, JAPEX could not be transformed into the new *kōdan*.[136] MITI overruled the initial objections of JAPEX president Okada and decided to absorb the company into the new *kōdan*. In a compromise reminiscent of the 1955 creation of JAPEX, MITI sweetened the deal with a promise that JAPEX would be divested "as soon as possible."[137]

In February 1967 the new Advisory Committee for Energy (Sōgō Enerugī Chōsakai) confirmed these prior negotiations by proposing a new *kōdan* as a "mother body" (*botai*) for domestic oil exploration firms. The committee reiterated earlier calls for national independence in a hostile international oil market and for effective policy regarding transportation and oil refining.[138] Enabling legislation was introduced in the

Diet within several months (Sekiyu Kaihatsu Kōdan Hōan) and passed in July 1967.

The 100 percent government-owned Japan Petroleum Development Corporation (JPDC), modeled directly upon *banks* rather than foreign national oil companies, began operations in October 1967. It was prohibited from undertaking exploration on its own but was authorized to provide both loan and equity capital to private firms and to guarantee their debts. It also provided auxiliary services related to technology procurement and sharing, machinery leases, exploration subsidies, and other forms of support. This compromise JPDC was a pump-primer, designed to stimulate overseas investments by *private* Japanese exploration and production firms. The new availability of low-risk capital quickly increased the number of firms involved in these ventures.[139] JPDC funds, derived from special oil tariffs, expanded with demand and inflation. A budget of 800 million yen in 1967 had grown to 82 billion yen by 1980.[140] Between 1967 and 1982, seventy-nine separate projects received JPDC/JNOC equity or loans, and seventy of them were overseas. Japan's major industrial groups responded with multifirm consortia to develop overseas oil which they established within months of each other just before the 1973 oil crisis.[141]

On at least three separate occasions MITI undertook to integrate the industry and extend the state's role in the market by expanding the JPDC mandate. In December 1971, for example, the Petroleum Committee of the Advisory Committee for Energy called for pooled risk, joint facilities, and state leadership for vertical integration through the consolidation of domestic firms.[142] The proposal called for state financial assistance to firms that collaborated in the market place and would allow the JPDC to administer foreign oil concessions on its own. Despite its numerous political setbacks, MITI persisted in its goal of nurturing a firm that would act in accordance with national policy. The government was instructed to issue a "vision" of this restructured oil industry.[143]

Nothing came of it. The oil industry, with support from the financial community, continued to define its own structure and its own best interests. Just months before the first oil crisis the Basic Problems Roundtable within MITI's Advisory Committee for Energy (Kihon Mondai Kondankai) tried again. In June 1973 it assailed the fragmentation of the Japanese oil industry. The central problem was Japan's lack of bargaining power in the international oil market and, as so often before, MITI's solution was to strengthen the JPDC and reexamine the role of the state: "The important problem is the nurturing of an oil industry that is able to take actions from a position of strength vis-à-vis the international majors and the producing nations."[144] It was argued, as before, that general trading firms and other private companies lacked the power to bargain effectively, so an integrated, centralized national oil industry guided by the state and following its "vision" should be nurtured. Again there was no support from the industry.

MITI's next unrequited recommendation was issued after the OAPEC embargo had made oil four times more expensive and several orders of magnitude more central to national consciousness. In February 1974 MITI vice-minister Morozumi Yoshihiko announced plans for a new government agency tentatively called the Direct-Deal Crude Import Corporation.[145] The Morozumi Plan proposed a state monopoly to negotiate on a government-to-government basis for crude oil. In July, MITI's Advisory Committee for Energy endorsed the proposal. Arguing that the international oil market had been transformed into a seller's market, it suggested that Japan prepare for an era when the majors would be less important than the producing countries themselves. MITI called for 1) the diversification of petroleum sources; 2) the promotion of government-to-government transactions; 3) the promotion of "direct deals" by establishing a single channel for such transactions; 4) demands for "transparency" (clearer, earlier indications of supply plans) from the international majors; and 5) a renewed call for consolidation and vertical integration of the Japanese oil industry.

The committee seemed to signal a tactical change by MITI. Although its report clearly stated that "where private industry lacks initiative there should be government leadership for structural reorganization,"[146] it was also newly conciliatory:

> At base, the structure of the [oil] industry is a problem that has to be addressed by the firms on their own, and it goes without saying that we are looking forward to voluntary progress toward its reorganization. However, the interests of individual capital are very complex, making it difficult to expect any actual movement (toward restructuring). If this is the case, and in light of the present experience with the oil crisis and rapidly changing international conditions, it is necessary to grapple with these problems by achieving a joint public-private consensus.

But the report also seemed impatient with private recalcitrance. "The people," it argued, "can no longer wait for spontaneous action by the firms to consolidate the industry."[147] MITI's senior bureaucrat, Morozumi, was trying to resurrect public support for a state-owned oil corporation. As a JNOC official later recalled, "his stated preference (*tatemae*) was for the consolidation of the industry with private firms at the core. His actual intention (*honne*) was that the JPDC would become an integrated national oil champion."[148] Unhappily for the proposal, Morozumi left MITI to take up the presidency of the EPDC in June 1975, just as the Advisory Committee began formal debate on upstream consolidation. The committee was split, and lacking industrial support the plan died.

Opposition parties found the energy issue an attractive banner under which to rally antigovernment sentiment. In fact energy was the only area where all of the opposition parties agreed that some form of national ownership was critical.[149] Their preferences varied, however, regarding the extent and nature of state intervention. The Communists called for a comprehensive state oil company (Sōgō Enerugī Kōsha) that would bring together under one roof direct state management of coal, oil, gas, and electric power. The Democratic Socialists stressed national planning rather than ownership but did use the term nationalization (kokuyūka and kōshaka) in favorable reference to the Socialist party program under way in West Germany. The Socialists, whose very first policy program in November 1945 had called for the nationalization of energy industries,[150] wanted an expansion of JPDC powers, including a direct and integrated market presence. Kōmeito echoed the idea.

Still the industry did not budge. Even the chaotic international oil market of the mid-1970s was not enough to make Japanese refiners and distributors seek new structural arrangements. Perhaps the oil shock did not propel firms into merger agreements because MITI had already given them separate opportunities for collusion on prices, allocation, and production. Even before MITI began scrambling in late 1973 to assure supplies of crude, it had helped work out an arrangement with the Petroleum Association for a price cartel and the stabilization of domestic supplies of refined product. At two separate meetings of the association, in October 1972 and April 1973, agreements were made to limit competition by allocating crude among twenty-four firms. Subsequently the twelve largest, accounting for 80 percent of the market, met five times in 1973 to agree to price hikes for various distillates.

These actions brought almost instant disapproval from the Japanese Fair Trade Commission. In February 1974 it rules that the twelve firms had violated the Antitrust Law.[151] The case would have profound implications for the oil industry, and for business-government relations more generally, for the firms based their defense upon a claim that in colluding they were merely following MITI's administrative guidance. In 1980 the Tokyo High Court ruled that the Petroleum Association had been acting on its own; "even if [collusion] was carried out according to the administrative guidance of MITI's responsible officials, it was not done merely to cooperate with administrative guidance."[152] Nine of the firms were convicted of forming a price cartel; all were acquitted of charges of production fixing. MITI guidance was, however, recognized as long as it does not lead to illegal collusion, a decision upheld by the Supreme Court in early 1984. As MITI refused to assist in the defense of the twelve firms at any point in their trials or appeals, relations between MITI and the industry deteriorated considerably.

So did business conditions. Growth in demand dropped sharply. New refinery construction had continued throughout the high growth of the 1960s but was postponed after 1973. The financial stability of the Japanese industry itself was shaken: equity/capital ratios deteriorated sharply. In August 1975 the Advisory Committee for Energy issued a report filled with contradictions, calling alternately for the "modification of the competitive principle" and for "freedom of choice" for industry. It argued for the "strengthening of the public management structure of petroleum" at the same time that Japan "should aim at a nucleus of domestically capitalized private firms."[153] Both the industry and MITI were clearly groping for an answer to market dislocations for a commodity that had come to account for 80 percent of Japan's energy supply.

By the time MITI and the industry had sorted through the alternatives, talk of state management had again disappeared from public documents.[154] MITI henceforth would focus upon state support for the voluntary consolidation of the downstream industry. The overt nurturing of domestic firms was abandoned. MITI's incentives for consolidation (*shū yakuka*) would no longer discriminate against foreign-affiliated firms. As the head of the Agency for Natural Resources and Energy would later remark, "whether it is a white cat or a black cat, a cat that brings oil is a welcome cat."[155] For the first time MITI was betting on market conformity rather than market control. But, as we shall see, efforts to cajole industrial consolidation had no more success than efforts to direct it. When it came to reorganization, the Japanese oil industry continued to march to its own drummer.

MITI's tactical shift was first reflected by the Advisory Committee for Energy in December 1975. The committee acknowledged that the industry had become atomized and that disparities in capability among thirty-one refining firms and thirteen distributors had contributed to excessive competition. It recommended (again) the consolidation of the industry but adjusted its expectations: "business relations and fuel choices of each firm are different, and for these reasons as well as for a variety of other circumstances, it is impossible to expect such a consolidation in the short-term."[156] The revised approach encouraged consolidation into several groups rather than a single unified firm. As a first step MITI would encourage joint stockpiling in accordance with evolving national commitments to the International Energy Agency.

In June 1975 the JPDC had been authorized to engage directly in joint stockpiling with private firms. The oil firms had been unwilling to finance ninety-day stockpiles on their own. The Petroleum Association agreed that stockpiling was a form of insurance for the economy which had high but necessary premiums, but it succeeded in getting the state to bear the bulk of the financial burden. The government agreed to pay two-thirds of the costs of land acquisition. The JPDC was also authorized to provide concessionary loans to joint stockpiling firms, finance up to 90 percent of the total cost of crude oil earmarked for stockpiling, and provide subsidies to local governments that cooperated in tank siting. Once again the state's role had been expanded to placate the private sector.[157]

A second outcome of the committee's December 1975 report is even more revealing of business-government relations and the political economy of structural transformation of the oil industry. Ten billion yen was allocated to the JPDC in the FY 1976 budget for "improving the refined product retailing management structure." For the first time the JPDC had resources to apply downstream. The same allocation has appeared in the budget ever since, but not once has a refining firm accepted any of the money. It is reported that these funds were included because the Petroleum Planning Department within MITI overruled the Petroleum Development Department, and forced the funds upon the upstream officials while keeping the funds away from their control: "JNOC has loaned its body to the cause, but has nothing to do with these funds. . . . The money has never been spent because the firms do not want state control."[158] A Petroleum Association official states the problem more directly: "Ten billion yen is not enough money to overcome the resistance of private firms to cooperate with each other and to submit to the state direction that would inevitably accompany its acceptance."[159]

In June 1978 the JPDC became the Japan National Oil Corporation (JNOC), and the national stockpile program began in earnest. In the mid-1980s stockpiling was JNOC's largest budget item. More than half of its expenditures are related to the financing and construction of facilities for oil stockpiles or to the purchase of stock. The refinery finance program, by contrast, remains unwelcomed and unused.[160]

JNOC is authorized neither to explore for oil nor to produce oil under its own name. Formally it cannot second officers or make personnel decisions. It is limited by law to serving as a financial organ in support of private firms, what one JNOC director called "oyakata hinomaru," a sort of protective government umbrella.[161] Although JNOC has power through its review of annual project plans, most private participants are satisfied that state control has been contained.

The instruments of this containment are suggested by the two ways in which JNOC participates in consortia: it may provide loans, or it may hold equity.[162] Private firms can choose any combination of the two. In some cases equity participation, unadorned by requirements for collateral and fees that accompany loans, may be desirable, but JNOC equity is an unde-sirable constraint to many private investors. Characteristically investors want the state's money but not its control. Of the seven major industrial groups whose consortia accept JNOC support for overseas oil exploration, only one (Mitsui) accepts JNOC equity.[163] The rest have opted to raise their own equity while allowing the state to provide loans and under-write their debts. As one leading energy planner puts it, "The basic principle behind the *kōdan* is simple. 'I'll take the risk with the state behind me. If I win, I'll pay back the state and keep the profits. If I lose, the state takes the losses.'"[164]

One-third of the equity capital of Japanese overseas oil exploration firms comes from JNOC, most of it accepted by firms and consortia that are not affiliated with their own financial institutions.[165] When we com-bine JNOC loans and equity, however, we find that the state finances nearly *two-thirds* of all Japanese-owned overseas exploration. By 1985 petroleum development firms supported by JNOC accounted for over three-quarters of the crude oil imported by Japanese-owned ventures, although this supply still contributed only 11 percent to the total Jap-anese market.[166]

Significantly, however, firms accept equity with the expectation that JNOC will divest its holdings when commercial operations start or when private shareholders demand it.[167] The JNOC legislation does not require divestitute, but uncirculated operating regulations very clearly *do*. These regulations explicitly require JNOC divestiture when stock values rise beyond acquisition prices. Failure to divest can be excused only by dis-agreements over price and value of holdings. Separate, less formal "statements of intent" initialed by JNOC and the principals additionally stipulate that divested shares be offered first to the private partners.[168]

This has raised problems. Although JNOC cannot provide equity for production companies or tender its shares freely, there is no explicit formula for divestiture when exploration becomes exploitation. Accord-ing to one JNOC official, "in most cases we lead our private partners to believe that we will retire our shares after production begins, but in some cases disagreements about share prices have stalled divestiture."[169] What results is a gap between the spirit and the actual implementation of these agreements. The spirit of JNOC participation, in which JNOC retires its equity upon commercialization, has obtained only twice.[170] In six instances JNOC has demanded share prices that its private partners have judged exorbitant. Negotiations have been protracted, giving JNOC a very limited, indirect, and temporary market presence.[171]

Unlike foreign oil exploration firms that organize vertically as parent and subsidiary, Japanese ventures are much more diverse. A separate enterprise is created for each project, resulting in smaller, more limited

Table 5.5. Distribution of upstream equity in the Japanese oil industry, 1983

Sector	Percentage of Total	Billion Yen
JNOC	35.1%	249.6
Private exploration	23.4	166.6
Refining firms	8.2	58.5
Financial institutions (banks, insurance, securities)	8.4	59.6
Trading firms	7.2	50.9
Electric utilities/gas firms	2.1	14.8
Steel	2.0	14.0
Coal, metal mining	2.7	19.5
Shipbuilding, auto, electrical	2.5	18.0
Petrochemical/textiles	1.4	9.9
Foreign governments	1.3	9.2
Other	5.8	40.9
Total	100.1%	710.9

SOURCE: Sekiyu Kōgyō Renmei 1983:160–67.

firms. Whereas most of the majors take upstream profits and tighten downstream belts, the structure of Japanese projects makes this difficult (capital-short Japanese refining firms are not interested in upstream integration). Exploration firms find it difficult to attract capital from refiners. In only six of Japan's more than five dozen oil exploration and development firms do refiners collectively own more than 30 percent of the equity. Moreover, the combined capitalization of these six firms is less than half the capitalization of Japan's single largest firm, the Japan Oil Development Company (which has no refinery capital). Upstream investments by Japanese refiners (8 percent of total upstream Japanese capital) are smaller than what banks or oil-consuming heavy industries provide. JNOC, therefore, even if limited in function and control, has stepped into a significant breach (see Table 5.5). Nonetheless the Japanese petroleum industry is no closer today than it was in the 1930s to the vertical integration that economic planners have consistently sought. In some respects it is further away. Proposals for a vertically integrated, state-owned Japanese major (*wasei mejā*) ended with what might best be called two unintegrated "Japanese minors," the JNOC upstream and Kyōdō Oil downstream.

As JNOC was evolving upstream, MITI continued to promote downstream consolidation. In October 1978 the Petroleum Committee of the Advisory Committee for Energy sought mergers and business tie-ups through mutual assistance among private firms.[172] As with JNOC's untapped fund of 10 billion yen for refinery assistance, nothing happened beyond a further financial deterioration of the industry.

Three years of debate and cajolery accomplished little toward the consolidation of the industry. Finally, in December 1981, MITI came to terms with the market, indicating that it was ready to consider the unthinkable. Citing slower economic growth, persistent excessive competition, and increased alternative energy, the Advisory Committee for Energy recommended that the government "respect the vitality of the private sector and progressively reduce and eliminate administrative intervention."[173] It was a clear turning point in public-sector thinking about the petroleum industry. In May 1983 MITI formally recommended that "in principle the upgrading of secondary facilities should be left to each company's own judgment in the light of their individual financial positions."[174] In this shift lies a "half-negation" of the Petroleum Industry Law, which has been at the heart of administrative and industrial planning for a quarter-century. Explaining it requires a revision of accepted explanations for how the Japanese petroleum market came to be so fragmented.

EXPLAINING FRAGMENTATION

The Japanese petroleum industry is the second most fragmented in the industrial world today. Only in the United States do more production, refining, and distribution firms occupy a significant share of the market (see Table 5.6).

As late as mid-1984 Japan had thirteen major downstream firms in refining, wholesale, and distribution (*motouri gaisha*), only three of which occupied more than 10 percent of the market: Nippon Oil at 17.9 percent, Idemitsu Kōsan at 14.7 percent, and Kyōdō Oil at 13.2 percent.

The most widely accepted explanation for the fragmentation of the Japanese oil industry holds that MITI used its licensing powers under PIL-II to pull profits away from refiners. It did so to give heavy industry the lowest possible factor costs and thereby enhance Japan's international competitiveness. The position is stated best by Yoshi Tsurumi:

> A fragmented oil industry—the result of permitting free entry into both the refining and wholesaling of oil but deliberately keeping refining capacity out of balance with wholesaling capacity in order to impede vertical integration—was expected to compete vigorously and thus to be relatively weak in price bargaining with highly concentrated user industries. Because oil firms were politically too weak to influence planning policy, the deliberate creation of monopsonistic buyers of industrial oil products proved an effective mechanism for guaranteeing strategic growth industries access to cheap energy. A few large industrial buyers, most notably steel and petrochemicals, were able to drive hard bargains by playing one oil firm off against the other.

Table 5.6. Market share of top five oil firms in selected nations, 1980–83

	Refining	Product Sales
Japan	44.5% (1983)	59.6% (1982)
FRG	66.3% (1982)	62.0% (1981)
France	93.8% (1981)	84.3% (1981)
U.K.	74.5% (1981)	70.2% (1980)
United States	35.5% (1982)	30.4% (1981)

SOURCE: Tanaka 1983:21.

As Amelia Porges has added, "By allowing new entry, MITI was also able to weaken oligopoly in the industry . . . and thus weaken private control of oil. . . . This has been MITI's strongest weapon, as it bottlenecks growth in an industry based upon economies of scale."[175]

A different interpretation is possible, indicated, and preferred for several reasons. First, MITI's purportedly unmitigated commitment to cheap fuel is at variance with consistent postwar government policy: raising tariffs on crude to subsidize the coal industry. Crude oil tariffs were raised six times between 1951 and 1977, from zero to 750 yen/kl. Chapter 3 has already documented more than a decade of indeterminant policy before MITI and the coal producers found a compromise on the shift toward petroleum. Taxes on residual oil for industrial use rose almost twice as fast in Japan as in Western Europe between 1970 and 1982.[176] Largely as a result, factor costs to industry in Japan have not been consistently lower than in most other industrial nations (see Table 5.7).[177]

Second, even if fragmentation has served to reduce factor costs to heavy industry and has had its supporters within MITI, it may not be attributable to MITI policy alone. Fragmentation may have been little more than the natural result of competitive market conditions during a period of rapidly expanding demand. Alternatively, other policies might have achieved the same end. Many were indeed considered, but none

Table 5.7. Relative price index of heavy fuel oil for selected nations, 1960–80 (ratio of fuel oil C [heavy fuel oil] price to average retail refined product prices, excluding tax)

Year	Japan	West Germany	France	Italy	U.K.
1960	.75	n.a.	.71	n.a.	.68
1965	.76	n.a.	.77	.61	.73
1970	.73	n.a.	.75	.47	.75
1975	.65	.69	.69	.79	.78
1980	.71	.65	.79	.80	.76

SOURCES: Japan 1960–70, Sekiyu Kōgyō Renmei 1982. Japan 1975–80 and Western Europe, OPEC 1982.

218

proved politically acceptable. In fact the policy record is one of many false starts, of a hesitant groping toward consolidation, especially by the MITI advisory commissions. More planners argued for a vertically integrated oil industry, with restrictions on downstream competition and administered prices, than argued for fragmentation. Equally, integration might have restrained factor costs for heavy industry. It is by no means clear that fragmentation was a necessary or even a sufficient instrument to achieve this end. It is clear, however, that there has never been broad political support for such a program. Indeed, if MITI had sought fragmentation, it would not have needed licensing powers, which are better suited for blocking new market entrants (consolidation) than for splintering them.

Third, MITI was never united to pursue a single program for the petroleum industry. Perhaps the only major agreement was the view that the dominance of foreign majors should somehow be lessened. It is correct, as Caldwell says, that "policy intervention by MITI was clearly oriented as much if not more toward promoting the expansion of the user industries as it was toward strengthening the oil industry."[178] But this divided focus can be explained only by divisions within MITI that users' demands exacerbated. The principle of price over security reflected an alliance between one group of energy planners and energy consumers. As the MITI advisory commission reports clearly indicate, many in the inner circle of state planners preferred more complete controls and more effective security. Parts of MITI's Mining Bureau, in the mid-1960s most notably the Development Section, vigorously promoted vertical integration and the creation of a national oil champion. But the Planning Section and its allies believed it would be dangerous to disrupt relations with the majors, which were supplying abundant, inexpensive crude to Japanese refiners. This group sought to maximize the benefits of a buyers' market. To that end they established guidelines for refinery construction permits which gave priority to joint facilities, to consolidate refining firms whose crude sources were untied.[179]

Such incentives did not entice firms to coalesce because projections promised rapid expansion and great profits. Firms, confident about their prospects in a growth economy, proliferated.[180] Application for refining licenses were routinely approved; according to one former senior MITI planner, "It was politically very difficult for us to give a firm 'no' to applications for permission to build refineries, especially when financing was available for individual firms. We often reduced the scale of firms' plans, but seldom refused to grant permission. The result was fragmentation."[181] The record does not allow us to rule out MITI weakness any more than it allows us to posit MITI strength. Clearly those within MITI promoting downstream fragmentation and price competition had powerful allies in heavy industry and electric power. They also benefited from financial institutions avid to invest in refinery projects.

In sum, there is no a priori reason to credit MITI with fragmenting the industry. The real test for the evaluation of state capacity would be evidence that MITI succeeded either in fragmenting or in consolidating the market in the absence of powerful allies in the private sector and market incentives. In a century of structural change in the Japanese petroleum industry, no such case exists. Instead, we have a history of thwarted and splintered government efforts to overrule rather than to conform to the market place. Although in each case MITI policy has ultimately been market-conforming, it has occasionally (though certainly not always) started as market-distorting. We do better to attribute the structural fragmentation of the Japanese oil industry to preferences articulated by market players and their allies within the state than to the prescience or capacity of state actors alone.

A historic transformation currently under way may fulfill goals long held by those within MITI who seek to consolidate the industry. Although government policy will vigorously abet this transformation, change will not happen according to MITI blueprint. This, too, deserves explanation.

EXPLAINING CONSOLIDATION

After the second oil crisis, price increases for petroleum products led to a sharp decline in domestic demand and an underutilization of Japan's refining facilities.[182] Excess capacity quickly became excessive competition, made more severe by significant reductions in Japan's overall dependence upon petroleum as a primary fuel and feedstock.[183] Oil company profits on sales declined from an already meager 1.45 percent in 1973 (compared to 6 percent for all manufacturing companies) to 0.81 percent in 1982 (compared to 3.9 percent for all manufacturing companies).[184] The equity position of Japanese oil-refining firms deteriorated, moreover, even as Japanese manufacturing firms were beginning to wean themselves away from their traditionally heavy dependence upon debit financing.[185] The current reordering of the Japanese oil industry is an overdue response to deteriorating market conditions and the specter of fratricidal competition.

The refining and primary distribution firms, judging deterioration to be structural and decline of profitability to be permanent, have at long last begun to consolidate. The recombination currently under way will restructure the industry by reducing the number of market participants from thirteen to six. Such an outcome would be consistent with the December 1981 report of MITI's Petroleum Council, which called for precisely that reduction. But MITI is not setting the terms for this reorganization.

The earliest discussions of downstream consolidation were between Shell Oil and Shōwa Oil, rumored for a decade but first disclosed publicly in December 1982.[186] Agreement was delayed, however, by opposition from retail station owners and their lead bank, Daiichi Kangyō.[187] In the meantime the first significant step toward consolidation came from a different quarter: in October 1983 Daikyō Oil and Maruzen Oil publicly announced concrete plans to merge. Both were in deep financial trouble. Two years earlier MITI had tried to persuade Nippon Oil to acquire Maruzen, but the market leader reportedly "turned a deaf ear and refused."[188] Instead, as MITI monitored the Shell/Shōwa negotiations, Daikyō and Maruzen, under the guidance of their lead banks, the Industrial Bank of Japan (IBJ) and Sanwa, reached a separate accommodation. From MITI's perspective, it was an imperfect union.

Ikuta Toyoaki, chairman of MITI's Petroleum Council, was publicly miffed because the agreement held no promise for downstream consolidation. Responding to the announcement, he stated that it "has no meaning unless it is extended to retail sales. The intentions of these firms in that regard is unclear. In fact, I worry that this will lead to an increase in refinery competition for market share. It is necessary to secure the consent of the Petroleum Council for such a merger of refining firms, but there were no prior consultantions. This was done without the slightest notice."[189] MITI hopes, nonetheless, that this merger (creating Cosmo Oil) will ultimately incorporate Kyōdō Oil as well. The IBJ, lead bank of Cosmo, is also lead bank of Nippon Mining, which holds nearly half the equity of Kyōdō. In October 1986 Kyōdō announced its intention to merge with Cosmo.[190]

The announcement of the Daikyō/Maruzen merger activated negotiations to secure a competitive position in the restructured market place. In December 1983 Nippon Oil (the number one firm) and Mitsubishi Oil (number five) announced their intetion to tie up from crude transport to sales.[191] The next month General Oil and Esso Standard announced a similar intention, and Mobil Oil and Kygnus followed suit in February. Only Idemitsu Kōsan, historically a lone wolf, is expected to seek no accommodation with former competitors. In February 1984 MITI's Petroleum Committee formally confirmed these moves, announcing that it would recommend new incentives for consolidation through priorities for license applications and special Development Bank financing.[192] MITI began to promote sales agreements (*hanbai kyōtei*) instead of mergers. It was merely accelerating a process already well under way.

The large banks and their client refineries had seized the initiative for two reasons. First, the banks had to protect themselves against bankruptcies by the weakest firms, in which they have very vulnerable financial and equity positions. Japanese banks are shareholders (up to 5 percent) as well as lenders; the prospect of bankruptcy therefore forces particularly difficult choices upon them.[193] Second, the profitability of oil (particularly for banks) had dropped. Despite earlier MITI exhortations to consolidate, there was a substantial lag between the two oil crises and active moves toward industrial reconstructing. This lag was related to the way in which the increase of crude prices after the first two crises and the yen-dollar float after 1971 produced record oil-related profits for the banks. Not even during the period of rapid demand growth had the banks made so much money financing oil purchases and refinery expansion. Their profits were linked directly to usance fees from the sharp rise in refineries' short-term financing needs and from inflated currency transactions necessary for yen-earning firms to acquire dollar-denominated petroleum. In addition they were asked to finance new, expensive, and legally required desulphurization and stockpile facilities—the latter often with state debt guarantees.

For a time, then, even as the financial condition of the industry deteriorated and borrowing became the only reliable source of capital for the refiners, the oil-related profits of the banks increased. The more firms there were in business, the more foreign exchange transactions, short-term loans, and facilities needed to be financed. As long as even moderate growth could be projected and the regulatory structure (PIL-II) remained intact, the banks, each with their own refining firms, had incentive to block industry consolidation.

Figure 5.2 suggests the strong relationship between oil price increases and bank profitability that obtained after each of the first two oil crises.[194] Subsequent reductions in crude oil volumes and f.o.b. prices, combined with declining exchange commissions and interest rate margins, have been reinforced by the increasing tendency of the stronger firms to switch dollars for yen. These firms have increased yen-funded transactions to reduce exchange risks and to take advantage of yen-denominated interest rates. All this suggests an explanation for the timing of the current industrial restructuring which is independent of oil crises and national security issues alone.

Senior MITI energy planners and oil industry officials unanimously confide that the most significant obstacle to reorganization was the banks. Typical is a senior member of MITI's Advisory Committee on Energy: "We said 'Do it, do it' many times, but the main banks wouldn't budge. They shilly-shallied around instead . . . collecting usance fees."[195] The oil industry lends support to a more general finding: MITI has never been able to assume the control it has occasionally sought over allocative decisions by banks.[196]

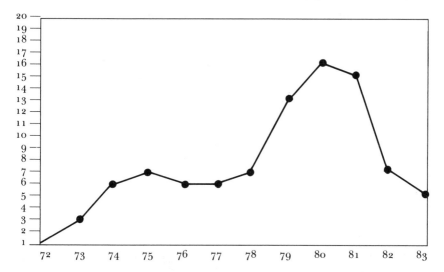

Figure 5.2. Estimated banks' oil-related profits, 1972–83 (top nine firms)

SOURCE: Industrial Bank of Japan. See note 194.

Index (1972=1)

For these several reasons, financial institutions and firms were finally ready to stimulate reorganization. Attention then turned toward PIL-II, which had served to sustain the fragmentation of the petroleum industry long beyond its market rationality. By carefully balancing and coordinating market players, PIL-II had helped calcify a fragmented industrial structure, especially under conditions of low growth. The same fragmentation that may have reduced factor costs during high growth became excessive capacity during low or no growth. With MITI as a gatekeeper, PIL-II contributed to structural depression for Japanese oil refiners. It distorted production planning, for refiners often preferred (rationally) to run at less than capacity, and even to incur losses, rather than to scrap facilities and thereby surrender their allocated market shares. The most profitable oil firms often prefer smaller, weaker firms to be propped up, because the provisions of PIL-II raise prices for *all* firms. These disincentives are widely recognized, even by some architects of PIL-II who now advocate its dismantling. In August 1982 the influential Administrative Reform Commission (Rinchō) formally proposed that PIL-II be relaxed.[197]

No sooner had MITI begun musing openly about PIL-II than major shifts in world oil markets sent energy planners back to their drawing boards. New intervention has been crafted to stabilize markets and to satisfy the refineries and banks, in response to two developments that unfolded in 1985.

The first is related to import pressure from Middle Eastern "export refineries." By the mid-1980s the oil-producing nations had completed a move downstream to add some 25–50 million tons/year of refined products to world markets. The industrial consumers, in the International Energy Agency (IEA), sought to share the new product without sacrificing refining capacity unevenly across member states. In late 1984 the IEA pressured Japan to reverse its policy of refining at the doorstep of the consumer. European and American refining firms would not accept the brunt of OPEC export competition. But Japanese refineries a decade earlier had surrendered much of the market for naphtha to imports when Japanese electric utilities and petrochemical firms banded together to force a relaxation in MITI policy. Lighter products such as kerosene and gasoline were their last profitable business, for they were the last products protected by MITI policy. Japanese refineries, given their precarious financial state, were reluctant to compromise further.

The second was the political *cause célèbre* of Lion's Oil and its president, Satō Taiji, who saw opportunity in this glutted market for refined product. Satō, who owns several independent retail stations in Kanagawa Prefecture, decided to test MITI policy. Formally, after all, the Japanese market was open: there were no legal restrictions, no quotas, and no prohibitive tariffs to prevent importation of petroleum product. Yet although Japanese gasoline prices remained well above world levels, imports were zero. Clearly the Japanese market was not, in fact, open. When Satō attempted to deliver a leased tanker of Singaporean gasoline for resale at his service stations (after first properly notifying MITI of his cargo), MITI intervened with administrative guidance to cut off his financing. Refining firms, including foreign ones now nestled comfortably within the existing regulatory structure, and overextended banks heaved a collective sigh of relief.

They also sat down with MITI to work out a more permanent solution to the specter of free trade in petroleum products. In January 1986 the Temporary Measures Law for Specified Petroleum Product Imports became effective.[198] Answering IEA demands for open markets and refiners' demands that the opening be painless, the new legislation stipulated that petroleum imports would be "liberalized," but only licensed firms would be permitted to engage in this business. Not surprisingly, only the refining firms would receive licenses. As in 1962, a state jurisdiction was constructed to ameliorate the worst effects of liberalization.

The Scylla of cheap foreign competition and the Charybdis of maverick importers were navigated successfully by putting MITI at the wheel. But the *Oil Industry Maru* is a leaky craft that floats only at the sufferance of consumers who profess outrage but remain unorganized. The suddenly strong yen of 1986 helped ameliorate consumer discomfort, for prices declined precipitously. In fact the electric utilities reaped windfall profits; they gave industrial customers a $6.2 billion dollar rebate.[199] The future of PIL-II and related MITI jurisdictions in the oil market are subject to permanent negotiation. Indeed the very structure of that market is itself undergoing profound change. The evidence is clear: this change is paced more by market players than by economic bureaucrats.

CONCLUSIONS

The history of structural transformation in the Japanese oil industry is a record of continuity no less striking than in the coal and electric power cases. The activist Japanese state has failed at nearly every juncture—in peace and war, as early as 1902 and as recently as 1984—to entice the private sector to consolidate on its terms and under its control. Economic bureaucrats (and in the prewar period, military planners) repeatedly aimed for a vertically integrated, nationally unified petroleum industry. What emerged instead was horizontally fragmented and vertically truncated. Of this, Inokuchi Tōsuke has observed that state power and mobilization merely accelerated a process already under way in prewar and wartime Japan:

> The goal of consolidating the refining firms was inherent in the creation of the oil control companies, but owing to the diverse positions and interests of each of the firms, it could not be achieved. . . . The consolidation and concentration of the Japanese oil industry followed a capitalist route of development. Compared to the consolidation of the production and sales sectors, the separation of the refining sector into eight blocs was . . . not a reflection of the weakness of capital in that sector, but evidence of the ferocity with which private capital competed internally.[200]

But we need not assume inexorability to appreciate this politics of reciprocal consent. Disputes over the nature and extent of state intervention in the oil business usually ensured conformity to the market; but for the structurally diverse oil industry the question remains, To whose market did state policy conform? In the prewar period it was the market of the large oil firms, most of which grew even larger with state encouragement. Upstream private firms welcomed state action. These entrepreneurs, growing impatient with the government's limited commitment to a national fuels policy and increased drilling subsidies, lobbied earliest and most vigorously for a public policy company. The result was

225

a government policy not merely market-conforming and risk-reducing but market-guaranteeing and risk-eliminating. In refining, however, military planners could not make private capital accept unification of the industry. The state had to settle for much less than it sought, and ultimately it had to cope with much more than it bargained for.

But a market also belonged to rural interests, and it too had to be respected and preserved. Agricultural interests displayed considerable tenacity when their commercial rights were threatened in 1939 and again in 1954. These interests, by no means those of big capital, were nonetheless successful. Competitive fragmented markets clearly limited state intervention.

Above all else was the military market for petroleum. The relative unimportance of oil for the civilian economy distinguishes the wartime politics of oil from those of electric power and coal. The navy held three-quarters of Japan's total refined inventories when the Pacific War started, and by 1942 military refineries were producing nearly half of the nation's petroleum products. The state may have failed to centralize and consolidate Japanese oil, but its officers (military and civilian) intervened in every phase of the industry. There is little evidence of the corresponding intervention from banks, heavy industry, and national commercial federations which redirected state planning in coal and electric power until after the war.

Once petroleum became important to heavy industry and financial institutions, negotiations over state intervention became more complex. Oil became only one of several key players, and infiltration of the industry by foreigners helped ensure that oil would not always be the most important. Nonetheless, consolidation would continue to elude the Japanese state. The objects of state efforts, which often involved collaboration with parts of private industry, were domestically capitalized oil firms. But for all the nationalistic posturing by MITI in the 1960s and 1970s, and despite PIL-II, the domestic firms' share of the nation's refining capacity increased by only 5 percent between 1965 and 1982 and actually *declined* after 1975.[201] MITI ultimately learned that its postwar welcome in the market place was not much changed from its prewar welcome. Government proposals to restructure the industry were successively diluted; plans for a state-owned Japanese major became in practice two separate, barely viable Japanese minors. Banks replaced oil firms as the main obstacle to market restructuring.

In oil, as in electric power and coal, public policy was both ubiquitous and central in the transformation of the industry. As a result some have observed, in the words of Porges, that "government intervention has been more pervasive in the oil industry than in any other."[202] If so, then the political struggles over state intervention in the Japanese oil industry confirm the important difference between jurisdiction and control, between state support and state leadership, and between market conformity and market displacement. Although MITI's intervention in the oil market has been pervasive, it has been constrained consistently by bureaucratic politics, market fragmentation, and the vulnerability of the Japanese economy to external economic crises. The record of state efforts to restructure a fragmented industry, both up- and downstream, in oil as in coal and electric power, is punctuated by blunted initiatives, compromised ambitions, and outright failures that owe as much to conflict within the state itself as to conflict between business and state.

CHAPTER SIX

A Political History of
Alternative Energy in Japan

Two international oil crises in the 1970s clearly illuminated the contours of Japan's widely familiar energy dilemma. The Japanese economy had come to account for 10 percent of global production but was precariously dependent upon imported energy, mostly oil from the Gulf states. Industry consumed more than half of Japan's primary energy (compared to only one-quarter in Britain and one-third in the United States), accentuating the danger of Japan's foreign petroleum dependence. Nowhere are there greater incentives to develop alternative energy.

What are Japan's alternatives? The response depends on answers to two corollary questions long central to Japanese business and the state: Alternatives *to* what? Alternatives *for* what? Each generates separate energy choices for Japan. The former invokes petroleum and Japan's energy dilemma; the latter invokes commercial possibilities and Japan's energy opportunity.

With petroleum as the referent, analysts focus upon Japan's need to diversify both by geographic origin (supplier) and by energy source (supply). The problem shaped Japan's militarist ambitions just as it shaped responses to crises fifty years later. In the 1930s as in the 1980s *supplier* policies included accommodations with the majors, direct deals with producer countries, and acquisition of foreign oil fields. *Supply* policies in this same half century have included exploitation of nonoil energy resources, development of new energy technologies, and conservation.

Broader, more fundamental strategic goals are also involved, especially in a postwar Japan whose energy pregnability is matched by its military impotence. The American alliance has abetted policy planners in their benign neglect of military security. Japanese "comprehensive

228

security" makes energy and industrial policy central to discussions of national security. Thus when one considers alternatives to petroleum, the issue involves not only energy supply but also additional *commercial* alternatives. The challenge for Japanese government and industry is obvious: to ameliorate vulnerabilities in energy supply by developing commercially viable energy technologies that might also enhance Japan's international competitiveness.

The significance of this commercial component in national energy strategies is not unique to Japan, but the emphasis in Japan is important. It is entirely consistent with the shift toward information and technology, and away from raw materials, as the key factor in Japanese industrial development. It is a corrective to popular conceptions of Japan as a "fragile blossom," conceptions that emphasize only vulnerability. Energy security, narrowly defined, may be the "push" for an active search for alternative energies, but national security, broadly constituted and inclusive of commercial considerations, acts as the "pull." The development of alternative fuels therefore looms large in Japan's energy future as it has in Japan's energy past. In the history of alternative energy markets in Japan, as this chapter shows, conflicts between businessmen and economic bureaucrats have limited the nature and extent of state intervention despite many incentives for "strong" state leadership.

SYNTHETIC FUELS

The first evidence that Japan was concerned about its need for alternative sources of liquid fuel came soon after domestic oil production peaked in 1915. The Imperial Navy, following the British lead, converted the fleet to oil boilers and began research on coal liquefaction in 1919. In 1921 the South Manchurian Railway Company (Mantetsu) joined a navy project to develop oil shale. By 1926 the navy had taken the lead, establishing the basic program for petroleum outlined in Chapter 5, but in addition to that program the government hoped to develop synthetic fuels and other alternatives. The latter effort was expanded in 1928, when the navy and the Mantetsu built a pilot synfuels plant.

After the outbreak of hostilities in China in 1937, petroleum supply became more uncertain. Inspired by apparent German successes and ignoring the failures of the navy/Mantetsu synfuel projects, the government promulgated the Synthetic Fuels Industry Law in August 1937.[1] The law authorized Japan's first public energy corporation since state-owned mines had been privatized in the 1880s. The Imperial Fuels Industries Corporation (Teikoku Nenryō Kōgyō K. K.) was formally established the following January. The Ministry of Commerce and Industry (MCI) secured the cooperation of private investors in the normal Japanese way, by guaranteeing dividends and exempting profits from taxation—no minor incentives in an uneconomical project. The Finance Ministry purchased 50 percent of the initial 400 million yen of equity; the next ten shareholders, half of which were Mitsui or Mitsubishi affiliates, together purchased less than 25 percent of initial shares. The MCI set targets of more than 40 million barrels for 1943, but less than 10 percent of that amount was produced in the seven years of operation.[2] The wartime synfuels effort was a critical failure. No effort was made to reconstruct the industry for postwar commerce. Instead, SCAP converted the plants to produce ammonium sulphate fertilizer.

Alternative liquid fuels were irrelevant to an economy that had domestic coal and access to unlimited cheap petroleum—conditions that obtained for most of the 1950s and 1960s. Japan had virtually no alternative energy program until the first oil crisis (with the exception of nuclear power, discussed below). In 1973 MITI established the Agency for Natural Resources and Energy (ANRE) in an effort to coordinate energy policy planning.[3] Within a year ANRE and the MITI Agency for Industrial Science and Technology (AIST) established the Sunshine Project to support research in non-nuclear technologies for energy supply. In 1975 the Japan Petroleum Development Corporation was authorized to engage in oil shale and oil sands projects, and in 1978 ANRE and AIST created the companion Moonlight Project to focus on conservation technologies. Before the 1973 oil embargo the total MITI budget for alternative energy R&D had been 400 million yen. A decade later it was more than 100 billion yen, three orders of magnitude greater.

But it was not until the Iranian revolution and the second oil crisis that the nation significantly expanded its efforts in new energy technologies. Government and industry organizationally redefined and technologically reoriented their efforts. An unprecedented 2.9 trillion yen over the next decade was allocated to achieving energy security. Central to this rearrangement was the Alternative Energy Law of 1980; central to the law was a debate over state intervention which was resolved in favor of private industry.

MITI bureaucrats proposed an early form of this legislation in the first draft of their "1980s Vision" in autumn 1978. During the Iranian revolution and after the nuclear reactor accident at Three Mile Island in early 1979, senior representatives from the MITI Ministerial Secretariat, AIST, and ANRE met to discuss the development of new energy technologies. They agreed to promote a state-owned *kōdan* (public corporation) for alternative energy over which MITI would enjoy full supervisory control. MITI officials worked on proposals throughout the summer but withheld formal announcement until after the general election in October and Prime Minister Ōhira Masayoshi's pledge that energy policy would receive his government's highest priority. Actually Prime Minister Ōhira gave his new cabinet four policy priorities, the first two of which, energy policy and financial reconstruction, were incompatible. The former demanded substantial increases in government spending in the search for alternative energy technologies; the latter demanded restraint and austerity. The two priorities defined opposing constituencies in the debate over Japanese energy policy in 1979 and 1980.

MITI proceeded in the hope that the energy priority would prevail. In late November it announced a four-part program that would have significantly enhanced MITI's power in energy policy making (see Figure 6.1). The first pillar of the program was the Alternative Energy Introduction and Promotion Special Measures Law, which would allow the MITI minister to establish legally binding targets for private industry in the conversion from oil to alternative energy. The law would authorize MITI to issue nationwide energy targets and develop incentive policies for industry and consumers to meet them. Industries would be required to report all plans involving energy use in excess of these targets, and the MITI minister would provide guidance for energy conversion.[4] The second and third pillars both addressed finance. MITI proposed to establish new special accounts earmarked for alternative energy R&D and funded by new taxes on petroleum and electricity consumption. The fourth pillar of the program entailed the creation of an alternative energy public corporation, the proposed MITI-supervised *kōdan* mentioned above. None of these four proposals survived intact.

The first public opposition to the MITI proposal was voiced by Keidanren chairman Dokō Toshio, who also headed Japan's fiscal reorganization, the Administration Reform Council (Rinchō). In a speech to senior Keidanren leaders Dokō tied the energy issue to fiscal reform: "I have doubts about the idea of an Alternative Energy Public Corporation. While we do have to make energy policy a priority in the 1980 budget, the creation of a new tax structure would present many problems. We need first to reconsider the existing energy tax system."[5] The Administrative Management Agency (AMA), the bureaucratic organ responsible for administrative reform, concurred. On November 17, AMA officials announced their opposition to an additional public corporation at a time of fiscal retrenchment. Moreover, they took the offensive, proposing to eliminate the Coal Mine Damage Corporation, the Rationalization of Coal Industry Corporation, and the Electric Power Development Corporation, the three existing energy-related public corporations that MITI supervised.

The Ministry of Finance soon joined in what was becoming a chorus of

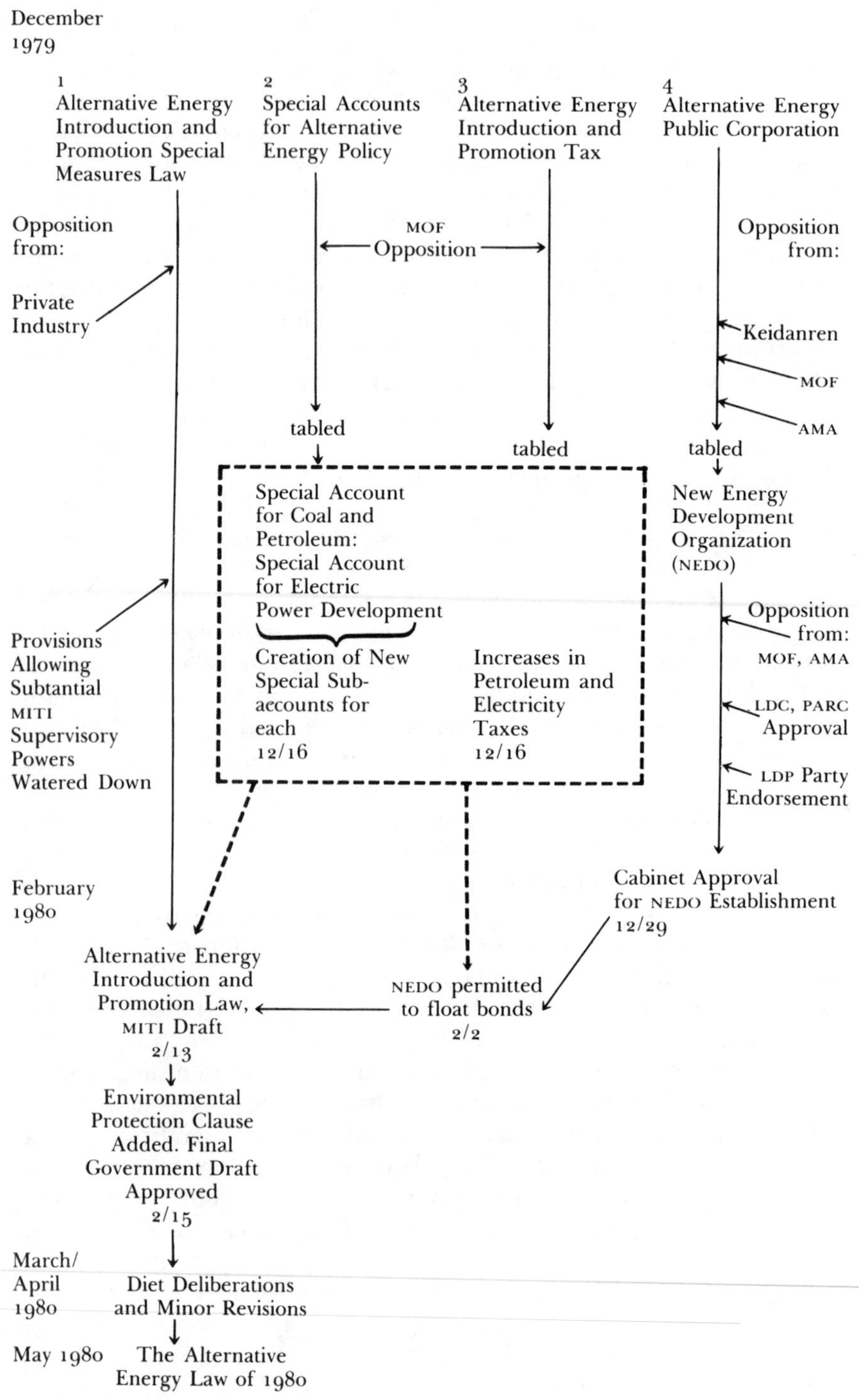

December
1979

1
Alternative Energy
Introduction and
Promotion Special
Measures Law

2
Special Accounts
for Alternative
Energy Policy

3
Alternative Energy
Introduction and
Promotion Tax

4
Alternative Energy
Public Corporation

Opposition
from:

MOF
←——— Opposition ———→

Opposition
from:

Private
Industry

←Keidanren

←———MOF

←AMA

tabled

tabled

tabled

Special Account
for Coal and
Petroleum:
Special Account
for Electric
Power Development

New Energy
Development
Organization
(NEDO)

Provisions
Allowing
Subtantial
MITI
Supervisory
Powers
Watered Down

Creation of New
Special Sub-
accounts for
each
12/16

Increases in
Petroleum and
Electricity
Taxes
12/16

Opposition
from:
MOF, AMA

←LDC, PARC
Approval

← LDP Party
Endorsement

February
1980

Cabinet Approval
for NEDO Establishment
12/29

Alternative Energy
Introduction and
Promotion Law,
MITI Draft
2/13

NEDO permitted
←——— to float bonds
2/2

Environmental
Protection Clause
Added. Final
Government Draft
Approved
2/15

March/
April
1980

Diet Deliberations
and Minor Revisions

May 1980

The Alternative
Energy Law of 1980

Figure 6.1. The Alternative Energy Law of 1980: MITI's Four-Point Program

opposition. Finance, like the AMA, opposed any increase in government bureaucracy.[6] It refused to incorporate the MITI plan into the budget proposal it submitted later in December. Keidanren opposition, however, was rather different in kind. AMA and Finance wanted reductions in the bureaucracy for the sake of the public sector; Keidanren also guarded against encroachment upon the private sector. On November 27 both Dokō and Inayama Yoshihiro, his successor as Keidanren chairman, met with Prime Minister Ōhira. For Keidanren they insisted that alternative energy development was a matter for the private sector, and they rejected the idea of a new public corporation. Prime Minister Ōhira reportedly understood: "Mr. Sasaki [Sasaki Yoshitake, then MITI minister] has explained his proposal for a new Alternative Energy Public Corporation, but I have to question the wisdom of establishing a new public corporation at a time when we are also trying to reorganize existing ones."[7]

Yet all parties seemed to agree about the need for reform of the energy tax system. After all, of the 3 trillion yen generated in FY 1979 from energy-related taxes, over three-quarters went to the maintenance of roadways and only 13 percent to energy R&D.[8] On December 16, less than one week before submission of the final draft budget, representatives of MITI and the Finance Ministry met to negotiate. In compromise MITI abandoned its proposal for new taxes and new special accounts but received additional revenues from existing taxes. In addition, Finance consented to establish four new special subaccounts for R&D.

As financial compromises were being struck between MITI and Finance, the leadership of the LDP was proposing a means to satisfy Keidanren. Top party officials met on December 13 to discuss a hybrid public/private enterprise. Apparently under pressure from the LDP, Sasaki revealed on the twentieth that MITI was abandoning its plans in favor of the "third sector" New Energy Development Organization (NEDO).[9] To placate private-sector opposition, he announced that the new organization would be administered by a policy committee of distinguished leaders from industry, government, and the academic world. To placate AMA and the Finance Ministry, he announced that NEDO would absorb one of MITI's energy public corporations, the Rationalization of Coal Industry Corporation, thereby streamlining the MITI bureaucracy.

As if to confirm the arrangement between business and state, MITI announced in July 1980 that NEDO's board of directors would be chaired by Dokō Toshio. Likewise, Watamori Tsutomu, the vice-president for heavy industries at Hitachi, was made NEDO president. Toshiba, Dokō's former firm, and Hitachi are Japan's leading vendors of nuclear plants. Both Dokō and Watamori ware among Japan's most respected advocates of nuclear power, the only alternative to petroleum *excluded* from the NEDO charter. These appointments do more than simply confirm Keidanren's ability to frustrate MITI control of synfuels and other new energy technologies. NEDO also represents significant check on MITI interference with the nuclear power industry.

NUCLEAR POWER

MITI *Ambitions and Private Priorities*

Nowhere have MITI ambitions been frustrated more thoroughly than in nuclear power. Unlike other alternative energies nuclear power was big business in Japan long before the oil crises of the 1970s. In 1966 Japan commissioned its first nuclear reactor, and by 1973 Japan had already "indigenized" most of the foreign nuclear technologies it had originally licensed. By 1987 more than one quarter of Japan's electric power was generated in atomic plants built almost entirely by Japanese firms. Japan has the fourth-largest nuclear power program in the world, with 25 gw of installed capacity distributed among thirty-five privately owned and operated commercial power plants. Its nuclear power industry is as technologically diverse and independent of government control as any in the world. Plant vendors and electric utilities have separated state aid from state control to a significant degree. Total government funding for nuclear power development, a mere 250 million yen in 1954 when it first appeared in the General Account Budget, reached 1.6 trillion yen in 1982.[10] How has private industry managed so consistently to have the state socialize the risks of nuclear development?

The earliest public champion of nuclear power in Japan was Nakasone Yasuhiro. In January 1951, as a young but already ambitious Dietman, he petitioned John Foster Dulles to permit Japan to begin developing a nuclear industry.[11] There were others not far behind the future prime minister. In October 1952 Kosaka Junzō, having lost his battle for a national electric utility (see Chapter 4), created the Electric Power Economics Research Institute (Denryoku Keizai Kenkyūjo) with assistance from former ministers of state, private business leaders, and leading scientists.[12] This institute would be instrumental in promoting nuclear power when President Eisenhower's Atoms for Peace initiative touched off a full-scale nuclear fever in Japan. Kosaka's institute, created initially to counter Matsunaga's Central Electric Power Research Institute, was soon joined by private utilities and equipment manufacturers.

In January 1953 the Japan Science Council (Nihon Gakujutsu Kaigi), representing the academic community, created its first special committee on nuclear power. Social scientists strongly opposed nuclear power, physicists were anxious to return to their wartime research; but natural scientists and engineers came to dominate the council. They took a cautious position, urging extensive R&D before commercialization. In fact the caution of the academic community would obstruct rapid exploitation of nuclear power by the private sector.[13]

But even before these groups had a chance to coalesce, Nakasone and Keidanren president Ishikawa Ichirō forced the pace. In January 1954 Ishikawa visited the United States for laboratory tours and briefings, and he returned an advocate of Atoms for Peace. Three months later Nakasone secured suprapartisan support for a supplemental 300 million yen science and technology budget, three-quarters of it earmarked for nuclear power. This first "atomic power budget" passed the Lower House after only perfunctory debate, and when the House of Councillors failed to act in thirty days, it became law. Only afterward did the bureaucrats begin to consider how to spend the money. For its part, the scientific community was offended by the lack of consultation surrounding Diet action. Their reservations seemed all the more compelling when, just days after the budget was approved, a Japanese tuna-fishing boat was showered with radioactivity during an American nuclear bomb blast on Bikini Atoll. The budget may have passed, but the storm over nuclear power was just beginning to gather.

Within a month the Science Council presented formal objections to Diet. By autumn the council had formally adopted Three Nuclear Principles, affirming that nuclear power R&D should be open, democratically managed, and independent of foreign control.[14] These items, however, were not of primary concern to industrialists and allied conservative politicians, who refused to relinquish the initiative. Less than a month after the nuclear budget passed, Shōriki Matsutarō, president of *Yomiuri Shimbun*, launched his own Committee for the Peaceful Use of Atomic Power (Genshiryoku Heiwa Riyō Kondankai), led by Keidanren chairman Ishikawa and Matsunaga Yasuzaemon.[15] Ishikawa lobbied actively for the Japanese government to sign the accord on the peaceful use of atomic power offered by the United States. That agreement was signed in June: the United States would supply nuclear fuel for an experimental reactor and the government would establish an agency for atomic energy research. The bureaucracy bickered over jurisdiction, so Ishikawa took matters into his own hands. Before the end of August he had secured the agreement of private-sector leaders to contribute 20 million yen toward the establishment of a nonprofit atomic energy research institute (Nihon Genshiryoku Kenkyūjo, JAERI). The nine utilities together assumed half of this institute's initial expenses. When JAERI began operations in November to receive enriched uranium from the United

States, it was, some observers argued, very much "under the leadership of the business community."[16] Its chairman was Ishikawa himself.

Within a year the Kosaka group and the Shōriki group reached a modus vivendi and joined with others as the Japan Atomic Industrial Forum (JAIF), an association of several hundred vendors, suppliers, and industrial consumers of nuclear power.[17] In its early years the JAIF spent more than 100 million yen annually to publicize and promote nuclear power.[18] Over the next decade the JAIF, more than any other group, public or private, set the shape, pace, and direction of nuclear power development in Japan. Its principal conflicts would be with academics and with MITI.[19]

While private industry was sorting itself out, Nakasone took responsibility for organizing government jurisdiction. In August 1955 he was one of Japan's four participants in the first International Conference on Peaceful Uses of Atomic Power, held in Geneva. He returned to form a suprapartisan group of Dietmen to promote nuclear power. With Miki Bukichi he also played a key role in molding the third Hatoyama Cabinet (formed in November), which on the atomic power issue moved forcefully and in the direction Keidanren wanted. Shōriki was made minister of state in charge of atomic energy, and two members of the Dietmen's group became parliamentary vice-ministers at the Economic Planning Agency and the Administrative Management Agency.

Nakasone's group was well ahead of the bureaucracy. The Economic Planning Agency had finally issued the first government plan for atomic power development in September; within a month both the Ministry of Education and MITI issued their own independent programs.[20] Concerned that bureaucratic resolution might locate authority somewhere undesirable, particularly within MITI, Nakasone and his allies introduced legislation to create the Science and Technology Agency (STA) and two nuclear power–related public corporations under its jurisdiction in January 1956.

Earlier that same month, on New Year's Day 1956, the Japanese Atomic Energy Commission (JAEC) was, like the STA, formally established within the Prime Minister's Office. This affiliation was significant, for Ishikawa and Shōriki, two of the first five commissioners, had successfully guided formal jurisdiction for nuclear power R&D away from MITI.[21] JAEC chairman Shōriki wasted no time. On January 5, without consulting his fellow commissioners, he publicly proclaimed that Japan would build and operate a reactor within five years. The only way that could be accomplished was through the importation of reactor technology. The academics, especially Yukawa who already held misgivings about the JAEC, were stunned. Yukawa's first words as commissioner reportedly were, "If this is the way it is going to be, I quit."[22] It was announced that he was leaving for reasons of health.

This controversy did not slow the private sector. Industrial leaders understood that basic research was going to be both necessary and costly, so their first order of business was to reconstitute JAERI to maximize public funding and minimize public control. At a meeting in February, Shōriki and Ishikawa opposed the establishment of JAERI as a "government-owned, government-operated" research institute, preferring a "special legal entity." Ishikawa insisted upon this latter designation, more "convenient" for private industry, over the objections of the Ministry of Finance, which preferred JAERI as a national research laboratory over which it could have direct budgetary control.[23] Sentiment in Diet also supported the reconstitution of JAERI as a fully public corporation (*kōsha*). Ishikawa and other Keidanren leaders, with the support of the Economic Planning Agency, preferred a "special legal entity" for three reasons. First, the form provided access to state funds while preserving managerial flexibility for the laboratory managers. Second, with the waiver of civil service requirements, top researchers could be recruited with private-sector salary levels. Finally, budgets would be relatively unconstrained by Diet or Finance Ministry deliberations.[24]

The formula paid off handsomely. Private industry rushed headlong to commercialize foreign reactor technology. With a minimal capital investment of 250 million yen, it helped control a national research institute, 92 percent of whose budget in the ensuing decade came from the public treasury. The "new" JAERI formally began operations in June 1956, attached to the prime minister's new Science and Technology Agency. By design, MITI initiative and MITI control were still conspicuously absent.

Additional legislation created the Nuclear Fuels Public Corporation (Genshi Genshiryoku Nenryō Kōsha, NFPC) at the same time. Unlike JAERI, this was a 100 percent state-owned entity charged with development and secure supply of nuclear fuel. Despite assurances from the United States and Britain, there was considerable concern in Japan about the stability of overseas uranium supplies. It was judged best, because of international controls and low absolute levels of demand, to let the state take responsibility for uranium prospecting, mining, and refining. The JAEC under Shōriki proposed the *kōsha* formula. MITI proposed to license and manage the effort but was rebuffed. The final compromise was a *kōsha* not subject to public enterprise labor-management laws and Diet budgetary resolutions. To make things even more comfortable for Shōriki and Ishikawa, the first NFPC director-general, Takahashi Saisaburō, was a mining engineer from Mitsubishi Mining. Hara Tamashige, his first vice-director, was likewise a private-sector leader.[25]

By that same month, June 1956, five major industrial groups had consolidated to compete for the technology and capital that would make

Table 6.1. Japan's five nuclear power industrial groups

Group	Date	Reactor type[a]	Foreign affiliation	Number of firms
Mitsubishi	10/55	PWR	Westinghouse (U.S.)	27
Hitachi	3/56	BWR	General Electric (U.S.)	24
Sumitomo	4/56	PWR/BWR	United Nuclear (U.S.)	37
Mitsui (Toshiba)	6/56	BWR	General Electric (U.S.)	41
Daiichi (Fuyō)	6/56	GCR/AGR	Nuclear Power Group (U.K.)	25

[a]PWR = pressurized water reactor; BWR = boiling water reactor; GCR = gas-cooled reactor; AGR = advanced gas reactor.

nuclear development possible. Each was centered on a major manufacturer of electrical machinery with origins in the prewar *zaibatsu*. Each tied itself to a foreign source of nuclear technology (see Table 6.1).

Although Westinghouse and General Electric had an early advantage from prewar ties to the major Japanese vendors and utilities, Shōriki and Ishikawa were impressed with the British Calder Hall reactor.[26] Four days after the JAIF was formally established, Shōriki's newspaper company initiated a series of visits to Japan by Britain's leading nuclear power officials, including cabinet minister Geoffrey Lloyd and Christopher Hinton, chairman of Britain's state-owned nuclear power corporation. The British promised extraordinarily cheap (2.5 yen/kwh) electric power from their magnox-type reactor. The utilities accepted these estimates; preferring "proven economy" to both indigenous reactor development and the still precommercial American reactors, they discarded plans to import demonstration reactors in favor of importing large-scale commercial reactors at the earliest opportunity. All subsequent JAEC reports stressed the importance of bringing a Japanese Calder Hall reactor on line as quickly as possible.

The only issue outstanding was to designate an organization to import the reactor. There were several candidates. Some at JAERI sought the responsibility, but the Finance Ministry refused to go along. The Socialist party proposed a new state-owned utility. In the early spring Shōriki and the private utilities proposed new nuclear power generation operating company (Genshiryoku Hatsuden Shikō Kaisha) under private control. More determined than ever to seize a measure of control, MITI challenged the claims of safety and economy made by British and Japanese private utilities. Much of MITI's determination came from its desire to provide the EPDC with a raison d'être beyond the impending exhaustion of hydropower projects. Arguing that Calder Hall power would be nearly twice as expensive as the utilities were claiming and that Shōriki's claims for Calder Hall safety were mere "prayers," MITI insisted that a state agency, its EPDC, import Japan's first reactors. The contradictions in MITI's position were not lost on public opinion: the press openly wondered why MITI insisted on EPDC control if the technology were truly untested and uneconomical.[27]

MITI and the EPDC appealed to Kōno Ichirō for help. Like Shōriki, Kōno was an influential member of the Hatoyama faction and a cabinet minister. Like many other conservative politicians, Kōno had ties with construction firms that might be well served by public control of nuclear power budgets. A fabled Summer's Battle over control of nuclear power was joined, between Shōriki as proxy for Keidanren and the private utilities and Kōno as proxy for the construction industry and MITI. Shōriki's JAEC ruled in August that state funds should be used for R&D but that private firms should handle technology importation. Shōriki was, however, willing for the EPDC to participate as a minority partner in a new firm. Kōno seemed about to accept this compromise, but he did an abrupt about-face, insisting upon a new "special corporation" under state control if the EPDC were not assigned the responsibility for technology imports. At this point the nine utilities flatly refused to participate in or cooperate with such a state-controlled entity. The JAIF backed them up, and Kōno (and MITI) backed down.[28]

The final compromise was the new Japan Atomic Power Company (JAPCO). During the EPDC battle MITI had enjoyed the support of heavy industry, but this time the utilities did. The new power firm, like the EPDC, was limited to wholesale power generation and was created to receive reactor technology. Unlike the EPDC, however, it was not the product of special legislation, and its majority shareholders were private firms.[29] The first president was Yasukawa Daigorō, a leading electrical equipment manufacturer. JAPCO was capitalized at one billion yen, 20 percent of it from the EPDC, the rest from the private sector (see Table 6.2).

Although the Kōno-Shōriki deal had made private industry the operator of Japan's nuclear power plants, private firms refused to accept full financial responsibility for accidents. Eventually, despite efforts by the

Table 6.2. JAPCO initial capitalization (parentheses are 1982 distributions)

Shareholders	% total	Number of firms
Private utilities	42% (75%)	9
(TEPCO = 20.2%; Kansai = 10.1%; others = 1.3% each)		
EPDC	20% (10%)	1
Five nuclear groups	20% (12%)	59
Others	18% (4%)	123
TOTALS	100%	192

SOURCES: Kawai 1961:38; JAPCO Annual Report 1984.

Finance Ministry to limit public liability, the Atomic Power Indemnification Law was passed in June 1961 giving the atomic power firm "complete responsibility" in the event of an accident but requiring the operator to carry only a five-billion-yen insurance policy. Any indemnification in excess of that sum became the responsibility of the state "within the extent of the budget."[30] The private sector had again prevailed, blocking formal state control while taking refuge in the guarantees provided by limited state participation.

Government and industry should not have ignored academic criticisms that JAPCO was moving too fast in the wrong direction. JAPCO's gas-cooled 166 mw Calder Hall was a conspicuous failure. The JAEC, using its considerable political influence, overruled strenuous objections from the scientific community and granted each license JAPCO sought. Calder Hall came on line in 1966, three years late and 50 percent over initial budget because of a dozen major design and safety problems. Calder Hall power per kwh was nearly twice as expensive as that of conventional, thermal generating plants. Even before Calder Hall came on line, the Japanese utilities had bailed out, convinced by American vendors that light water reactors such as the GE boiling water reactor or the Westinghouse indirect cycle pressurized water reactor were more attractive.

The Calder Hall mistake was never repeated. In May 1963, more than three years before the British-designed reactor came on line, JAPCO announced that Japan's second reactor would be a U.S.-designed light water reactor. The announcement touched off vigorous competition among vendors and groups. In September 1965, still ten months before Calder Hall came on line, the award was made for a General Electric design.[31] Even before this second reactor was constructed at Tsuruga, both Tokyo and Kansai Electric announced plans to build their own reactors independently of JAPCO. The scaffolding for commercial nuclear power had been completed, and the utilities were anxious to strike out on their own.[32] Every commercial reactor built in Japan since the Calder Hall has been light water design. The private utilities now operate thirty-five reactors and have five more under construction; JAPCO operates three with only one under construction.

The decision to import the first American light water reactor was taken even though JAERI's own light water demonstration reactor was still under construction. JAERI and its scientists, working to develop indigenous technology, were left behind; the accelerating commercialization of nuclear power in the early and mid-1960s brought a major change to the Japanese nuclear power industry. JAERI apparently was not getting anywhere fast enough. Its scientists had wandered down a series of technological culs-de-sac, among them the design of a "semi-homogeneous" reactor and failure to develop a refrigerant for a natural uranium–fueled heavy water reactor.[33] Private industry, which had championed JAERI and effectively used it as a first market for its experimental facilities, found that "after all, a research center is but just that—a research center. It cannot suffice as a market for the business community."[34] Industry began urging JAERI to undertake more applied research.

This, of course, was not the scientists' business. Strikes and other labor disturbances were common in JAERI's early years. Between June 1959 and March 1964 there were sixty-six work stoppages, and in 1963 alone there were forty-four strikes. Workers complained about low wages and their isolation at the research center in Tōkai Mura. So unsettling was the labor situation that in October 1963 General Electric, lacking confidence in management, ordered the shutdown of Japan's first experimental reactor. At about the same time the JAERI labor union embarrassed management by sharply criticizing visits by American nuclear submarines and the LDP government's nuclear policies. JAERI director Kikuchi Masashi, an academic, was forced to resign by STA chief (and therefore ex officio JAEC chairman) Satō Eisaku. In a move as symbolic as it was substantive, he was replaced by Mitsubishi Shipbuilding chairman Niwa Chikao.

For all this conflict, the basic message from the academics was not entirely lost. By the mid-1960s most industry leaders were acutely aware that planning was incoherent, that reactor choice required coordination, and that a continued rush to build commercial reactors would speed the industry ahead of its own technological capabilities, thus dangerously increasing dependence upon foreign technologies. In September 1964 the JAIF convened a meeting of the industry's top representatives to coordinate indigenization of conventional power reactors (*kokusanka*) and to reevaluate new reactor development. Debate centered upon whether or not a fast breeder reactor could be developed for the long term in parallel with advanced thermal reactors for the medium term. The private utilities favored a direct path from light water to fast breeder reactors, believing that it was too late and too expensive for Japan to develop advanced thermal reactors. They argued that "if you chase two rabbits at once you will not catch even one."[35] The vendors generally preferred to continue development of conventional light water reactors. They recognized that indigenous technologies would be profitable in the long run, but they were unwilling to assume the risks involved without funding from either the state or the utilities.

The JAEC issued an interim report in July 1965, entitled "Ways to Proceed with the Power Reactor." Reflecting incomplete consensus in the private sector, it called for industry-led indigenization of conventional reactor technology and state-led measures for safety and fuel. The JAEC found the advanced thermal reactor attractive enough to justify

R&D, but a lack of consensus on the fast breeder reactor precluded a forceful statement of purpose. Even so, by 1966–67 it was abundantly clear that the existing ten-year nuclear power program, issued in 1961, was obsolete. Japanese utilities had proved to be the best overseas market for U.S. vendors. The 1961 plan had projected only 6–8 gw of installed capacity by 1985, but the utilities were now prepared to contract for five to six times that amount. JAIF ambitiously estimated that 40 percent of all electric power would be nuclear-generated by 1985. "To justify the government's authorization of massive reactor importation," undertaken by the utilities at their own pace, argued Satō Hideo, the JAEC prematurely revised its ten-year plan in 1967.[36] At the same time it began to advocate a national project for a new style of Japanese-designed reactor.

Once again the sticking point was who got responsibility. JAERI volunteered to coordinate the new reactor's development, but the utilities strongly opposed the idea. JAERI's new president, Niwa, proposed that he personally head a new organization modeled after the General Headquarters of the Imperial Navy (*kansei honbu*) to supervise contract research if JAERI were not selected. Satō Eisaku and Fukuda Takeo intervened at the utilities' behest to quash both ideas.[37] JAPCO, a utility created to import foreign technology, was not a strong candidate because, like the EPDC, it had no reactor design staff. The utilities would not even consider the EPDC (and thereby MITI). Instead they proposed that a new agency for fast breeder development be created with 100 percent state capital; they would manage it. After more than a year's negotiations, dominated by JAIF leaders and the JAEC commissioners, it was finally agreed that advanced thermal and fast breeder reactors would be developed simultaneously by a new special public body (*tokushu hōjin*), funded jointly by public and private capital.[38]

This new organization was the Power Reactor and Nuclear Fuel Corporation (PNC), legally established in October 1967. It absorbed the NFPC because the Finance Ministry would not authorize an increase in the total number of public agencies. An unusual set of basic agreements determined the character of the new organ. First, personnel would be the responsibility of the private sector. Second, budgeting would be as far removed from bureaucratic control as possible. The JAIF preferred "flexible and politically responsive budgeting" and succeeded in having PNC carry-over budgets decided at the cabinet level.[39] Third, R&D spending would be left to the state, but reactor construction costs would be shared evenly with private firms. Finally, the director-general received unusually sweeping powers to assign external research and appoint directors. Nothing like these stipulations had ever appeared before in a public corporations law.⁴⁰ Richard Suttmeier has correctly pointed out that

> The underlying philosophy behind PNC is that it serve as a mechanism for undertaking very expensive high risk R&D projects which industry is unwilling to undertake. At the same time it is expected to facilitate the development of the technological capabilities of industry by an extensive use of contracts, let to the major nuclear industrial groups in a judiciously balanced fashion.⁴¹

Behind that philosophy has been the active intervention and guidance of private-sector leaders. Like JAERI before it, and undoubtedly for the same reasons, the PNC was assigned to the administrative jurisdiction of the STA and the Prime Minister's Office. MITI and its EPDC remained on the sidelines, eager but unrequited suitors.

The first director-general of the PNC was Chūbu Electric Power Company president Inoue Gorō, the nominee of JAIF chairman Suga and TEPCO president Kikawada. Inoue's vice-director was Hitachi's Kiyonari Susumu. Even before the PNC had designed or built anything, its directorate, a private-sector union of utilities and vendors, was ensuring that the reactors once constructed would be transferred to private ownership. The point had been left unspecified in the legislation, but at the request of the JAIF, the JAEC soon clarified the government's position. It acceded to the JAIF request that the 50 percent private share of reactor construction costs be considered "investment," recognizing the right of these private participants to claim the reactor when it is ready for commercial use.⁴² Almost immediately Toshiba was designated chief contractor for the fast breeder project and Hitachi for the advanced thermal reactor program.

In the meantime JAERI was left to atrophy. JAERI's share of Japan's nuclear development budget had been 56 percent as late as 1965, but by 1969, just two years after starting, the PNC's budget exceeded that of JAERI. By 1972 the PNC accounted for two-thirds of the nation's nuclear power budget and JAERI but one-fifth. Private-sector contributions to JAERI, already a mere token, hardly changed in twenty years and in 1984 amounted to 0.2 percent. JAERI requests for more were resisted.⁴³

The rationale for the PNC's national projects was obvious. A genuinely domestic fuel cycle in tandem with a Japanese-designed reactor would provide unprecedented energy security. Thus along with the advanced thermal prototype *"fugen"* (no experimental reactor was planned) and the experimental fast breeder *"jōyō,"* fuel policy attracted a great deal of attention from the JAEC and the PNC. Following the lead of the United

States and accompanying the creation of the PNC, nuclear fuel was privatized in 1968. For the first time private firms could fabricate and trade enriched uranium and plutonium. As Japan lacked fuel-refining and enriching facilities, the nation was still dependent upon American nuclear supplies. A revised U.S.-Japanese nuclear agreement that became effective in 1968 made it seem to JAIF leaders that "a thirty year supply of enriched uranium was guaranteed."[44] President Carter's application a decade later of stricter nonproliferation measures therefore met with great resentment.[45]

Japan is now the only nation actively committed to the development of an advanced thermal reactor.[46] This commitment comes partially from a fuel conversion ratio and fuel use efficiency significantly higher than those for conventional light water reactors. The advanced thermals can also burn plutonium, making them even more attractive for uranium-poor but light water–rich Japan. Finally, as noted above, an indigenous technology was also an important strategic consideration.

Nevertheless, the private utilities were reluctant supporters of the PNC's advanced thermal program. They preferred the cheapest available facilities to the development of new reactor technologies. Advantages to the vendors, in the form of contracts and technological development, were far more direct. The PNC distributed responsibility for *fugen* equitably among the five major nuclear groups. Hitachi was named main contractor and took responsibility for the reactor core and the electrical systems. Toshiba was awarded contracts for the turbines and equipment housings. Mitsubishi got the primary cooling system, Fuji Electric the safety and fuel systems as well as the conversion apparatus. Sumitomo was asked to develop the auxiliary cooling equipment.[47] The prototype reactor began full operation in 1979, supplying power to three prefectures in northern Japan. Actual construction costs borne by the utilities (two-thirds of the private sector's 50 percent share) far exceeded initial estimates.

The utilities were also concerned in the late 1960s about access to uranium ore. American multinational corporations and European state agencies were actively acquiring uranium mining rights around the world. The utilities proposed a mechanism by which they and Japanese mining firms might together receive government funds for overseas prospecting and mining. Their (now familiar) idea was a government agency to assume the early risks, allowing private firms to enter after projects had demonstrated commercial feasibility. (As noted in Chapter 3, the major Japanese mining companies, Mitsui and Mitsubishi, were eager to diversify away from coal.) A target of one-third of Japan's domestic demand for uranium was established, and in March 1968 the JAEC's nuclear fuel panel fully supported the utilities' preference for selective public intervention: "When prospecting and development cannot be executed on a commercial basis, the government should take the initiative in preliminary survey and other phase(s) of projects."[48] In 1971 the new special financing program was inaugurated. Uranium-prospecting companies could now receive, through the MITI-affiliated Metal Mining Public Corporation (MMPC), government loans redeemable only if uranium deposits were discovered.

A Place for MITI

Japan's nuclear power–related institutions were all in place by the early 1970s. MITI has jurisdiction over the licensing of power plants and setting of rates, and is responsible for most energy-related advisory commissions, so it is by no means peripheral to the nuclear power debates. Yet its EPDC has never achieved the leadership in nuclear power development that at least two generations of MITI bureaucrats have sought. Private industry and politicians artfully deflected EPDC and MITI ambitions in reactor development. But by the end of the 1970s persistence was rewarded, with a project that the utilities ultimately decided they did not want, the expensive advanced thermal demonstration reactor. Seldom has political struggle over state intervention been waged more transparently by shifting coalitions among the agencies of government and their business allies.

MITI first battled with the utilities in 1957, for control of reactor importation. The prospects for hydropower were clearly limited. If the EPDC was to stay in business, it would have to diversify. But TEPCO's Kikawada and Kansai's Ashiwara had already made it clear that the utilities objected to any EPDC diversification into light water reactors; their objections were formally communicated to MITI.[49] By February 1964 the EPDC was trying again with an R&D agreement with Canadian General Electric which allowed it to dispatch a researcher to study CANDU, the Canadian heavy water reactor.[50]

The EPDC had already outlived its hydropower mandate and seemed to be living on borrowed time. In September 1969 EPDC governor Fujinami Osamu announced that the EPDC would conduct research on the British advanced gas reactor. Because of technical failures on the British side, nothing ever came of this initiative.[51] The EPDC then turned to the high temperature gas reactor of the American Gulf General Atomic Corporation. Gulf General Atomic had already taken orders for six new-style reactors by the late 1960s, and the EPDC was eager to sign on. MITI allocated the construction contract to Mitsubishi (over the strenuous objections of Mitsui/Toshiba). Once again, however, engineering problems aborted the project.

Even before this failure in 1974 MITI made a final stab at the light water reactor market. In 1971 the EPDC sought authorization to import Japan's first large-scale boiling water reactor.[52] This 1100 mw plant, which eventually became JAPCO's Tōkai Daini reactor, went to JAPCO at the insistence of the private utilities. The casting vote was a formal memorandum signed by TEPCO chairman Kikawada "with the full support of MITI minister Miyazawa" on behalf of the Federation of Electric Power Companies and addressed to EPDC governor Ōbori.[53] The Kikawada Memo was straightforward: the EPDC was "requested" to stay clear of all light water projects, and the reactor was assigned to JAPCO. EPDC was "permitted" to construct other types of commercial reactor, but the utilities made it clear that they would oppose any EPDC prototype, research, or demonstration reactors. The implications were clear: the EPDC could compete with the private utilities if it could find a competitive technology; but the utilities had reserved the truly competitive technologies for themselves, and the EPDC could not develop any on its own. Only CANDU was left.

The first oil crisis was an unexpected shot in the arm for the EPDC. Sharp increases in the price of oil made coal-fired thermal power plants attractive once again. Ironically it was the EPDC's virtual monopoly on coal power plants and engineering expertise which saved it from administrative reform.

The prospects for nuclear power were also boosted by the oil crisis, which made nuclear fuel seem the most attractive alternative to petroleum for a resource-poor but technology-rich nation such as Japan. Nuclear power provides diversity and security of supply, cost advantages, a technology-based (and therefore high value-added) export, and the convenience of inexpensive stockpiling.[54] Considerable time and money were spent to convince the general population. The average lead time for licensing, siting, and construction of a nuclear power plant in Japan increased dramatically after 1975 as the environmental movement gathered momentum. By 1980 the average was 160 months, longer even than in the United States, to bring a plant on line.[55] Siting negotiations remain the single greatest cause of delay. Prime Minister Tanaka, avidly pro-nuclear and notoriously pro–pork barrel, in 1974 set up a special account derived from electricity taxes for the siting of nuclear power plants. The amount available more than doubled between 1976 and 1983. In 1977 alone it was greater than the total amount spent in the two decades between 1956 and 1975. In 1983 these funds, euphemistically called "cooperation money" and obviously designed to coopt residential opposition through large expenditures on public works, amounted to 14 percent of the nation's nuclear power budget.[56]

Siting and related problems were squarely, if lavishly, addressed by

the mid-1970s. It seemed as if MITI and the STA had come to a modus
vivendi on the supervision of nuclear power development. But an accident involving radiation leakage from Japan's first nuclear-powered
ship, the *Mutsu,* in August 1974 provided MITI a new opening in its
jurisdictional struggle with the STA. Using the *Mutsu* controversy, MITI
sided with the Transport Ministry in laying blame for the accident on the
STA and the Nuclear Safety Commission for insufficient safety inspec-
tions. Nuclear Safety commissioner Tajima Eizō resigned. MITI sought a
broad reorganization of nuclear power under its own direction, arguing
that nuclear policy should be related in administrative terms to electric
power and general energy policy. These in turn, it argued, are part of
industrial policy, an undisputed MITI responsibility. Opposing MITI were
STA and the Administrative Management Agency, which wanted all nuclear power administration consolidated in an atomic power agency in
the Prime Minister's Office.[57]

An advisory commission was appointed, chaired by Arisawa Hiromi.
In December 1975 he recommended that the JAEC be divided in two, an
idea based upon the recent reorganization of the American Atomic Energy Commission. The JAEC would retain responsibility for promotion
and planning, and the separate Nuclear Safety Commission (NSC) would
concentrate on safety issues—the JAEC would be the accelerator, the NSC
the brake, and the prime minister would remain the driver. Arisawa also
recommended that evolving but still uncoordinated administrative responsibilities be ratified: Transport would handle nuclear ships, the Science and Technology Agency would handle R&D reactors, and MITI
would be responsible for the regulation of commercial plants.

Bureaucratic politics ensured only glacial progress on these proposals.[58] Diet finally acted in October 1978, nearly two years after the
Arisawa Report, and as it turned out, did not so much clarify responsibility as adopt a convenient way to continue deferring administrative reform. R&D belonged to the STA, but MITI was responsible for the importation of commercial technologies. Different laws gave both agencies
responsibilities for inspection and safety. Nevertheless, the inauguration
of the new JAEC and the NSC ushered in a new era of safety checks, public
hearings, and stringent siting requirements, all to be secured first and
foremost through local political support.

For its efforts MITI clearly emerged with more formal authority than it
had previously enjoyed. But this entire battle was a red herring. The real
issue for MITI had little changed since 1957: how was it to secure control
over choice of technology and reactor development. MITI's last chance
was to take control of Japan's "transition" reactor. As related above, the
JAEC decided in 1967 to proceed with development of a prototype advanced thermal reactor; the *fugen* project was assigned to the PNC, cre-

ated expressly for the purpose. Although plagued by cost overruns and private-sector refusals to bear their full share,[59] *fugen* was about to come on line. The JAEC initiated formal discussions about responsibility for the next logical phase, a demonstration reactor.

In MITI's view, however, a demonstration reactor was not the necessary next step. The CANDU reactor was already in commercial operation in Canada and abroad. It could be imported with a stable supply of Canadian uranium, enhancing the Japanese search for fuel supply diversity and fuel cycle closure and reducing the need for plutonium imports just when the Carter nonproliferation regime was making such trade difficult. It had an additional domestic political advantage in that the utilities had not studied it carefully, and it also satisfied Foreign Ministry and MITI aims to increase imports from and thereby improve relations with Canada. In May 1977 EPDC governor Morozumi Yoshihiko, former administrative vice-minister at MITI, fired the first public volley by claiming that CANDU was economically and technologically the proven equal of the light water reactor.[60]

MITI was confronting the STA and the private utilities. The STA wanted to continue supervision of the advanced thermal reactor, the agency's largest and most prestigious development project. Many in the STA saw a commercially viable CANDU as a threat to their own survival.[61] CANDU had been exported only to less developed countries such as Korea and Romania with little nuclear experience, the STA pointed out, and Japan's stringent safety standards would delay it for at least a decade. Therefore, they argued, it would meet Japan's interim needs no more quickly than an indigenous reactor.[62] The STA stressed, moreover, that the lesson of the Carter initiatives and its International Nuclear Fuel Cycle Evaluation was the renewed strategic importance of development of a truly indigenous reactor. Japan must finally break its debilitating dependence upon foreign fuels and foreign technologies.

The private utilities, dissatisfied participants in the *fugen* project, did not share STA's avid commitment to reactor development. They feared that either new reactor would reduce profit margins. They did, however, share STA's concerns about MITI expansion into nuclear power.[63] The utilities preferred the advanced thermal reactor project at a pace they could control to buying CANDU power from the EPDC at MITI's price. They "supported" the advanced thermal reactor to block MITI and CANDU. The utilities took the position that limited funds and manpower made it foolhardy to promote both the CANDU and the advanced thermal, and because of their own difficult experiences with the imported Calder Hall they supported continuation of the latter.

The first joint victory for the utilities and the STA came in April 1978 when a JAEC report evaluating the choices for an interim reactor deferred a final recommendation. Another evaluation commission was established, chaired by JAERI director Murata Hiroshi. Deliberations continued quietly through the new fiscal year, but budget deliberations in the fall provoked the most direct confrontation over control of nuclear power since the Shōriki-Kōno fight back in 1957. As in that first battle, the utilities and their allies blocked MITI and redirected it to assume a supporting role.

The issue flared into the open on October 24, 1978, when the Nuclear Power Division of MITI's Advisory Committee for Energy called for the introduction of CANDU as soon as possible. MITI announced a budget proposal for FY 1979 which included 1.8 billion yen for "basic planning for CANDU importation."[64] All this happened without consulting the JAEC, causing discomfort even within MITI's own councils. The day after the announcement, influential members of MITI's own Advisory Committee for Energy chastised the ministry for its recklessness. Chastened but no less determined, MITI promised its committee and the public to put the CANDU issue on the "chopping block" of public opinion, adding only that it would be diligent in securing the support and understanding of all parties.

Nevertheless, the response from the STA and the JAEC was swift. On October 31, STA minister (and ex officio JAEC chairman) Kumagai Taizaburō declared his "extreme displeasure" with MITI's handling of the matter and stated STA's opposition to CANDU.[65] On November 10, acting JAEC commissioner Kiyonari added his protests. In the meantime unrest was brewing within the STA. Younger bureaucrats who had entered the agency after its formation in 1957 feared that they would be sold out by their seniors, most of whom had come from MITI. Forty of these officials formed a study group to evaluate the CANDU. Word of their activities reached Kumagai through newspaper reports.[66] Kumagai arranged an audience for them with Kiyonari on December 1, and Kiyonari assured them that the JAEC would make a final decision on the CANDU.

The December budget deadline was approaching, and MITI was fast losing its advantage. By mid-December the JAEC was hearing expert testimony that challenged MITI claims that CANDU-derived plutonium would close Japan's nuclear fuel cycle. It was learned, for example, that Canada was not reprocessing its own CANDU spent fuel, and the facilities to do so were a quarter of a century away. The vendors finally weighed in, expressing ambivalence about CANDU. In principle the vendors cared little about which reactors they built as long as they received enough orders to make their efforts profitable.[67] In practice, however, vendors testified before the JAEC on their reluctance to undertake the CANDU project. Mitsubishi, in particular, refused to cooperate, saying (some claim on behalf of Westinghouse) that it already had its hands full with its pressurized reactor program. Hitachi agreed to cooperate only if other vendors and the utilities agreed to make CANDU a national project.[68] On December 15 a JAEC sectional committee advised MITI to make a more deliberate study of CANDU, killing the project for FY 1979.

MITI did not give up. During the spring it increased pressure to gain acceptance of CANDU and even tried to circumvent the bureaucracy by drafting a cabinet resolution supporting the project. JAEC commissioner Kiyonari aborted that effort by threatening mass resignations.[69] In July a private-sector "summit" on nuclear development, chaired by Keidanren chairman Dokō Toshio, was held at Keidanren headquarters. Dokō, originally from Ishikawajima-Harima Heavy Industries and Toshiba, both leading nuclear vendors in the Mitsui Group, had long been a supporter of the advanced thermal reactor. He and other business leaders agreed that the recent Three Mile Island accident and other technical failures made foreign technology more unattractive than ever. There was no support for CANDU. Keidanren petitioned Prime Minister Ōhira and the JAEC to move ahead with the commercialization of the advanced thermal reactor.[70]

With this strong show of support, the JAEC formally decided on August 20 to kill the CANDU and move ahead on a *fugen*-type advanced thermal reactor. Indignant, MITI and the EPDC demanded all of the JAEC's evaluative data and filed a written inquiry about the CANDU decision. They also launched *ad hominem* attacks on Kiyonari. All was to no avail. With the full support of the prime minister, Kiyonari and the JAEC withstood the counteroffensive.

But MITI was not shut out of the nuclear business altogether, for responsibility for the advanced thermal demonstration reactor was still to be decided. Once the CANDU had been stopped, the coalition between the utilities and the STA fell apart. As an official MITI report stated, "The biggest problem vis-à-vis the commercialization of the advanced thermal reactor is that private industry's response has not been adequate.[71] TEPCO president Hiraiwa Gaishi complained that costs for *fugen* were nearly double those for a conventional reactor and that capital for reactors to which the utilities were already committed was scarce and expensive. Kansai Electric chairman Ashihara Yoshishige suggested that private-sector cooperation could most readily be secured by special tax measures to raise capital. The private utilities were stalling for time.

Fugen had begun commercial operation in March 1979. In August 1981 the JAEC issued its final evaluation: it recognized the utilities' claim that the advanced thermal could not compete economically with their light water reactors but insisted that energy security outweighed cost. It took another six months before JAEC chairman Nakagawa Ichirō formally appealed to Keidanren chairman Dokō to break the impasse. But the utilities continued to stall. They created a new evaluation committee, which deliberated until June 1982.

Finally, three full years after the advanced thermal had been chosen as Japan's next generation of reactor, the utilities took an extraordinary step. TEPCO's Hiraiwa proposed that the EPDC construct one advanced thermal plant and in exchange the government reduce the costs to the private sector of its construction.[72] It took EDPC president Morozumi only two weeks to consider and eagerly accept the utilities' proposal. The EPDC was officially in the nuclear power business. In 1984, when the second Administrative Reform Commission targeted the national railways, the national telephone monopoly, and other public agencies for privatization, the EPDC was not designated. It had a third lease on life.

The utilities also were satisfied. When the details were announced in August 1982, it was clear that they had negotiated well. They agreed to assume only 30 percent of the costs, less than they had committed to *fugen*.[73] Hitachi was selected as the lead contractor. The advanced thermal demonstration reactor, with a 600,000 mw capacity, is scheduled for completion by the early 1990s. Like the fast breeder prototype *"monju"* it is a large-scale engineering project undertaken by private industry with predominantly public funds for long-term energy needs.

The fast breeder remained unsettled. In 1977, when the *"jōyō"* experimental reactor came on line, the utilities limited their commitment for the next phase to 20 percent,[74] delaying the transition to the prototype. Three years later the PNC was awarded responsibility for the *monju* prototype, with most of its funding derived from the development account for electric power resources.[75] Almost immediately the EPDC began studying a demonstration reactor. Opposition from the utilities and STA mounted, guaranteeing that the fast breeder reactor would become the next focus of the struggle for political control of nuclear development in Japan.

The task of sorting out a division of labor in Japan for the development of nuclear power is as old as the technology itself. And like the technology, it is still evolving. Permanent solutions have been frustrated by permanently fluid political alignments, sketched out in Figure 6.2.

In the three most important battles for control of nuclear power (JAPCO in 1957, PNC in 1967, and CANDU in 1978), the principal protagonists have been MITI, the STA, and the private utilities. The utilities have enjoyed fairly consistent support from the vendors and from other state agencies, which has been the key to their success. It has also been the key to the evolving consensus in Japan on the division of financial responsibility for nuclear development. It was agreed from the beginning that R&D and the operation of experimental reactors would be the responsibility of the government, with cooperation and participation from the

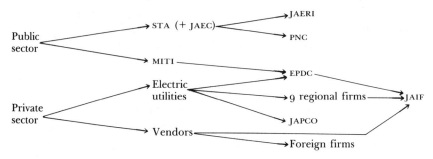

Figure 6.2. Nuclear power alignments in Japan, ca. 1982

private sector. The construction and operation of nuclear plants, as well as the introduction of new technologies, would be the responsibility of the private sector, with the support of the state. But we have seen many violations of these basic divisions. MITI often sought to foist technologies upon the industry, and even more often private industry backed away from its financial commitments for reactor development when costs increased beyond initial estimates.[76]

The JAEC's ten-year, long-term nuclear program announced in 1982 projects a total 5.4 trillion yen of public spending for nuclear power. It also forecasts that the private sector will invest an additional 14 trillion yen. The transfer of nuclear technology to the private sector and compensation to the state for bearing the costs of R&D remain unresolved questions. As a measure of how far and how fast the industry has come, much of the investment will be taken to enhance the "international competitiveness" of Japanese reactors produced for export.[77] Yet the distribution of institutional responsibility is as uncertain as ever. The regime inherited from two decades of debate within the bureaucracy and between the state and business appears in Table 6.3. But all is subject to negotiation. In that respect, little has changed.

CONCLUSION

Competition among business and state actors has decided control of investment in alternative energy in Japan. Confrontations and coalitions have shifted with perceptions of market opportunities. As a result, close business-government collaboration has been bought at a high price—both for the public purse and for the egos of MITI bureaucrats. In synfuels and in nuclear power, state intervention has been stimulated by the vulnerability of the Japanese economy and limited by an oligopolistic

Table 6.3. Responsibility for nuclear power development in Japan, 1984

Project	Public Sector	Private Sector
Light Water Reactor	*Fuel Cycle R&D (PNC, JAERI) *Safety (JAERI)	*Reactor operation *Education, training, operators *Quality control *Public confidence
Fast Breeder Reactor	*Operation of experimental reactor (PNC) *Construction/operation of Prototype Reactor (PNC) *Safety (PNC) *Training (PNC)	*Demonstration reactor
Advanced Thermal Reactor	*Operation of prototype reactor (EPDC, PNC) *R&D support for demonstration reactor (PNC) *Operation/construction of demonstration reactor (EPDC)	*Technological development to increase capacity and economy
Plutonium Recycled Light Water Reactor (thermal plutonium)	*Support private sector	*Test plutonium mixes for commercial reactors
Plutonium Fuel Fabrication	*Rationalization, capacity expansion (PNC)	*Participation in PNC facility and operation
FBR Fuel Reprocessing	*R&D (PNC) *FBR prototype, fuel reprocessing, construction, planning (PNC)	None
Uranium Supply	*Overseas prospecting (MMPC, PNC) *Subsidy for mine development	*Mine development
Uranium Enrichment	*R&D and operation of pilot plant (PNC) R&D, construction, and operation of demonstration plant (PNC) *Uranium fluoride conversion R&D (PNC)	*Participation in all PNC activities
Fuel Reprocessing	*R&D support (PNC) *Site survey (PNC) *Support for capital acquisition (PNC)	*Construction and operation of commercial plants

(*continued*)

Table 6.3. (*Continued*)

Project	Public Sector	Private Sector
Waste disposal	*Vitrification R&D (PNC) *Temporary storage (PNC) *High-level radioactive waste disposal (PNC)	*Low-level radioactive waste disposal
Fuel Storage	Under study	Under study
Multipurpose Heat-Utilizing Reactor	*R&D for high-temperature gas demonstration reactor (JAERI) *Support for siting and development of LWR multipurpose heat-utilizing reactor (MITI)	*Participation in these projects
Fusion	*Basic research (JAERI)	*Construction contract
Radiation Utilization	*Basic research (JAERI)	*Industrial applications

SOURCES: Kamiō 1984 and interviews.

configuration of political resources. Both cases illuminate the relationship between openness and market concentration, as well as the frustration of apparent imperatives of openness by bureaucratic politics. In short these cases suggest the political relevance of state and market structures. Let us explore each of these in turn.

Business offered no competition to state initiatives in synfuels until it became clear that alternatives to petroleum could provide attractive markets in their own right. State designs on private markets were moderated soon after the second oil crisis had made alternatives for competitiveness seem profitable. The market role of MITI's proposed Alternative Energy Public Corporation was transformed from producer to banker; the corporation's board of directors was immediately colonized by private-sector leaders. The same private elites that championed nuclear power assumed control of synfuels development. The same Japanese heavy industrial firms and private utilities that design and build nuclear reactors (with considerable state funding) help direct the public-funded development of alternative energy technologies.

These changes were facilitated by the oligopolistic politics of heavy industry. The capacity of utilities and vendors consistently to pressure the state contrasts markedly with what obtained in petroleum. This coordination seems to be related to lucrative and common markets and undoubtedly has contributed to the success of private industry in setting the pace, shape, and direction for Japan's alternative energies. Where commercial applications have been low in risk and immediately apparent, for example, as in light water reactors, development has involved the initiative of private industry coordinated with the (often grudging) support of the state. Where risks have been high and applications distant, as in advanced thermal reactors, fast breeders, and synfuels, the state has been enticed into accepting the bulk of financial responsibility without a commensurate degree of policy control. Roger Gale's observation about nuclear power applies to the synfuels program as well: "The private companies, while philosophically supportive of an ambitious nuclear power program, are reluctant either to finance the development of new technologies or to see them owned and managed by the government."[78]

State structure is relevant to the explanation of state intervention in alternative energy markets. Here private oligopoly is matched by divisions within the state, divisions that often have slowed the expansion of the state's role in these markets. Bureaucratic struggles, especially between the STA and MITI, have been as important as public-private disputes in determining the nature and extent of state intervention. The Science and Technology Agency, it should be recalled, originated in private and LDP moves in the 1950s to limit MITI jurisdiction in nuclear power. Industry and its associates in the conservative ruling party created in the STA their most important ally for blocking MITI's ambitions in both nuclear power and synthetic fuels.

Compared to many national experiences with synfuels and nuclear power, the Japanese story is one of success. In the United States the Federal Synthetic Fuels Corporation was abolished as soon as world oil prices softened in the mid-1980s. Yet although decreasing revenues from imported petroleum reduced its budgets, Japan's NEDO continues to fund private firms. On the nuclear side, Japanese reactors are among the world's most efficient.[79] They are also among the least expensive to construct and operate. The first half of the 1980s saw not a single new plant order in the United States; meanwhile Japan's nuclear power program moved steadily forward. Relatively minor accidents in 1982 and 1986 failed to slow its momentum.

One obvious lesson from these battles to control markets is that market success is not determined by prescient planners. It does not emerge organizationally from centralized, strong states or from pure market competition. Market and state are both products of the negotiated politics of reciprocal consent. State structures can be created by private preferences, just as private markets can be distorted by state intervention. There is ample evidence that the reverse proposition is also true: state structures can shape private preferences, and private markets can distort themselves. Japanese successes in alternative energy are no more derived from the collaborative instincts of state planners than they are

255

from the conciliatory politics of private interests. We do better to attribute those successes to the way state structures evolve to conform to private markets that are, ironically, distorted by oligopolistic collaboration among private interests. The concluding chapter attempts to develop this idea.

CHAPTER SEVEN

The Business of
the Japanese State

This book explores the ways businessmen and bureaucrats have sought to organize the economies of the industrial democracies. It has concentrated upon the nature and extent of state intervention in the energy market place as a critical case for theories of state leadership in capitalist economies in general and in Japan in particular. I have focused most closely upon the origins of state enterprise as a historical "point of compact" to explain the institutional differences that distinguish Japan from other cases. These institutional differences, in turn, have been located in the context of important questions about business-government relations.

In the mixed economies of Western Europe the state is predominantly a producer, either as a rival or as a partner to private industry. The Japanese state, despite a rich entrepreneurial history, is neither. Japan is singular, a case of extensive state jurisdiction without a competitive commercial presence in the energy market place. The United States exhibits less of the former, somewhat more of the latter. In Europe there is usually both. Europeans build national champions with state equity. The Japanese restructure private markets with public financial assistance.

More specifically, Japan's energy industries involve a peculiar concentration of market-conforming financial and regulatory institutions that attempt to guarantee the stability of private markets. In the rare event that the state extends equity to a productive enterprise, that firm is limited to wholesale production for private industrial consumption (for example, the Electric Power Development Corporation) and is explicitly prohibited from competing with private firms (for example, the Japan National Oil Corporation). Unlike in the European cases we have examined, no combination of strategic, political, or other incentives has led the Japanese state to adopt a competitive presence in the market. The state is virtually never an energy producer, except in so far as it supplies private markets at cost. It therefore does not displace but conforms to (and often reproduces) energy markets. In comparative and historical perspective these institutional differences offer insights into Japanese capitalism more generally. This final chapter explores these insights and suggests their relevance to my central purpose—the specification and explanation of the state's roles in structuring domestic markets.

THE JAPANESE STATE AS GUARANTOR

Chalmers Johnson has correctly observed that "Japan offers a panoply of market-conforming methods of state intervention, including the creation of government financial institutions . . . [and] an extensive reliance on public corporations . . . to implement policy in high-risk or otherwise refractory areas."[1] This configuration, unique among the industrial democracies, deserves explanation.

Why *is* the commercial role of the Japanese state so limited? Why *does* Japan, often paired with France as exemplar of the strong, centralized, planned, neomercantilist economy, depend so heavily upon market-conforming financial mechanisms of public intervention? What *do* the limitations upon commercial activities by the Japanese state reveal about relations between the private sector and what is reputed to be the most dominant central bureaucracy in all the industrial democracies?

The most popular answers posit bureaucratic dominance and state leadership. They acknowledge the role of the private sector but stress the power of the state. It is often an article of faith that Japanese economic bureaucrats are *primus inter pares*, directors of the Japanese economy. To one version the fact that Japanese public corporations are seldom market players matters very little; these firms are seen nonetheless as instruments of the state, populated by seconded bureaucrats who answer to their home ministries as they enforce state priorities over private ones.[2] The most extreme statement of this view is historical. Bernard Silberman, for example, concludes that the prewar Japanese state was able to "foreclose the whole notion of interests . . . [and] to incorporate those private interests into a public one dominated by the state bureaucracies."[3] A more moderate version portrays the Japanese state-as-guarantor emerging from the uniquely Japanese confluence of bureaucratic legitimacy, administrative centralization, information exchange, market reliance, and state capacity.[4]

Common to most assessments are MITI-men and other bureaucrats with a great and prescient faith in the market place. More important still, these bureaucrats are said to have exceptionally broad power to intervene, to use market forces as instruments of public policy.[5] It is often argued that economic bureaucrats wisely choose to intervene in moderation because of their awareness of the potential costs of market distortion. The state has no separate commercial presence because it does not need one: the state can control without owning, and if it wants to, it can achieve ownership with little effort. Raymond Vernon, for example, suggests that "when a special entrepreneurial push from the government has seemed useful, MITI has had no great difficulty in securing the needed authority to create a publicly controlled enterprise."[6] Johnson likens Japanese economic bureaucrats to their distant Venetian cousins: "The genius of modern Japan, much like that of medieval Venice, has been the ability to fuse in an ad hoc manner the effectiveness of the absolutist state with the efficiency of the bourgeois market."[7] Daniel Okimoto observes the Japanese state's lack of "institutionalized involvement in the marketplace" and argues that a "diversity of access points permits the Japanese government to stand back and watch the market function while retaining the flexibility to intervene at any time."[8]

In short, it is widely held that the Japanese state is not in business because the bureaucracy can regulate the market more efficiently than participate in it. Market conformity is widely understood as the industrial policy instrument of choice. It provides evidence of state capacity. Thus it is by virtue of bureaucratic choice and bureaucratic power that the Japanese state is less a market player than European states. Although the emphases on policy networks and public bureaucracies vary, analyses of Japanese economic and industrial policy are dominated by statist assumptions about bureaucratic power, whether labeled state-led capitalism, guided free enterprise, administrative guidance, or the developmental state.[9]

This view, in turn, has been widely accepted in the comparative literature on states and markets. Japan is the archetypical statist regime, virtually always paired with France.[10] And there is indeed much that is similar about French and Japanese patterns of economic policy making. Both countries have developed sector-specific planning mechanisms that systematically include big business and state bureaucrats and that seem to exclude labor and small business. Both rely upon an elite career bureaucracy that consistently favors scale and consolidation.[11] John Zysman speaks of the French and Japanese economies as "both tied to state-led growth," a model he characterizes as one in which "the government bureaucracy attempts to orient the adjustment of the economy by explicitly influencing the position of particular sectors, even of individual companies, and by imposing the solutions on the weakest groups in the polity."[12] He suggests that both are distinguished by the way in which "prices in crucial markets are determined by government." Peter

Katzenstein rejects the "Japan as *smart* state" hypothesis but celebrates the French and Japanese state structures and institutions that "preempt the costs" of economic adjustment.[13]

If one accepts these comparisons and the analyses of Japan specialists upon which they are based, one must conclude that institutional differences between the French state-as-rival and the Japanese state-as-guarantor are trivial. My evidence, however, suggests otherwise. The origins of the state-as-guarantor reveal political dynamics of policy making in Japan which suggest a reinterpretation of why Japanese economic policy is market-conforming. Although the Japanese state pervades the market, it does not lead, guide, or supervise private interests. There is little evidence that state actors have ever been able to resist political pressures in the absence of alliances with parts of the private sector. In three hundred years of coal markets and a century of oil and electric power, where have state actors systematically denied access to particular groups in the policy process? Where have they ignored the demands of labor or small business with impunity? Where have state initiatives been adopted without evisceration and without guarantees? Transformations of energy markets have always preceded state intervention, and state intervention has always conformed to and reconfirmed evolving energy markets. Again we ask, repeating the question posed in Chapter 1, not why the Japanese state is so pervasive in the economy but why the pervasive state is so congenial to private firms.

A paradox frames our answer. The Japanese state acts as guarantor because its power in the market place is enhanced and circumscribed simultaneously by the routines of mutual accommodation we refer to as reciprocal consent. It achieves jurisdiction and is denied control in an iterative process with private interests within an environment of unusually stable elites and extraordinarily durable institutions. The Japanese bureaucracy does not dominate, it negotiates.

So do bureaucracies elsewhere, of course. Reciprocal consent is not uniquely Japanese. In Western Europe similar negotiations over the nature and extent of state intervention have resulted in a market presence for the state—often with considerable support from industry and labor. In Japan the state has been diverted away from market competition entirely. What makes Japan different is the routinization of economic policy which the durability of elites and their constituencies makes possible. Japan is not merely a vat of competing interests; neither is Japan a European government in an American business environment. Rather, the institutionalized routine of negotiation, reciprocal consent, is the tie that binds. It deserves closer scrutiny.

The politics of reciprocal consent has been central to the development of Japanese capitalism. Earlier in this century politics centered upon the

Japanese state's failed effort to separate management from capital. More recent negotiations have centered upon the state's effort to augment private ownership with state control. Historically it has been a consistent dynamic: Japanese capital has struggled quite successfully, across wars and depressions, to separate state aid from state control. Reciprocal consent, therefore, is quite different from "consensus," that model of Japanese politics which stresses harmony and cultural adhesives instead of conflict and structural stability.

Conflict and stability have produced an undeniably pervasive, developmental state.[14] But the evidence from the energy industries makes any inference of state leadership problematic. Market objectives are more commonly achieved through the state than state objectives are achieved through the market. The pervasive Japanese state has nearly always been congenial to private interests, in large measure because private firms have learned how to surrender jurisdiction while retaining control of markets. By privately ordering markets to conform to a perpetually negotiated, state-sanctioned economic order, private investors have found one solution—some would say the optimal solution—to the vagaries of capitalist development.[15] Risk is frequently socialized, costs often transferred. This solution entails the intimate involvement of state agencies, of course, and as a result the politics of reciprocal consent is often confused with state leadership, mutual trust with the mutual sanction from which it is derived. Regulation and jurisdiction, in sum, are often confused with control. But the energy industries provide no evidence that the Japanese state was ever able to force the pace of market transformation or to shape markets in its own image.

On the contrary, in achieving jurisdiction without control the Japanese state merely enshrined bargaining and negotiation in the definition of and access to markets. Conflict over the mechanisms for this "private ordering" was public and consequential. Private firms have always encouraged the sort of state intervention that would permit them to limit production legally, to allocate markets, to control prices, and to collude in sales. Battles over state control (*kokka tōsei*) and self-control (*jishu tōsei*) before the end of the war were resolved by state-sanctioned cartels that guaranteed private ownership and private management. This solution profoundly affected the major institutions of the Japanese economy, and especially the limits on the state as market player, by defining the Japanese notion of what the capitalist state is and ought to be.

It is and ought to be pervasive. It does and ought to enjoy extensive jurisdiction in the economy. It can and must provide for the common defense through collective management of market diseconomies—especially excessive competition. Neither economic bureaucrats nor business leaders ever developed a deep faith in the salutary effects of the free market. The Japanese economic elite, as Okimoto aptly puts it, has long felt that the market was far from sacrosanct, that "capitalism needs the visible hand of the state."[16] In 1930 economic bureaucrats were suggesting that "in order to obtain the largest possible return from the capital investment, it is necessary, besides amalgamating enterprises in the various industries, to encourage the adoption of business agreements among the enterprises . . . concerning the amount of production, division of markets, sales process, and other measures for the prevention of unnecessary competition."[17]

Arguably matters are not much different today. The 1980s have witnessed as much concern among Japanese businessmen and bureaucrats about excessive competition as the 1930s did. Because of the stable and largely oligopolistic politics of reciprocal consent, Japan never developed the hostility to private monopoly that dominated policy debates in the United States. While the American state was invested with powers to regulate the trusts, the Japanese state was invested (often by the Japanese trusts themselves) with jurisdiction to assist in their healthy development. Even today concern about the evils of excessive competition dominates discussions of economic policy. Fratricidal hypercompetition is to Japanese economic planners every bit the *bête noir* that excessive concentration is to American antitrust officials. Clearly, as this book has shown, neither the Japanese government nor Japanese capital trusts the market. As in France, state bureaucrats or private firms have never held a priori that markets will adjust in the best interests of capital or citizens. This, then, has been a story of cartels, trusts, control, and other non-Smithian initiatives taken both by the state and by private actors. Yet markets and even oligopolies often prove impossibly undisciplined; whether the problem is producers, consumers, or the state, the Japanese have evolved a sophisticated system of negotiation whose results have been consistently market-conforming. Conflict does not get subsumed by consensus, it gets enshrined by reciprocal consent.

Thus emerges a Japanese guarantor-state, not from its own inherent capacity but from the complexity and stability of its interactions with market players. Comparisons to European strong states may misrepresent the fundamentally *conservative* character of the Japanese state. Indeed, comparisons to the United States may be more revealing about the origins of state intervention in the economy. Japan offers remarkable parallels to what Theodore Lowi has called "the state of permanent receivership." Lowi argues that the federal government of the United States increasingly and inexorably underwrites risk for established and well-organized interests: "Any institution large enough to be a significant factor in the community may have its stability underwritten. . . . Above all [the state of permanent receivership] respects the established jurisdictions of government agencies and the established territories of private corporations and groups."[18] In Japan, however, there is less pretense about respecting the sanctity of the free market. Ironically, a state that does not trust the market supervises interventions that consistently reproduce shifting market structures, while firms that insist on their autonomy in the market place welcome and help shape state jurisdiction. This irony is best illuminated by evaluating the comparative political histories presented in this book.

THE PROPOSITIONS AND THE EVIDENCE

At particular moments in history, relations between businesses and governments have dominated the politics of the industrial democracies. As we have seen, moreover, throughout industrial history democratic (and often antidemocratic) politics have shaped relations between business and the state. Yet business-state relations are not all that shape politics. No explanation for the distribution of public and private power in mixed capitalist economies can be as compelling as one that explores and incorporates struggles for a more basic unit of the political economy, control of productive resources.

This reminds us that the institutional outcome of struggles between business and the state can be a misleading test for analysis of the role of either in the market place. For one thing, analysts can draw the protagonists too sharply. We may reify Business and State drawing excessively Manichean portraits and ignoring such other determinants of market transformation as labor, consumers, international politics, and plain luck. This book has repeatedly documented the relevance of each of these factors. Second, analysts may unnecessarily presume that when private markets are the central mechanisms of adjustment, the state must have been unable or unwilling to intervene. The Matsukata Shock or the Bujun imports (both in 1932), or the creation of the Anglo-Persian Oil Company, all suggest how market solutions can involve much more than the obvious market players. Third, and conversely, when new state structures emerge from these struggles, the immediate presumption is that public authority has prevailed over private power. Yet consider the British coal reorganization in 1930 and the Important Industries Control Law of the following year in Japan. Here, as in virtually all of the dozens of cartels and legislated rationalizations examined in this book, depressed demand did more than legislation to encourage businessmen to cooperate. I have chosen not to infer process from structure. Rather, I build upon historical examination of the political conflicts and economic contingencies that constitute the policy record.[19]

Each policy record (the substance of Chapters 3–6) documents political conflict between and among actors public and private for control of separate sectors of the Japanese economy. Each struggle for control began with the very origin of the sector and reveals often striking correspondences with European state intervention (examined in Chapter 2). The British amalgamation of electric utilities during World War I, the politics that shaped the British Coal Mine Act of 1930, and the exclusion of autogenerators from the Italian and French nationalizations, all tell the same tale of politically inspired, privately led evisceration of state initiatives that we find in Japan in the 1955 coal rationalization, the creation of the Japan National Oil Corporation, or the Electric Power Development Corporation. Conflicts upstream and downstream, or between producers and consumers, helped structure state interventions in the cases of France's CFP, Italy's ENEL, or Germany's Ruhrkohle; they were echoed in Japanese experiences in all three sectors. Domestic producers supported state intervention in the formation of APOC and CFP; such support was similarly critical in the coal nationalizations of 1872 and in each of the postwar Japanese coal programs. In no nation, least of all Nazi Germany or authoritarian Japan, did private autonomy fully surrender to state control, even during wartime mobilization. Indeed, state control may have been more complete in Britain or the United States than in Germany or Japan.[20] In short, battles over the nature and extent of state intervention in the economy have been anything but unique to Japan. The political and economic history of market transformation in France, Britain, Italy, and elsewhere reveals similar struggles over the separation of management from capital, legislated rationalizations, depression cartels, state-sanctioned collective marketing agreements—and private cheating on them—and, above all else, generous state subsidies to noncompetitive but politically resourceful private enterprises.

Yet there is much diversity here as well, with different stories for different sectors. Unlike oil or electric power, coal was perceived by (and presented to) governments more as a social than as an economic or energy problem, especially in the postwar period—a problem related to the economic, political, and social viability of specific regions. Ownership, moreover, was usually several hundred years more entrenched than it was in the "latecomer" sectors.

Oil differs from electric power and coal in several fundamental ways. Private firms seldom existed before the state intervened in the sector. Indeed, oil is distinguished by its peripheral importance to the civilian economy and domestic politics in the industrial democracies in the early twentieth century. In most nations oil rarely accounted for even 5 percent of primary energy supply until mid-century. Yet military utility and emerging strategic significance consistently entangled oil matters in international affairs. In oil politics, for this reason, labor was always less relevant than diplomacy.

Finally, even in the single critical case of energy in Japan, there is significant diversity. Whereas the Japanese electric power industry originated with domestic private capital, free of government regulation, the coal industry originated under daimyo control during the Tokugawa period. The oil industry soon came under foreign domination. Each sector thus presents different arrays of interests and different solutions to the problems of business-government relations. Let us examine these parallels and differences more systematically, in the context of the propositions presented in Chapter 1.

I proposed that state intervention would be enhanced by six factors: market structure, centralization, developmental timing and finance, openness, the nature of the ruling coalition, and administrative tradition. The importance of some of these factors has been confirmed unambiguously. Electric power nationalization in Italy, for example, was an overt effort to broaden and stabilize the ruling coalition. Only the erosion of Christian Democratic support made nationalization compelling to industrial and party leaders; nothing else had changed. Likewise, vulnerability to foreign sources of energy, particularly of oil, clearly motivated such state actors as the British Admiralty in 1907 and Enrico Mattei in 1952 to negotiate vigorous intervention. Businessmen, it should be recalled, perceived the same vulnerability and vigorously encouraged intervention.

Other hypothesized relationships, however, may be ambiguous or even misleading, and certainly underspecified. I therefore begin by evaluating each factor individually against the evidence. (Ultimately, of course, our goal is to understand how these individual factors interact and combine to facilitate state intervention in the economy.) The evidence is drawn from several sectors, several countries, several centuries. It is clear that at any single point in a product or industrial life cycle "energy" is not a single business. We have explored "sunrise" businesses based on new technologies, such as synfuels and nuclear power; standardized commodities such as petroleum and electric power; and "sunset," mature businesses such as coal. Generalizations derived from these cases are more than the sum of experiences of isolated sectors. They incorporate state and society in complex, stable patterns of negotiated jurisdictions that are embedded in financial and product markets in ways that ensure that this case, while critical, is not exceptional. This diversity combines with the inherent strategic importance of energy to encourage rather than inhibit generalization.

Market Structure

I proposed in Chapter 1 that state intervention would be facilitated by the vertical fragmentation or horizontal isolation of the target sector. Diversified or integrated firms would fare well vis-à-vis the state, and oligopolistic sectors would do better than fragmented ones in thwarting or shaping state intervention. The evidence, however, is mixed on the political relevance of this simple measure of market structure.

First consider the structure of the electric power sector at the time of nationalization. Here (as in coal) lower barriers to entry, higher initial rates of return, and broader commercial markets resulted in larger numbers of private firms sooner than in oil. France had nearly two thousand private electric utilities at the time of nationalization; Britain had over five hundred. The consolidation of the Japanese sector under the Nippatsu arrangement resulted, by contrast, in the creation of nine regionally integrated utilities that resisted nationalization after the Occupation. These cases lend support to the proposition about fragmentation.

Italian experience brings us to reconsider that of Japan. Only thirty-three electric power firms existed when Nippatsu was created, and they had already been consolidated into five regionally integrated groups— by the commercial banks rather than by the state. MITI was allied with heavy industrial consumers, moreover, and was quite prepared to nationalize this consolidated utility sector; it might have succeeded but for a countervailing alliance between Matsunaga and SCAP.[21] Italy had more than three hundred electric utilities when ENEL was created, but 93 percent were affiliated with one of five major groups. The fragmentation argument thus looks less compelling.

Coal nationalizations are equally mixed about the relationship between fragmentation and state intervention. British coal was so fragmented in the prewar period that the firms could neither manage their relations with the state nor their collusion with one another. Nationalization nonetheless consumed nearly half a century of political struggle. Likewise, it was utterly impossible for Japanese coal producers to manage their own cartels, whether state-sanctioned or not. In France, however, twenty-three firms accounted for 90 percent of production in 1946, a concentration that is uncharacteristic of prenationalized coal industries. Again, we note how the consolidated Ruhrkohle syndicate could not be made to march to Hitler's drumbeat.

Oil is less diverse. State intervention there came earlier and more comprehensively than in electric power or coal. When the industrial democracies first considered nationalization, electric power was already a major source of primary energy and was already associated with staggering capital costs. Oil, on the other hand, was still incidental to the civilian economies. The oil market, unlike coal's, was not characterized by large numbers of regionally based producers. Entrenched private interests in coal and electric power ensured that debates over nationalization would be played out over decades. In contrast the Italian AGIP in 1926 and ENI in 1953, the British APOC in 1909, and the French CFP were each established with state equity where few or no private firms existed and where those that did exist were eager to accept and shape the protection of the state. This eagerness, as we shall see, was always associated more with vulnerability to foreign competitors than with market structure. Oil reminds us that the proposition about consolidation is useful only where private markets have already developed. Producers of a commodity of little consequence, no matter how concentrated they may be, are little protected from state intervention.

Oil provides a better window on to the variety of politically relevant ways in which markets can be fragmented. It moves analysis away from enumerating firms in narrowly defined product niches and toward competitive relationships among firms in broader markets. First consider the issue of interfuel competition. Industrial consumers need energy, but not necessarily a specific kind of energy. A substitutability between oil and coal, or between thermal and nuclear electric power, makes industrial consumers as relevant as producers to the domestic politics of energy. The creation of the British APOC involved an alliance between domestic oil firms and the military against coal interests. A marriage of convenience between domestic and foreign oil firms staved off French coal and viticultural opposition to the creation of CFP. Competition between coal and oil was clearly the defining characteristic of business-state conflict over energy policy in postwar Japan.

Second we consider the way that upstream and downstream divisions among oil interests have affected state policy in the industrial democracies. Burmah Oil used state equity to integrate downstream as APOC. Domestic French firms, protected as a distribution cartel until World War I, helped create CFP and ultimately used its authority to integrate upstream. But whereas European state intervention often served to create a consolidated industry or to consolidate a fragmented one, Japanese state intervention upstream created a fragmented overall industry. Ever since the creation of the Imperial Oil Company in 1939, and in large measure because of it, the political history of the Japanese oil industry has involved the state's unsuccessful attempts to consolidate the industry up- or downstream. Its many failures to do so have been among the most conspicuous failures of the strong Japanese state. Concerted and repeated efforts to establish a Japanese major have resulted in two Japanese minors; only one is state-owned, and neither is significant in the world oil market.

This "vertically fragmented intervention" characterizes the Japanese histories of all three energy sectors. It contrasts sharply with images of the comprehensive strategic targeting that is said to characterize Japanese industrial policy. In the prewar period national policy companies were established as joint public-private ventures (but always with state guarantees) in each sector. Imperial Oil and Nippatsu were established upstream with the support of banks or industrial consumers and at least some upstream firms, but only after efforts to establish a comprehensive state presence had failed. Both companies were restricted to energy production, both were explicitly prohibited from selling oil and electric power. State intervention in the coal industry, by contrast, was vertically fragmented downstream. Nittan was limited to sales; production was left to private firms.

This evidence suggests an unexpected relationship between market structure and state intervention. From protracted negotiations over the nature and extent of state intervention in Japan emerges a pattern of vertically fragmented, noncomprehensive intervention. The private sector consistently retained the most profitable portion of each business. Each national policy company was created as a compromise in which industrial consumers allied with the state and different energy producers allied with different parts of the state and with different groups of consumers. Nippatsu pitted generating firms against distribution firms; Nittan saw sellers oppose producers; and Imperial Oil found producers allied with the state against refiners and distributors.

The same pattern is common to many European cases. Energy-consuming industries often encouraged the state to take a commercial role in markets. Evidence shows that consumers supported the state's nationalization of electric power, coal, and oil in Britain, France, and Italy. But only in Japan did this coalition result in fragmented intervention rather than a consolidation of energy producers.

One way to explain this difference is to view the retention of market rights through fragmented intervention as a political solution to the split within oligopolistic markets between producers and consumers and among producers and distributors. Japan may owe its market-reproducing institutions of state intervention to the emergence of oligopoly politics.

M. W. Kirby writes of British industrial development that

> a major theme of British industrial history in the half-century before the outbreak of the Second World War was the movement in favour of what

Keynes termed "business collectivism"—the rise of the large scale company and of cooperative attempts by producers to stabilize their markets. . . . Arrangements for market-sharing were designed to preserve the existing structure of an industry.[22]

Yet business collectivism was far more advanced in Japan than in Britain, at least in the energy sector. British collieries, for example, were not part of companies as large and diversified as the *zaibatsu*. Labor, moreover, was politically more powerful in Britain than in Japan.[23] Nonetheless, oligopoly politics in prewar Japan was not fully consolidated; energy market segmentation coincided historically with the development of *zaibatsu* capital. Japanese energy markets were more oligopolistic than those in Europe but less vertically integrated. *Zaibatsu* interests were active in the mining of coal but not in its sale and distribution. They invested in refineries but not in upstream production. They financed electric utilities but seldom operated them. Individual *zaibatsu* and their postwar descendants could frustrate state programs that had broad support, as in Mitsubishi's recalcitrance vis-à-vis Kyōdō Oil in 1941, Mitsui's refusal to cooperate with the Uemura Program in 1968, or the undermining of coal rationalization by Sumitomo in 1955. These groups also coalesced around programs for nuclear power development or overseas oil exploration; but they typically did so as horizontally unconsolidated competitors rather than as vertically integrated sectors.

Marxist economic historians see monopoly capital where Keynes saw business collectivism. They depict an inexorable monopoly capital in the guise of *zaibatsu*-affiliated firms, "actively supported by the state," extending their domination of small producers by achieving control over most productive and technologically advanced businesses. The result is "excessive monopoly profits" derived from "differential rents" that are enforced through cartel arrangements with the blessing of the state.[24] But if businesses learned how to collude, they did so incompletely; if the *zaibatsu* welcomed a solution to market uncertainty, they often did so in spite of the state. Moreover, their solutions may now appear inexorable, but they are better understood as trials and errors in a highly volatile and fragmented market place.

Vertically fragmented intervention, then, can be explained as a political solution to the problems posed to producers by state efforts to consolidate, restructure, and control markets. Producers retained market rights as consistently as state planners attacked them. Their retention reinforced a market segmentation that is by European standards exaggerated—perhaps because these segmented markets persist among oligopolistic competitors. Ironically, political compromises that served targeted industries no less than they served state planners actually furthered market segmentation. They have brought market players no closer to the integration and consolidation that state planners have so often and so unsuccessfully sought.

On this first proposition, then, market structure matters a great deal, even if it matters in ways more subtle than we first imagined. Coalitions within and across fragmented markets do far more to determine how states intervene in markets than do fragmentation or consolidation simply defined. Clearly, we cannot understand state intervention in Japanese energy markets without understanding how markets were structured and how structured markets shaped interests to favor, entice, or oppose state intervention. In Japan, unlike Europe, these interventions reproduce segmented markets to sustain private control.

Centralization

My second proposition held that the interventionist state is highly centralized. State centralization is, I posited, the public-sector analogue to market concentration. Neo-Weberian assumptions suggest that rational, centralized states should be stronger vis-à-vis private interests than other states. Prospects for state intervention should be greatest where the state is centralized and private interests are divided.

Centralization, it is widely acknowledged, is more easily asserted than measured. Like state strength itself, centralization is a matter of degree. But though much of the literature on states and markets stresses the political relevance of state centralization, our evidence focuses attention on divisions within states. States are divided in diverse and politically relevant ways, just as markets are. The political fragmentation of markets is often reproduced in inter- and intrabureaucratic form. Is this cause or consequence, or both, of market structures?

Like markets, states can be fragmented horizontally and vertically. Horizontal fragmentation has been more relevant to state intervention, but we have seen more evidence of both than of unified state action. Europe seldom achieved consensus for the nationalization of oil, coal, or electric power. In fact, conflict between the British Admiralty and the Treasury (in the APOC case) or between Mattei and the Italian cabinet (in the ENI case) was as central to the outcome as was conflict between business and government. But this proposition and the deceptively simple observation upon which it is based find their most direct test in Japanese energy. Nowhere is there supposed to be a greater degree of central coordination and control.

Consider first the vertical component. The policy record of each energy sector reveals considerable divisions between central and local authorities. The actions of the Japanese central government are highly circumscribed by territorially based interests represented in local governments that have significant autonomy.[25] The center is poorly insulated from patronage, legislative bargaining, or the electoral and party systems themselves.

Local interests first appeared in energy markets during the Tokugawa period, when daimyo assumed control of the mines. In the one case when it overruled local authority, the young Meiji state "released" the mines to private entrepreneurs in 1869, just prior to the abolition of the *han* governments. These same mines were nationalized in 1872 with private support and in response to calls for protection. After reprivatization in the mid-1880s, and throughout the subsequent hundred years of state intervention in the coal industry, local interests—usually small, independent mineowners—have significantly affected the terms of state intervention. The coal business created some of the most influential political and business dynasties in Japan, among them the Aso and Yasukawa families of Chikuhō. Individuals of unassailable (and occasionally unethical) political influence, such as Kiso Shigeyoshi of Fukuoka, also emerged from the regional mines. Under Kiso's leadership, for example, Japan delayed compliance with ILO accords for more than a decade even though Japan was an early signatory. Kiso also masterminded the campaign to force concessions on the importation of Chinese (Bujun) coal in 1932. Again, it was Kiso and other locally based, non-*zaibatsu* coal interests that mobilized parliamentary support to emasculate state control of the mines in 1947 and destroy the fragile Socialist Democratic party government. For nearly twenty years mineowners worked through local politicians and LDP Dietmen dependent upon their support, frustrating all the central bureaucracy's efforts to abet the switch to oil. Throughout the history of Japanese coal mining, in short, local interests have wrested concessions from the state and shaped public policy. These interests failed only when the central bureaucracy allied itself with national, *zaibatsu* coal firms, or well-organized industrial consumers, or both.

Japanese coal provides the richest examples of local interests frustrating a nominally centralized state, but by no means the only ones. Agricultural and marine interests organized in 1939 to get their elected representatives to block the proposed Joint Sales Monopoly. This coalition reappeared in 1954–55, when the Fishing Industries Association used its political muscle to force MITI to allocate scarce currency for extra crude oil imports. Indeed, the success with which local interests protected their commerical rights stimulated the defensive formation of the Petroleum Association of Japan in 1955. The only case in which the central government overwhelmed the localities is the Nippatsu dissolution of 1945–50. Then localities joined with the left and industrial consumers to seek retention of the quasi-national utility; importantly it was SCAP, not MITI, that overruled them.

These cases illustrate how the Japanese state is vertically fragmented.

However, as noted above, it is *horizontal* fragmentation and intra-bureaucratic politics at the center that more commonly frustrate the centralizing aspirations of state planners. Market transformations that involve a well-coordinated Japanese state are exceptionally rare. This book has explored more than seventy market transformations in three energy sectors over hundreds of years, and in more than two-thirds of them I find evidence of politically relevant divisions within the central bureaucracy.

The classical confrontation is between "guardians" of the public treasury and "advocates" for special interests or special programs.[26] In Japan, of course, it takes the form of disputes between MITI and the Finance Ministry or the Administrative Management Agency. This confrontation has significantly affected state intervention in the creation of the New Energy Development Organization, for instance, every coal rationalization program from 1955 until 1968, and MITI's abortive efforts to establish an upstream state oil corporation from 1955 until the 1970s.

A second pattern of intrabureaucratic politics that belies characterizations of Japan as a centralized state involves the many confrontations among advocates. The best examples are the battles between the Science and Technology Agency and MITI over nuclear power, the struggles between army and navy for control of military refineries, and the disputes between the Ministry of Commerce and Industry and the Agriculture Ministry on behalf of their different clients. What Japanese often call "vertical administration" (*tatewari gyōsei*) is a competitive, sectional centralism. Characterized by insularity, it ensures duplicated programs as often as it engenders administrative stalemate and political intervention.[27]

Third, conflicts are frequent *within* MITI itself over the proper allocation of energy policy resources. MITI and its advisory commissions often speak with many tongues, and seldom has there been a single, consistent energy policy within MITI, much less the central government. In oil, confrontations between an upstream MITI and a downstream MITI, a producers' MITI and a consumers' MITI, have ensured inconsistency and confusion. Confusion was also evident in the debates over state control of coal in 1947 and over establishing the Electric Power Development Corporation in 1952.

In sum, although it is impossible to deny the pervasive presence of the Japanese state in domestic energy markets, the policy process that generates that presence is segmented as much by the state as by the market. MITI is neither a single fount of coordinated economic policy nor an impartial arbiter of conflicting societal interests. Expectations about state intervention which we derive from structural characterizations of centralization are frustrated by the evidence from these many cases.

Developmental Timing and Finance

My third proposition concerned relationships among timing of industrialization, concentration of capital, and intervention of the state. In Chapter 1, I noted Alexander Gerschenkron's hypothesis that late developers face large and "lumpy" entry costs, and so nations that amass large sums of investment capital gain an advantage. Usually state banks can most readily perform this investment function. Through their influence in financial markets, states gain control in industrial sectors where investment needs are great, usually where production is highly standardized. Energy sectors have exceptionally high capital costs and are exceptionally standardized, and so they should conform easily to our expectations.

The subsidiary hypothesis held that where capital is concentrated, private banks and states alike will want to promote the cartelization of industry, to protect their investments and avert what Gerschenkron calls "fratricidal struggles among their children."[28] The structure of industry, especially its cartelization in middle stages of development, should be linked to the ways in which financial markets are concentrated, which in turn should be highly susceptible to state influence. In short, we expect banks to play a disproportionately large role in the transformation of energy markets and states to play a disproportionately large role in the development of financial markets.

Various pieces of evidence confirm the first hypothesis. Without state capital and protection, both Britain and France would have missed opportunities to establish a viable domestic petroleum industry. When domestic capital ignored the development of Italian oil refineries, the Fascist state stepped into the breach. In Japan the state intervened most directly in energy (and other) markets early in industrialization, particularly as a direct commercial participant in the coal business. State intervention and the socialization of risk were invaluable to late-developing countries such as Italy and Japan, and to late-developing industries within Britain and France.

However, our evidence suggests that the concentration of *private* capital was of greater moment, and so findings related to the subsidiary hypothesis are more intriguing. Although the financial system in Japan structures choices for industry and provides leverage for the state, it does so in a political process through which usually private capital has *already* captured the benefits of socialized risk and parceled out debt. Let us consider the role of private financial institutions and the Japanese state in three energy businesses.

State capital as noted, was critical to the early development of the Japanese coal mines. But with the growth and development of private financial institutions, the importance of state finance receded. The mines were turned over to private investors once the public treasury had borne the initial capital costs. These mining ventures, in turn, became "cash cows" for the burgeoning *zaibatsu* empires of Sumitomo, Mitsubishi, and especially Mitsui. Also important during sundry mid-century crises, of course, were the financial guarantees that the state gave to banks and firms that invested in the coal business.

More interesting is a lesser-known relationship between public and private finance. The failure of MITI's postwar coal programs, as reported in Chapter 3, can be partly attributed to the evacuation of the coal business by city banks. In the 1960s mine indebtedness increased even faster than operating losses—but this increase did not reflect a commitment by private banks to salvage the mining firms. To the contrary, politicians and bureaucrats were replacing private with public debt in a desperate and doomed attempt to save the sector. But banks were determined to get out, and they did so while they could—with public funds. Neither the mining firms nor their erstwhile bankers paid as much for failure as the Japanese treasury did.

State intervention in electric power and in oil was late compared to coal. In electric power the state merely confirmed arrangements made earlier by the city banks. In February 1932 Mitsui Bank led a group of major creditors in proposing a national holding company to eliminate redundant facilities; the utilities would manage the company under bank supervision. The Denryoku Renmei, a self-control association under the nominal jurisdiction of the state, gave these banks the power to arbitrate in cases of excessive competition, participate in setting prices, and allocate markets. By the time the Japanese state assumed "control" of the electric utilities in 1938, the banks were already coordinating the world's third-largest electric power sector; they had secured state assistance to eliminate the massive foreign debts that had stimulated their direct intervention in the first place, and they were openly seeking more profitable markets. Despite numerous efforts by reform bureaucrats, the sector would not be consolidated until the banks were ready. In a manner quite consistent with European experience,[29] Japanese financial institutions worked together, in alliance with the state, to amalgamate the industry against the will of some of the firms themselves.

Half a century later the pattern repeated itself in the Japanese oil industry. Prewar financial circles showed little interest in oil exploration, preferring to process foreign crude under the protection of the state. Upstream, the few firms active in the business found themselves short of capital for exploration. In 1938, after Japanese banks had turned a deaf ear to them, these firms prevailed upon the state to create the Imperial Oil Resources Development Company. Subsequent state efforts to integrate the Japanese oil business vertically were numerous and unsuccessful. In 1939 the military had to settle for a refinery specializing in aviation fuel; in more than a dozen efforts civilian bureaucrats could not entice the industry to consolidate on their terms.

Certainly financial assistance from the state was welcome; indeed, the establishment of the Petroleum Resources Development Corporation in 1967 provided the financial guarantees that finally stimulated private banks to move into the market. But most striking was the clear relationship between bank profitability and the restructuring of the Japanese oil industry in the mid-1980s. Banks continued to profit from the fragmented Japanese oil industry through two international oil crises, and only after they judged this profitability to be exhausted did the industry begin to change. The second most fragmented oil market in the industrial democracies looked suddenly likely to become one of the most consolidated. The Japanese state supported this transformation, though it was one that it neither enticed nor could have managed on its own.

In sum, Japanese coal conforms to the initial hypothesis that the state will intervene more directly during the initial stages of late national development. That private investors in oil and electric power have been selective in relying upon state assistance does not disconfirm the idea. Nor does the fact that these investors have consistently separated assistance from control by negotiating state jurisdiction. Meiji Japan, as noted in Chapter 3, is replete with similar state intervention in other sectors, among them steel, railroads, chemicals, and munitions.

The evidence relating to the cartelization of industry once privatized is more intriguing. It suggests a relationship between state and financial markets different from our initial hypothesis. We expected the state, assuming a developmental mandate, to intervene when competition is excessive, to redirect, stabilize, and stimulate growth; but we observe a process in which markets adjust and market players then prevail upon the state to absorb the costs associated with adjustment. Cartels and collusive arrangements involving state, industry, and financial institutions are therefore linked to the evolving norms of reciprocal consent; private banks are disproportionately important in shaping the way the state intervenes in markets. The pervasive role of the state in Japanese development, we observe, was usually preceded by extensive accommodation to private interests, especially banks.

This conclusion helps clarify the significance of our observation that the chief institutional distinction between Japanese and European state intervention is a nearly exclusive reliance by the Japanese state upon financial mechanisms. In energy, as overall, government financial institutions, offering guaranteed loans at low interest rates, far outnumber the few remaining commercially active state enterprises. In the mid-1980s loans to industry from government-owned financial institutions accounted for more than 10 percent of all industrial loans in Japan: one-third were in primary industry and electric power, one-fifth in transportation. State banks in Europe are even more numerous, but their origins are different. Italy's Institutio Reconstruzzione Industriale (IRI), for example, was created in 1933 after the country's banking system collapsed. France nationalized banks for purposes of reform and consolidation. These and other states have a broad financial presence as creditors in industrial markets where they have a commercial presence as well. But in Japan the state became a guarantor only after consistently failing to control directly productive resources.

Why do Japanese banks not act like Japanese manufacturers and block competition from the state? In fact they have done precisely that: the Japanese state neither competes with nor determines allocations by private banks.[30] State financial institutions are more than additional creditors in Japanese financial markets, they are guarantors, protecting not just targeted industries but the banks as well. Protection is explicit in their charter, as one analyst has concluded:

> The government identified the need for specialized long-term credit banks in the early 1950s to relieve the pressures on ordinary banks for long-term funds. . . . There are twelve government financial institutions . . . established to provide finance for specific purposes judged to be in the national interest. *They are expressly prohibited from competing with the banks and other financial institutions.*[31]

In the prewar period national policy companies (*kokusaku gaisha*) institutionalized this role of guarantor. The state quietly but uniformly guaranteed the dividends of private partners in each of these joint ventures. After the Occupation the distinction between creditor and guarantor was reaffirmed in two separate struggles, one with the Finance Ministry in 1955 and one with MITI in 1963.[32] Finance drafted a bill that authorized it to compel banks to invest in public bonds; the measure was killed by vigorous private opposition before being submitted to Diet. Eight years later Sahashi Shigeru, the advocate of state control who as MITI Coal Bureau chief in 1954 had hoped to nationalize the coal mines, wrote the Special Measures Law for the Promotion of Designated Industries. He hoped to invest MITI with market authority that would have rivaled anything known during the halcyon days of state control. The key provision required private lenders to finance industries designated by MITI. The law was eviscerated by bankers even before it went to Diet, where it died in full public view.[33]

The relationship between Japanese financial markets, state intervention, and state leadership remains among the least understood aspects of business-government relations in modern Japan. Considerable evidence shows that financial markets in Japan were as much the product of negotiation and reciprocal consent as they were elsewhere, but the view persists that Japanese policy makers systematically controlled financial institutions to promote economic growth. Andrew Spindler, for example, argues that "Japan's leading banks, although concerned primarily with commercial gain, have . . . of necessity recognized the dominant role of the state in the Japanese financial system, and they have deferred to official wishes as a matter of sound business judgment."[34] John Zysman writes that "the market for industrial loans is structured by the government. . . . *Prices in all but the very short term money markets are artificially maintained by the government.* . . . In Japan a rational banker *must* wish to follow the lead of the central bank. The government's industrial priorities of growth and exports will be met."[35]

These views are not confirmed by the evidence presented in this book. On the contrary, the timing of the development of oligopolistic Japanese finance capital seems to be both cause and consequence of the Japanese state-as-guarantor.

Openness

The fourth explanation proposed for state intervention concerned the vulnerability of domestic markets to foreign competition. Those states with the most open markets should have the most active public sectors. When a state cannot, for whatever reason, effectively protect domestic producers, it may need to own or regulate all or significant parts of strategic sectors. In smaller, trade-dependent states, openness may also be associated with variants of liberal corporatism because such states need domestic solidarity to compete and survive in world markets.

Because European states are relatively self-sufficient in coal and electric power, only oil provides a cross-national test of these hypotheses. The earliest state interventions in domestic petroleum markets were linked either to military strategy or to demands by domestic firms for protection or subsidies. Behind both loomed the possibility that foreign, multinational oil companies would come to accumulate vast financial power. As the strategic utility of petroleum became clear, so states increasingly embraced the demands of domestic firms. In short, openness and vulnerability shaped state intervention regarding petroleum in ways significantly different from those in other energy sectors.

Political demands were married to developmental strategy in different ways, of course. In Italy the Fascist state intervened before a domestic industry had formed. After 1945 progressives directed the Italian industry, but for essentially similar purposes. Distributors in France organized their domestic market before World War I, but they could not protect themselves from being absorbed by vertically integrated firms beyond the discipline of their cartel. Penetration of their market by foreign majors led French firms to seek upstream integration in Poland, Rumania, and Mesopotamia. This last (and greatest) prize required state protection as much as it required partnership with the majors themselves. A subsequent and similar vulnerability led French producers and the state downstream toward their 1928 Petroleum Industry Law. Meanwhile, across the Channel, the British state was judging the strategic imperatives of oil sufficient to overrule producers of other fuels; it established itself in the oil business.

States adjust to international markets in different ways.[36] Some hegemons, such as Britain in the early twentieth century, are able (and prefer) to transform international markets. The Japanese, on the other hand, have consistently directed their attention inward, toward domestic structures that they could more effectively negotiate. In the Japanese case the scarcity of domestic resources contributed to a widespread perception of vulnerability that led in turn to a more uniform rejection of openness as a strategy of economic development. Dependency theorists predict that industries tied to foreign capital will be powerful vis-à-vis the host state. But Japanese oil, apparently because foreigners dominated it, was the energy sector least effective in achieving the state policy it wanted. Historically in Japan political coalitions that support protectionism have arisen to preclude rather than cope with the most onerous effects of openness.[37]

Fear of foreign control through ties to foreign capital has consistently and profoundly motivated Japanese economic policy over the past century. All three energy sectors have seen much "fear of the blue eyes" (*aome kyōfu*). Evidence appears earliest in the Meiji nationalization of the coal mines and other strategic sectors. The massive foreign debt of electric power in the 1930s led the state and city banks to intervene, and despite the attractions of foreign capital, postwar reconstruction of the industry never attained the same degree of foreign dependence. Indeed, no private electric utility ventured to raise capital abroad even though Occupation legislation expressly permitted capitalization on foreign money markets. Politicians and bureaucrats made domestic capital more attractive by extracting scarce resources from state financial institutions newly created for the purpose. Reliance on foreign capital was thereby limited to the Electric Power Development Corporation, which was perceived as less vulnerable because it was a joint MITI-private venture.

Oil even more unambiguously presents vulnerability begetting collusive solutions and protection in the guise of liberalization. Unlike electric power or coal, the oil business was coveted by foreign investors. By 1953 the extent to which foreign interests held equity in Japanese firms was already anomalous. A decade later Japan was finally ready (and therefore willing) to take advantage of liberalized world trade. MITI created the Energy Roundtable to debate and design precisely such a strategy for post-GATT Japan to liberalize markets while simultaneously protecting them. The action paralleled Sahashi's ham-handed attempt in the early 1960s to establish MITI control of the economy to preclude "colonization" by the United States. Sahashi's plan was rejected by business because it tried to do too much, but its stepchild, the Petroleum Industry Law of 1962, was acceptable once jurisdiction had been substituted for control. Postwar debates on petroleum policy were dominated by schemes to preclude the onerous consequences of liberalization without sacrificing access to foreign markets for competitive Japanese goods. This was a subtle balance, requiring persistence and energy to negotiate collaborative solutions.

In sum, openness is clearly associated with state intervention in all the sectors examined in this book. In Japan, however, it is the vulnerability that openness engenders, breeding protectionist coalitions, rather than the political logics inherent in an open economy which seems to stimulate protracted efforts to manage markets through state intervention. The consistent success of these efforts is attributable to the nature of the ruling coalition in Japan.

Ruling Coalition

The fifth proposition concerned the relationship between state intervention and the nature of the ruling coalition. Coalitions of bureaucrats, businessmen, and politicians vary, I proposed, in the breadth and identity of their constituencies and in the stability of their authority. State intervention should thus be market-conforming where the politics of reciprocal consent are inclusive and where these broadly representative actors are stable over time. Conversely, coalitions that are sharply discontinuous and more narrowly constituted should be associated with a more competitive state presence and with market-displacing state intervention.

Evidence from both Europe and Japan sustains this relationship. The European cases examined in Chapter 2 are especially clear vis-à-vis the second half of the proposition. British state intervention in coal and electric power was extended further with each shift of power in the half decade that preceded nationalization. Ultimately these nationalizations were abetted by the shift between Labour and Conservative governments after World War II. The same was true of the French mines. In postwar France a discredited elite was displaced by a government of counterelites intent upon a broad program of nationalization. A leftist plurality and labor unrest in the French mines translated into a program of state control.

Italy's nationalization of electric power is the archetype for understanding how shifts in or erosion of a ruling coalition can stimulate state intervention. Beneath a veneer of hyperinstability a broad and stable DC coalition governed Italy in the early postwar years with business support. Four separate efforts to nationalize the electric utilities in the 1950s were stillborn. But by the early 1960s the coalition had narrowed significantly, directly affecting the political calculus of the DC. The creation of a national electric utility, ENEL, was the political price exacted by the left wing of the Socialist party for participation in the newly stabilized and broader ruling coalition. The observation of the leading DC economist of the period bears repeating: "If the nationalization is judged politically wise, neither its cost nor its financial consequences should render it inadvisable."[38]

State intervention in Japan has also been abetted by shifts in the ruling coalition. As the development of the Japanese state has been nearly linear, however, with broadening and increasing stability since the Meiji restoration, these shifts have had less dramatic effects than in Europe. Indeed, the relatively regular expansion of the ruling coalition in post-Meiji Japan helps explain the peculiar dynamics that I have called reciprocal consent. In the evidence at hand the role of labor provides a measure of breadth and the way financial circles coalesced in support of the state acts as a measure of stability.

The most narrow and unstable ruling coalition in modern Japan was that of early Meiji. The tenuousness of the young oligarchy contributed to its assumption of a direct role in the market. Certainly this was so with coal. The demands of state building at first led the oligarchy to privatize the mines to frustrate the emergence of competing centers of power. Shifting strategic concerns, specifically perceptions of foreign threats, thereupon led to nationalization. As entrepreneurs subsequently appeared, the mines were again transferred to private control.

Emerging stability was not always accompanied by a broadening of the coalition, however. Labor was excluded throughout the prewar period, an exclusion that helped consolidate the ruling coalition in Japan as it veered toward its authoritarian experiment. Except for the mobilization of mineworkers by small mineowners in 1932, organized labor would matter only occasionally in energy politics until unleashed by the Occupation in 1945. Then it mattered very much, and nowhere did it matter more to national politics than in electric power and coal.

The most dramatic case of labor's importance to policy outcome was that of state control of the mines. As in the France of the same time, the installation of a leftist plurality contributed to a period of instability and to an abortive experiment with state mine management. This intervention was conspicuously abetted by labor unrest (miners, their ranks swelled by convicts and Korean corvée laborers, were arguably the most exploited workers in Japan). This experiment was as close as the Japanese state would ever come to a comprehensive and direct commercial presence in the energy market place. The debates would topple the delicate coalition of Socialists and "progressive" capitalists, and ultimately the whole episode contributed to the consolidation of the postwar conservative coalition.

A similar story can be told about the electric power workers. They too remained an unorganized, repressed, and therefore trivial political force during the prewar period. The Occupation's initial encouragement of organized labor, however, brought often violent struggles for control of the industry. Densan, led by Sasaki Ryōsaku, turned off the nation's electric power on several occasions during these turbulent years; but these workers would exercise their power only as long as Nippatsu remained the national electric utility. With the establishment of the SCAP-Matsunaga private monopoly system, Densan lost leverage. The only other evidence that energy-sector labor was uneasy with the evolving regime was in nuclear power development. But the battle in the Japan Atomic Energy Research Institute was joined by academics and scientists, much less of a match for industry than Densan had been.

The Miike coal mine strike of 1959–61 was the final paroxysm of labor unrest in postwar Japan. It proved to be the most protracted and futile dispute in the history of Japanese labor relations. Mitsui's lockout successfuly broke the Tanrō strike, but the success with which Tanrō cultivated public opinion and elicited state support for miners suggests that the terms of labor's exclusion may already have shifted. Each of the six subsequent public efforts to salvage the domestic coal industry was as much to assist miners as to bail out mineowners and their financiers.

To what extent is labor excluded from the ruling coalition? The matter is much debated in analyses of Japanese politics. Certainly, organized labor is not formally a part of the LDP's "grand coalition,"[39] but LDP hegemony has depended as much upon electoral as upon interest group inclusiveness. The ruling party has used incumbency to reward support from all manner of societal interests. Sometimes its reach is indirect; labor may not be incorporated by the conservative mainstream, but it surely may be coopted, for labor has shared considerably in Japan's postwar economic growth. At other times the reach of the coalition is direct; we have seen how opponents to nuclear power were bought off. Ellis Krauss and Michio Muramatsu have found, moreover, that the groups excluded from the ruling coalition—especially labor and citizens' groups—enjoy independent, direct, and apparently efficacious access to the bureaucracy.[40]

The political efficacy of labor has profound implications for the nature and extent of state intervention in Japanese energy markets. Reciprocity among the parts of a routinized system is the core of conservative dominance and reciprocal consent in Japan, derived in part from the most important struggles for control of the market. In Europe, the struggle was class-based, labor versus management. When labor won, as in France and Britain in the late 1940s, it entered the ruling coalition through the front door, and the state intervened directly in the economy. In Japan, on the other hand, battles between capital and the state were more significant, largely because capital had already snuffed out labor's political aspirations. In shaping state intervention the struggle between large and small mines or between coal and oil were more important than the confrontation between miners and owners. Likewise electric power did not experience the confrontations between utility owners and organized labor which racked European politics; rather, the state typically ratified accommodations decided among banks, utilities, and heavy industry. These are segmented rather than Manichean struggles. They take place in a political stew of fragmented but stable balances within a broad conservative coalition. Labor is incorporated, albeit in a peculiar way: it has entered the conservative mansion through the tradesman's entrance.

Organized business, on the other hand is more than an invited guest. The Japanese government responds to pressures for private ordering of energy markets exerted by a conservative coalition involving all segments of the businesses involved, up- and downstream as well as producers and consumers. The institutional manifestation of this business coalition (and indeed of postwar business-government collaboration more generally) is the Federation of Economic Organizations, Keidanren. No other institution so dominates the politics of energy or economic policy more generally (besides MITI itself). We have seen Keidanren wield veto power, as it blocked the Sahashi Program in 1962 as well as all efforts before 1967 to establish a state petroleum corporation up- or downstream. We have seen its counsel transform other initiatives toward market conformity, as in the second Petroleum Industry Law and the creation of the New Energy Development Organization. We have also seen its deliberations enshrined as public policy, most strikingly in the way its bitterly contested internal allocations of domestic coal purchases in 1959 and price levels in 1961 became the standard for MITI's own First Coal Program.

The breadth and stability of Japan's ruling coalition seems to be fundamental to any convincing account of state intervention in Japan. It is commonly characterized as Japan, Incorporated, a term just as commonly rejected by Japan specialists.[41] If we appreciate how difficult it is for large, diversified corporations to coordinate and implement strategic decisions, I am not sure that the image is wholly misleading. The evidence of this book suggests that the extent to which we can "unbundle" Japan, Inc., is the extent to which we can profitably apply it. "Japan, Inc." has to *include* rather than exclude labor. Also, it has to consider the political relevance of segmented private markets, which regime stability can mask. Japanese elites are stable representatives of diverse interests and therefore have to confront their diversity with concession and compromise. In short, "consensus" rests more upon a structure of stability than upon a culture of harmony, for as Vernon argues, "with the stability of the various participants assured, none can as readily afford to win an isolated decision through evasive action."[42]

Administrative Tradition

I hypothesized that states will be likely to intervene when they have a history, or administrative tradition, of intervention. Some states are more likely to intervene in markets than others, I suggested, because domestic structures have been conditioned by previous intervention. Surely this book shows that different domestic structures are associated with different solutions to problems of capitalist development. We have identified a variety of ways in which states intervene in markets. Different states have at different times intervened as partners, guarantors, creditors, and rivals of private firms. They have intervened to displace or to conform to shifting markets. Our explanations for these differences have included aspects of market structure, bureaucratic centralization, developmental timing, openness, and the nature of ruling coalitions. Administrative tradition can be used to differentiate among general patterns of state intervention.

But it is not always obvious how these patterns condition intervention. The elite corps of the Grandes Ecoles—the men of the Polytechnique and St. Cyr—may distinguish the statist French from Italian or American bureaucrats. As we have seen, however, the proximate determinants of French intervention have closely resembled those in other industrial democracies. Oil supplies grow indeterminant, it seems, and ruling coalitions grow unstable without respect to tradition. Our accounts of state intervention in coal and electric power in transwar Britain often apply to Japan with only minor amendment; the American state of permanent receivership has many parallels to the Japanese guarantor state. Administrative traditions depend upon the politics of state intervention as much as they shape them. I conclude, therefore, that this variable was badly underspecified in Chapter 1.

The basic problem is imagining that a single factor is at work when states intervene in markets. Detailed analysis shows how in each case specific factors modify the influence of a specific independent variable. Although some hypotheses were confirmed in particular cases, others were rejected; some have proved wholly misspecified. Explanations for state intervention based upon such sectoral characteristics as substitutability, product homogeneity, production scale, or product life cycle, for example, fail to account for observed cross-national (or even intranational) variations. Fragmentation of market structure in France and England impeded state intervention in electric power, yet in Japanese coal a similar fragmentation invited alliances between industrial consumers and the state which abetted intervention.

Centralization is equally problematic in predicting state response. In Japan the bureaucracy was first diverted from its nationalization schemes and then had to supply cheap factors of production as its only chance to become a market player. In Italy, on the other hand, the bureaucracy created a national champion where no domestic firm existed. But before we can think of the Italian economy as dominated by a strong state, we have to appreciate that its success in oil was linked to problems of openness and foreign domination in the early 1950s, and it owed its success in electric power to a shift in the ruling coalition a decade later.

In short these factors do not provide competing monocausal explanations for observed variation in the nature and extent of state intervention. They clearly interact in a variety of ways that require better specification if comparative and historical study is to respond to calls for "middle-range generalizations" about the roles of states in markets.[43]

For example, the effects of timing and openness on patterns of state intervention are modified by the structural characteristics of states and markets. Equally open economies respond very differently to their vulnerabilities. Italy, France, and Japan are all vulnerable to disruptions in the energy supply, but their different oil markets have produced different adjustment strategies. The two most fragmented oil markets, the United States and Japan, experience the least intervention, despite very different levels of vulnerability and self-sufficiency. I repeat the conclusion from Chapter 2: state intervention depends not only upon openness and vulnerability but upon *who* is vulnerable and *where* that vulnerability resides in a particular political economy.

Markets and states intervene in the same way to mitigate the effects of timing. Late development helps explain patterns of intervention through state and private investment banks. But the development of oligopolistic finance does not automatically generate market conformity or market displacement by public institutions. The state must reproduce consolidated markets in ways that reinforce the stability and expand the breadth of the ruling coalition before the business of the state can be determined. Patterns of intervention differ significantly among late developers.

The independent effects of state and market structures are likewise modified by a process of reciprocal consent that both constrains and invites intervention. From the degree of market fragmentation or state centralization we cannot predict the roles of states in markets. Each role is both cause and consequence of different coalitional struggles, which can produce very different patterns of state intervention. The nature and extent of state intervention derive most proximately from the breadth and stability of ruling coalitions. These coalitions can reflect market and state structures that are shaped initially by developmental peculiarities, especially timing and openness. Taken together, these interactions are the administrative traditions that, assisted by detailed historical and comparative analysis, predict little but explain much—especially if they are not posited as competing monocausal explanations.

Explanation still remains to be done. We have yet to answer the empirical questions about state identity, autonomy, capacity, and development set out in the first chapter of this book. We now turn to this final task.

ANSWERING THE EMPIRICAL QUESTIONS

This book is about the relationships between businesses and states; the central unit of analysis is market transformation rather than industrial or economic policy because government intentions, actions, and reactions assume a disproportionate emphasis when we make state policy the dependent variable. By focusing upon market transformation, I have assumed a more neutral vantage point from which to observe business-government concertation in economic and industrial policy making. Marino Regini justifies this perspective by imploring us to look

> at the other, less well-known, side of the moon . . . [to focus] on the strategies of interest organizations rather than on the role of the state. . . . Neo-corporatist writers pay very little attention to the conditions which may lead organized interests to move autonomously into a corporatist path as a part of *their own* strategy of exchange, by exercising self-restraint in their market actions, and by even implicitly inducing governments to grant them a public status.[44]

Changes in political and economic relations between buyers and sellers, between suppliers and producers, or among firms in the same business were systematically explored for evidence that state actors and structures mattered. The evidence that they do matter is overwhelming. State initiative is ubiquitous in the policy records of Japanese oil, coal, and electric power. In the seventy separate cases of attempted or actual transformation of Japanese energy markets that this book has explored in detail, the Japanese state assumed the initiative alone or in coalition with private actors more than 90 percent of the time.

Our interpretation of this initiative must depend, however, upon answers to the empirical questions posed in Chapter 1 regarding state identity and autonomy. Analytically it is useful to separate state structures from social structures, using conventional distinctions among bureaucracies, political parties, and interest groups. But the interactions among these groups suggest that what is useful for analytical purposes evades a fundamental theoretical problem: the clear identification and separation of state and social structures.

What we call "the state" is consistently a central actor in the energy policy networks of the industrial democracies. But our limited test of the "statist" perspective in historical cases suggests that there can be no purely theoretical specification of the extent to which and the conditions under which state preferences are autonomous. We cannot attribute autonomous motives to bureaucrats, even if policy outcomes that enhance state power suggest such motives. States and markets belong to businessmen and bureaucrats alike; state power and private power frequently enhance each other. The observation may make problems with analytically convenient distinctions between state and society, but it makes the politics of reciprocal consent comprehensible.

In the Japanese case this politics joins the delicate balancing of state jurisdiction with private control to belie monolithic misinterpretations of Japan, Inc., on the one hand, and belief in state leadership of quiescent businessmen, on the other. State and private actors have clashed often and with widespread effects; so have businessmen and so have bureaucrats among themselves. Any clear identification of state and private interest must therefore be limited by an appreciation of how each is structured and how much each infiltrates the other. Clearly the Japanese state evolved as an autonomous player in energy and financial markets. With its "visions" and goals it has more often than not assumed a strategic position in political negotiations over markets. Yet our evidence suggests that its autonomy was induced through a process of reciprocal consent—that is, the Japanese state has a strategic role less because it leads than because it negotiates its authority. Identifiable state actors, to the extent that they actually lead, select (and sometimes create) demands for authoritative response; they ally themselves with private actors (occasionally of their own creation) whose demands conform to their own

286

view of proper economic adjustment. State autonomy in Japan has always been buttressed by congenial private interests. The identity and the autonomy of the state have been under perpetual negotiation. Negotiated jurisdictions become routinized in the context of a broad and stable ruling coalition.

Japanese political stability thus depends upon the same interpenetration of elites that makes identification of the state so problematic. The Japanese state can create and manipulate interests, but it can also be colonized by them. Although Japanese elites combine for mutual benefit to confront market perturbations, it is impossible to judge a priori who in specific policy settings is the client of whom. By relying upon stable and evolving structures of support and exchange through the politics of reciprocal consent, Japanese elites combine in a variety of ways. We need to specify that variety, to "unbundle" everyone's favorite strawman.[45]

We start to understand Japan, Inc., with an acknowledgment that the metaphor is misspecified. No student of the modern, diversified corporation would assume decision processes as mechanistic as those posited by some observers of Japan. Evolving and more appropriate structural models of the Japanese political economy properly shift analysis from state policy to the subgovernmental processes that create policy.[46] In the Japanese policy system we need to look beyond the obvious and easy characterizations of unity and state leadership just as we need to appreciate the formal and informal policy networks that confer "autonomy" upon the state. Clearly, we must seek underlying dynamics and understand how private interests are invited into the interior processes of government;[47] but we must also understand how the government is invited into the interior processes of the market.

This reciprocity is embedded in the notion of administrative guidance (*gyōsei shidō*), the informal policy mechanism often invoked as evidence of state control in Japan. I argue for a more nuanced understanding of business-government relations. Michael Young points out that administrative guidance is effective only to the extent that the regulated parties participate in determining the regulatory regime. This "private ordering" is in turn enforced by the stability of the coalition itself:

Administrators often leave largely to the parties the task of determining many of the details of the regulatory scheme and, on occasion, even the appropriate degree of regulation. Frequently, regulation amounts to little more than an administrative organ's structuring of a bargaining situation in which the parties are compelled to negotiate with each other over the proper allocation of the benefits and burdens of regulation. . . . Administrative guidance issued without such consultation may meet with disobedience and, in rare instances, litigation. Agencies avoid this result by committing much of the actual formation and implementation of guidance to the regulated parties themselves.[48]

What structural characterization should we choose for this subgovernment-based private ordering? Daniel Okimoto uses the term "network state" to capture the way in which the state derives strength from the convergence of public and private interests within a network of formal and informal interactions.[49] Takashi Inoguchi speaks of "bureaucratic inclusionary pluralism," by which he accommodates the role of the state in policy deliberations without sacrificing the outcome to private conflict alone.[50] Krauss and Muramatsu develop a similar notion of "patterned pluralism."[51] There are multiple points of access to the Japanese policy process, they argue; actors whose influence is widely distributed and who are distant from state control often battle one another. But the authors acknowledge a bureaucratic role and insist that the stability of the ruling coalition in Japan combines with a multiplicity of interests to structure Japanese pluralism and to provide containers for conflict. David Friedman prefers to speak of "bureaucratic clientelism," by which he refers to the mechanism that enshrines and institutionalizes bargaining in Japan.[52]

These all amount to the same idea, that understanding the Japanese policy process requires a prior appreciation of political conflict within and across subgovernments rather than direct confrontation between unified actors. In this book I have termed that process "reciprocal consent," a formulation not completely inconsistent with Japan, Inc. To the extent that it can accommodate diversity and conflict, and to the extent that it can be disaggregated, Japan, Inc., may yet be the most elegant characterization of the Japanese political economy. William Lockwood, speaking of Japan's New Capitalism, evoked the now common metaphor of a seamless web of elite interactions to explain the interdependence of business and government in Japan. The metaphor remains apt, but what is seldom remembered is its final insight, which addresses squarely the issue of identity and autonomy: "A web it may be, but a web with no spider."[53]

State capacity, in turn, is derived from these same business-government interactions rather than from abstractions about state power. We have assembled little evidence that states or markets reflect unified interests; similarly we have little support for the notion that state capacity is consistent over time or across sectors. The ubiquity of the state in the market neither reflects a generalized state capacity nor consistently predicts policy choice. Moreover, as anticipated, state ownership provides no measure of state capacity. It has too many subtleties, and there are too many other instruments of state power inherited from prior struggles over state intervention. Undifferentiated notions of state capacity that posit strength and weakness misdirect inquiry and profoundly underestimate the possibilities for public policy in particular nations.[54]

Our evidence, in fact, impugns the article of faith that Japan is the archetype of the strong state. The most important empirical lesson of this book is the consistency with which state programs for market control and direct intervention were transformed. In *no* case did the state prevail against private interests. In the 1885 concessions in the Miike and Takashima colliery disputes, and in the CANDU reactor debate a century later, the Japanese state has never been insulated effectively from private interests. These and numerous other failures, including the impossibly politicized postwar coal programs, suggest that strong states require strong interests in society. They also suggest that we should stop asking why the Japanese state is so strong and start asking why its capacity is so often mischaracterized.

These observations in turn answer our final empirical questions about national development. In Japanese studies these questions are framed narrowly, as a choice between change and continuity. War and foreign occupation in twentieth century Japan make it convenient to speak of distinct prewar and postwar structures. Much research begins with 1945, as if an entirely new set of actors and institutions appeared with the end of the war. The justification for doing so is that the American Occupation acquired for the Japanese state powers that had eluded it for decades.

Recent studies of the Japanese political economy stress further changes. Analysts argue that the 1970s saw, in Okimoto's words, "an erosion of MITI's once imperial powers."[55] It is often argued that the stability of LDP power has invested particular politicians with significant experience and expertise in particular policy areas. As a result, "specialist politicians" (*zoku giin*) are more independent and more influential than ever before. The bureaucratic dominance of the 1950s has given way, as part and parcel of the structural evolution of the Japanese economy, to a more balanced distribution of power and influence.[56]

One can accept these shifts and still be more impressed with the way that private prerogatives have been elaborated and made manifest in a public role for politicians. State intervention in Japan has not been transformed from control to suasion; rather, its negotiated origins have become more transparent. After all, most MITI powers were bestowed by the Occupation. They were not organic to the system. That system, although it has differentially bestowed political resources that have changed over time, is marked by fundamental continuity in the distribution of those resources. The terms "prewar" and "postwar" seem handier for description than for analysis. The Japanese state has historically been both pervasive and constrained; efforts to separate state aid from state control were a part of economic policy making from the beginning. Students of the twentieth-century Japanese political economy would do well, therefore, to adopt a transwar perspective on the policy process. Nakamura Takafusa places this in its proper, nonteleological context: "the postwar social and economic system, technologies, lifestyles, customs, and so on, took shape during and were passed on from the war years. Even if these institutions were not established with a view to the longer term in mind, they cast the die for the postwar period."[57]

Nakamura has in mind such institutions as the financial groups, MITI, and the Bank of Japan, as well as such practices as subcontracting, life-time employment, and company unions. This book adds numerous examples from the energy sector. There were cases of overt institutional transfer across the war, as from Nippatsu to the EPDC, from the *haiden* to the nine private utilities, from Imperial Oil to JAPEX, from the first to the second Petroleum Industry Law, and from Shōwa Sekitan to Shin Shōwa Sekitan. Control associations became industry associations with democratic charters—but without structural change. Distribution systems were reinforced by the Occupation. More than a few wartime institutions of the state were renamed and reinvested with broad powers in the postwar economy. In fact, these continuities reach into a past even deeper than "transwar" allows. One important example is the historiographic parallels between the development of the Japanese coal industry and the development of the Japanese state that began in the Tokugawa period.

When we view continuities and these final empirical questions in comparative perspective, however, we sharply confine their importance. Possibilities for national development can be explained by post hoc process tracing, but they cannot be predicted by conflated assumptions about national development. Most limiting is the widely accepted assumption that societies travel toward a common goal. It is based upon a technological determinism that posits centralization of both industrial and bureaucratic organization. Our observation of persistent, multiple, and conflicting centers of industrial and bureaucratic power, even in Japan, calls such assumptions into question and raises an alternative of multiple futures.

Stephen Jay Gould speaks of the migration of turtles and evolutionary theory in words that hold particular import for this book:

> Results rarely specify their causes unambiguously. . . . If we are forced to infer a process only from its modern results, then we are usually stymied or reduced to speculation about probabilities. For many roads lead to almost any Rome.[58]

And, I would add, they lead to almost any Tokyo as well.

Notes

CHAPTER 1. *States, Markets, and the Politics of Reciprocal Consent*

1. Nettl 1968:562. In Evans et al. 1985, see Theda Skocpol's introductory essay, which acknowledges important early exceptions to society-centered assumptions in the social science literature.

2. From the dictum that the state is the "committee which manages the common business of the bourgeoisie" both Marx and Engels retreated, later amending what Nettl (1968:571) calls "one of the least adequate generalizations Marx ever made." For a modern approximation, the state as the "boardroom of the bourgeoisie," see Miliband 1969 and 1977.

3. See Nordlinger 1981; the literature cited in Skocpol 1985; and Freeman forthcoming.

4. On the instrumentalist view see Miliband 1969 and O'Connor 1973. I speak here of the so-called functionalist school identified with Poulantzas 1978; Offe 1975; Becker 1983. For critiques of neo-Marxism see Carnoy 1984.

5. Becker 1983:6.

6. The best collection from this perspective is Evans et al. 1985. Monographs include Krasner 1978; Gilpin 1975; and Katzenstein 1985. For a thoughtful critique see Gourevitch 1978. Also note Almond 1986, who argues that neo-statists misrepresent the literature they are attacking.

7. E.g., Skocpol 1985:28.

8. As Katzenstein 1978:16 notes, this research is in the tradition of Moore, Bendix, and Gerschenkron. The publication of *Between Power and Plenty* coincided with Krasner 1978, Zysman 1977, and Gourevitch 1978, whose influence has been strongly felt in subsequent work. See Ikenberry 1982, 1983; Zysman 1983; Kurth 1979; Evans et al. 1985; Katzenstein 1985b. Rueschemeyer and Evans 1985 attempt to specify the conditions under which "effective" state intervention is possible.

9. Krasner 1978:3.

10. See, on nuclear power, Frost 1984; on bureaucracy, Suleiman 1974; on agriculture, Berger 1972; on regional policy, Tarrow 1977; and on small business, Berger and Piore 1980.

11. On the New Deal see Karl 1963; see also Skocpol 1980 for an application of neo-Marxist theories.

12. But see Gourevitch 1978; Evans et al. 1985:chap. 11; Zysman 1983.

13. Cf. Schmitter 1977:14.

14. Postwar liberalism borrowed from sociology to model modernization (see Parsons 1951; Lerner 1958; Deutsch 1961; Pye 1966), but its optimistic assumptions were challenged by later theorists, notably Gusfield 1967 and Huntington 1968. Broader explanations of social and political change arose from the work of Gerschenkron 1962 on the timing of industrialization. Notable Marxist analyses of development include Sweezy 1962 and Wallerstein 1974.

15. Gourevitch 1978:900. This is what Dore 1974 discovered, causing him to reconsider the central thesis of *British Factory, Japanese Factory* (1973). See also Goldthorpe 1984 for a critique of liberal models of industrial pluralism and convergence; and Piore and Sabel 1984.

16. Gould 1980:16.

17. Skocpol 1985:20.

18. Feigenbaum 1985:25 captures this point nicely.

19. Heclo 1978 speaks of issue networks in this context. Gourevitch (1978:907) puts the question succinctly: where business and the state work closely together, "Who has coopted whom?" The literature on subgovernments is instructive. On the American case see J. L. Freeman 1965; Heclo 1978; Milward and Wamsley 1979. On the Japanese case see Campbell 1984.
Reciprocal consent is related to several extant approaches to business-government relations. It accepts the notion of "business privilege" from Lindblom 1977 and other neo-Marxists who use the relatively unconstrained capacity of private enterprise to invest, to disinvest, and to accumulate capital as an analytically useful boundary between state and society. It rejects, however, the metaphysical attribution of "hegemony" (Gramsci 1973) to business-government interactions and the positing of a "pact of domination" (Rueschemeyer and Evans 1985). Also, it treats the unity of a capitalist class as an empirical question. It is related to the bargaining enshrined in corporatist solutions to economic organization, especially vis-à-vis the autonomous role played by state planners that this literature emphasizes. But by emphasizing that these arrangements are plastic, imperfectly structured, often informal, and symptomatic of a great range of permutations of power relationships and participants, it also resonates well with pluralism. Ultimately, I avoid "corporatism" and "pluralism" because their semantic entanglement has rendered them more confusing than enlightening. Compare, for example, Frank Wilson's (1983:896) definition of neocorporatism and Nordlinger's (1981:158–59) definition of neopluralism. See also Krauss and Muramatsu forthcoming, who speak of "patterned pluralism," and the discussion of societal, liberal, and democratic corporatism in Schmitter and Lembruch 1979; Berger 1981; Almond 1983; and Katzenstein 1985b.

20. See the work of Cameron 1978; Duvall and Freeman 1981; Moe 1979; Monsen and Walters 1980; Pryor 1976; note also Myrdal 1960, who argues that regulation and planning make nationalization unnecessary. In addition, note Evans et al. 1985:360, who suggest using public corporations as objects of analysis for understanding business-state relations.

21. Gelinas 1978.

22. Lindblom 1977:175; see also Katzenstein 1985 for the Austrian case.

23. Gourevitch 1984 uses "crises" in the same way.

24. See Seidman 1975, 1980; Walsh 1978.

25. Seidman 1975:94. See also Sharkansky 1979 for a comparative treatment of these issues.

26. The Labour party spokesman for this position was Britain's Herbert Morrison; see Holland 1974. But conservative governments may be equally comfortable with state ownership insofar as it promotes economic nationalism. Mercantilist states will establish state enterprises as revenue sources and as national champions for strategic ends in the international economy. Others will bail out ailing sectors or firms, as in the Conservative buy-out of Rolls Royce in Britain in 1971.

27. See Feigenbaum 1982, Laux 1983, and Vernon 1984 for a review of these justifications.

28. See, for example, Mansfield 1980; Tupper and Doern 1981; Holland 1974; Pryor 1976. For exceptions see John Freeman 1982; Laux forthcoming.

29. Shonfield 1965.

30. Gerschenkron 1962; Moore 1966; Gourevitch 1978; Kurth 1979.

31. On the former see Offe 1975, 1985; O'Connor 1973; Mandel 1975; Przeworski 1980. On the latter, Fagan 1960; Miliband 1969.

32. Miliband 1969:57–58.

33. There have been numerous efforts to describe the role of the state in economic policy making. Most widely cited is Marx, the state as the "boardroom of the bourgeoisie." Nettl 1968 speaks of a doorkeeper. Ikenberry 1982 has written of the state as strategist. Klapp 1982 distinguishes between the state as landlord and the state as entrepreneur. Zysman 1983 posits three roles: regulator, administrator, and player. Each subsumes other activities variously characterizing the state as umpire, overseer, guide, investor, facilitator, certifier, and producer. Perhaps the most graphic metaphor is that of Hoffmann 1974:450, quoted in Zysman 1977:7, who describes the rise of industrial policy in France as a case in which "the watchdog became a greyhound." This profusion of metaphors is evidence of a more fundamental concern, viz., the need to move beyond "Who governs?" to "How?" and "For whom?" in order more effectively to characterize the ways states and markets are related.

34. No algorithmic rationality helps us sort through these roles. Like most maps, although this one "traces the contours of the terrain the traveler will encounter, it does not explain them" (Katzenstein 1985b:30). Explanation, my ultimate goal, will be guided by these typological musings but has to be built upon empirical evidence. Note also that the model's utility is complicated by the way in which a state-owned oil company can be a "partner" of heavy industry by supplying a cheap factor of production at the same time that it is a "rival" of private refineries.

35. National Academy of Public Administration 1981:16. Lowi 1979 refers to the American "permanent state of receivership."

36. See Zysman 1983.

37. For Marxist views see Hilferding 1981; Dupuy and Truchil 1979; see Chandler 1978 for the liberal view. On the crucial variable see Regini 1984. Neoclassical theory, of course, makes the apolitical case that no intervention is necessary when competition exists.

38. There is room for disagreement on this point. Krasner (1978:10) turns this argument on its head, suggesting that the state may enjoy greater flexibility and greater influence in shaping private markets when it is confronted by "oligopolistic, diversified corporations than when it must deal with sectors composed of large numbers of small owner-operated producing units."

39. In some historical cases this latter relationship has been an explicit element in the politics of reciprocal consent, as in the Italian Fascist Charter of

Work, which allowed "intervention of the state in production only when private initiative is absent" (as quoted in Freeman forthcoming:chap. 2). In work in progress Ernest Wilson argues that the presence of a merchant class can have a chilling effect upon the nature and extent of state intervention.

40. Kurth 1979:12.

41. Katzenstein 1985b:24; Cameron 1978.

42. Chandler 1978; David Vogel 1978.

43. Ikenberry 1986 explores this irony in a comparative context.

44. See Eckstein 1975:116.

45. This is closely tied to Krasner's 1978 argument about geopolitics and foreign economic policy as relatively "insulated parts of the state's domain." As Sampson 1975:73 puts it in the case of petroleum: "Oil was too important to be left to the oil companies" (quoted in Feigenbaum 1982:111).

46. The criticality of energy as a test of state strength and state autonomy can be overstated. Indeed, American political historians familiar with the operation of the Texas Railroad Commission (see Nordhauser 1979 and Lovejoy and Homan 1967) and the frequent collusion among private multinationals and the State Department (Adelman 1972; Vernon 1983; Anderson 1981) might not recognize energy as a sector where autonomous state power necessarily prevails over private interests. Nonetheless, in few sectors of the American economy is state regulation more intrusive. Recent analysts of American energy policy have emphasized the state's regulatory capacity and the indirect but significant instruments of state leadership in setting energy policy goals (Neff et al. 1983; Ikenberry 1986). Moreover, the United States is in many ways the extreme case. Virtually every other industrial state, both self-sufficient in energy and not, intervene more directly and (sometimes) more profitably in their oil, coal, and electric power industries than in any other.

47. Cf. Nordlinger 1981:147.

48. Sumiya and Taira 1979:189.

49. James Abegglen was the first to use the term.

50. See Kaplan 1972 for the most important popularization of Japan, Inc.

51. See, for example, Patrick 1986; Trezise 1982; Saxonhouse 1986; and Pepper et al. 1985.

52. Krauss et al. 1984; Horne 1985; Steiner et al. 1980; Fukui 1970; Okimoto forthcoming.

53. Silberman 1982:229; Pempel and Tsunekawa 1979:244. See also Hadley 1970 for an account that stresses state leadership.

54. Cohen 1949:3, 31. Smith 1965 and Marshall 1967 are excellent and balanced accounts of this period.

55. Hoshino 1956; Tōhata 1960.

56. The seminal works are Lockwood 1955; Allen 1946; Bisson 1945; Cohen 1949; and Nakamura 1961. Also see Duus 1984 and Tiedemann 1971.

57. Moore 1966:301. See also the Japanese *Kōza-ha* tradition of Marxist economics, as well as Yanaga 1968. Few who have looked carefully at the implementation of industrial control legislation, beginning in 1931 with the Important Industries Control Law, fail to acknowledge that large capital retained significant control of the hundreds of state-licensed cartels. The number of cartels expanded from under 100 in 1930 to over 625 in 1935 (see Fujita 1935:67); the Mitsubishi Economic Research Bureau 1936 provides a comprehensive list. It notes that "control through these cartels rested merely on mutual consent, and

there were frequent cases of violation of agreements, particularly by outsiders. On the other hand, there still were many large-scale industries in which no cartel had been formed owing to the conflicting interests of the manufacturers concerned." Lockwood 1955:568 notes that only on one occasion prior to 1937 was the state able to use its legislated powers to enforce cartel formation, and even then it was unsuccessful. Johnson 1982:153 notes that invariably the president of each control association was the chief executive of the largest firm in that sector, "and as a result, the control associations were utterly dominated by the *zaibatsu.*"

58. Johnson 1982:24.

59. Pempel and Tsunekawa 1978:258. For accounts of the wartime economy that stress the independence of private enterprise despite controls common to all the belligerent economies, see Cohen 1949.

60. Respectively Ezra Vogel 1978; Pempel 1982; Tsurumi 1978; Young 1984; and Inoguchi 1983.

61. See, for example, the *Asahi Shimbun* survey of September 12, 1983, in which only 10 percent of those surveyed felt that the bureaucracy held power, whereas the LDP and big business together accounted for 53 percent. "Bosses" (*kuromaku*) got 12 percent. For more on the role of bosses (*kuromaku*) in Japanese politics, see Samuels 1983.

62. Johnson 1982:20 and 1986:564.

63. See Dore 1973 for the most sophisticated statement of this proposition. See Vogel 1979, Ouchi 1981, and Athos and Pascale 1981 for more popular accounts. Friedman 1986 vigorously rebuts the proposition with historical evidence from the machine tool industry.

CHAPTER 2. *State-owned Energy Corporations in the Industrial Democracies*

1. Smith 1965; Marshall 1967; Chap. 3 below.

2. Cross-sectional data have been collected for the member nations of the OECD (excluding Iceland). When possible, they have been supplemented by case study materials and interviews. I have constructed the tables from various primary and secondary sources, including annual reports, government documents, and personal correspondence.

3. Sheahan 1976:132.

4. See Pryor 1976; Walters and Monsen 1979:160–70.

5. Wilson 1980:128.

6. For more on ATIC see Bruce et al. 1981.

7. The following account is derived primarily from Fagan 1960; Kirby 1977; Kelf-Cohen 1969; Krieger 1983; Robson 1962.

8. Quoted in Kirby 1977:186.

9. Kirby 1977:197.

10. Quoted in Kelf-Cohen 1969:41.

11. Fagan 1956:25.

12. For details on the French coal nationalization see Bye 1955, Einaudi et al. 1955, and Frost 1983.

13. This short discussion is based upon Gillingham 1985.

14. See Keck 1981 on the West German fast breeder reactor program and the striking similarities with the Japanese case reported in Chap. 6 below.

15. Vining 1981:175.

16. This account is drawn from Kelf-Cohen 1969 and Robson 1962.

17. The same had applied mutatis mutandis to the British Coal Mines Reorganization Commission.

18. This account is based upon Frost 1983 and Bye 1955.

19. Frost 1983:147.

20. Frost 1983:153.

21. André Marty, quoted in Frost 1983:164.

22. Prodi 1974:45, for example. The other was the 1905 railway nationalization, also involving sizable lump-sum payments to private capitalists. Ironically, most of these funds were invested in hydropower generation and transmission facilities.

23. Rossi 1955:222–23. Stories are told for example of Edison chairman Valerio, who would predict corporate profits by measuring the snowfall in the Italian mountains.

24. For these parliamentary activities see Fedi 1981:104–14.

25. Rossi 1955:222.

26. See Di Palma 1977:chap. 3 for an eloquent political history of this period.

27. Quoted in Fedi 1981:110.

28. Quoted in Fedi 1981:112.

29. Posner and Woolf 1967:41.

30. Goodermote and Mancke 1983; Jacoby 1974. For a more comprehensive review of the strategic concerns prompting states to establish themselves in the oil business, see Bell 1982. For state-owned oil firms in the Third World, see Levy 1982; Heller 1980; Klapp 1987.

31. Data supplied by Michael Lynch—MIT Energy Laboratory. OPEC state–owned export refineries began to come on line by the late 1980s, dramatically increasing the world market share of refined products by state-owned firms.

32. Bell 1982:104.

33. See Grayson 1981:chap. 13.

34. E.g., Grayson 1981:1.

35. Gracey 1968:25–74; Pratt 1981:95–148; Sheahan 1976; Grayson 1981. The evidence seems rather more mixed in the case of ENI than in the others. See also Holland 1972 and Grassini 1981.

36. See Heller 1980:9.

37. An alternative was coal-gas-powered engines. But oil had already been adopted by the Russian and Italian navies and had some performance advantages over coal, if only supplies could be made as reliable as British coal.

38. The Shell Transport and Trading Company, specializing in oil transport, was owned by Briton Marcus Samuel; Royal Dutch Oil, which had significant interests in Indonesia and Transcaucasia, was principally Dutch. The two companies combined in 1907 into one holding group, in which Royal Dutch gained 60 percent controlling interest. Royal Dutch Oil's subsidiary, Asiatic Petroleum Company, often worked with the French Rothschild-owned production facilities in Transcaucasia to market oil in Europe and Asia. In 1911 the Rothschilds sold their holdings to Shell, for which they were paid in shareholdings in the two companies. See Nowell 1983:233. On the British market see Williamson et al. 1963:255.

39. This discussion is based upon Ferrier 1982, especially 159–260.

40. Quoted in Ferrier 1982:159.

41. Kent 1976:6.

42. Quoted in Ferrier 1982:182.

43. Quoted in Ferrier 1982:218.

44. Nowell 1987.

45. The *Report of the Royal Commission* on the coal industry published in 1926 indicated the possibility of meeting Great Britain's liquid fuel requirements with synthetic fuel, and in 1931 Oswald Mosley argued that synthetic oil was necessary to preserve Britain's great stake in the coal industry (Mosley 1931:37–38). Synthetic oil manufacture was in the Labour party's platform as late as 1939 (Addison 1975:51).

46. There is some evidence that the British coal industry gained a different kind of support; it profited from its worldwide dominance. In the immediate postwar period high export prices subsidized low domestic prices. In 1919 coal's export price was three times greater than its domestic price in Great Britain. Profits from this "reverse dumping" may have lessened coal industry incentives to fight government oil policy during the early years of APOC's growth.

47. Later the French would establish a second state oil company modeled upon the Italian ENI (see Feigenbaum 1982:110). French intervention in the oil market has taken two forms: direct participation in the market through state-owned oil companies, and import regulation. The Compagnie Française des Pétroles, which now markets under the name Total, became a legal entity in 1924 and entered refining and production over the course of the next decade. The company now known as Elf-Aquitaine evolved through a series of mergers of public and private companies after World War I. Protective legislation designed to encourage refining in the domestic market was enacted in 1928 and placed under the administrative tutelage of the Office Nationale des Combustibles Liquides, or ONCL, which was rebaptized the Direction des Carburants, familiarly known as DICA, in 1939.

48. See Nowell 1983:256–67.

49. Murat 1969:8–9.

50. Faure 1939:84–89.

51. Nowell 1987. Grayson's secondary account (1981:49) argues that the French state took equity in CFP to stave off a left-wing government.

52. Sources are mixed. Grayson 1981:49 suggests an initial reluctance by private investors; Feigenbaum 1985 disagrees, as does Nowell 1987.

53. Kuisel 1967:31–32. This move solved the problem of who would have access to Mesopotamia and who would participate in the profits therefrom. But if the immediate creators of the CFP were Poincaré and Mercier, Shell and its ally, the Armenian oil magnate Calouste S. Gulbenkian, both desirous of a French presence in Mesopotamia to counter the predominance of British (Anglo-Persian) interests, had been lobbying for just such a corporate entity since at least 1919 (see Nowell 1983:250–51). The initiative was not all the French government's.

54. Grayson 1981:48; Feigenbaum 1985:57–58.

55. See Feigenbaum 1985:57.

56. Rondot 1962:36.

57. Fontaine 1967:60–63; Nowell forthcoming.

58. Magini 1976:21–25.

59. See Alimenti 1937.

60. Magini 1976:45.

61. Alimenti 1937:49.

62. Magini 1976:49.

63. See Alimenti 1937.

64. ASIA 1927:761–64.

65. Senato 1953:7.
66. Quoted in Alimenti 1937:33.
67. Alimenti 1937:29.
68. Squarzina 1958; Senato 1953.
69. See Squarzina 1958; Alimenti 1937; Cottino 1978; Magini 1976.
70. Ratiglia 1982.
71. Alimenti 1937:38.
72. Ratiglia 1982:4.
73. Today ENI controls 39 percent of the Italian market for refined products (see ENI 1981) and accounts for 53 percent of direct petroleum imports (see Ratiglia 1982). Its closest competitor in the marketing of refined petroleum products, Exxon, has only 10 percent of the Italian market. Shell's holdings were acquired by ENI in the 1970s.
74. See Colitti 1979 and Votaw 1964, for example.
75. See Squarzina 1958.
76. Ratiglia 1982:6.
77. Votaw 1964:13.
78. See, for example, the thirty-six volumes of press commentary, *Stampa e Oronero,* that Mattei had his staff compile.
79. See Colitti 1979.
80. Lockwood 1955:90.
81. Kirby 1977:151.
82. Cf. Kirby 1977:169.

CHAPTER 3. *A Political History of the Japanese Coal Industry*

1. The most detailed economic history of coal is Sumiya 1968. For the legal philosophy of the mining industry, see Ishimura 1960. Other portions of this discussion are derived from general histories by Imai 1966 and Yada 1977. An excellent local history of Chikuhō is Nagasue 1973. The company history of the Hokkaido Mine and Steamship firm, Nanajū Nenshi Iinkai ed. 1958, is also helpful. I have drawn freely from these sources.
2. First was Fukuoka; soon Kōkura, Karatsū, and Satsuma followed suit.
3. See Kuboyama 1942b. Tokugawa era *han* also managed Japan's earliest textile and shipbuilding plants. Although coal technologies such as dry distillation production of tar were developed before 1830 by these publicly owned mines, mechanization had to await the Restoration's foreign specialists. The first modern shaft in Japan (over 45 meters deep) was sunk at the *han*-managed Takashima colliery in 1868 under the guidance of the Englishman Thomas Glover, who later served the Restoration government (and Mitsubishi) so faithfully. American engineers had produced the first Hokkaido mining survey even earlier, and in 1864 the first Hokkaido colliery opened.
4. Cf. Smith 1965:36 and Sumiya 1968:112–13.
5. Marshall 1967:20–24.
6. Vernon 1983:86.
7. Sumiya 1968:115–22.
8. Imai 1966:appen. notes two rebellions, one in September 1883 and another in March 1884.
9. Sumiya 1968:125; see p. 264 for a record of Mitsui Bussan profits. By 1880 half of Miike's production was for the steamship (export) trade.

10. Sumiya 1968:116. This discussion is based upon pp. 127–35.
11. Sumiya 1968:261.
12. Horie 1939:78 quotes from the preamble to this Act.
13. Asahi . . . Honsha 1970:58.
14. Sumiya 1968:267–68.
15. Cf. Smith 1965:43.
16. E.g., Yada 1977; Sumiya 1968.
17. Sumiya 1968:121.
18. Asahi . . . Honsha 1970:58.
19. Ibid.
20. Sumiya 1968:257.
21. Note the role played by the Briton Glover in Kyushu and by the American Benjamin Lyman, who came to Hokkaido in 1872 at the invitation of the Meiji government. Lyman produced the first detailed geological surveys of the Hokkaido coal deposits and, later, of the Niigata oil fields (Kiyomiya 1952:239).
22. Sekitan Tsūshin 1959:56. National coal production exceeded one million tons for the first time in 1884, nearly quintupling in the first decade of recorded statistics.
23. Yada 1977:15.
24. In Chikuhō, for example, three families emerged that wielded great political power well into the second half of this century. The Yasukawa family, progenitor of the electronics manufacturer Yaskawa Electric was descended from Matsumoto Jirauchi, designer of the *shikumihō*. The others were Asō and Kajima, non-*zaibatsu* local capitalist families of enormous influence.
25. Yada 1977; Imai 1966.
26. By contrast, as early as 1870 British mines were already producing 110 million tons.
27. Shibagaki Kazuo estimates that by the late Meiji period 50–80 percent of all Mitsubishi profits came from its mining enterprises. Likewise, mining profits subsidized early manufacturing losses by Mitsui firms. See Yada 1977:37, who also notes that the Furukawa and Sumitomo *zaibatsu* were also centered on mining in their early years. The best detailed exploration of the expansion of *zaibatsu*-affiliated mining companies in the most productive mining regions is Sumiya 1968:325–36.
28. Sekitan Tsūshin 1959:57; Nanajū Nenshi . . . 1958:65–104. For an account of the Sino-Japanese War and World War I in the development of the Japanese economy, "when Japan seemed near the end of her rope," see Lockwood 1955:18–19, 38.
29. Asahi . . . Honsha 1970:276–83 mentions the role of entrepreneur Shibusawa Eichi in promoting this society; Scalapino 1983 is an excellent political history of the Yūaikai. Seldom did mine explosions kill fewer than one hundred miners.
30. Kiso would later help eviscerate a state control bill and land in jail for his (apparently successful) efforts to bribe future prime minister Tanaka Kakuei and others. See interview in Kondō and Osanai 1978.
31. Interview, January 17, 1984. The labor contract system was known as *rōdō teikyōgyō*. "Double harness" was *tomo kasegi*. Wages for miners actually declined by nearly 40 percent between 1929 and 1933 at a time when labor costs accounted for 60 percent of total production costs (see Mitsubishi Economic Research Bureau 1936:207).
32. Sekitan Tsūshin 1959:58–59 provides a comprehensive overview of these producers' activities.

33. For a full list of members, see Horikubō 1939:5–8.
34. See Ōki 1961:235–42 for additional information on the relationship between the SKR agreements and the activities of the smallest mining firms.
35. Kuboyama 1942b:228–30.
36. My account of the Bujun case is based upon Asahi Shimbun Seibu Honsha 1970:302–5. See also Ōki 1961 and Kuboyama 1942b.
37. Kuboyama 1942b:242–43.
38. See Johnson 1982 for the best treatment in English of this legislation.
39. Ōki 1961:245. See Gillingham 1985 for details about Ruhrkohle.
40. On business-government relations throughout this period see Nezu 1958.
41. See the memoirs of Matsumoto in Kiyomiya 1952:209. Matsumoto was born in Fukuoka in 1870. His father was Yasukawa Keiichirō, one of Japan's most powerful coal industry leaders. After marrying into the Matsumoto family and studying finance at the University of Pennsylvania, Matsumoto became a coal entrepreneur. He was chairman of Shōwa Sekitan and in 1940 became the first president of Nippon Sekitan, the national coal control organ. He became a member of the House of Peers in 1945. See Kiyomiya 1952:253–70.
42. Quoted in Nezu 1958:14.
43. For full details see Nezu 1958:137–41; Ōki 1961:245–47; Nagasue 1973:175.
44. Nagasue 1973:175.
45. Nakamura and Miyazaki 1961:26.
46. Ōki 1961:246.
47. Ōki 1961:246–47.
48. Nezu 1958:11.
49. This account is based on Nezu 1958.
50. Kiyomiya 1952:213.
51. Kondō and Osanai 1978:112.
52. Ōki 1961:300.
53. Nezu 1958:28.
54. A former control association official offers an interesting but different explanation for not unifying sales and production control. He claims that Mitsui Bussan, thelargest coal sales firm in Japan at that time, promoted Nittan, while Mitsui Mining was "selfishly opposed" to any cooperation with the military. He claims that no integrated national coal corporation appeared because of this split within the Mitsui zaibatsu itself. Interview, February 20, 1984.
55. Yada 1977:25; Nagasue 1973:177–78.
56. See the account in Sekitan Tsūshin 1959:61, which stresses the cartel's continued power.
57. See Matsumoto's memoirs, Kiyomiya 1952:212.
58. Interview, February 20, 1984.
59. Nakamura and Miyazaki 1961:26.
60. At least six separate mergers involving major mining firms took place during wartime, paid for by mine consolidation subsidies (tankō seiri). See Nakamura and Miyazaki 1961:28; Yada 1977:27; Sekitan . . . Jigyōdan 1965:91. For details of one such merger, that of the Iriyama and Iwaki mines, see the September 1943 issue of Sekitan Tōsei Kaihō, the official journal of the Coal Control Association.
61. Nakamura 1957:225–27.
62. Kunisaki 1943:3.

63. See Samuels 1983:2.
64. Kunisaki 1943:3.
65. Nakamura 1957:227.
66. Nezu 1958:593.
67. See Nagasue 1973:178–87. See also Yada 1977:25–26.
68. See figures in Harada 1981, Imai 1966, and Cohen 1949.
69. Ōki 1961:254.
70. Nakamura 1957:208–9.
71. Monthly statistics show the dramatic drop in the number of foreign mine workers: see Nakamura 1957:209. The drop does not seem to have been the direct result of the SCAP order.
72. Hein 1986; Moore 1983.
73. Nakamura 1957:217–18.
74. Included were many other young economists, such as Ōkita Saburō, Inaba Hidezō, Tsuru Shigeto, and Kojima Keizō, who would deeply influence energy and economic policy for the next thirty years. See Johnson 1982:179–90 for a broad perspective on priority production and its relationship to Japanese economic planning, past and future.
75. Andō 1973:282. The familiarity of the problem no doubt suggests why the solution of priority production so closely resembled the 1938 revised materials mobilization plan. See Johnson 1982:182 and Nakamura 1981.
76. Johnson 1982:182.
77. GHQ-SCAP 1951a:3.
78. GHQ-SCAP 1951b:85 and No. 45:46.
79. GHQ-SCAP 1951b argues this was *not* the case, but the evidence presented below suggests otherwise.
80. Sonoda 1970:22.
81. Hein 1986.
82. Johnson 1982:177.
83. Much of the following is derived from Shinobu 1967:623–66. See also Saitō 1948 for the full record of Diet deliberations. Kojima 1957 is an insider's view of the economic policy process, especially for coal, in the immediate postwar period. For the view of Socialist party secretary general Nishio, see Andō 1973.
84. Some Liberals, then governing under Prime Minister Yoshida, initially seemed ready to concede the principle of state control in an effort to placate SCAP. They reneged on that concession upon becoming an opposition party the following spring. Yoshida, backed squarely and generously by private mining interests, succeeded in preventing any such measure during his tenure.
85. See the institutional history by Johnson 1982.
86. See the review by Kojima 1957:289–93, which discusses the pros and cons of five different permutations in detail. This section is also based upon an interview with one of these MCI officials on March 1, 1984. See also Kojima 1957:284–307 for a discussion of bureaucratic disputes over coal nationalization.
87. The first *sekitanchō chōkan* was Suga Reinosuke, president of Furukawa Mining. His top administrative officer was Hirai Tomisaburō, a career bureaucrat who later became administrative vice-minister of MITI and president of Nippon Steel.
88. Quoted in Kondō and Osanai 1978:113.
89. Interview, February 17, 1984.
90. For a detailed if one-sided account, see Harada 1981. It is also a matter of

record that Kiso was unable to account for eight million yen he was supposed to have spent on travel to promote the anti–state control movement. Tanaka admitted to receiving one million yen from Kiso but claimed it was an advance payment for a construction contract. As he was unable to produce any contract as evidence, he and Kiso became classmates (*dōsōsei*) at Sugamo prison. Kiso, later affectionately referred to as "the last small mine operator in Japan," also had ties to Sasakawa Ryōichi. Kiso was chairman of the Fukuoka Motorboat Racing Association, one of Sasakawa's main activities (see Kondō and Osanai 1978:122).

91. Yanaga 1968:80–81.

92. Draft Bill Art. 16.6; for the full text see Saitō 1948:193–98.

93. See Shinobu 1967:641–42. See Saitō 1948 for a verbatim record of Diet interpellations and the active opposition of these representatives. Prime Minister Hatoyama used the lure of a cabinet post in 1955 to secure Nishida's support in placating opposition to a different piece of coal legislation.

94. Kiso claims that even Ashida was sympathetic. Ashida, he claims, "invited us to his home and asked us to suspend the opposition movement, assuring us the bill would not pass" (quoted in Kondō and Osanai 1978:113). Katayama also remembers that "Ashida only came along in the end at our insistence for the sake of the cabinet" (quoted in Andō 1973:267).

95. Cf. Kojima 1957:299.

96. Cohen 1949:473.

97. The full text of this letter is in GHQ-SCAP 1951a:appen. 10.

98. Saitō 1948:199–201.

99. See testimony in Saitō 1948:134, 140–42.

100. *Yomiuri Shimbun*, November 16, 1947.

101. Kondō and Osanai 1978:113.

102. Tuchman 1978:6 uses this phrase to describe Christianity in sixth-century France.

103. Quoted in Andō 1973:268.

104. Imai 1966:15. See Kojima 1957:305–38 for details of the actual operations of state control.

105. This was a one-of-a-kind experiment in Japan. Although "descent from heaven" (*amakudari*), by which bureaucrats come to populate top positions in the private sector, is widely known, it is most irregular for private-sector employees to work in, much less dominate, a public bureaucracy in Japan.

106. Interviews, February 10 and March 1, 1984.

107. Interview, February 20, 1984. See also the analysis of Nakamura 1957:223, who sees "the failure of state control of coal [as] related to the fact that large capital was able to use effectively priority production as a lever for its own reconstruction."

108. Nakamura 1957:221; Sonoda 1970:4–5.

109. Johnson 1982:191 draws this comparison.

110. Imai 1966:16 shows this graphically.

111. Most explanations ignore the coincidence, suggesting that stockpiles increased only because the Dodge Line permeated the economy and demand grew slack. See, for example, Imai 1966:16–17; Sonoda 1970:8; Shigen . . . Sekitanbu 1982:26. Despite a lack of any actual increase in production, they argue that the coal industry entered a time of "excessive production" and that the unusually large stockpiles indicated that rationalization was necessary. Even if slackening demand accounted for some short-term stockpiling, however, it cannot account for reductions just as controls were lifted, at least a year before the Korean War restimulated general demand.

112. The same account can be found in Sonoda 1970:8–9; Sekitan Tsūshin 1959:55; Ōki 1961:302.

113. Imai 1966:201.

114. Interview with coal journalist, February 29, 1984.

115. Interview, February 20, 1984.

116. For a brief but comprehensive review of market conditions from 1950 to 1955, see Sekitan Tsūshin 1959:28–33.

117. Nearly identical accounts of the "63 Strike" can be found in Imai 1966, Sonoda 1970, and Yada 1977.

118. Quoted in Imai 1966:22.

119. Sonoda 1970:13.

120. See Sekitan Tsūshin 1959:37, 85, on the cyclical sales strategies of the large mining firms. Firms dumped excess production on the market when demand fell, through brokerage houses, and they increased their direct sales to industrial consumers when demand was high. The small and medium-sized firms were buffers for the largest firms.

121. Hirschman 1970.

122. Ōki 1961:311 dates this in October 1952.

123. Ōki 1961:311; Imai 1966:52; Sonoda 1970:28–29.

124. Kondō and Osanai 1978:123–33 provide interesting material on how one firm, Ube Kōsan, successfully made the transition from coal to chemicals. Kiso Shigeyoshi (ibid.:114) tells of his buying the Nakajima Tankō Co. in 1955 after the owner had nearly driven the mine into bankruptcy by spending all his capital on unprofitable nonmining ventures.

125. Noted in Sekitan . . . Jigyōdan 1965:89.

126. Sekitan . . . Jigyōdan 1965:82, 88–89, 91.

127. See Chapter 5 below and Caldwell 1981:71–72.

128. Sonoda 1970:14–15.

129. As early as January 1953 the Coal Bureau had issued a sober assessment of the advantages of heavy oil entitled "Policy Problems Regarding High Coal Prices."

130. Sekitan . . . Jigyōdan 1965:80–114 is an interesting retrospective discussion among the top MITI coal planners, touching on all these points.

131. Johnson 1982 provides details on the career of this extraordinary man. He was a highly controversial advocate of state control in both prewar and postwar periods. For details of the Sahashi Plan, see Sonoda 1970:45–46.

132. Interview with MITI bureau chief and proponent on this plan, March 1, 1984.

133. The oil-refining companies and the electric utilities, of course, *did* have reason to oppose these measures. But their natural allies, the steel and cement industries, won special exemptions from the boiler law. The utilities' opposition was moderated, as we shall see in the next chapter, by MITI promises of selective and flexible enforcement, a fixed five-year time limit, and as yet competitive coal prices. The petroleum refining industry, an untrusted stepchild of the Occupation, was still politically ineffectual in the 1950s. Keidanren, following the coal industry's lead, supported the measure (*Nihon Keizai Shimbun*, July 10, 1955). See also Caldwell 1981:75.

134. Sekitan . . . Jigyōdan 1965:47.

135. Sonoda 1970:49.

136. Sekitan Tsūshin 1959:79. Indeed, in the subsequent boom, market prices shot up without reference to these targets. See Sekitan Tsūshin 1959:80; Ōki 1961:312. State intervention in pricing was not attempted again until 1963,

then as a ratification of prior Keidanren agreements. These were the so-called "standard prices" (*kijun*) that accompanied the creation of the Coal for Electric Power Distribution Public Corporation. See below.

137. Sekitan . . . Jigyōdan 1965:90–92. Coal Bureau chief Saitō remembers (ibid.:86) that it was a visit from Takeuchi to the MITI administrative vice-director that pressured him to back away from eliminating the most inefficient mines.

138. See *Economisto*, April 16, 1955.

139. *Nihon Keizai Shimbun*, July 10, 1955. See also *Asahi Shimbun*, July 19, 1955, evening ed.; *Ekonomisto*, July 16, 1955; *Mainichi Shimbun*, May 25, 1955. See the 22d Diet testimony of the Liberal party's Kanda, Furuchi, and Ono: in *Ekonomisto*, July 30, 1955.

140. Nishida had been a leader in the battle over "standard prices," and it seems to have been his ultimate support, as cabinet minister, for the measure that made an agreement possible.

141. The actual number of mines increased from 668 in March 1955 to 784 in March 1958. But 137 mines were scrapped during that period, so the number of new mines was 253 (Imai 1966:25).

142. Sonoda 1970:60. See also Hokutan president Hagiwara's own account of his 1955–59 investments in coal chemicals and tourism, in Kondō and Osanai 1978:97–99.

143. The most famous transaction of the period was the long-term supply contract concluded between Hokutan and Tokyo Gas, which kept Hokutan alive and well through ten subsequent years of price reductions. The scarcity of coal during the Korean War boom had frightened Tokyo Gas into a long-term, fixed-price deal just before the full implications of cheap oil were recognized.

144. In the autumn of 1959 IMF and GATT conferences saw sharp criticism of Japan and demands for liberalization of its markets. The implications of these demands are explored in Chapter 5 below.

145. Caldwell 1981:76.

146. Sekiyu Renmei 1962:96–97. A Coal Bureau Policy Section chief at that time recalls how he even resurrected the idea for several forms of state ownership, including the Tangyō Kōdan and the Seisan Kōdan ideas that had failed in the past. He wanted private industry to surrender its mining rights to the state, letting a *kōdan* take responsibility for all production. The only support among the large mineowners came from maverick Hagiwara of Hokutan. Industry objections led him to discard the notion (interview, March 1, 1984). Young LDP leader Nakasone Yasuhiro, as chairman of a group of LDP Dietmen interested in energy policy, likewise proposed that the Japan Mining Law be revised to provide state control for all resource development, as part of a comprehensive energy policy program administered by an energy public corporation (*enerugī kōdan*). See Oi 1972:5.

147. See Imai 1966:35–36. The Miike mines were located on the coast.

148. See accounts in Sonoda 1970:82–83; Imai 1966:38–40; and Shigen . . . Sekitanbu 1982:27.

149. Uemura figures often in this book. Born in 1894 in Tokyo, he grew up in Hokkaido, where his father worked in a variety of ministries associated with Hokkaido development. Uemura was an economic bureaucrat, serving key posts. In 1941 Matsumoto Kenjirō summoned him to become executive director for the Coal Control Company. He worked closely there with MCI minister Kishi and with Shiina Etsusaburō, the MCI vice-minister during the wartime coal mobilization. On Matsumoto's recommendation he became the executive director of

Keidanren's secretariat but was immediately purged for his association with wartime economic policy. After 1951 he returned to Keidanren as a vice-chairman. He was a key adviser to chairman Ishizaka (1956–68) and succeeded him as chairman in 1968. He served in that capacity until Dokō Toshio took over in 1974.

150. Imai 1966:33–34.

151. Sonoda 1970:79.

152. This refund (*kanpu*), generated by tariffs on oil and other special subsidies to the electric utilities and the steel industry as compensation for "compulsory" purchases of domestic coal, would amount to more than 23 billion yen between 1962 and 1967 (Sonoda 1970:116).

153. The instrument created in this legislation to oversee transaction prices for domestic steaming coal and to ensure the execution of long-term coal trade contracts was a special public entity (*tokushu hōjin*), the Steaming Coal Payment Liquidation Company (Denryoku Yōtan Daikin Seisan K. K.). MITI and the Coal Association sought a policy-induced rationalization of coal distribution through joint storage, transport, and sales coordination; but the private utilities, with the support of the Finance Ministry, refused to cooperate. They settled for an organ that served merely as sole agent for the distribution of subsidies to the electric power companies. Imai 1966:186; interview with former MITI Coal Bureau chief, March 8, 1984.

154. Nakamura 1981:79.

155. Shigen Enerugīchō Sekitanbu 1982:27. Vogel 1985 offers a similar account.

156. See time-series data in Sonoda 1970:127.

157. Sonoda 1970:132–34.

158. In June 1965 Nihon Tankō was similarly designated, and by August, Meiji Kōgyō and Kishima Tankō were demanding similar designations.

159. See Shigen . . . Sekitanbu 1982:38–39. It is ironic that this policy was announced just when Japan went into almost permanent surplus on its balance of payments.

160. Sonoda 1970:121.

161. This joint public-private sales company lasted until June 1977, when high oil prices and pressure for administrative reform made its dissolution attractive. It was absorbed into the Rationalization of the Coal Industry Corporation, a public agency that was itself absorbed into the New Energy Development Organization in 1979. See Chapter 6 below.

162. Quoted in *Mainichi Shimbun*, December 17, 1964.

163. Noguchi 1965, 1964, 1966. See also the debate in *Ekonomisto*, January 12, 1965, and Sasaki 1965.

164. Hagiwara reports that Kōno, then head of the Economic Planning Agency, responded favorably to the idea (Kondō and Osanai 1978:99). Hagiwara also resuscitated the Meiji-era term *sekitan hōkan*, referring to the restoration of property and administrative authority to the emperor, and called for the return of all mining rights to the state, whereupon the state would "pay coal companies the full amount to develop the fields and sink the shafts by delegation" (ibid.:100).

165. Interview with a former Coal Mine Bureau chief, March 1, 1984.

166. Quoted in Kondō and Osanai 1978.

167. *Energy in Japan*, December 1966. Also see *Ekonomisto*, June 14, 1966.

168. *Nihon Keizai Shimbun*, November 8, 1965.

169. *Nihon Keizai Shimbun*, November 20, 1965.

170. *Nihon Keizai Shimbun*, November 9, 10, 1965.

171. *Nihon Keizai Shimbun*, November 8, 1965.

172. *Energy in Japan*, December 1966, p. 13.

173. Sonoda 1970:148.

174. Sonoda 1970:173. The firms were Kyushu Kōzan and Ōtsuji Tankō. See *Zaikai*, February 15, 1969.

175. Quoted in *Asahi Jaanaru*, October 6, 1968.

176. Sonoda 1970:172.

177. Quoted in Kondō and Osanai 1978:118–19.

178. For the full text of the Hagiwara Plan, see Hagiwara 1968. The best review of all these plans is *Asahi Janaaru*, October 6, 1968, and Sonoda 1970:184–92. Also note that Kiso sought the creation of a 100 percent public agency to buy out all the nation's mines, including a 5–7 percent profit at the same time. He claimed (self-servingly) that "times had changed since when I had been involved in the anti-state control movement. This is not control, but should be considered just like the rice price subsidy system" (see Kondō and Osanai 1978:120).

179. See Sonoda 1970:186 and *Energy in Japan*, August 1968.

180. He alleges that even Mitsui Bank chairman Koyama ordered Mitsui Mining president Kurada to "keep quiet and fall in line behind the Hagiwara plan," but that Mitsui Mining simply dug in its heels in opposition. Hagiwara's own account appears in Kondō and Osanai 1978. An interview with a leading Lower House Commerce and Industry Committee member, March 29, 1984, confirmed that the Mitsui Bank, the leading bank of Hagiwara's Hokutan Mines as well as of Mitsui Mining, did give "passive understanding" to his plan (*rikaisha*).

181. Quoted in Kondō and Osanai 1978:103.

182. Hagiwara says *he* authored the LDP program. See Kondō and Osanai 1978:100.

183. Kondō and Osanai 1978:121; *Zaikai*, February 15, 1969.

184. Kondō and Osanai 1978:100.

185. *Jitsugyō no Nihon*, December 15, 1968. Interview with Energy Advisory Commission member, February 9, 1984.

186. For details see *Energy in Japan*, August 1968; Sonoda 1970:186–89.

187. Although Hagiwara's "One Company Plan" was, as noted above, a central restructuring proposal, once it was blocked within the industry Hagiwara turned his support toward the Uemura Program as the "lesser of two evils." See *Jistugyō no Nihon*, November 30, 1968. For his initial critiques of the Uemura Plan, see Hagiwara 1968.

188. *Asahi Janaaru*, October 6, 1968.

189. *Nihon Keizai Shimbun*, June 29, 1968; *Energy in Japan*, November 1968.

190. Cf. *Nihon Keizai Shimbun*, June 20, 1968; interview with a former MITI Mining Bureau chief, January 27, 1984.

191. Uemura's ascendence to the Keidanren chairmanship should have strengthened the chances for the acceptance of his coal program. Ironically, it had the opposite effect, because in becoming chairman of Japan's most influential business interest group, he had to pay closer attention to the concerns of the steel and electric power firms. Interviews with a Dietman, March 29, 1984, and with an Uemura lieutenant, February 20, 1984.

192. Unpublished, undated, and unsigned internal MITI document, entitled "Memo," pp. 4.3–4.4.

193. *Nihon Keizai Shimbun,* August 16, 1968.
194. Speaking to this theme of abandonment by the Finance Ministry, financial institutions, and consumer industries, a leading private-sector coal planner, and supporter of the Uemura Plan, remarked in an interview on February 20, 1984, that "we in the coal industry were terribly jealous of the success of the German Ruhrkohle. In Japan, the large users simply discarded us (*mikigiru*)."
195. Horiuchi 1984:46.
196. *Jitsugyō no Nihon,* November 30, 1968.
197. *Energy in Japan,* July 1969.
198. Sonoda 1970:203–4.
199. Shigen . . . Sekitanbu 1982:38–39; *Nihon Keizai Shimbun,* July 28, 1968.
200. *Zaikai,* February 15, 1969.
201. Kishima, Meiji, and Aso had all supported the Uemura Plan; they now retired from the coal business altogether. See *Energy in Japan,* July 1969.
202. Sonoda 1970:220–22.
203. Zenkoku . . . Kyōgikai 1971c and Nihon Sekitan Kyōkai 1971.
204. Zenkoku . . . Kyōgikai 1971a.
205. The internal records of the Advisory Council make fascinating reading. See the summaries in Zenkoku . . . Kyōgikai 1971a–d.
206. Nihon Tekkō Renmei 1971. Imports of coking coal had trebled between 1966 and 1975. Thus quite apart from whether it was already being fully reimbursed for domestic coal purchases, the steel industry's 8 million ton "compulsory" purchase was a negligible portion (10–13 percent) of its total demand.
207. Zenkoku . . . Kyōgikai 1972c. On May 19, 1972, the council's electric utility representative bluntly declared "we will cooperate on volume, but not on price" (Zenkoku . . . Kyōgikai 1972e). He was supported by the steel spokesman, and further discussion about a new public agency was deferred.
208. Shigen . . . Sekitanbu 1982:38–39; *Energy in Japan,* September 1972.
209. Not one of the five big coal mining companies (Mitsui, Mitsubishi, Sumitomo, Taiheiyō, and Matsushima) was still affiliated with its parent firm by the early 1980s. Coke and coal sales, which had accounted for 95.6 percent of the parent firms' total business in 1957, accounted for less than half their total business in 1982. Real estate, petroleum products, building materials, machinery sales, supermarkets, and leisure industries have filled the breach. These firms, accounting for 80 percent of Japan's coal production by the mid-1980s, recorded losses of 8 billion yen (more than 600 yen/ton) in FY 1984. Subsidies from the government amounted to 18 million yen per miner. (Data compiled from company reports.)
210. *Mainichi Shimbun,* February 21, 1986.
211. Recall Silberman's (1982:247, 229) characterization of interest groups in the 1930s as having been "foreclosed" by the state and of small business interests in particular as "conflated into the structure of large-scale economic organizations." Vogel (1985:chap. 4) presents a more seamless web of creative state policies and "clear vision" that transformed Japan's largest coal mining district. He is impressed with "how quickly state leaders achieved policy changes in response to changing world conditions."
212. Interview, January 27, 1984.
213. Johnson 1978:130.
214. Interview, March 8, 1984.

CHAPTER 4. *A Political History of the Japanese Electric Power Industry*

1. Johnson 1978:132.

2. For comparison, ENEL, the Italian national utility, and the Tokyo Electric Power Company, the world's largest private utility, have a nearly identical generating capacity (30–40 thousand mw). Note also that privately owned Tokyo Electric sells more power and employs fewer workers (40,000) than state-owned ENEL (114,000).

3. The first hydroelectric power plant in Japan (5 kw) was constructed in 1888 for Miyoshi Electric by Shibaura Electric. Within seven years Fukushima Electric Light had built a 60 kw plant. See Otake 1980, 1:756–57.

4. Williamson and Daum 1963. The early electric power industrialists were among the most influential of Japan's emerging business elite. Perhaps most distinguished was Shibusawa Eichi (1840–1931), known as the architect of modern Japanese banking, who held 2 percent of the shares of Tokyo Electric Light Company (Tokyo Dentō) when it was founded in 1886 as Japan's first electric utility. It was but one of over 500 firms in which Shibusawa was an important participant. He was never affiliated formally with a *zaibatsu* family.

Many in the emerging elite, among them Shibusawa and Tokyo Dentō's first president, Yajima Sakurō, were sent to study abroad to acquire knowledge and technical skills that could be put to the service of Japan's industrial transformation. Perhaps the most important single figure was Fujioka Ichisuke, who in 1884 became Japan's first professor of electrical engineering. As an entrepreneur (he held the same number of original shares in Tokyo Dentō as did Shibusawa) and a publicist, he was more responsible than any other for selling electric power to investors and consumers alike. In 1890 he helped develop the first Japanese light bulb and eventually became president of Shibaura Electric, forerunner of Toshiba Corporation.

5. For an intimate account of this period in Tokyo, see Lockwood 1955:329–30 and Seidensticker 1983.

6. According to one account, however, the only businesses that could afford to keep their lights on throughout the night were brothels. A director of Tōhō Electric once observed that he could accurately guess the number of electric lights in a town if he knew the number of geisha (Ōtani 1978:19–20).

7. Otake 1980, 1:130–32.

8. The first major exception was the capital and technology agreement between General Electric and Fujioka in 1905—the basis for the close ties between Toshiba and GE that continue to this day.

9. See Williamson et al. 1963.

10. See Otake 1980, 1:212; Ōtani 1970:25.

11. These regulations are reprinted in Otake 1980, 1:148–56. Industry may have wanted these regulations to avoid conflicting regulations being passed by many local governments.

12. An industry group was established in 1897, but it never spoke as a voice for the entire industry. See the official account in Nihon Denki Kyōkai 1975:1–9.

13. Sakai 1965:165.

14. Otake 1980, 1:212–13. See also Sakai 1965:71–92 for an outline of the legislation.

15. Sakai 1965:169.

16. Tokyo Denryoku Shashi Henshū Iinkai 1983:69.

17. Ozawa 1979:59–61.
18. See Sakai 1965:93–130.
19. Ōtani 1978:22–23.
20. Ōtani 1978:26–27.
21. Otake 1980, 1:483; Sakai 1965:169, Seiji Keizai Kenkyūjo 1959:14–15.
22. Otake 1980, 1:483.
23. Sakai 1965:169.
24. Otake 1980, 1:394–95.
25. Otake 1980, 1:402.
26. Otake 1980, 1:459.
27. This may have been ensured by the presence of seven *zaibatsu*-affiliated representatives out of eighteen members on the Lower House oversight committee, and by a majority of *zaibatsu*-affiliated peers on the Upper House committee. See Tiedemann 1971:283; 1979:62–63.
28. Nihon Denki Kyōkai 1975:13.
29. Lockwood 1955:49.
30. Estimates vary. See Ozawa 1979 and Otake 1980, vol. 1.
31. In 1926, 100 yen = U.S. $50. In 1932, 100 yen = U.S. $20.
32. The most complete accounts of the creation of the Denryoku Renmei are Komamura 1966; Tokyo Denryoku Shashi Henshū Iinkai 1983; Nihon Denki Kyōkai 1975; Ōtani 1978; Otake 1980, vol. 1; Ozawa 1979; Seiji Keizai Kenkyūjo 1959. *Yomiuri Shimbun,* April 20, 1932, has an account as well.
33. Ōtani 1978:29.
34. Ōtani 1978:23.
35. Ozawa 1979:62.
36. Interview with a director of Tokyo Electric Power Company, October 7, 1983.
37. This account is based on Komamura 1966:303–11.
38. Tokyo Denryoku Shashi Henshū Iinkai 1983:75.
39. Quoted in Ozawa 1979:61.
40. Between 1931 and 1933 electric power generating capacity expanded by over 30 percent. Japan ranked behind only the United States and Germany in power generation (Mitsubishi Economic Research Bureau 1936:54–55).
41. Two important points should be noted. First, virtually all the world's industrial nations were rationalizing national electric power systems in the 1930s. This period marked the first appearance of power pools and joint high-voltage lines in the United States. In Britain a national grid has been introduced several years earlier. Second, Japan's first two national policy companies in the electric power sector were regional utilities in Tohoku in 1936, modeled directly upon the 1935 Tennessee Valley Authority in the United States.
42. Ozawa 1978:206.
43. On this so-called *genbutsu shusshi* formula see Tokyo Denryoku Shashi Henshū Iinkai 1983:92.
44. Ōtani 1978:34–35.
45. Otake 1980, 1:489–90. Others have noted that the railways minister, Maeda Yonezō, strongly opposed the nationalization. He did not want to surrender the National Railways' own considerable number of power stations.
46. Johnson 1982:126.
47. Ōtani 1978:12 has a partial text of that speech.
48. *"Ningen no kuzu."* Quoted in Matsuzaka 1980:192 and in Ōtani 1978:3. The most complete accounts of Matsunaga's leadership of private opposition to

state control are Usami 1981 and Matsuzaka 1980. As noted above, Matsunaga had often argued in the past for a unified national utility. Okamura, therefore, apparently had the impression that even Matsunaga would come around to support the Ministry of Communications program if state control seemed the only way to integrate the national power system. The bureaucrats badly under-estimated Matsunaga's opposition to state control.

49. Ōtani 1978:36.

50. Johnson 1982:126.

51. Allen 1946:146–47. Even the controlled press voiced reservations about the state control program; see *Tokyo Nichi Nichi Shimbun*, September 4, 1936.

52. For the full account see Sakai 173–74; Otake 1980, 1:497. Also see Tokyo Denryoku Shashi Henshū Iinkai 1983:96–102.

53. See Ōtani 1978:46. Johnson 1978:133 has a slightly different version.

54. Quoted in Ōtani 1978:44.

55. For a comparison see Tokyo Denryoku Shashi Henshū Iinkai 1983:102.

56. Quoted in Ōtani 1978:47.

57. Duus 1984:826 notes a strange bedfellowship in Diet. He reports that all political parties strenuously opposed the original Nippatsu bill—with the exception of the left-wing Social Masses party.

58. See Sakai 1965:169–92 for a full discussion of the parliamentary debates.

59. Interview with a director of Tokyo Electric Power Company, October 7, 1983.

60. Duus 1984:826.

61. Ōtani 1978:30.

62. Ōtani 1978:30; Nakamura and Miyazaki 1961:25.

63. Nakamura and Miyazaki 1961:25.

64. Ōtani 1978:30.

65. Nakamura and Miyazaki 1961:25 use the term *katagawari*, the "shoulder-ing of another's debts," introduced vis-à-vis the coal industry in Chapter 3.

66. Ōtani 1978:60–61.

67. Ōtani 1978:32; Otake 1980:483, Komakura 1966. See also Nippon Hassōden Shashi 1944.

68. They were Masuda Jirō of Daidō and Ikeo Yoshizō of Nippon Denryoku, former chairman of the industry association.

69. Matsunaga sat out the war at his country home. Many credit him with a strong commitment to the free market. Yet Matsunaga frequently championed collusive industrial restructuring, and the facilities of his Tōhō Denryoku were the most widely dispersed of any of those held by the large utilities. Thus they were poorly suited for amalgamation into a single firm under state control (Ōtani 1978:68–74).

70. Yamada 1977:93.

71. Ōtani 1978:65–66. The black market purchases resulted in scandals that forced the resignation of President Masuda and also involved top Electricity Agency officials.

72. One was Urayama Jōtarō, leader of the Kantō regional branch of the electricity association. Another was Kosaka Junzō, a Minseitō peer and president of Nagano Electric Power, who would become Matsunaga's most difficult foe in the postwar reconstruction of the electric power industry.

73. Ōtani 1978:86–87.

74. Yamada 1977:91; *Asahi Shimbun*, May 8, 1976. "Progressive" bureaucrats took the initiative in creating dozens of such joint public-private ventures during

this period, including Nippon Steel, Imperial Oil, South Manchurian Railroad, and others in heavy industry. All guaranteed dividends to private shareholders.

75. The leading figure in Densan in the early postwar years was Sasaki Ryōsaku, chairman of the Democratic Socialist party (1977–85).

76. GHQ-SCAP 1952a:3.

77. The most complete review of these programs is in Shinobu 1967. See also Ōtani 1978 and Otake 1980.

78. For a review of the relationships between these organizations and among these and other representatives of local interests, see Samuels 1983:21–27.

79. Otake 1980:101. The Ōyama Commission was concerned with far more than questions of industrial structure and state control, of course. It also reviewed rate structure, finance, and so forth. Useful reviews of its work are in Otake 1980:107; Ōtani 1978:126–30; Nihon Denki Kyōkai 1975:148–49.

80. Otake 1980:106.

81. GHQ-SCAP 1952a:33.

82. Ibid.

83. Seiji Keizai Kenkyūjo 1959:4–6. Americans had a negligible investment in Japanese electric utilities.

84. Quoted in Usami 1981:19. For Matsunaga's own reflections on the reconstruction debates, see Andō 1973:367–79. The most useful biographies of Matsunaga are Matsuzaka 1980 and Usami 1981.

85. See Shinobu 1967:1204.

86. Ōtani 1978:152. Examples of the regional coalitions are the Kyūshū Denryoku Juyōsha Taikai Jikō Iinkai and the Hokkaidō Denryoku Mondai Renraku Kyōgikai.

87. Ōtani 1978:156. This same explanation seemed plausible several years later, in Kōno Ichirō's support for state control of the nuclear power industry. See Chapter 6 below.

88. The press by and large opposed privatization. See the editorials in *Asahi Shimbun*, January 28, 1950, and in *Mainichi Shimbun*, January 23, 1950.

89. Johnson 1978:135.

90. Ōtani 1978:163.

91. Ōtani 1978. There has been speculation as to who conceived the Potsdam strategy. Johnson 1978 suggests it was MacArthur himself. One former MITI Electric Power Section chief and Public Utilities Commission official claims it was Matsunaga who sold the idea to SCAP (interview, February 10, 1984).

92. Ōtani 1978:179. Kosaka is an enigmatic figure. A private businessman active in electric power and chemical manufacturing in Nagano, he had served in the House of Peers during the war. As noted above, he had also worked with Matsunaga in 1940 to block the state's Nippatsu consolidation effort. After the war, however, he became the final president of Nippatsu at Yoshida's request and Matsunaga's staunchest foe.

93. Ōtani 1978:185.

94. Densan unrest continued after SCAP's dismissal of more than 2,000 electric power industry workers, 20 percent of those purged in the private sector. Yet, as Densan had feared, the dissolution of Nippatsu hastened the disintegration of the electric power labor movement. By the fall of 1952 defections and cooptation had debilitated Densan.

95. See Samuels 1983:169–71.

96. Like Matsunaga, Ichimanda enjoyed the confidence of SCAP leaders. He served as governor of the Bank of Japan for almost nine years, through the

tenure of nine finance ministers and seven cabinets. The actual annual rate of increase in electric power demand between 1951 and 1961 was nearly 12 percent, half again as much as even Matsunaga had projected.

97. Nihon Denki Kyōkai D. N. I. 1982:31.

98. In Japanese variously referred to as a "dengen kaihatsu tokushu kaisha" and a "dengen kaihatsu kōsha." It ultimately became the Dengen Kaihatsu Kabushiki Kaisha, the Electric Power Development Corporation.

99. Matsunaga 1983, 513.

100. The government's Japan Development Bank held 99 percent of EPDC's initial capital. In 1969 the nine private utilities increased their holding from 1 percent to 7.5 percent and today hold over a quarter of EPDC shares. It is often suggested they increased their exposure in order to reduce MITI control (see *Denki Shimbun*, May 20, 1983, and Sanjū Nenshi Henshū Iinkai 1984). Although the EPDC never operated at a loss, it was designated for privatization (along with the debt-ridden national railways) by the Administrative Management Agency during the first administrative reform in 1970. The relationship between the private utilities and MITI over the EPDC and their division of labor has been most uneasy over the decades. See Gale 1981.

101. Note also that an additional 1.5 percent of the nation's total is generated by public enterprises of a different sort. These are the thirty-two hydropower stations managed by local governments, which, like the EPDC, are required to sell their power to the nine private utilities.

102. Nihon Denki Kyōkai D. N. I. 1982:31.

103. Sanjū Nenshi Henshū Iinkai 1984:88–93.

104. See Chapter 3 above.

105. Tsūshō Sangyōshō Shigen Enerugīchō Kōeki Jigyōkyoku 1983:43.

106. *Yomiuri Shimbun,* October 29, 1954; Seiji Keizai Kenkuȳjo 1959:76.

107. Nihon Denryoku Kyōkai D. N. I. 1982:24–25.

108. Yomiuri Shimbunsha Seijibu 1981:203–5.

109. Ōtani 1978:222–23.

110. Suzuki 1983:81–84; interview with TEPCO official, October 21, 1983.

111. See Steiner et al. 1980 for background on Japanese political opposition in the period.

112. *Akahata,* June 13, 1977. See also Chapter 5 below for a more comprehensive examination of these nationalization programs.

113. See Yamada 1977:89–98 for a rebuttal of the nationalization advocates written pseudonymously by a TEPCO official. His data showed the privately owned American and Japanese utilities to be more efficient than the state-owned French, Italian, and British. There were fewer power stoppages and strikes in Japan than in these European countries as well.

CHAPTER 5. *A Political History of the Japanese Oil Industry*

1. The use of oil for illumination is recorded in the *Nippon Shoki,* Japan's first written history prepared over thirteen hundred years ago. Commercial records from the Edo period report barter values and transport prices (Uehara 1981:84–85).

2. For the origins of the Japanese oil industry, see Inokuchi 1963 (the author is sometimes cited as Iguchi; both readings of the Chinese characters are possi-

ble, but Japanese libraries use Inokuchi). For an intimate account of the early years of the industry, see the essays by Okuda Hideo in *Sekiyu Bunka*, 1981–83; Naitō 1957:70–90 is a personal account of the founder of Nippon Oil.

3. It is perhaps misleading to speak of "giants" in an industry as small and as peripheral to the economy as petroleum was in its early years. Relative to the profusion of tiny enterprises, however, these two firms loomed large in both capital and technology. Neither was associated with a *zaibatsu* (Tsūshō Sangyō . . . Sekiyuka 1958:229); both were very successful. Nippon Oil authorized annual shareholder dividends that averaged over 25 percent between 1888 and 1902 (Inokuchi 1963:33–34).

4. Naitō 1957:194–95.

5. Between 1891 and 1907 Hōden alone absorbed 124 firms (Tsūshō Sangyō . . . Sekiyuka 1958:229). Hōden acquired eighteen smaller firms in September 1904 when share prices plummeted because of the Russo-Japanese War (Henshūshitsu 1958:245–46).

6. Demand for fuel oil would more than quadruple between the last Meiji years before World War I and the beginning of the Shōwa period in 1925 (Okamoto 1979:95).

7. Thus the Allies' embargo of petroleum, often identified correctly as a proximate cause of the attack on Pearl Harbor, had less to do with the civilian economy than with the military (see Lockwood 1955:93). The Army paid little attention to petroleum until after the Manchurian Incident in 1931.

8. Uehara 1981:177–78. This political victory notwithstanding, the military achieved technological advantages over private firms with the establishment of the naval refineries in Tokuyama and later in Yokkaichi and Ōfuna, especially in synthetic fuels development.

9. See Tsūshō Sangyō . . . Sekiyuka 1958:23–31, as well as the personal account of Hōden president Hashimoto Keizaburō 1958:170, the person credited with finally engineering the merger.

10. Hashimoto, president of Nippon Oil and a former bureaucrat, was a peer. So were Naitō Hisahiro, the founder of Nippon Oil, and Kuhara Sannosuke, a leading entrepreneur whose diverse activities included the Nissan *zaibatsu* and Kuhara Mining (today's Nippon Mining). Perhaps the most active lobbyist among these oil executive Dietmen was Hasegawa Shōichirō, founder and president of Taiyō Oil. In 1919 he began to organize industry groups to press for subsidies (see Hasegawa 1936 for his complete program). Most important, he argued that the state should supply funds for drilling exploratory wells and turn operation of proven sites over to private entrepreneurs. He also stressed the importance of acquiring foreign fields, developing synthetic fuels, and controlling foreign imports. (Coal liquefaction research was begun by the Manchurian Railways in 1928.) See Inokuchi 1963:55. The government was unwilling to subsidize private purchase of oil fields in the South Pacific. Hashimoto recalls that the Finance Ministry could not be convinced of the value of these "treasure houses" and suggests in his memoirs that such a measure would have avoided the Pacific War (Hashimoto 1957:176). According to one account, MCI was willing to provide more funds sooner, but the Finance Ministry consistently intervened to block its requests (Yuki 1938:313–14).

11. Mitsubishi Shōji became a 50 percent partner of Associated Oil (later Tidewater, then Getty) in 1924. Mitsubishi Oil was created in 1931 with predominantly foreign capital, establishing an important precedent for the postwar

petroleum industry. The Mitsubishi Group did not gain complete ownership of Mitsubishi Oil until 1984, when Getty was acquired by Texaco and subsequently sold.

12. Mitsubishi Economic Research Bureau 1936:211, 214.

13. Nippon Sekiyushi Henshūshitsu 1958:298–99; Inokuchi 1963:245.

14. A fair amount of debate concerned what to consider Mitsubishi Oil, whose largest shareholder by this time was Tidewater Oil.

15. Nakamura and Miyazaki 1961:21. A similar effort by petroleum *retailers* to gain state recognition for their plight in 1930 was quashed by producers and refiners, who viewed solidarity among vendors with extreme suspicion. The state did not recognize sales associations until January 1932. See Zenkoku Sekiyu . . . Kyōdō Rengōkai 1974; Ōi 1972:4–5.

16. Ōi 1972:6 suggests that the maverick Matsukata may have been acting on behalf of the military.

17. *Asahi Shimbun,* September 19, 1932.

18. *Asahi Shimbun,* September 25, 1932, and Nippon Sekiyu Henshūshitsu 1958:307–8.

19. Nakamura and Miyazaki 1961:21.

20. Inokuchi 1963:247–48.

21. Nippon Sekiyu Henshūshitsu 1958:310–13; *Asahi Shimbun,* June 9, 1933.

22. *Asahi Shimbun,* May 4, 1933. Several Imperial naval officers were highly placed in the MCI bureaucracy, among them the Synthetic Fuels Division chief. Interview with former MITI official, November 30, 1983.

23. The initial draft made no mention of guaranteed dividends, only that dividends would receive a "priority." Inokuchi 1963:251 has the full text.

24. As in France, the state responded with control legislation when domestic firms suffered at the hands of foreign competition and when security of supply was seriously threatened. Japanese planners were impressed with the provisions in French law that approached these problems by requiring stockpiles and using licensing authority to give priority to domestic refiners. See Chapter 2 above and Grayson 1981:24 for details.

25. Inokuchi 1963:252.

26. Interview with former Mitsubishi Oil executive, December 1, 1983. See also the memoirs of Ogura Oil president Nakahara Nobuhei (Okuda 1981) and the account by Ōi 1972:6, which stresses "domestic political conditions" over international relations as the basis for the state's abandonment of its "more thorough plan."

27. The best account of PIL-I in English, especially in an international context, is Anderson 1975. Okamoto 1979:97 (see also *Asahi Shimbun,* February 15, 1934). Numbers of firms from Inokuchi 1963:57–58.

28. Gaining these funds took extended MCI lobbying at the Finance Ministry. Nippon Sekiyu Henshūshitsu 1958:3–4.

29. Stanvac, created in 1933 through the marriage of Standard's refinery operations with the distribution network of Socony-Vacuum, was the largest U.S. direct investment in East Asia before World War II. Standard became Exxon and Socony-Vacuum became Mobil (see Anderson 1975).

30. Cohen 1949:23–24.

31. Anderson 1975:82.

32. The month before PIL-I was implemented, the Japanese puppet government in Manchukuo had created the Manchuria Petroleum Company in which Japanese interests held 80 percent and the government held 20 percent. Foreign

firms were shut out by a prohibition on unauthorized transfer of shares. Nippon Oil's Hashimoto was made chairman of the board (see Anderson 1975:52–53; Hashimoto 1958:189). Also contributing to the growing estrangement was the June 1935 establishment of the Chōsen Oil Company in Korea. Previously Stanvac and Rising Sun had had this market to themselves, but Nippon Oil, Idemitsu Shōkai, and the colonial government now conspired to fix a tariff system to make Japanese petroleum competitive. Again, Hashimoto Keizaburō became the firm's first chief executive officer (see his memoirs, Hashimoto 1957:187–88).

33. *Asahi Shimbun*, March 3, 1936.

34. Inokuchi 1963:245. See 267 for more on downstream cartels established in this period in kerosene, residual fuel oil, asphalt, and lamp oil.

35. *Asahi Shimbun*, May 2, 1936.

36. Nippon Sekiyushi Henshūshitsu 1958:357.

37. Inokuchi 1963:273. It is easy to get the two firms confused. The Japanese pronounce both names Kyōdō Kigyō; the English translation of both is exactly the same. Only the first Chinese character differs: the second Kyōdō Kigyō is written with the character *tomo*, not *kanau* (see Nippon Sekiyushi Henshūshitsu 1958:365). Both joint enterprise companies provided a "single channel" system for crude oil importation and storage under the supervision of the MCI Fuels Bureau.

38. One wartime petroleum planner used Hashimoto to compare industrial policy and business-state relations in wartime Japan and Nazi Germany: "Just like the Nazis, if we could find an appropriate individual who shared our views, we would leave direction of that sector to him, as it was to Hashimoto. If not, then the military would have to use one of its own" (interview, January 19, 1984). Hashimoto was originally a bureaucrat, known as the "father of the state salt and tobacco monopoly." He served as finance vice-minister in 1911 and agriculture vice-minister in 1913 before retiring in 1914 at age fifty. At that point he became a peer and joined Hōden Oil. He was president or chairman of every major government control company, joint venture, or overseas oil project until he was purged by SCAP in 1946, the result, he claims, "of Machiavellian plotting by a certain section chief in a certain ministry" (Hashimoto 1958:195–96; see also Okuda 1981:161–62).

39. See the account by Nakahara in his memoirs, Okuda 1981:161–79.

40. Nippon Sekiyushi Henshūshitsu 1958:382–83.

41. Inokuchi 1963:280–81. See also Cohen 1949:25.

42. The best account of this is Inokuchi 1963:282–88 and Zenkoku Sekiyu . . . Kyōdō Rengōkai 1974:13–25; see also the press accounts of the day, which were remarkably detailed about rural opposition to the MCI program: *Asahi Shimbun*, October 6 and 27, and December 1, 1939.

43. For another glimpse of this powerful postwar politician, see Chapter 6 below.

44. Zenkoku Sekiyu . . . Kyōdō Rengōkai 1974:17.

45. Regulations on the consumption side were far more complete than on the supply side. See Zenkoku Sekiyu . . . Kyōdō Rengōkai 1974:7–8 and Nippon Sekiyushi Henshūshitsu 1958:367–72.

46. Nippon Sekiyushi Henshūshitsu 1958:392.

47. Hasegawa 1936:9–10.

48. Cohen 1949:25; Nippon Sekiyushi Henshūshitsu 1958:392–95.

49. Teikoku Sekiyu Kabushiki Kaisha Rōmubu 1982:197.

50. This account is based upon Hasegawa's memoirs, 1958:196–97.

51. For details on the policy process and personalities involved in the creation of Imperial Oil, see Teikoku Sekiyu Kabushiki Kaisha Rōmubu 1982:201.

52. Of this the company history of Daikyō Oil makes an interesting observation: "Government guarantees and the pooled accounts of the industry got us through by the skin of our teeth after crude supplies from the South became impossible" (Daikyō Sekiyu K. K. 1976:18).

53. Quoted in Daikyō Sekiyu . . . Iinkai 1980:58; Cohen 1949:146.

54. The phrase is from Hein 1982:8.

55. See Zenkoku Sekiyu . . . Kyōdō Rengōkai 1974:43–46 for this temporary agency. See also Chapter 3 above for details of the Economic Stabilization Board and other *kōdan* programs for product distribution.

56. Inokuchi 1963:373–74.

57. GHQ-SCAP 1952b:9.

58. GHQ-SCAP 1951a; GHQ-SCAP 1952b.

59. See Brown 1983 for an excellent overview of this period.

60. GHQ-SCAP 1952b:18.

61. GHQ-SCAP, Natural Resources Section 1951a:52.

62. GHQ-SCAP, Natural Resources Section 1951a:50.

63. GHQ-SCAP, Natural Resources Section 1951a:51.

64. Chen 1965.

65. See Brown 1983 for an excellent summary of these reports and reversals. He also notes the composition of the PAG: three from Stanvac, four from Shell (originally Rising Sun), one each from Caltex, Tidewater, and Union. Caldwell 1981 is also a useful review.

66. Quoted in Kondō and Osanai 1978:30, 31, 40.

67. Porges 1979:19.

68. Interview with wartime government energy planner, January 19, 1984, who suggested that Mitsubishi Oil faithfully held Tidewater royalties in an escrow account throughout the war.

69. Johnson 1978:129. Caldwell 1981:78–81 shows that MITI's control could be politically influenced. A prominent case in the oil sector was the acceptance by MITI of demands by Zengyōren, the Fishing Industries Association, in 1954–55 for an independent currency allocation. In a move strikingly reminiscent of the 1939 conflict over the joint sales monopoly, the fishing industry demanded and was granted its own quota. The oil industry feared that such demands would spread to other politically influential oil-consuming groups but found itself politically disadvantaged. There was no oil industry association until late 1955, when the Petroleum Association of Japan was established. But MITI had by then already made its concessions. The fishing industry was granted guaranteed supplies of currency outside the formal industry allocation system.

70. For an excellent discussion of the way in which MITI exercised its currency allocation powers vis-à-vis the oil industry during this period, see the three-part series by Ōi 1972; Caldwell 1981; and Brown 1983.

71. Initiative for this plan, which would have created a public-private joint venture and joint use of the facility by the eight refining companies, reportedly came from Maruzen Oil president Katayama. Interview with former MITI section chief, December 6, 1983. See also Nippon Sekiyushi Henshūshitsu 1958:520–22.

72. Interview with a director of the Japan National Oil Corporation, November 30, 1983.

73. In fact, as early as November 1946 MCI and PAG sponsored a petroleum exploration advisory commission (Sekiyu Shigen Kaihatsu Sokushin Kaihatsu Shingikai) known as PEAC.

74. Johnson 1978:124 reports that "all vestiges of government ownership" had been eliminated in 1950. In fact Finance Ministry shareholding was retained when private subscriptions for the venture fell short of expectations.
75. Sekiyu Kōgyō Renmei 1982:4; Sekiyu Shigen Kaihatsu 1967:8.
76. Sekiyu Shigen Kaihatsu 1967:8.
77. Sekiyu Kōgyō Renmei 1982:5; Inokuchi 1963:420.
78. See *Nihon Keizai Shimbun*, July 10, 1955.
79. *Nihon Keizai Shimbun*, February 25, 1960; Inokuchi 1963:69.
80. The other important venture was in north Sumatra in 1958.
81. For a complete account see Brown 1983. Mizuno Sōhei, Yamashita's son as well as his successor, claims that several domestic refiners, including those with foreign ties, were positive about collaborating with Arabian Oil. See Kondō and Osanai 1978; Tsūsho . . . Sekiyuka 1958.
82. See the accounts in Vernon 1983, Brown 1983, Caldwell 1981, Sekiyu Renmei 1962, and Ōi 1972.
83. For Arisawa's account of this group's work, see Kondō and Osanai 1978:25.
84. Sekiyu Renmei 1962:75–76.
85. The euphemism "special crude" (*tokushu genyu*) was used for oil from Arabian and other Japanese-controlled fields that would enjoy a reserved market.
86. Sekiyu Renmei 1962:100.
87. Ōi 1972:7–8, first essay.
88. Shigen Enerugīchō Sekiyubu 1980:194.
89. Ōi 1972:11, first essay. See also p. 4 of second essay.
90. Ōi 1972:10.
91. Sekiyu Renmei 1962:77. Also see Brown 1983 for an account of government intervention to assist in the disposition of Arabian Oil. In the end foreign-affiliated refineries agreed to accept shipments if the *force majeure* clauses of their contracts could be invoked. Interview with a director of Japan National Oil Corporation, December 5, 1983.
92. Sekiyu Renmei 1962:76. A member of the Roundtable told me in an interview that "most of [the others in] that group knew nothing about petroleum. They had no knowledge of how the industry had developed. They knew about coal, but not much about oil" (interview, January 19, 1984).
93. Interviews with Roundtable members, February 9, 1984, and April 4, 1984.
94. Tsūshō . . . Sekiyuka 1962:198.
95. All four are described in Tsūsho . . . Sekiyuka 1962:199–201.
96. Tsūsho . . . Sekiyuka 1962:199. The Petroleum Association was incensed that PIL-II would be submitted to Diet without any prior consultation with industry. See its own account in Sekiyu Renmei 1962:101–3.
97. Interview, January 9, 1984.
98. Shūgiin Ōbei Enerugī Chōsadan 1961; Ōi 1972:4–5, third essay.
99. Sekiyu Kōgyō Renmei 1982:28.
100. This group was established in the midst of debate, in November 1961, by Arabian Oil, JAPEX, and the few other Japanese oil exploration and production firms. Some in MITI have claimed credit for guiding the creation of this group. The JPDA was said to be the brainchild of Petroleum Division chief Takase Mitsuya, who promoted it as a means to influence the Finance Ministry and politicians. Interview with MITI official, November 30, 1983; see also Samuels 1983 for an exploration of "cheerleading" groups in a different context.

101. Sekiyu Renmei 1962:102.
102. The account is from Sekiyu Renmei 1962:102. Ōi 1972, second essay, provides a fuller account of opposition to the legislation as initially drafted.
103. Ōi 1972:10, second essay.
104. See Tanaka 1983:35.
105. Japanese National . . . Congress 1982:16.
106. Ōi 1972:14, second essay. See also Caldwell 1981:117, who observes that PIL-II represented "an accommodation to existing market conditions" as well as "to the control of the majors."
107. Vernon 1983:94.
108. Interview with a former MITI Refining Section chief, December 6, 1983. President Idemitsu soon established himself and his firm, the leading independent refining and product sales firm in Japan, as a thorn in MITI's side. Idemitsu blames MITI and PIL-II for the problems that came to plague the industry: "The very reason why the oil industry is unprincipled, without policy, and otherwise is treading the wrong path is due to the PIL-II. Bureaucrats aren't suffering; they think that if you have power you can do anything. That is the way of the idiot son. If one doesn't suffer one cannot succeed in one's work. . . . How can you manage wisely if, like bureaucrats, you simply graduate from college, back into national power, wave it about, and hang on?" (Kondō and Osanai 1978:52).
109. Matsui 1969:8–9.
110. Caldwell 1981:119.
111. MITI's Petroleum Department historically has been more concerned with the downstream industry than with exploration and production, first through its control of currency allocations and later through the administration of PIL-II. Refining and marketing is the province of its Petroleum Distribution Division (Sekiyu Ryūtsūka). Upstream was often left to the technical staff (gikan) in the Petroleum Development Division (Sekiyu Kaihatsuka).
112. Sekiyu Kōgyō Renmei 1982:31–32.
113. Brown 1983; Kondō and Osanai 1978:84.
114. Sekiyu Kōgyō Renmei 1982:31.
115. Petroleum Council, internal memorandum, "Sekiyu Sangyō Taisei ni Kansuru kore made no Seisaku no Kangaekata no Keifu" (A record of the thinking about policy toward the structure of the oil industry until the present) (October 1983), p. 2.
116. Sekiyu Kōgyō Renmei 1982:36; interview with a director of Japan National Oil Corporation, December 5, 1983.
117. Sekiyu Seisaku, June 10, 1982, p. 40.
118. Petroleum Council, October 1983 memorandum.
119. Sekiyu Kōgyō Renmei 1982:38–39.
120. Sekiyu Kōgyō Renmei 1982:37.
121. Ōjimi Kōsō. Ōjimi later became MITI's administrative vice-minister, the top career post in the ministry. After retiring, he became chairman of Arabian Oil. See Kondō and Osanai 1978:84; Sekiyu Kōgyō Renmei 1982:54–55.
122. A large portion of this tariff had already been earmarked for the coal industry.
123. Sekiyu Kōgyō Renmei 1982:55.
124. Sekiyu Renmei 1962:104–7.
125. See Campbell 1977 for details on the Japanese budget process.
126. Interview with a former MITI Petroleum Division official, December 1, 1983.

127. See Brown 1983. Caldwell 1981:113 attributes the initiative to the Japan Development Bank.
128. Brown 1983:63.
129. *Sekiyu Seisaku,* June 10, 1982, p. 40.
130. Internal document of the Agency for Natural Resources and Energy dated April 25, 1974.
131. Sekiyu Kōgyō Renmei 1982:47.
132. Quoted in Kondō and Osanai 1978:25.
133. Sekiyu Kōgyō Renmei 1982:57–59, emphases added.
134. Fujioka was also president of Getty-affiliated Mitsubishi Oil. See the articles by JAPEX president Mimura Kiichi 1966a, 1966b.
135. Interview with a director of the Japan National Oil Corporation, December 5, 1983.
136. Relations between the two firms had never been smooth, even though Imperial Oil had a large holding of JAPEX stock. By the early 1960s JAPEX had discovered more gas than Imperial, even though the initial compromise was designed to deliver the most promising domestic gas fields to Imperial Oil. JAPEX denied the existence of any prior agreements. Imperial protested and threatened court action. MITI was inclined to support JAPEX, for if JAPEX surrendered its gas fields to Imperial, it would lose its raison d'être, and the state would be out of the business entirely. In 1962, therefore, MITI intervened and instructed JAPEX to reach a new accommodation with Imperial Oil. JAPEX would turn over Niigata sales to Imperial and agree not to encroach upon Imperial's customers. Interview with a director of Japan National Oil Corporation, December 5, 1983.
137. In fact, the separation was always clear between JAPEX and the rest of the *kōdan* after it was absorbed. It was designated the "operations headquarters" (*kōdan jigyō honbu*) and was divested and reestablished as JAPEX in April 1970. Once separated, it lost its status as special corporation (*tokushu kaisha*) and became a normal joint stock company. The shares held by the Finance Ministry were transferred to the *kōdan* (interview with former MITI section chief, November 30, 1983).
138. This committee began deliberations in August 1965 as successor to the Comprehensive Energy Division in the Industrial Structure Council. It soon became the most influential MITI organ in energy planning; its cast has changed little in thirty years. The chairman in 1984 was still Arisawa Hiromi.
139. For the full decision rules related to project participation by the new agency, see Sekiyu Kōgyō Renmei 1982:62–67.
140. Sekiyu Kōgyō Renmei 1982:421. By this time the JPDC had become the Japan National Oil Corporation (JNOC).
141. The first was the January 1973 formation of a thirty-six-firm consortium of major firms in the Fūyō Group, such as Nippon Kokan, the Fuji Bank, and Marubeni.
142. The term used to describe the desired consolidation, "*daidō danketsu,*" was first used by the army in 1938 in its own unsuccessful effort to consolidate the oil industry.
143. *Sekiyu Sekisaku,* June 10, 1982, pp. 40–41.
144. Petroleum Council, October 1983 memorandum.
145. Mochizuki 1975:109.
146. *Sekiyu Seisaku,* June 10, 1982.
147. Petroleum Council, October 1983 memorandum.
148. Interview with JNOC official, December 1, 1983.

149. Kunimasa 1974:57–70 has collected all the platforms vis-à-vis nationalization as the parties prepared for (unrealized) coalition government in the early 1970s. In addition see *Denki Shimbun*, February 18–19, 1976; *Sekiyu Seisaku*, March 5, 1974, pp. 24–25; Nihon Kyōsantō Chūō Iinkai 1973:38; Nihon Shakaitō Seisaku Shingikai 1973:7. By the 1980s only the Communist party still proposed nationalization; see *Enerugī Fuōramu*, July 1983.

150. Nihon Shakaitō 1965:25.

151. See Tanaka 1983 for additional details; also see Young 1984.

152. Quoted in Tanaka 1983:37.

153. *Sekiyu Seisaku*, June 10, 1982, pp. 41–42.

154. Mochizuki 1975:164–67 speaks of a summer 1975 proposal by the Advisory Committee for Energy for a new study of public control of oil, a proposal that met with general support by Keidanren leaders. He claims that it was never pursued because of mistrust between the oil industry and MITI, opposition from foreign firms, and the foot dragging of the major banks.

155. Quoted in *Shūkan Tōyō Keizai*, January 28, 1984.

156. Petroleum Council, October 1983 memorandum.

157. See *Energy in Japan* no. 34, September 1976; no. 39, December 1977.

158. Interview with MITI Petroleum Division official, December 5, 1983.

159. Interview, November 21, 1983.

160. Since 1975 JNOC has offered direct financial assistance to foreign governments seeking to expand exploration and development projects. To that end JNOC finances geological surveys, leases exploration equipment, and provides technical assistance in the acquisition of exploration rights for Japanese firms overseas.

161. Interview, December 5, 1983.

162. In principle JNOC loans (extended at less than market rates) may amount to 70 percent of an overseas project; if a Japanese firm is the principal operator, they can be even higher. For domestic projects the limit is 80 percent. In 1982 these loans totaled 140 billion yen. JNOC is also authorized to guarantee 60 percent of private bank loans secured by a Japanese firm for overseas exploration. See Sugihara 1983:27.

163. Complete shareholding data appears in Sekiyu Kōgyō Renmei 1983.

164. Interview with an Energy Roundtable member, January 19, 1984.

165. Sekiyu Kōgyō Renmei 1983:160–67.

166. See *Japan Petroleum and Energy Weekly*, December 23 and 30, 1985, p. 2. Some estimates are higher; see *Asahi Shimbun*, November 29, 1983.

167. Interview with oil exploration company finance officer, December 7, 1983.

168. Based upon interviews with JNOC, MITI, and Ministry of Finance officials and with oil company executives.

169. Interview, December 5, 1983.

170. Internal JNOC documents. In some cases, such as JAPEX and Nippon Peru Oil Development, no JNOC divestiture was ever intended.

171. At the same time, however, JNOC has found itself short of cash because of budget deficits and austerity. Cash shortages provide incentives to sell shares, but they advise maximization of cash flow through dividends from equity holdings. In several new ventures JNOC opted for cash dividends over stock dividends for precisely this reason. Interview with oil production company official, December 7, 1983.

172. Petroleum Council, October 1983 memorandum.

173. *Sekiyu Seisaku,* June 10, 1982, pp. 39–45.

174. Japanese National Committee 1982:2.

175. Tsurumi 1978:128; Porges 1979:19–20. Caldwell 1981 concurs but comes closer to placing these choices in their political context. She argues that Japanese policy makers, by accommodating foreign majors, opted for price over security, a perspective she and the Japanese call "energy economics." In this view MITI planners saw the oil industry "as second to but necessary for Japan's high growth industries." They therefore devised a policy that "worked to preclude the emergence of a strong and unified domestic oil industry" (p. 5).

176. OPEC 1982:86, 99.

177. Adelman 1972:242–43 has a different explanation for higher prices in Japan after 1962.

178. Caldwell 1981:110.

179. *Energy in Japan* no. 15 (December 1971), p. 4.

180. Particularly medium-sized refineries, producing feedstocks for the petrochemical industry and heavy fuel for the utilities. In most cases the thirteen major refining firms held equity in these so-called *kombinato* refineries, which were little more than "teapot" facilities, unburdened with expensive capacity to upgrade product. The larger portion of their output was "captive" production, supplied to parent heavy industries. Although the thirteen major firms have long held close to 100 percent of the merchant market, they have come to produce only slightly less than half of the nation's refined petroleum products (data are for 1982; see Sekiyu Kōgyō Renmei 1983). The *kombinato* refineries came on line in the late 1960s under the assumption that the high demand growth of that decade would continue. For a short time the nations' refineries operated profitably at nearly full capacity.

181. Interview, January 10, 1984. Mochizuki (1975:133) concurs: "fragmented, hence financially weak refining companies" were an *"unwelcome result* of MITI's policy to promote domestic capital" (emphases added).

182. In 1983 the capacity utilization rate, already low, plummeted to barely 50 percent (see Tanaka 1983:16).

183. In the decade after the first oil crisis, oil's share of Japan's primary energy supply was reduced by more than one-fifth, from 77.6 percent to 61.6 percent. The most optimistic 1985 projections for 1995 showed petroleum accounting for barely 50 percent of Japan's energy supply.

184. Tanaka 1983:1.

185. The average Japanese equity/capital ratio, 25 percent among manufacturers, is only 4.5 percent among refining firms. Moreover, this aggregate figure masks the precariously high debt being carried by particular companies. The combined debt of Maruzen and Daikyō Oil in 1984, for example, was nearly *nineteen* times the total of their shareholders' equity. After half a decade of steady decline in demand and an unprecedented decline of 5 dollars per barrel in the price of crude, the Japanese refining industry lost 100 billion yen in the first half of FY 1983 alone. See *Shūkan Tōyō Keizai,* January 28, 1984.

186. *Japan Petroleum Energy Weekly,* December 20, 1982.

187. *Asahi Shimbun,* January 8 and April 20, 1984.

188. *Asahi Shimbun,* October 26, 1983.

189. Quoted in *Asahi Shimbun,* October 27, 1983.

190. See *Japan Petroleum and Energy Weekly,* October 20, 1986. Kyōdō Oil is already (unhappily) related to Daikyō Oil in three ways. First, the refined products of Ajia Oil, which moved from Kyōdō to Daikyō in 1981, are still sold by

Kyōdō Oil. Second, as noted above, the IBJ is the lead bank of both. Third, Daikyō owns significant shares of Kyōdō's Fuji Oil and Kagoshima Oil. Relations deteriorated in 1981 when Ajia Oil defected. A Daikyō/Maruzen/Kyōdō merger, something that IBJ may promote, would make this group number one in the Japanese market. Moreover, MITI has never fully abandoned its designs for a Japanese major. This consolidation may fit nicely with its efforts to integrate JNOC downstrem. If such an unprecedented integration takes place, it would reflect IBJ strategy as much as MITI administrative power.

191. Complicating this arrangement was the acquisition of Getty Oil, Mitsubishi's partner since the prewar period, by Texaco, a partner in Caltex, the holder of 50 percent of Nippon Oil's equity. As noted above, several months after this acquisition, in the summer of 1984, Texaco sold its inherited equity in Mitsubishi Oil to the Mitsubishi Group. For the first time ever, Mitsubishi Oil became a fully Japanese-owned firm.

192. See *Shūkan Tōyō Keizai*, January 28, 1984; *Asahi Shimbun*, February 28, 1984.

193. This is best illustrated in the Maruzen-Daikyō case. In late 1983 Maruzen faced the prospect that the Tokyo Stock Exchange would suspend all trading of its shares. (Regulations stipulate such action if a firm shows three consecutive years of cumulative losses in shareholders' equity.) Had trading been suspended, Maruzen would have faced significant problems on other capital markets and hundreds of its smaller lenders, such as regional savings banks, might have panicked, increasing the likelihood of bankruptcy. In the past Maruzen had sold facilities to show paper profits. This time it joined with Daikyō to create a new refinery (Cosmo) to which they sold facilities, for which they received payment derived from IBJ loans, from which they would both show a profit, and with which (in a purely circular transaction) they would pay back the IBJ. In April 1986 the marketing business of Daikyō and Maruzen merged with Cosmo Oil. This "son of Cosmo Oil" suddenly became number three in the downstream sector of the Japanese oil industry (see *Japan Petroleum and Energy Weekly*, April 6, 1986). It has also expanded into entirely new businesses. In May 1986 a Cosmo subsidiary entered a joint venture with Alfa-Romeo to import cars to Japan (*Japan Economic Journal*, May 24, 1986).

194. Figure 5.2 is derived from the consolidated balance sheets and income statements for nine oil firms, all customers of the IBJ. It is built upon five separate elements: 1) the volume of crude petroleum purchased by refineries, 2) the f.o.b. price of these purchases, 3) interest rate margins, 4) exchange commissions, and 5) the shifting balance between dollar-funded and yen-funded import financing. The index was constructed using several key assumptions, all conservative. Short-term debt as reported in these documents has a heavy dollar component; the dollar portion of short-term debt was calculated at current exchange rates for each period. Using current exchange commission rates and current interest margin rates (which deviated variably from posted rates) against this total dollar borrowing, I have estimated IBJ profits. I believe that IBJ lending is representative and therefore that these results can be generalized to the industry as a whole. Data are not available before 1972.

195. Interview with a former member of the Advisory Committee on Energy, February 9, 1983.

196. Horiuchi 1984 details the most famous MITI failure, the banks' successful resistance to the 1963 Special Measures Law for the Promotion of Designated Industries, which died in Diet. Slack demand and declining profitability also

stimulated this consolidation. The liberalization of Japan's capital markets, begun under foreign pressure in the early 1980s, has transformed bank-firm and interbank relations. Previously the city banks managed what appeared to oil company managers in effect an import finance cartel (interview with oil company executive, October 3, 1984). This arrangement maintained usance fees and margin rates for banks, which under Japan's "main bank" financial system went unchallenged by firms that were growing dependent upon them. These relationships, protected from competition by foreign lending institutions, limited firms' borrowing options. Capital market protection was dismantled, however, precisely as oil firms' foreign exchange needs plummeted because of reduced import volumes. Competition led, predictably, to reduced margin rates and commissions. At first, these were extended to the more profitable oil firms. By 1982, however, the banks could no longer generate profits even from the weaker oil refiners to whom foreign banks would not extend loans. Their foreign exchange needs were simply too low. With healthy firms attracting foreign bank assistance and weaker firms propped up by creditors to avoid bankruptcy, restructuring and consolidation made eminent good sense.

197. *Shūkan Tōyō Keizai*, January 28, 1984.

198. For an analysis of this legislation from the perspective of the Japanese refining industry, see Takai 1986. For background on the Lion's Oil case see *Japan Petroleum Energy Weekly*, January 14, 1985. For Satō's own account, see Satō 1986.

199. See *Financial Times Energy Economist*, June 1986.

200. Inokuchi 1963:310, 311–12.

201. From 49.6 percent in 1975 to 47.9 percent in 1982. See Sekiyu Renmei 1983.

202. Porges 1979:19.

CHAPTER 6. *A Political History of Alternative Energy in Japan*

1. See Nippon Sekiyushi Henshūshitsu 1958:400.

2. Cohen 1949:137.

3. MITI had the prescience to establish ANRE in July, several months *before* the oil shock. Takano (1980:27) unfairly calls this a fluke.

4. See *Nihon Keizai Shimbun*, November 24, 1980.

5. Quoted in *Nihon Keizai Shimbun*, November 14, 1979.

6. Nearly 40 percent of the general account budget in FY 1979 was funded by national bonds. Debt financing had been introduced in FY 1966, marking Japan's transition from surplus to deficit budgeting. By 1979 "financial reconstruction" was a business and government priority. See Noguchi 1981:30 and Johnson 1987.

7. Quoted in *Nihon Keizai Shimbun*, November 28, 1979.

8. *Nihon Keizai Shimbun*, December 10, 1979.

9. This sort of hybrid is known as a *dai san sekutā* (third sector) company in Japan. It is a frequent resort of industry, when government seems to be resisting private-sector pressures to create a public corporation, and of government, when industry seems to be unwilling to cooperate with a government proposal for the creation of a public corporation. In this case it was clearly the latter. For a detailed case of the former, see Samuels 1983. The third sector company, de-

signed to maximize private-sector managerial and technological expertise in conjunction with joint public-private capital, was important to many government plans during the high-growth decade. For relations between third sector firms and other forms of more purely public or private enterprise, see Johnson 1978. The American counterpart of NEDO, the Synthetic Fuels Corporation, established at the same time for the same reasons, was dismantled in 1986.

10. Kamiō 1984:10.

11. Much of the following is drawn from Satō forthcoming.

12. This group of luminaries included former home minister Gotō Fumio, former justice minister Iwata Chūzō, former agriculture minister Ishiguro Tadaatsu, and the presidents of *Sankei Shimbun* and the Mitsubishi Bank, as well as Tokyo University professor Kaya Seiji and Inaba Hidezō who, next to Arisawa Hiromi, has probably been the most active and influential energy policy planner in postwar Japan. Kosaka claims his first inspiration to promote nuclear power came in December 1948, the night he was released from Sugamo Prison with Kishi Nobusuke and others (see Nihon Genshiryoku . . . Kaigi 1971, 1:7–9).

13. Kawai 1961 has the best early account.

14. *Asahi Nenkan*, 1955:35.

15. Shōriki had first come to public attention two generations earlier as the police commander injured dispersing the 1918 Hibiya riots. He was an accomplished publicist credited in Japan as father of both professional baseball and commercial television (see Seidensticker 1983:261). He was also known in some circles as the "devil of atomic power" for his efforts to reverse Japanese public opinion and cure Japan's "nuclear allergy" (see Yanaga 1968:chap. 7 and Kawai 1961:28).

16. Nakajima and Anzai 1979:41.

17. As a measure of the nuclear fever that gripped Japanese industry, the JAIF boasted seven hundred members within one year of its establishment in March 1956. Few firms even remotely related to this new industrial frontier wanted to get left behind. Even such commercial firms as Tokyo's largest kabuki theater, Kabukiza, and its leading hostelry, the Imperial Hotel, became JAIF members (see Kawai 1961:76 and Satō forthcoming).

18. Kawai 1961:77 says "to buy supporters for nuclear power."

19. See Nihon Genshiryoku . . . Kaigi 1971, 1:140–43. Shōriki himself suggested that the JAIF was established to confront academic opposition to nuclear power (see Kawai 1961:44).

20. *Asahi Shimbun*, October 27, 1955.

21. Kanazawa 1955. Other commissioners included Fujioka Yoshio, representing the Science Council, Arisawa Hiromi, the choice of the right-wing Socialist leader Asanuma Inejirō, and the Nobel laureate Yukawa Hideki, who only reluctantly agreed to participate. Apparently the public relations value of Yukawa was so great that Nakasone personally intervened to convince him to participate. Yukawa agreed to do so only on condition that Fujioka also be selected (see Nihon Genshiryoku . . . Kaigi 1971, 1:55–63 for private industry's account). The academic community had first proposed an independent JAEC in 1952. Politicians dissatisfied with their lack of control of similar "independent commissions," most notably Matsunaga's Public Utilities Commission, vetoed the idea. As finally accepted, the JAEC was an authoritative advisory body attached to the Prime Minister's Office, whose chair would be filled ex officio by the cabinet-level minister of the new Science and Technology Agency. This too was Nakasone's doing. See Ishikawa 1983:32 and Satō forthcoming.

22. Quoted in Nihon Genshiryoku . . . Kaigi 1971, 1:58–63; Kawai 1961:39–42; Nakajima and Anzai 1979:25.

23. See Yanaga 1968:chap. 7; Kawai 1961:68.

24. Nakajima and Anzai 1979:41–42. The weakest point in this "special entity" formulation from the perspective of private industry was the exemption of JAERI employees from the Public Employees Law, which banned strikes by public employees. Labor unrest plagued JAERI early on; industry lost confidence in it and turned elsewhere. Nihon Genshiryoku . . . Kaigi 1971, 1:76.

25. Nihon Genshiryoku . . . Kaigi 1971, 1:81; interview with a Power Reactor and Nuclear Fuel Corporation official, March 26, 1984.

26. During the war Mitsubishi had carefully reserved royalities owed to Westinghouse (interview with a member of the Nuclear Advisory Commission, April 17, 1984).

27. Kawai 1961:35. See Nihon Genshirysku . . . Kaigi 1971, 1:108, for the range of politically inspired claims about generation costs.

28. Some suspect that Kōno was influenced by funds from the utilities as well as by British promises to buy more salmon and sea trout from Japan. Kōno was a leading spokesman for the Japanese fishing industry and had gone to Britain to negotiate a trade package. See Genshiryoku . . . no Kai 1981 and Satō forthcoming.

29. At Kōno's insistence the agreement also gave the state the right to nationalize the firms in the future and reserved the right to approve appointments to JAPCO's board of directors. Neither stipulation has ever amounted to anything. Three-quarters of the initial senior management were on loan from the private utilities. Of thirty directors, only six came from EPDC; the rest came from the utilities and the large vendors (Kawai 1961).

30. Nihon Genshiryoku . . . Kaigi 1971, 1:121–28. Similar legislation to limit the liability of utilities in the event of a nuclear accident, the Price-Anderson Act, was passed in the United States in 1957.

31. Many suggest that it was no accident that General Electric was awarded this contract, for JAPCO's leading shareholder, TEPCO, long had technical ties to General Electric (see Satō forthcoming).

32. Nihon Genshiryoku . . . Kaigi 1971, 1:300–301.

33. Nihon Genshiryoku . . . Kaigi 1971, 2:27.

34. Nakajima and Anzai 1979:45–46.

35. Nihon Genshiryoku . . . Kaigi 1971, 2:35.

36. Satō forthcoming.

37. Interview with a member of the Advisory Committee for Energy, April 17, 1984.

38. Nihon Genshiryoku . . . Kaigi 1971, 2:46–48.

39. Even today much of the budget for PNC's *monju*, the fast breeder prototype, is "buried" in indirect accounts (interview with STA official, May 3, 1984).

40. Nihon Genshiryoku . . . Kaigi 1971, 2:46–47.

41. Suttmeier 1981:112. The parallels with the German breeder reactor program are compelling. Keck 1981 and Nelson 1984 both describe similar state subsidies for nuclear power research in which utilities have limited interest but for which vendors are happy to accept contracts.

42. Suttmeier 1981:53–55.

43. Interview with a JAERI director, May 3, 1984. This official claimed that the PNC was created "to punish" JAERI. He noted that the utilities were dissatisfied with JAERI's personnel practices and cautiousness, but only because they had "no

experience with nuclear power" and had "a lot to learn." Today, half of JAERI's budget is devoted to the 300 mv JT-60 *tokamak* fusion reactor built by private industry.

44. Nihon Genshiryoku . . . Kaigi 1971, 2:67.

45. See Ishikawa 1983:180–234 for a thorough treatment of Carter's policies and their impact on Japan. See also Ebinger 1984 for a general discussion of these policies and the International Nuclear Fuel Cycle Evaluation.

46. The advanced thermal reactor is a variety of the steam-generating heavy water reactor described in Keeny et al. 1977:392–93. It is based upon a British design.

47. Tsūshō Sangyōshō . . . Sangyōka 1981:33.

48. Quoted in *Energy in Japan* no. 5, August 1968.

49. Interview with a member of the Nuclear Power Advisory Committee, April 17, 1984.

50. Dengen Kaihatsu Kabushiki Kaisha 1984:249–50. An EPDC researcher was resident at Canadian General Electric every year until 1978, when the JAEC finally rejected the CANDU.

51. Nihon Genshiryoku . . . Kaigi 1971, 2:19–20.

52. The boiling water is a type of light water reactor that employs a direct cycle in which the water coolant that passes directly through the reactor is converted to steam to power the turbine. See Keeny et al. 1977:392–95.

53. Interview with a former JAPCO president, April 18, 1984.

54. Suttmeier 1981 lists these and other advantages; he also explores the social costs of nuclear power in Japan.

55. Lesbriel 1985 reviews the issues and procedures associated with power plant siting in Japan.

56. Genshiryoku Iinkai annual.

57. Ishikawa 1983:95–101.

58. Suttmeier 1981:123; Ishikawa 1983:119–25.

59. Unanticipated rises in construction costs led the vendors to demand an extra 20 billion yen for materials in 1974. The utilities refused to pay their full share (Satō forthcoming).

60. EPDC and MITI officials were growing so enthusiastic about the prospects for the CANDU that they were led to extraordinarily un-MITI-like pronouncements, such as the claim that "the more different types of reactors we have, the better it will be for our atomic energy development" (quoted in Satō forthcoming). MITI, of course, is associated with crusades to standardize and to eliminate "excessive competition," and it had never been known for promoting diversity. See Nihon Genshiryoku . . . Kaigi 1971, 1:143–49 for a discussion of MITI's efforts to rationalize nuclear development.

61. Ishikawa, 1983:152.

62. Ishikawa 1983:161–62. *Asahi Shimbun,* December 19, 1978, reported that many were concerned that the importation of CANDU, seen as a "Third World reactor," would be a blow to Japan's prestige.

63. Ishikawa 1983:145.

64. *Asahi Shimbun,* December 19, 1978. Some suspect that Morozumi had already secretly initialed a licensing agreement with the Canadians (interview with a member of the Nuclear Power Advisory Committee, April 17, 1984).

65. Ishikawa 1983:137.

66. *Nihon Keizai Shimbun,* November 25, 1978. Their group was called the Asenkai, literally Frog and Locust Club.

67. They were already moving personnel from their depressed shipbuilding operations to power reactor projects. Ishikawa 1983:146 claims that these personnel were moved under the "administrative guidance" of MITI, but others argue they needed little incentive beyond the market to relocate permanent employees where future growth was indicated (interview with Nuclear Committee member, April 16, 1984).

68. See *Asahi Shimbun*, December 19, 1978.

69. Ishikawa 1983:164–65.

70. Jishu Gijutsu Kenkyūkai 1981:51–52; Ishikawa 1983:168–69.

71. Tsūshō Sangyōshō . . . Sangyōka 1981:35.

72. *Energy in Japan* no. 59 (September 1982); Ishikawa 1983:290.

73. Kamiō 1984:11.

74. *Energy in Japan* no. 39 (December 1977).

75. This is why the PNC budget appears to have declined in relative terms in recent years: much of the fast breeder funding is buried in a separate account (interview with an STA official, May 3, 1984).

76. Kamiō 1984:1.

77. Kamiō 1984:2; Tsūshō Sangyōshō . . . Sangyōka 1981:30–31.

78. Gale 1981:90.

79. The unit capacity factor of Japanese nuclear reactors, 76 percent in 1985, was behind only those of West Germany and Sweden (*Japan Petroleum and Energy Weekly*, April 7, 1986).

CHAPTER 7. *The Business of the Japanese State*

1. Johnson 1982:318. See Johnson 1978 for a short review of the varieties of public companies. I have not differentiated among the Japanese euphemisms for "nationalization," "state-owned corporation," or "public policy company." (Consider the following list: *kokuyūka, kōyūka, shakaika, minshuka, kokkakanri, tokushu hōjin, kokusaku gaisha, kōsha, eidan,* and *kōdan.*) Lockwood (1965:493) labels the Japanese proclivity to finance but not to own commercial enterprise "sponsored capitalism."

2. The most exhaustively researched and best-argued representation of this view is Johnson 1982. See also Johnson 1978:11. Additional evidence to support this "bureaucratic dominance" thesis is in Pempel 1982.

3. Silberman 1982:230–31.

4. Okimoto forthcoming is a comprehensive and sophisticated political economy of Japan, focusing most closely upon telecommunications and electronics. Okimoto is less willing than others to look exclusively at the economic bureaucracy. His analysis incorporates private interests and explores their formal links to one another and the state. See also Okimoto 1984:78–133 and Inoguchi 1983. Most "pluralist" accounts of Japanese politics, however, are not comparative, nor do they examine economic policy making. See, for example, the essays in Krauss 1985 and Krauss and Muramatsu forthcoming.

5. See Katzenstein 1980.

6. Vernon 1983:88.

7. Johnson 1984:64.

8. Okimoto forthcoming:chap. 3.

9. "State-led capitalism" was coined by Pempel 1982; "guided free enter-

prise" is from Ezra Vogel 1978; "developmental state" is from Johnson 1982; "administrative guidance" is widely used in Japan and discussed below.

10. The most prominent among these are Krasner 1977, Zysman 1983, and Katzenstein 1985b.

11. See Cohen 1977:chaps. 1–5.

12. Zysman 1983:91.

13. Katzenstein 1985b:21–23. Elsewhere (1980:37) he distinguishes between "Hegelian" French statism, which emphasizes political leadership and bureaucratic initiative, and "Weberian" Japanese statism, which is derived from closer business-government ties and mitigates the need for forceful political leadership.

14. Johnson 1982 speaks of this developmental role for state bureaucrats who, through their market jurisdiction, contribute to economic growth and to the competitiveness of particular sectors of the economy. Some challenge this view on the grounds that the developmental state has been anything but effective. See Patrick 1986, Pepper et al. 1985, Saxonhouse 1986, Trezise 1982, and Friedman 1986.

15. On private ordering see Young 1984.

16. Okimoto forthcoming:chap. 1. Note that the 1884 *Kōgyō Iken* has a nearly identical statement.

17. Fujita 1935:72.

18. Lowi 1979:280.

19. See Ikenberry 1983.

20. Suggested by Cohen 1949 and Gillingham 1985.

21. A former MITI Electric Power Section chief insisted that "a national electric utility would have been a 70–80 percent certainty if we had had our way and if Matsunaga had not won the confidence of SCAP" (interview, February 10, 1984).

22. Kirby 1977:1.

23. See Krieger 1983.

24. Yada 1977:22–34, speaking of prewar coal, is representative.

25. Steiner et al. 1980.

26. See Wildavsky 1964.

27. See Craig 1975 for more on *tatewari gyōsei*. On this point, and for a theoretical treatment of these linkages within the Japanese administrative system, see Samuels 1983:chaps. 1 and 3. Reed 1986 calls it functional fragmentation.

28. Gerschenkron 1962:15.

29. Cf. Hilferding 1981:223.

30. The extent to which this can be generalized is a matter of dispute. For support of this view, see Patrick 1986, Saxonhouse 1986, Horiuchi 1984, and Friedman 1986. For the contrary view, see Zysman 1983.

31. Vittas 1978:275, emphases mine.

32. See Horiuchi 1984.

33. Johnson 1982 has more on this and on Sahashi in particular.

34. Spindler 1984:175.

35. Zysman 1983:248, emphases in original.

36. See Ikenberry 1986 for an interesting essay on these strategies.

37. See Boltho 1983 for a splendid comparison of openness in Japanese and Italian postwar development strategies.

38. Pasquale Saraceno, quoted in Fedi 1981:110.

39. The standard reference for this argument is Pempel and Tsunekawa 1979. I have also found useful the insights of Okimoto forthcoming:chap. 4.

40. Krauss and Muramatsu forthcoming.

41. Virtually every monograph on Japanese politics and society since the early 1970s (including my own) has paid lip service to the deficiencies of this metaphor. See for example Vogel 1975 and Krauss et al. 1984.

42. Vernon 1983:86. On p. 85 Vernon compares Japanese and American bureaucratic politics with apt reference to different structural constraints imposed by the federal bureaucracy and the U.S. Senate: "The rivalries, animosities, and alliances that are the bread and butter of Washington bureaucratic politics have fairly close counterparts in Tokyo, but with one profound difference: whereas the common strategy of the strangers who make up the U.S. government is to try to avoid and circumvent the opposition, the Japanese approach is to find a process of decision making in which all the affected parties have participated. . . . In this sense, one might say that the Japanese government behaves rather like the highly socialized U.S. Senate, whose members are aware that they must live with one another over the long pull."

43. Skocpol 1985:28 calls this her "programmatic conclusion."

44. Regini 1984:127, emphases in original.

45. I am grateful to William Rapp, formerly of the U.S. Department of Commerce, for suggesting this term.

46. This builds upon the critique of Allison 1970 that helped redirect policy studies toward policy networks and subgovernments. It is best developed and applied to Japan by Campbell 1977, 1984, and Okimoto forthcoming.

47. Nordlinger 1981:159.

48. Young 1984:983, 940.

49. In Okimoto forthcoming.

50. See Inoguchi 1983. This is, of course, quite close to the separation of control and jurisdiction in this study.

51. In Krauss and Muramatsu 1983.

52. See Friedman 1986.

53. Lockwood 1965:503.

54. This is consistent with the conclusions to Evans et al. 1985. See chap. 11.

55. Okimoto forthcoming:chap. 4.

56. This argument is best articulated by Satō and Matsuzaki 1986. See also Muramatsu 1981; Krauss and Muramatsu forthcoming.

57. Nakamura 1981:20. The only major study of modern Japan by a political scientist that adopts this perspective is Johnson 1982. For studies by economists or economic historians (in addition to Nakamura), see Lockwood 1955, Noguchi and Sakakibara 1977, Tiedemann 1971, and Duus 1984.

58. Gould 1980:34.

References

Abegglen, James C., and Thomas M. Hout. 1978. "Facing Up to the Trade Gap with Japan." *Foreign Affairs* 57, 1: 146–68.

Ackerman, Edward A. 1953. *Japan's Natural Resources and Their Relation to Japan's Economic Future.* Chicago: University of Chicago Press.

Addison, Paul. 1975. *The Road to 1945.* London: Cape.

Adelman, M. A. 1972. *The World Petroleum Market.* Baltimore: Johns Hopkins University Press.

Administrative Management Agency. 1982. "Administrative Reform in Japan." Tokyo.

Alimenti, Cesare. 1937. *La questione petrolifera italiana* (The question of Italian petroleum). Turin: Einaudi.

Allen, G. C. 1946. *A Short Economic History of Modern Japan, 1867–1937.* London: Allen & Unwin.

Allison, Graham. 1970. "Conceptual Models and the Cuban Missile Crisis." *American Political Science Review* 63, 3: 689–718.

Almond, Gabriel. 1983. "Corporatism, Pluralism and Professional Memory." *World Politics* 25, 2: 245–60.

———. 1986. "The Development of Political Development." In S. P. Huntington and M. Weiner, eds., *Understanding Political Development.* Boston: Little, Brown.

Anderson, Irvine H., Jr. 1975. *The Standard-Vacuum Oil Company and United States East Asian Policy, 1933–1941.* Princeton: Princeton University Press.

———. 1981. *Aramco, the United States and Saudi Arabia: A Study of the Dynamics of Foreign Oil Policy, 1933–1950.* Princeton: Princeton University Press.

Andō, Yoshio, ed. 1973. *Shōwa Seiji Keizaishi E No Shōgen* (Testimony related to the political and economic history of the Shōwa era). Tokyo: Mainichi Shimbunsha.

Arisawa, Hiromi, ed. 1961. *Gendai Nihon Sangyō Kōza* (Lectures on modern Japanese industry), III. Tokyo: Iwanami Shoten.

———. 1966. *Enerugī Seisaku no Shinchitsujo* (The new order for energy policy). Tokyo: Daiyamondo.

Asahi Shimbun Seibu Honsha, ed. 1970. *Sekitan Shiwa* (Historical stories of coal). Tokyo: Kenkōsha.

REFERENCES

Asahi Shimbunsha, ed. 1977. *Gendai Jinbutsu Jiten* (Modern biographical dictionary). Tokyo: Asahi Shimbun.

ASIA (Associazione fra le Società Italiane per Azioni), ed. 1927. *Annvarion delle società associate* (The annual report of associated companies). Roma: Castaldi.

Athos, Antony G., and Richard T. Pascale. 1981. *The Art of Japanese Management.* New York: Simon & Schuster.

Becker, David G. 1983. *The New Bourgeoisie and the Limits of Dependency: Mining, Class, and Power in "Revolutionary" Peru.* Princeton: Princeton University Press.

Bell, Joel. 1982. "Government Oil Companies: Quo Vadis?" *Journal of Business Administration* 13, 1–2: 99–126.

Berger, Gordon Mark. 1977. *Parties out of Power in Japan, 1931–1941.* Princeton: Princeton University Press.

Berger, Suzanne. 1972. *Peasants against Politics.* Cambridge: Harvard University Press.

Berger, Suzanne, and Michael J. Piore. 1980. *Dualism and Discontinuity in Industrial Societies.* Cambridge: Cambridge University Press.

Berger, Suzanne, ed. 1981. *Organizing Interests in Western Europe.* Cambridge: Cambridge University Press.

Bisson, T. A. 1945. *America's Far Eastern Policy.* New York: Macmillan.

——. 1949. *Prospects for Democracy in Japan.* New York: Macmillan.

Block, Fred. 1977. "The Ruling Class Does Not Rule: Notes on the Marxist Theory of the State." *Social Revolution* 33 (May–June): 6–28.

Boltho, Andrea. 1983. "Italian and Japanese Postwar Growth: Some Similarities and Differences." In Gianni Fodella, ed., *Japan's Economy in a Comparative Perspective.* Tenterden, U.K.: Norbury.

Brown, Mark S. 1983. "The Emergence of Japanese Interests in the World Oil Market." Harvard Center for International Affairs, Program on U.S.-Japan Relations, Occasional Paper 83–1. Cambridge.

Brown, Sidney Devere. 1966. "Ōkubo Toshimichi and the First Home Ministry Bureaucracy." In H. D. Harootunian and B. S. Silberman, eds., *Modern Japanese Leadership.* Tucson: University of Arizona Press.

Bruce, Harry J., Mel Horwitch, and Pedro Nueno. 1981. "The Evolution of the International Coal Trade: A Strategic and Decision-Making Perspective." Paper for the Academy of International Business/European International Business Association Joint International Conference, Barcelona, December 17–19.

Bye, Maurice. 1955. "Nationalization in France." In Mario Einaudi et al., eds., *Nationalization in France and Italy.* Ithaca: Cornell University Press.

Caldwell, Martha. 1981. "Petroleum Politics in Japan: State and Industry in a Changing Policy Context." Diss., University of Wisconsin.

Cameron, David R. 1978. "The Expansion of the Public Economy." *American Political Science Review* 72: 1243–61.

Campell, John C. 1977. *Contemporary Japanese Budget Politics.* New York: Columbia University Press.

——. 1984. "Policy Conflict and Its Resolution within the Governmental System." In E. Krauss et al., eds., *Conflict in Japan.* Honolulu: University of Hawaii Press.

Carnoy, Martin. 1984. *The State and Political Theory.* Princeton: Princeton University Press.

Chandler, Alfred D., Jr. 1978. *The Visible Hand: The Managerial Revolution in American Business.* Cambridge: Harvard University Press.

Chen, Ching Chih. 1965. "Crude Oil Prices and the Postwar Japanese Oil Industry." Diss., MIT.

Cianci, Ernesto. 1977. *Nascita dello stato imprenditore in Italia* (The birth of the entrepreneurial state in Italy). Milan: Mursia.

Cohen, Jerome B. 1949. *Japan's Economy in War and Reconstruction*. Minneapolis: University of Minnesota Press.

———. 1952. *Economic Problems of Free Japan*. Princeton: Princeton University Center of International Studies.

———. 1958. *Japan's Postwar Economy*. Bloomington: Indiana University Press.

Cohen, Stephen. 1977. *Modern Capitalist Planning: The French Model*. Updated ed. Berkeley: University of California Press.

Colitti, Marcello. 1979. *Energie e sviluppo in Italia* (Energy and development in Italy). Bari: De Donato.

Cottino, Gastone. 1978. *Ricerca sulle participazioni statale* (Research on the state holdings). Milan: Einaudi.

Coumbe, Albert T., Jr. 1924. "Petroleum in Japan." *Oil Engineering and Finance*, August.

Craig, Albert M. 1975. "Functional and Dysfunctional Aspects of Government Bureaucracy." In Ezra Vogel, ed., *Modern Japanese Organization and Decision-making*. Berkeley: University of California Press.

Curtis, Gerald L. 1975. "Big Business and Political Influence." In Ezra Vogel, ed., *Modern Japanese Organization and Decision Making*. Berkeley: University of California Press.

———. 1977. "Japan's Opposition Parties: How Close to Power?" *Japan Foundation News*, December: 6–10.

Daikyō Sekiyu Kabushiki Kaisha, ed. 1976. *Daikyō Sekiyu Kabushiki Kaisha 30 Nenshi* (The thirty-year history of the Daikyō Oil Corporation). Tokyo.

Daikyō Sekiyu Kabushiki Kaisha Shashi Henshūsan Iinkai, ed. 1980. *Daikyō Sekiyu 40 Nenshi* (The forty-year history of Daikyō Oil). Tokyo.

Dengen Kaihatsu Kabushiki Kaisha, ed. 1984. *Denpatsu 30 Nen Shi* (The thirty-year history of the Electric Power Development Corporation). Tokyo.

Denki Jigyō Kōza Henshū Iinkai, ed. 1969. *Denki Jigyō No Nenryō Mondai* (Fuel problems of the electric power industry). Tokyo: Denryoku Shimpōsha.

Denki Jigyō Rengōkai, ed. 1971. "Sekitan Mondai ni Taisuru Yōbō" (Demands concerning the coal problem). October.

Denki Jigyō Rengōkai Tōkei Iinkai, ed. Annual. *Denki Jigyō Binran* (Electric industries Handbook). Tokyo: Nihon Denki Kyōkai.

Destler, I. M., et al. 1976. *Managing an Alliance: The Politics of U.S.-Japanese Relations*. Washington, D.C.: Brookings.

Destler, I. M., Haruhiro Fukui, and Hideo Sato. 1979. *The Textile Wrangle: Conflict in Japanese-American Relations, 1969–1971*. Ithaca: Cornell University Press.

Deutsch, Karl. 1961. "Social Mobilization and Political Development." *American Political Science Review* 55, 3: 493–514.

Di Palma, Giuseppe. 1977. *Surviving without Governing: The Italian Parties in Parliament*. Berkeley: University of California Press.

Di Pasquantonio, Filippo. 1962. *La nazionalizzazione dell'industria elettrica*. Milan: Riuniti.

Dore, Ronald. 1973. *British Factory, Japanese Factory: The Origins of National Diversity in Industrial Relations*. Berkeley: University of California Press.

———. 1974. "Late Development—or Something Else? Industrial Relations in

333

Britain, Japan, Mexico, Sri Lanka, Senegal." Unpublished paper no. 61, August.

Drucker, Peter. 1971. "What We Can Learn from Japanese Management." *Harvard Business Review*, March–April: 110–22.

——. 1980. "Japan Gets Ready for Tougher Times." *Fortune*, November 3.

Dupuy, A., and B. Truchil. 1979. "Problems in the Theory of State Capitalism." *Theory and Society* 8.

Duus, Peter. 1984. "The Reaction of Japanese Big Business to a State-Controlled Economy in the 1930s." *International Review of Economics and Business* 31, 9: 819–32.

Duus, Peter, and Daniel Okimoto. 1979. "Fascism and the History of Prewar Japan: The Failure of a Concept." *Journal of Asian Studies* 39, 1: 65–76.

Duvall, Raymond D., and John R. Freeman. 1981. "The State and Dependent Capitalism." *International Studies Quarterly* 25, 1: 99–118.

Ebinger, Charles K. 1984. "U.S.-Japanese Nuclear Energy Relations: Prospects for Cooperation/Conflict." In Ebinger and R. A. Morse, eds., *U.S.-Japanese Energy Relations: Cooperation and Competition*. Boulder: Westview.

Eckstein, Harry. 1975. "Case Study and Theory in Macropolitics." In Fred Greenstein and Nelson Polsby, eds., *Handbook of Political Science*. Menlo Park: Addison-Wesley.

Economist. 1978. "Special Report on 'The State in the Market.'" December 30.

Einaudi, Mario, Maurice Bye, and Ernesto Rossi. 1955. *Nationalization in France and Italy*. Ithaca: Cornell University Press.

Ekonomisuto. 1982. "Sengo Sangyō Seisaku no Naka no Keizaigakusha." August 8.

ENI, ed. 1981. "Rapporto sull' energia." Report presented to the assembley of CNEN. December 16.

——. 1982. "The System of State Holdings in Italy: Problems and Strategies." Mimeo.

Evans, Peter B., Dietrich Rueschemeyer, and Theda Skocpol, eds. 1985. *Bringing the State Back In*. New York: Cambridge University Press.

Fagan, H. 1960. *Nationalization*. London: Lawrence & Wishart.

Faure, Edgar. 1939. *Le pétrole dans la paix et dans la guerre*. Paris: Nouvelle Revue Critique.

Fedi, Publio. 1981. *Bilancio in rosso: MITI e realta nell'esperienza della nazionalizzazione elettrica, 1962–1977* (Budget in red: Myths and reality of the experience with the nationalization of electricity, 1962–1977). Florence: Le Monnier.

Feigenbaum, Harvey B. 1982. "Public Enterprise in Comparative Perspective." *Comparative Politics* 15, 1: 101–22.

——. 1985. *Politics of Public Enterprise: Oil and the French State*. Princeton: Princeton University Press.

Ferrier, R. W. 1982. *History of the British Petroleum Company: The Developing Years, 1901–1932*. Cambridge: Cambridge University Press.

Fontaine, Pierre. 1967. *L'aventure du pétrole français*. Paris: Sept Couleurs.

France, C. W. 1978. "Public Enterprises in the United Kingdom." In A. Gelinas, ed., *Public Enterprise and the Public Interest*. Toronto: Institute of Public Administration of Canada.

Freeman, J. Leiper. 1965. *The Policy Process: Executive Bureau–Legislative Committee Relations*. Rev. ed. New York: Random House.

Freeman, John. 1982. "International Economic Relations and the Politics of

Mixed Economies." Paper presented at the Annual Meeting of the International Political Science Association, Rio de Janeiro.

Freeman, John R. Forthcoming. *The Politics of Mixed Economies.* Ithaca: Cornell University Press.

Friedman, David. 1985. "The Misunderstood Miracle: Politics and Economic Decentralization in Japan." Diss., MIT.

Frost, Robert L. 1983. "Alternating Currents: Technocratic Power and Workers' Resistance at Electricité de France, 1946–1970." Diss., University of Wisconsin.

—. 1984. "France's False Start in Nuclear Power, 1954–1969." Paper presented to the Annual Meeting of the Society for the History of Technology, Cambridge, Mass.

Fujita, Keizō. 1935. "Cartels and Their Conflicts in Japan." *Journal of the Osaka University of Commerce* 3.

Fukui, Haruhiro. 1970. *Party in Power: The Japanese Liberal Democrats and Policy Making.* Berkeley: University of California Press.

Furuta, Keizō. 1940. "Nihon Sekitan Kaisha no Sōritsu to Sekitan Tōsei Kikō no Kakumeiteki Hatten" (The revolutionary development of the coal control organization and the establishment of the Japan Coal Company). *Nichimanshi Sekitan Jihō* no. 2 (June): 431–37.

Gale, Roger W. 1981. "Tokyo Electric Power Company: Its Role in Shaping Japan's Coal and LNG Policy." In R. Morse, ed., *The Politics of Japan's Energy Strategy.* Berkeley: University of California Institute of East Asian Studies.

Gelinas, André, ed. 1978. *Public Enterprise and the Public Interest.* Toronto: Institute of Public Administration of Canada.

Gendai Nihon Sangyō Hattatsushi Kenkyūkai, ed. 1963. *Gendai Nihon Sangyō Hattatsushi, II: Sekiyu* (History of the industrial development of modern Japan, vol. 2: Petroleum). Tokyo.

GHQ-SCAP (General Headquarters, Supreme Commander for the Allied Powers). 1949. "A Brief Progress Report on Political Reorientation of Japan." December 31.

—. 1951a. "Coal." *Historical Monograph* no. 45.

—. 1951b. "Price and Distribution Stabilization: Non Food Program." *Historical Monograph* no. 34.

—. 1951c. "Rehabilitation of the Nonfuel Mining Industries." *Historical Monograph* no. 44.

—. 1952a. "Expansion and Reorganization of the Electric Power and Gas Industries." History of the Nonmilitary Activities of the Occupation of Japan, *Monograph* no. 46. Washington D.C.: National Archives.

—. 1952b. "The Petroleum Industry." History of the Nonmilitary Activities of the Occupation of Japan, *Monograph* no. 41. Washington, D.C.: National Archives.

GHQ-SCAP (General Headquarters, Supreme Commander for the Allied Powers), Natural Resources Section. 1951a. "Petroleum and Natural Gas Production, 1950." Weekly Summary no. 284 (March 18–24). Tokyo.

—. 1951b. "Petroleum Producing Industry Monthly Review." Weekly Summary no. 285 (March 25–31). Tokyo.

Genshiryoku Iinkai, ed. Annual. *Genshiryoku Hakusho* (Nuclear power white paper). Tokyo: Ōkurashō Insatsu Kyoku.

Genshiryoku Jiyanarisuto no Kai. 1981. *Jiyanarisuto no Shōgen* (Journalists' testimony). Tokyo: Denryoku Shinpōsha.

REFERENCES

Gerschenkron, Alexander. 1962. *Economic Backwardness in Historical Perspective.* Cambridge: Harvard University Press.
Gillingham, John R. 1985. *Industry and Politics in the Third Reich.* New York: Columbia University Press.
Gilpin, Robert. 1975. *U.S. Power and the Multinational Corporation: The Political Economy of Foreign Direct Investment.* New York: Basic.
Goldthorpe, John H., ed. 1984. *Order and Conflict in Contemporary Capitalism.* London: Oxford University Press.
Goodermote, Dean, and Richard B. Mancke. 1983. "Nationalizing Oil in the 1970s." *Energy Journal* 4, 4: 67–80.
Gould, Stephen Jay. 1980. *The Panda's Thumb.* New York: Norton.
Gourevitch, Peter. 1978. "The Second Image Reversed: The International Sources of Domestic Politics." *International Organization* 32, 4: 881–912.
———. 1984. "Breaking with Orthodoxy: The Politics of Economic Policy Responses to the Depression of the 1930s." *International Organization* 38, 1: 95–129.
Gramsci, Antonio. 1973. *Letters from Prison.* New York: Harper & Row.
Grassini, Franco A. 1981. "The Italian Enterprises: The Political Constraints." In R. Vernon and Y. Aharoni, eds., *State-Owned Enterprise in the Western Economies.* New York: St. Martin's.
Grayson, Leslie E. 1981. *National Oil Companies.* New York: Wiley.
Gusfield, Joseph R. 1967. "Tradition and Modernity: Misplaced Polarities in the Study of Social Change." *American Journal of Sociology* 72 (January): 351–62.
Gyōsei Kanri Kenkyū Sentā. 1979. *Kōsha, Kōdan nado ni Kansuru Chōsa Kenkyū Hōkokusho* (A research report concerning public corporations). March.
Gyōsei Kanrichō. 1981. *Tokushu Hōjin Sōran* (Directory of Public Corporations). Tokyo.
Hadley, Eleanor M. 1970. *Antitrust in Japan.* Princeton: Princeton University Press.
Hagiwara Kichitarō. 1968. "Sekitan Sangyō no Shintaisei Ron" (Arguing for a new structure for the coal industry). Plan presented to LDP Policy Affairs Research Council, Special Coal Policy Committee, March 2.
Haliday, Jon, and Gavan McCormack. 1973. *Japanese Imperialism Today.* New York: Monthly Review Press.
Harada, Taneo. 1981. *Takeuchi Reizō Denki* (The biography of Takeuchi Reizō). Tokyo: Azusa Shoin.
Haraki, Ehud. 1973. *The Politics of Labor Legislation in Japan: National-International Interaction.* Berkeley: University of California Press.
Hasegawa, Shōishi. 1936. *Sekiyu Kokusaku Ronshū* (Collected essays on a national oil policy). Tokyo: Hasegawa Jinushō.
Hashimoto, Keizaburō. 1958. *Waga Kaikoroku* (My memoirs). Tokyo: Sekiyu Bunkasha.
Heclo, Hugh. 1978. "Issue Networks and the Executive Establishment." In Anthony King, ed., *The New American Political System.* Washington, D.C.: American Enterprise Institute.
Hein, Laura Elizabeth. 1982. "Reconstruction and the Development of Energy Policy in Japan, 1945–1955." Thesis, University of Wisconsin.
———. 1986. "Energy and Economic Policymaking in Postwar Japan, 1945–1960." Diss., University of Wisconsin.
Heller, C. A. 1980. "The Birth and Growth of the Public Sector and State Enterprises in the Petroleum Industry." In United Nations Centre for Natural

Resources, Energy, and Transport, ed., *State Petroleum Enterprises in Developing Countries.* New York: Pergamon.

Hilferding, Rudolf. 1981. *Finance Capital: A Study of the Latest Phase of Capitalist Development.* Trans. M. Watnick and S. Gordon. Ed. Tom Bottomore. London: Routledge & Kegan Paul.

Hiroshima Tsūshō Sangyō Kyoku Ube Sekitan Shikyoku, ed. 1969. *Yamaguchi Tanden Sanbyaku Nenshi* (The three-hundred year history of the Yamaguchi coal fields). Ube: Ube Shimbun.

Hirschman, Albert O. 1970. *Exit, Voice, and Loyalty: Responses to Decline in Firms, Organizations, and State.* Cambridge: Harvard University Press.

Hoffmann, Stanley. 1974. *Decline or Renewal? France since the 1930s.* New York: Viking.

Hokkaidō Kisen Tanko K. K., ed. 1958. *Sekitan Kokka Tōkeishi* (History of state control of coal).

Holland, Stuart, ed. 1972. *The State as Entrepreneur.* London: Weidenfeld & Nicolson.

——. 1974. "Europe's New Public Enterprises." In Raymond Vernon, ed., *Big Business and the State.* Cambridge: Harvard University Press.

Horie, Yasuzō. 1939. "Government Industries in the Early Years of the Meiji Era." *Kyoto University Economic Review* no. 1: 67–87.

Horikubō, Masaji. 1939. *Senji Sengo no Sekitan Mondai* (Wartime and postwar coal problems). Tokyo: Shōwa Tosho.

Horiuchi, Akiyoshi. 1984. "Economic Growth and Financial Allocation in Postwar Japan." Brookings Institution Discussion Paper in International Economics. Washington, D.C. August.

Horne, James. 1985. *Japan's Financial Markets: Conflict and Consensus in Policymaking.* Sydney: Allen & Unwin.

Hoshino, Yoshirō. 1956. *Gendai Nihon Gijutsushi Gaisetsu* (An outline of the history of modern Japanese technology). Tokyo: Dainippon Tosho.

Huntington, Samuel P. 1968. *Political Order in Changing Societies.* New Haven: Yale University Press.

Ichinose, Tomoji, et al. 1979. *Kōsha, Kōdan, Jigyōdan* (Public corporations). Tokyo: Kyōikusha.

Idemitsu Kōsan, ed. 1983. *Idemitsu Sekiyu Shiryō* (Idemitsu oil data). Tokyo.

Iguchi, Tōsuke. *See* Inokuchi, Tōsuke.

Iidamura, Yoshiji. 1971. "Genryō no Jukyū" (Supplies of coking coal). *Tekkokai,* April: 12–18.

Ikenberry, G. John. 1982. "State Strength and Capacities: Comparative Responses to the Oil Crisis." Paper presented to the Annual Meeting of the American Political Science Association, Denver.

——. 1983. "International Change, State Structure, and Policy Response: U.S. Energy Adjustment Strategy in Comparative Perspective." Paper presented to the Annual Meeting of the American Political Science Association, Chicago, September 2.

——. 1986. "The Irony of State Strength: Comparative Responses to the Oil Shocks in the 1970s." *International Organization* 40, 1: 105–38.

Ikuta, Toyoaki. 1976. "An Analysis of the Recession in the Oil Industry." Supplement to *Energy in Japan* Quarterly Report no. 34, September.

Imai, Kōzō. 1966. *Sekitan* (Coal). New ed. Tokyo: Yūhikaku.

Inoguchi, Takashi. 1983. *Gendai Nihon Seiji Keizai no Kōzu* (The composition of the political economy of contemporary Japan). Tokyo: Tōyō Keizai.

Inokuchi, Tōsuke. 1963. *Gendai Nihon Sangyō Hattatsushi, II: Sekiyu* (The history of modern Japanese industrial development, vol. 2: Oil). Tokyo: Gendai Nihon Sangyō Hattatsushi Kenkyūkai.

Ishikawa, Kinya. 1983. *Genshiryoku Iinkai no Tatakai* (The battle of the Atomic Energy Commission). Tokyo: Denryoku Shimpōsha.

Ishimura, Zensuke. 1960. *Kōgyō no Kenkyū* (Research on mining rights). Tokyo: Keisō Shobō.

Itami, Toranosuke. 1950. "Teikoku Sekiyu Zōsan Seisaku Hihan" (A criticism of Imperial Oil's production increase policies). *Shinkeizai,* June 1.

Jacoby, Neil H. 1974. *Multinational Oil.* New York: Macmillan.

Japanese National Committee of the World Petroleum Congresses, ed. 1982. *Petroleum Industry in Japan.* Tokyo.

Jishu Gijutsu Kenkyūkai, ed. 1981. *Nihon no Genshiryoku Gijutsu* (Japanese nuclear power technology). Tokyo: Nikkan Kōgyō Shimbunsha.

Johnson, Chalmers. 1966. *Revolutionary Change.* Boston: Little, Brown.

——. 1978. *Japan's Public Policy Companies.* Washington, D.C.: American Enterprise Institute, 1978.

——. 1982. *MITI and the Japanese Miracle: The Growth of Industrial Policy, 1925– 1975.* Stanford: Stanford University Press.

——. 1984. "La Serenissima of the East." *Journal of the Israel Oriental Society* 18, 1: 57–73.

——. 1986. "The Nonsocialist NICs: East Asia." *International Organization* 40, 2: 557–65.

——. 1987. "MITI, MPT, and the Telecom Wars: How Japan Makes Policy for High Technology." In BRIE, ed., *Creating Advantage: American and Japanese Strategies for Adjusting to Change in a New World Economy.* Berkeley, Calif.

Kamiō, Kyōichi. 1984. "Kanmin Buntan Gijutsu Iten no Mondaiten" (Problems associated with transferring technology and responsibility between public and private sectors). Manuscript. Tokyo.

Kanazawa, Yoshio. 1955. "Genshiryoku Hōan no Kentō" (Debate over nuclear power legislation). *Juristo,* December.

Kaplan, Eugene. 1972. *Japan: The Government-Business Relationship.* Washington D.C.: U.S. Department of Commerce.

Karl, Barry D. 1963. *Executive Reorganization and Reform in the New Deal: The Genesis of Administrative Management, 1900–1939.* Cambridge: Harvard University Press.

Katzenstein, Peter J., ed. 1978. *Between Power and Plenty: Foreign Economic Policies of Advanced Industrial States.* Madison: University of Wisconsin Press.

——. 1980. "State Strength through Market Competition: Japan's Industrial Strategy." Manuscript. Ithaca, N.Y.

——. 1985a. "Small Nations in an Open International Economy: The Converging Balance of State and Society in Switzerland and Austria." In Peter Evans et al., eds., *Bringing the State Back In.* Cambridge: Cambridge University Press.

——. 1985b. *Small States in World Markets: Industrial Policy in Europe.* Ithaca: Cornell University Press.

Kawai, Takeshi. 1961. *Fushigi Na Kuni no Genshiryoku* (A strange nation's nuclear power). Tokyo: Kadakawa Shoten.

Keck, Otto. 1981. *Policymaking in a Nuclear Program: The Case of the West German Fast Breeder Reactor.* Lexington, Mass.: Lexington Books.

Keeny, Spurgeon M., et al., eds. 1977. *Nuclear Power Issues and Choices.* Cambridge, Mass.: Ballinger.

Kelf-Cohen, R. 1969. *Twenty Years of Nationalization: The British Experience.* London: Macmillan.

Kent, Marian. 1976. *Oil and Empire: British Policy and Mesopotamian Oil, 1900–1920.* New York: Harper & Row.

Kirby, M. W. 1977. *The British Coal Mining Industry, 1870–1946: A Political and Economic History.* London: Macmillan.

Kitada, Yawanari, and Masajima Tokujirō, eds. 1970. *Teikoku Kōgyō Kaihatsu Kabushiki Kaisha Shashi* (The corporate history of the Imperial Mining Company). Tokyo: Kinko.

Kiyomiya, Ichirō, ed. 1952. *Matsumoto Kenjirō Kaikyūdan* (Reminiscences of Matsumoto Kenjirō). Tokyo: Masushobō.

Klapp, Merrie G. 1982. "The State—Landlord or Entrepreneur?" *International Organization* 36, 3: 575–607.

———. 1987. *The Sovereign Entrepreneur.* Ithaca: Cornell University Press.

Kojima, Keizō. 1957. *Nihon Keizai To Keizai Seisaku* (The Japanese economy and economic policy). Tokyo: Tsūshō Sangyō Kenkyūsha.

Komamura, Yūsaburō. 1966. *Denryokusen Kaiko* (Recollections of the electric power wars). Tokyo: Denryoku Shinpōsha.

Kondō, Kanichi, and Hiroshi Osanai, eds. 1978. *Sengo Sangyōshi E no Shōgen,* III (Testimony related to postwar industrial history vol. 3). Tokyo: Mainichi Shimbunsha.

Krasner, Stephen D. 1978. *Defending the National Interest: Raw Materials Investments and U.S. Foreign Policy.* Princeton: Princeton University Press.

Krauss, Ellis S., and Michio Muramatsu. 1983. "The Structure of Interest Group Influence on Public Policymaking in Japan." Manuscript.

———. Forthcoming. "The Conservative Policy Line and the Development of Patterned Pluralism." Vol. I of Japan Political Research Committee Publications. Stanford: Stanford University Press.

Krauss, Ellis S., Thomas P. Rohlen, and Patricia G. Steinhoff, eds. 1984. *Conflict in Japan.* Honolulu: University of Hawaii Press.

Krieger, Joel. 1983. *Undermining Capitalism: State Ownership and the Dialectic of Control in the British Coal Industry.* Princeton: Princeton University Press.

Kubota, Akira. 1969. *Higher Civil Servants in Postwar Japan.* Princeton: Princeton University Press.

Kuboyama Yūzō. 1942a. *Sekitan Taikan* (A general view of coal). Tokyo: Kōronsha.

———. 1942b. *Sekitan Kōgyō Hattatsu Shi* (The history of the development of the coal industry). Tokyo: Kōronsha.

Kuisel, Richard F. 1967. *Ernest Mercier: French Technocrat.* Berkeley: University of California Press.

Kunimasa, Takeshige. 1974. *Kakushin Rengō Seiken* (Progressive coalition government). Tokyo: Gakuyō Shobō.

Kunisaki, Shinsui. 1943. "Nihon Sekitan Kaisha Jibai Gyōmu no Hossoku ni Saishite" (The inauguration of the sales function for the Japan Coal Corporation). *Sekitan Tōsei Kaikō* 1, 4–5: 2–7.

Kurth, James. 1979. "The Political Consequences of the Product Cycle: Industrial History and Comparative Politics." *International Organization* 33, 1: 1–34.

Laux, Jeanne Kirk. 1983. "Expanding the State: The International Relations of State-Owned Enterprises in Canada." *Polity* 15, 3: 329–50.

Laux, Jeanne Kirk, and Maureen Appel Molot. Forthcoming. *State Capitalism: Comparative Perspectives on Public Enterprise in Canada.* Ithaca: Cornell University Press.

Lehmbruch, Gerhard. 1984. "Concentration and the Structure of Corporatist Networks." In John H. Goldthorpe, ed., *Order and Conflict in Contemporary Capitalism*. London: Oxford University Press.

Lerner, Daniel. 1958. *The Passing of Traditional Societies*. Glencoe, Ill.: Free Press.

Lesbriel, S. Hayden. 1985. "Energy Power Plant Leadtimes in Japan." Griffith University Japan Research Center, Research Paper no. 118. Brisbane.

Lester, Richard K. 1982. "U.S.-Japanese Nuclear Relations: Structural Change and Political Strain." MIT International Energy Studies Program Working Paper. Cambridge, February.

Levy, Brian. 1982. "World Oil Marketing in Transition." *International Organization* 36, 1: 113–33.

Lindblom, Charles E. 1977. *Politics and Markets*. New York: Basic.

Lockwood, William. 1955. *The Economic Development of Japan: Growth and Structural Change, 1868–1938*. London: Oxford University Press.

——. 1965. "Japan's 'New Capitalism.'" In William W. Lockwood, ed., *The State and Economic Enterprise in Japan*. Princeton: Princeton University Press.

Lombardo, Antonio. 1983. "Japan's and Italy's Political Systems: Developmental and Comparative Perspectives." In Gianni Fodella, ed., *Japan's Economy in a Comparative Perspective*. Tenderden, U.K.: Norbury.

Lovejoy, W. F., and P. T. Homan. 1967. *Economic Aspects of Oil Conservation Regulation*. Baltimore: Johns Hopkins University Press.

Lowi, Theodore J. 1979. *The End of Liberalism: The Second Republic of the United States*. 2d ed. New York: Norton.

Magini, Manlio. 1976. *L'Italia e il petrolio*. Milan: Mondadori.

Mandel, Ernest. 1975. *Late Capitalism*. London: New Left Books.

Mansfield, Harvey. 1980. "Special Government Corporations: A Middle Way." In Harold Orleans, ed., *Nonprofit Organizations: A Government Management Tool*. New York: Praeger.

Marshall, Byron K. 1967. *Capitalism and Nationalism in Prewar Japan: The Ideology of the Business Elite, 1868–1941*. Stanford: Stanford University Press.

Matsui, K. 1969. "An Analysis of Capital Investment and Profitability of Japanese Petroleum Industry in the Postwar Period." Supplement to *Energy in Japan* Quarterly Report no. 9, December.

Matsunaga, Yasuzaemon. 1983. *Matsunaga Yasuzaemon Sakkashū Dai Yonken* (The collected works of Matsunaga Yasuzaemon, vol. 4). Tokyo: Gogatsu Shobō.

Matsuzaka, Naomi. 1980. *Waga Jinsei Wa Tōsō Nari: Matsunaga Yasuzaemon no Sekai* (My life is a struggle: The world of Matsunaga Yasuzaemon). Tokyo: Kōsui Sangyō.

Miliband, Ralph. 1969. *The State in Capitalist Society*. New York: Basic.

——. 1977. *Marxism and Politics*. Oxford: Oxford University Press.

Milward, H. Bunton, and Gary T. Wamsley. 1979. "Policy Networks: Key Concept at a Critical Juncture." Paper delivered to the Annual Meeting of the Midwest Political Science Association. Chicago, April 19–21.

Mimura, Kiichi. 1966a. "Kaigai Sekiyu Shigen no Kaihatsu no Kyūmu ni Tsuite" (Concerning the pressing need for the development of overseas petroleum resources). *Keidanren Geppō*, March.

——. 1966b. "Sekiyu Jijō to Sekiyu Shigen Kaihatsu no Mondaiten" (The petroleum situation and problems with oil resource development). *Keidanren Geppō*, December.

Ministero della Partecipazioni Statali. 1980. *Rapporto sulle partecipazioni statali*. Venice: Marsilio.

Ministry of State Participation. 1982. "The System of State Holdings in Italy: Problems and Strategies." Mimeo. Rome.

Mitsubishi Economic Research Bureau. 1936. *Japanese Trade and Industry: Present and Future*. London: Macmillan.

Miyake, Haruteru. 1954. *Nihon no Denki Jigyō* (The Japanese electric power industry). Tokyo: Denki Shimbun.

Mochizuki, Kiichi. 1975. "National Interests and International Extractive Business: A Case of Japanese Oil." Mimeo. Harvard University Center for Middle Eastern Studies. Cambridge.

Moe, Ronald. 1979. "Government Corporations and the Erosion of Accountability." *Public Administration Review*, November–December: 566–71.

Monsen, R. Joseph, and Kenneth D. Walters. 1980. "State Owned Firms: A Review of the Data and Issues." *Research in Corporate Special Performance and Policy* 2: 125–56.

Moore, Barrington, Jr. 1966. *Social Origins of Dictatorship and Democracy: Lord and Peasant in the Making of the Modern World*. Boston: Beacon.

Moore, Joe. 1983. *Japanese Workers and the Struggle for Power, 1945–1947*. Madison: University of Wisconsin Press.

Mosley, Oswald. 1931. *A National Policy: An Account of the Emergency Programme*. London: Macmillan.

Muramatsu, Michio. 1981. *Sengo Nihon no Kanryōsei* (Postwar Japan's bureaucratic system). Tokyo: Tōyō Keizai.

Murat, Daniel. 1969. *L'intervention de l'état dans le secteur petrolier en France*. Paris: Technip.

Myrdal, Gunnar. 1960. *Beyond the Welfare State*. London: Duckworth.

Nagasue, Toshio. 1973. *Chikuhō: Sekitan Chiikishi* (Chikuhō: The history of a coal mining region). Tokyo: NHK.

Naitō, Hisahiro. 1957. *Shupu Shūu Roku* (The memoirs of Naitō Hisahiro). Tokyo: Sekiyu Bunkasha.

Nakagawa, Shunshi. 1961. "Wagakuni Enerugī Seisaku ni Taisuru Iken" (An opinion concerning our nation's energy policy). Report of the House of Representatives, Commerce and Industry Committee. Tokyo.

Nakajima, Tokunosuke, and Ikurō Anzai. 1979. *Nihon no Genshiryoku Hatsuden* (Atomic power in Japan). Tokyo: Shin Nihon Shuppansha.

Nakamura, Takafusa. 1957. "Sengo Tōsei ni Okeru Sekitan Kogyō no Chikuseki Katei" (The process of capital accumulation by the coal industry under postwar controls). *Shakai Kagaku Kiyō* no. 6. Tokyo: Daigaku Kyōyō Gakubu.

——. 1961. *Senzen no Nihon Keizai Seichō no Bunseki* (An analysis of prewar Japanese economic growth). Tokyo: Iwanami Shoten.

——. 1981. *The Postwar Japanese Economy: Its Development and Structure*. Tokyo: University of Tokyo Press.

Nakamura, Takafusa, and Miyazaki Isamu. 1961. "Nihon no Enerugī Mondai" (Japan's energy problems). In Arisawa Hiromi, ed., *Gendai Nihon Sangyō Kōza III*. Tokyo: Iwanami Shoten.

Nakane, Chie. 1970. *Japanese Society*. Berkeley: University of California Press.

Nanajū Nenshi Henshū Iinkai, ed. 1958. *Hokkaidō Tankō Kisen Kabushiki Kaisha Nanajū Nenshi* (The seventy-year history of the Hokkaido Mine and Steamship Company). Tokyo.

National Academy of Public Administration. 1981. *Report on Government Corporations*. 2 vol. Washington, D.C.

Neff, Thomas, et al. 1983. "Energy and Security: An Analysis for the State of

California." MIT Energy Laboratory, Center for Energy Policy Research Working Paper. Cambridge, July.

Nelson, Richard R. 1984. *High Technology Policies: A Five Nation Comparison.* Washington D.C.: American Enterprise Institute.

Nettl, J. P. 1968. "The State as a Conceptual Variable." *World Politics* 20, 4: 559–92.

Nezu, Tomoyoshi, ed. 1958. *Sekitan Kokka Tōsei Shi* (The history of state control of coal). Tokyo: Nihon Keizai Kenkyūjo.

Nichimanshi Sekitan Jihō, ed. 1940. "Nichimanshi Sekitan Renmei Gaiyō" (Outline of the Japan-Manchuria-China coal alliance). *Nichimanshi Sekitan Jihō* no. 1: 1–17.

Nihon Denki Kyōkai, ed. 1975. *Gojū Nenshi* (Fifty-year history). Tokyo.

Nihon Denki Kyōkai Denryoku Nenpō Iinkai, ed. 1982. *Denki Jigyō no Jōkyō to Sanjū Nen no Ayumi* (The conditions of the electric power industry and its thirty years of progress). Tokyo.

Nihon Genshiryoku Sangyō Kaigi, ed. 1971. *Nihon no Genshiryoku: 15 Nen no Ayumi* (Japan's nuclear power: Fifteen years of progress). 3 vols. Tokyo.

———. 1984. *Genshiryoku Pokettobukku* (Nuclear energy pocketbook). Tokyo.

Nihon Kōgyō Shimbunsha, ed. 1981. *Enerugī Sōgō Binran* (Comprehensive energy handbook). Tokyo.

Nihon Kyōsantō Chūō Iinkai, ed. 1973. *Nihon Kyōsantō Dai Jūnikai Taikaigi Anshū* (A compilation of the program of the 12th convention of the Japan Communist party). Tokyo.

Nihon Sekitan Kōgyō Rengōkai, ed. 1936. *Sekitan Kōgyō Rengōkai Sōritsu 15 Nenshi* (A fifteen-year record since the establishment of the Coal Industry Association). Tokyo.

Nihon Sekitan Kyōkai. 1971. "Shin Sekitan Seisaku Sōki Juritsu no Onegai ni Tsuite" (Concerning a request for early establishment of a new coal policy). October 20. Tokyo.

Nihon Shakaitō, ed. 1965. *Nihon Shakaitō 20 Nen no Kiroku* (The twenty-year record of the Japan Socialist party). Tokyo.

Nihon Shakaitō Seisaku Shingikai, ed. 1973. *Sōgō Enerugī Seisaku* (Comprehensive energy policy). Tokyo, October 4.

Nihon Tekkō Renmei, ed. 1971. *Kokunaitan no Hikitori ni Tsuite no Yōbō* (Demands related to procurement of domestic coal). November. Tokyo.

Nippon Sekiyushi Henshūshitsu, ed. 1958. *Nippon Sekiyushi* (The history of Japanese oil). Tokyo.

Noguchi Yūichirō. 1964. "Enerugī Seisaku wa Doko e Yuku" (Where is energy policy going?). *Asahi Jānaru*, December 27.

———. 1965. "Sekitan Kokkan e no Tenbō" (Prospects for state management of coal). *Asahi Jānaru*, June 20.

———. 1966. "Sangyō Kokuyūka e no Tenbō: Sekitan Kiki o Sukuu Nano" (Prospects for nationalization of the industry: Something to rescue coal from its crisis). *Sekai*, April.

Noguchi, Yukio. 1981. *Gyōzaisei Kaikaku* (Administrative and fiscal reform). Tokyo: PHP.

Noguchi, Yukio, and E. Sakakibara. 1977. "Ōkurashō, Nichigin Ōchō no Bunseki" (Analysis of the MOF and BOJ dynasties). *Chūō Kōron*, August.

Nordhauser, Norman E. 1979. *The Quest for Stability: Domestic Oil Regulation, 1917–1935.* New York: Garland.

Nordlinger, Eric A. 1981. *On the Autonomy of the Democratic State.* Cambridge: Harvard University Press.

Nowell, Gregory P. 1983. "The French State and the Developing World Oil Market: Domestic, International and Environmental Constraints, 1864–1928." In Paul Zarembka, ed., *Research in Political Economy* vol. 6. Greenwich, Conn.: JAI.

——. 1987. "Political Economy of the World Oil Market: The Integration of France into a World System." Diss., MIT.

——. Forthcoming. "International Relations Theories and Technological Development: The Oil Market and the Case for Nondeterminate Outcomes." In Paul Zarembka, ed., *Research in Political Economy* vol. 8.

O'Connor, James. 1973. *The Fiscal Crisis of the State*. New York: St. Martin.

Offe, Claus. 1975. "The Theory of the Capitalist State and the Problem of Policy Formation." In Leon Lindberg et al., eds., *Stress and Contradiction in Modern Capitalism*. Lexington, Mass.: Heath.

——. 1985. *Disorganized Capitalism*. Cambridge: MIT Press.

Ōi, Ryūaki. 1972. "Sekiyu Gyōhō Shikōka no Sekiyu Sangyō" (The petroleum industry under the operation of the Petroleum Industry Law). *Sekiyu Seisaku* 11, 237 (August 20), 239 (September 20), and 243 (November 20).

Okamoto, Ryūzō. 1979. *Sekiyu Gyōkai* (The oil industry). Tokyo: Kyōikusha.

Ōki, Yōichi. 1961. "Sekitan Kōgyō no Kōzō" (The structure of the coal industry). In Arisawa Hiromi, ed., *Gendai Nihon Sangyō Kōza* III. Tokyo: Iwanami Shoten.

Okimoto, Daniel I. 1984. "Political Context." In Okimoto et al., eds., *The Comparative Edge: The Semiconductor Industry in the U.S. and Japan*. Stanford: Stanford University Press.

——. Forthcoming. *Between MITI and the Market: Japanese Industrial Policy for High Technology*. Stanford: Stanford University Press.

Okuda, Hideo, ed. 1981. *Nakahara Nobuhei Den* (The diaries of Nakahara Nobuhei). Tokyo: Tōa Nenryō Kōgyō K. K.

OPEC (Organization of Petroleum Exporting Countries), ed. 1982. *Petroleum Product Prices and Their Components in Selected Countries*. Vienna.

Osawa, Etsuji. 1978. *Denryoku Jigyōkai* (The electric power industry). Tokyo: Kyōikusha.

Oshima, Keichi. 1980. "International Cooperation in Industrial Technology." In H. Inose, ed., *Kagaku Gijutsu To Seisaku ni Taisuru Gakusaiteki Kokusaiteki Sekkin* (An international and interdisciplinary approach to science and technology policy). Special Research Report. Tokyo: Ministry of Education.

Otake, Sokuichi, ed. 1980. *Denryoku Hyakunen Shi* (The hundred-year history of electric power). 2 vols. Tokyo: Seikeisha.

Ōtani, Ken. 1978. *Kōbō: Denryoku o Meguru Seiji to Keizai* (Rise and fall: The politics and economics of electric power). Tokyo: Sangyō Nōritsu Tanki Daigaku.

Ouchi, William. 1981. *Theory Z: How American Businessmen Can Meet the Japanese Challenge*. Reading, Mass.: Addison-Wesley.

Ozawa, Etsuji. 1979. *Denryoku Jigyōkai* (The electric power industry). 2d ed. Tokyo: Kyōikusha.

Parsons, Talcott. 1951. *The Social System*. New York: Free Press.

Patrick, Hugh. 1985. "Japanese High Technology Industrial Policy in Comparative Context." Paper presented at the Columbia University Seminar on Modern Japan. New York, December 13.

——. 1986. "Japanese High Technology Industrial Policy in Comparative Perspective." In Patrick, ed., *Japanese High Technology Industries: Lessons and Limitations of Industrial Policy*. Seattle: University of Washington Press.

Peck, Merton J., and S. Tamura. 1976. "Technology." In H. Patrick and H. Rosovsky, eds., *Asia's New Giant*. Washington, D.C.: Brookings.

Pempel, T. J., ed. 1977. *Policymaking in Contemporary Japan*. Ithaca: Cornell University Press.

———. 1982. *Policy and Politics in Japan: Creative Conservatism*. Philadelphia: Temple University Press.

Pempel, T. J., and K. Tsunekawa. 1979. "Corporatism without Labor? The Japanese Anomaly." In P. C. Schmitter and G. Lembruch, eds., *Trends toward Corporatist Intermediation*. Beverly Hills: Sage.

Pepper, Thomas, et al. 1985. *The Competition: Dealing with Japan*. New York: Praeger.

Peterson, Peter G. 1971. *The United States in a Changing World Economy*. Washington, D.C.: U.S. Department of Commerce.

Petroleum Association of Japan. 1986. *Petroleum Industry in Japan*. Tokyo.

Petroleum Dept., Agency of Natural Resources and Energy, Ministry of International Trade and Industry. 1982. "The Petroleum Report." Tokyo, August.

Piore, Michael J., and Charles F. Sabel. 1984. *The Second Industrial Divide: Possibilities for Prosperity*. New York: Basic.

Porges, Amelia. 1979. "On Import Cartels and Industrial Organization in Japan." Memorandum prepared for the Office of the Special Representative for Trade Negotiations. Washington, D.C., August.

Posner, Alan R., and S. J. Woolf. 1967. *Italian Public Enterprise*. London: Duckworth.

Poulantzas, Nicos. 1978. *State, Power and Socialism*. London: New Left Books.

Pratt, Larry. 1981. "Petro-Canada." In A. Tupper and G. B. Doern, eds., *Public Corporations and Public Policy in Canada*. Montreal: Institute for Research on Public Policy.

Prodi, Romano. 1974. "Italy." In R. Vernon, ed., *Big Business and the State*. Cambridge: Harvard University Press.

———. 1976. "Public Ownership: Some Quantitative Dimensions." In William G. Shepherd, ed., *Public Enterprise: Economic Analysis of Theory and Practice*. Lexington, Mass.: Lexington.

Przeworski, Adam. 1980. "Material Interests, Class Compromise, and the Transition to Socialism." *Politics and Society* 10, 2: 125–54.

Pye, Lucian W. 1966. *Aspects of Political Development*. Boston: Little, Brown.

Rapp, William V. 1984. "Unbundling Japan, Inc." *Creative Computing* 10, 8: 43–48.

Ratiglia, Fabio. 1982. "The History and Role of the Italian National Oil Corporation: The ENI." Paper presented at the Colloquuium on Energy organized by the Malaysian National Committee of the World Energy Conference in cooperation with the Italian government. Kuala Lumpur, October 26–28.

Reed, Steven. 1986. *Japanese Prefectures and Policymaking*. Pittsburgh: University of Pittsburgh Press.

Regini, Marino. 1984. "The Conditions for Political Exchange: How Concertation Emerged and Collapsed in Italy and Great Britain." In J. H. Goldthorpe, ed., *Order and Conflict in Contemporary Capitalism*. London: Oxford University Press.

Report of the Royal Commission on the Coal Industry. 1926. London: HMSO.

Rispoli, Maurizio. 1977. "L'evoluzione dell'industria della raffinazione del petrolio in Italia nel periodo della 'grande crisi'" (The evolution of the Italian petroleum refining industry during the period of the "great crisis"). In G. Toniolo, ed., *Industria e banca nella grande crisi, 1929–1934*. Milan: Etas Libri.

Robson, William A. 1962. *Nationalized Industry and Public Ownership*. London: Allen & Unwin.

Rondot, Jean. 1962. *La Compagnie Française des Pétroles: Du franc—or au au pétrole franc*. Paris: Plon.

Rossi, Ernesto. 1955. "Nationalization in Italy." In M. Einaudi et al., eds., *Nationalization in France and Italy*. Ithaca: Cornell University Press.

———. 1962. *Elettricita senza baroni* (Electricity without barons). Bari: Laterza.

Rueschemeyer, Dietrich, and Peter Evans. 1985. "The State and Economic Transformation: Toward an Analysis of the Conditions Underlying Effective Intervention." In Evans et al., eds., *Bringing the State Back In*. New York: Cambridge University Press.

Saitō, Masatoshi, ed. 1948. *Rinji Sekitan Kōgyō Kanrihō no Kaisetsu* (An explanation of the temporary coal mining control law). Tokyo: Shōkōkyōkai.

Sakai, Yoshio, ed. 1965. *Denki Jigyō Hōseishi* (The history of electric power legislation). Tokyo: Denryoku Shimpōsha.

Sampson, Anthony. 1975. *The Seven Sisters*. London: Coronet.

Samuels, Richard J. 1983. *The Politics of Regional Policy in Japan—Localities, Incorporated?* Princeton: Princeton University Press.

Sanjū Nenshi Henshū Iinkai, ed. 1984. *Denpatsu Sanjū Nenshi* (The thirty-year history of the Electric Power Development Corporation). Tokyo: Dengen Kaihatsu Kabushiki Kaisha.

Saraceno, Pasquale. 1955. "IRI: Its Origin and Its Position in the Italian Industrial Economy, 1933–1953." *Journal of Industrial Economics*, July: 197–221.

———. 1956. *L'Instituto per la Riconstruzione Industriale, 3: Origini, ordinamenti, e attivita svolta* (IRI, 3: Its origin and its position in the Italian industrial economy). Rome: Ministero dell'Industria e del Commercio.

Sasaki, Jōtarō. 1965. "Sekitan Kigyō Jiritsu e no Michi" (The road to an independent coal industry). *Ekonomisuto*, December 21.

Satō, Hideo. Forthcoming. "The Politics of Technology Importation in Japan: Case of Atomic Power Reactors." In Gary Saxonhouse, ed., *Japanese Technology Transfer and Innovations*. Boulder: Westview.

Satō, Seizaburo, and Tetsuhisa Matsuzaki. 1986. *Jimintō Seiken* (The LDP regime). Tokyo: Chuo Kōronsha.

Satō, Taiji. 1986. *Ore Wa Tsūsanshō ni Barasareta* (I was murdered by MITI). Tokyo.

Saxonhouse, Gary. 1983. *The Early Japanese Labor Movement: Labor and Politics in a Developing Society*. Berkeley: University of California Institute for East Asian Studies.

———. 1986. "Why Japan Is Winning." *Issues in Science and Technology*, Spring.

Schmitter, P. C. 1977. "Modes of Interest Intermediation and Models of Societal Change in Western Europe." *Contemporary Political Studies* 10. April.

Schmitter, P., and G. Lembruch. 1979. *Trends toward Corporatist Intermediation*. Beverly Hills: Sage.

Seidenstecker, Edward. 1983. *Low City, High City*. New York: Knopf.

Seidman, Harold. 1975. "Government Sponsored Enterprise in the United States." In Bruce L. R. Smith, ed., *The New Political Economy: The Public Use of the Priate Sector*. New York: Wiley.

———. 1980. *Politics, Position, and Power: The Dynamics of Federal Organization*. 3d ed. New York: Oxford University Press.

Seiji Keizai Kenkyūjo, ed. 1959. *Nihon no Denryoku Sangyō* (Japan's electric power industry). Tokyo: Tōyō Keizai.

Sekitan Kōgyō Gōrika Jigyōdan, ed. 1980. *Sekitan Kōgyō 35 nen no Ayumi* (The coal industry's past 35 years). Tokyo.
———. 1965. *Danshi* (History of the Coal Mining Rationalization Corporation). Tokyo.
Sekitan Tsūshin, ed. 1959. *Sengo no Sekitan Shijō* (The postwar coal market). Fukuoka.
Sekiyu Dōkō Kenkyūkai, ed. 1983. *Sekiyu Nenpan* (Petroleum yearbook). Tokyo: Sogō Intanashiyonaru Sha.
Sekiyu Kōgyō Renmei, ed. 1982. *Sekiyu Kōgyō Renmei 20 nen no Ayumi* (Twenty years of progress by the Japan Petroleum Development Association). Tokyo.
———. 1983. *Wagakuni Sekiyu Kaihatsu no Jōkyō* (The current status of Japan's oil development). Tokyo.
Sekiyu Renmei, ed. 1962. *Sekiyu Gyōkai no Suii* (Transition in the oil industry). Tokyo.
———. 1983. *Sekiyu Kankei Kiso Shiryō* (Basic petroleum-related data). Tokyo.
Sekiyu Shigen Kaihatsu Kabushiki Kaisha, ed. 1967. *Sekiyu Shigen Kaihatsu Kabushiki Kaisha 10 Nenshi* (The ten-year history of the Petroleum Resources Development Company). Tokyo.
Senato della Repubblica. 1953. "Relazione di maggioranza della V Commissione Permanente (Finanze e Tesoro)" (Majority report of the 5th Permanent Commission for Finance and Treasury). N. 2489-A. Rome.
Sharkansky, Ira. 1979. *Wither the State? Politics and Public Enterprises in Three Countries.* Chatham, N.J.: Chatham House.
Sheahan, John B. 1976. "Experience with Public Enterprise in France and Italy." In William G. Shepherd, ed., *Public Enterprise: Economic Analysis of Theory and Practice.* Lexington, Mass.: Lexington.
Shigen Enerugīchō Chōkan Kanbō Sōmuka, ed. 1982. *Enerugī Tōkei* (Energy statistics). Tokyo: Tsūshō Sangyō Kenkyūsha.
Shigen Enerugīchō Sekitanbu, ed. 1982. *Kōru Nōto* (Coal notes). Tokyo: Shigen Sangyō Shimbunsha.
Shigen Enerugīchō Sekiyubu, ed. 1980. *Sekiyu Seisan no Genjō* (The current status of the oil industry). Tokyo: Sekiyu Tsūshin.
Shinobu, Seizaburō. 1967. *Sengo Nihon Seijishi* (The postwar political history of Japan). Tokyo: Keisō Shobō.
Shinohara, Miyohei. 1976. "MITI's Industrial Policy and Japanese Industrial Organization." *Developing Economies* 14, 4: 366–80.
Shōkōshō Sekitanchō, ed. 1949. *Sekitan Kokkakanri Ikkanen no Sokuseki* (The course of state control of coal after one year). Tokyo.
Shonfield, Andrew. 1965. *Modern Capitalism: The Changing Balance of Public and Private Power.* New York: Oxford University Press.
Shūgiin Ōbei Enerugī Chōsadan. 1961. "Ōbei no Enerugī Seisaku ni Kansuru Hōkoku" (A report concerning European and American energy policies). October. Tokyo.
Silberman, Bernard. 1982. "The Bureaucratic State in Japan: The Problem of Authority and Legitimacy." In T. Najita and J. V. Koschman, eds., *Conflict in Modern Japanese History: The Neglected Tradition.* Princeton: Princeton University Press.
Silberman, Bernard S., and H. D. Harootunian, eds. 1966. *Modern Japanese Leadership: Transition and Change.* Tucson: University of Arizona Press.
Skocpol, Theda. 1980. "Political Responses to Capitalist Crisis: Neo-Marxist

Theories of the State and the Case of the New Deal." *Politics and Society* 10, 2: 155–202.

——. 1985. "Bringing the State Back In: Strategies of Analysis in Current Research." In P. Evans et al., eds., *Bringing the State Back In.* New York: Cambridge University Press.

Smith, Thomas C. 1965. *Political Change and Industrial Development in Japan: Government Enterprise, 1868–1880.* Stanford: Stanford University Press.

Sōgō Enerugī Chōsakai, ed. 1974. "Sekiyu Gyōhō Seiteiji ni Okeru Haikei to Konnichi no Jōkyō" (The background at the time of the petroleum industry law and conditions today). Report prepared by MITI for the Basic Problems Study Group. Tokyo. June 7.

Sonoda, Minoru. 1970. *Sengo Sekitan Shi* (Postwar history of coal). Fukuoka: Sekitsū.

Spindler, J. Andrew. 1984. *The Politics of International Credit.* Washington, D.C.: Brookings.

Squarzina, Federico. 1958. *Le ricerche di petrolio in Italia* (Petroleum exploration in Italy). Rome: Jandi Sapi.

Steiner, Kurt, Scott Flanagan, and Ellis Kraus, eds. 1980. *Local Opposition in Japan: Progressive Local Governments, Citizens' Movements, and National Politics.* Princeton: Princeton University Press.

Sugihara, Keiji. 1983. "The Recent Energy Policy in the USA and a Description of the U.S. Synthetic Fuels Corporation." Mimeo. Cambridge, Mass.

Sugimoto, Yoshio. 1981. *Popular Disturbances in Postwar Japan.* Hong Kong: Asian Research Service.

Suleiman, Ezra. 1974. *Politics, Power, and the Bureaucracy in France.* Princeton: Princeton University Press.

——. Forthcoming. *Politics, Power, and State Structures.* Princeton: Princeton University Press.

Sumiya, Mikio. 1968. *Nihon Sekitan Sangyō Bunseki* (Analysis of Japan's coal industry). Tokyo: Iwanami Shoten.

Sumiya, Mikio, and Koji Taira, eds. 1979. *An Outline of Japanese Economic History, 1603–1940: Major Works and Research Findings.* Tokyo: University of Tokyo Press, 1979.

Suttmeier, Richard P. 1981. "The Japanese Nuclear Power Option: Technological Promise and Social Limitations." In Ronald A. Morse, ed., *The Politics of Japan's Energy Strategy.* Berkeley: University of California Institute for East Asian Studies.

Suzuki, Tatsuru. 1983. *Denryoku Sangyō no Atarashii Chōsen* (The new challenges to the electric power industry). Tokyo: Nihon Kōgyō Shimbunsha.

Sweezy, Paul. 1962. *The Present as History: Essays and Reviews on Capitalism and Socialism.* New York: Monthly Review Press.

Takai, Yoshio. 1986. "Gasoline Import and Its Implications for the Japanese Petroleum Industry." Thesis, Sloan School of Management, MIT.

Takano, Takeshi. 1980. *Tsūsanshō no Yabō* (MITI's ambitions). Tokyo: Weekend.

Tanaka, Norio. 1983. *Waga Kuni Sekiyu Sangyō no Sabaibaru Senryaku* (Strategies for the survival of our nation's petroleum industry). Tokyo: Institute for Energy Economics.

Tarrow, Sidney. 1977. *Between Center and Periphery.* New Haven: Yale University Press.

Teikoku Sekiyu Kabushiki Kaisha Rōmubu, ed. 1982. "Sekiyu no Ayumi" (The path of oil). Manuscript. Tokyo.

347

Tiedemann, Arthur E. 1971. "Big Business and Politics in Prewar Japan." In J. W. Morley, ed., *Dilemmas of Growth in Prewar Japan*. Princeton: Princeton University Press.

Tōhata, Seiichi. 1960. "Keizai Shutai no Keiseishi" (A typological history of economic actors). *Keizai Shutaisei Kōza* (Readings on economic policy, vol. 3). Tokyo: Chūō Kōronsha.

Tokyo Denryoku Shashi Henshū Iinkai, ed. 1983. *Tokyo Denryoku 30 Nenshi* (The thirty-year history of the Tokyo Electric Power Company). Tokyo: Dainippon Insatsu.

Trezise, Philip. 1982. "Industrial Policy in Japan." In Margaret E. Dewar, ed., *Industry Vitalization: Toward a National Industrial Policy*. Elmsford, N.Y.: Pergamon.

Tsuchiya, Kiyoshi. 1983. *Chūtō to Ōbei no Sekiyu to Keizai* (Oil and economics in the Middle East, Europe, and the United States). *Sōgō Seisaku Kenkyū* no. 784, August 10.

Tsurumi, Yoshi. 1978. "The Case of Japan: Price Bargaining and Controls on Oil Products." *Journal of Comparative Economics* 2: 126–43.

Tsushō Sangyōshō, ed. 1981. *Enerugī 1981* (Energy, 1981). Tokyo.

Tsūshō Sangyōshō Kōzankyoku Sekiyuka, ed. Annual. *Sekiyu Sangyō no Genjō* (The current state of the petroleum industry). Tokyo: Sekiyu Tsūshinsha.

Tsūshō Sangyōshō Shigen Enerugīchō Chōkan Kanbō Genshiryoku Sangyōka, ed. 1981. *Wagakuni Genshiryoku Sangyō no Kadai to 80 Nendai no Tenbō* (The problems of our nation's nuclear power industry and prospects for the 1980s). Tokyo.

Tsūshō Sangyōshō Shigen Enerugīchō Kōeki Jigyōkyoku, ed. Annual. *Denryoku Jukyū no Gaiyō* (An outline of electric power supply and demand). Tokyo.

Tuchman, Barbara. 1978. *A Distant Mirror*. New York: Knopf.

Tupper, Allan, and G. Bruce Doern, eds. 1981. *Public Corporations and Public Policy in Canada*. Montreal: Institute for Research on Public Policy.

Uehara, Masuo. 1981. *Sekiyugaku Nyūmon* (An introduction to the study of oil). Tokyo: Nikkan Kōgyō Shimbunsha.

United Nations Centre for Natural Resources, Energy and Transport, ed. 1980. *State Petroleum Enterprises in Developing Countries*. New York: Pergamon.

United States Dept. of Energy, Office of International Affairs. 1977. *The Role of Foreign Governments in the Energy Industries*. Washington, D.C.

Usami, Shōgō. 1981. *Denryoku no Oni Jinsei no Oni Matsunaga Yasuzaemon ni Manabu* (Learning from Matsunaga Yasuzaemon). Tokyo: Jitsugyō no Nipponsha.

Vacca, Sergio. 1981. "La politica energetica nazionale e i ruoli strategici delle imprese a partecipazione statale" (National energy policy and the strategic roles of the state enterprises). In G. De Michelis et al., eds., *Rapporto sulle partecipazioni statale*. Milano: Angeli.

Vernon, Raymond. 1983. *Two Hungry Giants: The United States and Japan in the Quest for Oil and Ores*. Cambridge: Harvard University Press.

Vernon, Raymond, and Yair Aharoni, eds. 1981. *State-Owned Enterprises in the Western Economies*. New York: St. Martin's.

———. 1984. "Linking Managers with Ministers: Dilemmas of the State-Owned Enterprise." *Journal of Policy Analysis and Management* 4, 1: 39–55.

Vining, Aidan R. 1979. "An Overview of the Origins, Growth, Size, and Functions of Provincial Crown Corporations." Vancouver: Institute for Research on Public Policy.

——. 1981. "Provincial Hydro Utilities." In Allan Tupper and G. Bruce Doern, eds., *Public Corporations and Public Policy in Canada.* Montreal: Institute for Research on Public Policy.

Vittas, Dimitri, ed. 1978. "Borrowing Systems Abroad: The Role of Large Deposit Banks in the Financial Systems of Germany, France, Italy, the Netherlands, Switzerland, Sweden, Japan, and the United States." London: Inter-Bank Research Organization.

Vogel, David. 1978. "Why Businessmen Distrust Their State." *British Journal of Political Science* 8: 45–78.

Vogel, Ezra. 1975. "Introduction: Toward More Accurate Concepts." In Vogel, ed., *Modern Japanese Organization and Decisionmaking.* Berkeley: University of California Press.

——. 1978. "Guided Free Enterprise in Japan." *Harvard Business Review*, May–June: 161–70.

——. 1979. *Japan as Number One.* Cambridge: Harvard University Press.

——. 1985. *Comeback.* New York: Simon & Schuster.

Votaw, Dow. 1964. *The Six-legged Dog: Mattei and ENI, A Study in Power.* Berkeley: University of California Press.

Wallerstein, Immanuel. 1974. *The Modern World System.* New York: Academic.

Walsh, Annamarie Hauk. 1978. *The Public's Business.* Cambridge: MIT Press.

——. 1979. "State Owned Business Abroad: New Competitive Threat." *Harvard Business Review*, March–April: 160–70.

Ward, Robert E. 1978. *Japan's Political System.* 2d ed. Englewood Cliffs, N.J.: Prentice-Hall.

Wheeler, James, et al. 1982. *Japanese Industrial Policy in the 1980s.* New York: Hudson Institute.

Wildavsky, Aaron. 1964. *The Politics of the Budgetary Process.* Boston: Little, Brown.

Williamson, Harold F., and Arnold R. Daum. 1963. *The Age of Illumination, 1859–1899.* Evanston: Northwestern University Press.

Williamson, Harold F., et al. 1963. *American Petroleum Industry, 1899–1959: The Age of Energy.* Vol. 2. Evanston: Northwestern University Press.

Wilson, Carroll L. 1980. *Coal: Bridge to the Future.* Cambridge, Mass.: Ballinger.

Wilson, Frank L. 1983. "French Interest Group Politics: Pluralist or Neo-Corporatist?" *American Political Science Review* 77, 4: 895–910.

Yada, Toshifumi. 1977. *Sekitan Gyōkai* (The coal industry). Tokyo: Kyōikusha.

Yamada, Ichitarō. 1977. *Nippon Daiteiden* (Japan's great electricity stoppage). Tokyo: PHP.

Yanaga, Chitoshi. 1968. *Big Business in Japanese Politics.* New Haven: Yale University Press.

Yomiuri Shinbunsha Seijibu, ed. 1981. *Gyōsei Kaikaku* (Administrative reform). Tokyo: Chōbunsha.

Yoshihara, Tadashi. 1965. *Sekitan Sangyō no Ikiru Michi* (The road toward life for the coal industry). *Ekonomisuto*, January 12.

Yoshino, Toshihiko. 1961. "Nihon Ginkō Sōritsu no Rekishiteki Igi" (The historical significance of the establishment of the Bank of Japan). *Banking* 10, 163: 27–38.

Young, Michael. 1984. "Judicial Review of Administrative Guidance: Governmentally Encouraged Consensual Dispute Resolution in Japan." *Columbia Law Review* 84, 4: 923–83.

Yuki, Hajime. 1938. *Honpō Sekiyu Shi* (Our petroleum history). Tokyo: Nippon Kōronsha.

Zaikai Kenkūjo, ed. 1983. *Kaisha Yakuin Roku* (Register of company directors). Tokyo.

Zanetti, Giovanni, and Giovanni Fraquelli. 1979. *Una nazionalizzazione al buio: L'ENEL dal 1963–1978* (Nationalization in the dark: ENEL from 1963 to 1978). Bologna: Il Mulino.

Zenkoku Sekiyugyō Kyōdō Kumiai Rengōkai and Zenkoku Sekiyu Shōgyō Kumiai Rengōkai, eds. 1974. *Zensekiren 20 nenshi* (The twenty-year record of the National Federation of Petroleum Commercial Associations). Tokyo.

Zenkoku Tankō Shokuin Rōdō Kumiai Kyōgikai, ed. 1971a. "Dai 12 Kai Taisei Iinkai no Keika Ni Tsuite" (Concerning the proceedings of the 12th structure committee meeting). Internal memorandum, September 10.

———. 1971b. "Dai 13 Kai Taisei Iinkai no Keika ni Tsuite" (Concerning the proceedings of the 13th structure committee meeting). Internal memorandum, September 16.

———. 1971c. "Dai 1 Kai Taisei Iinkai, Shōiinkai no Keika ni Tsuite" (Concerning the Proceedings of the 1st structure committee subsubcommittee meeting). Internal memorandum, November 2.

———. 1971d. "Dai 14 Kai Taisei Iinkai no Keika ni Tsuite" (Concerning the proceedings of the 14th structure committee). Internal memorandum, December 11.

———. 1972a. "Sekitan Kōgyō Shingikai Dai 15 Kai Taisei Iinkai no Keika ni Tsuite" (Concerning the proceedings of the 15th structure committee of the Coal Industry Council). Internal memorandum, January 20.

———. 1972b. "Dai 17 Kai Taisei Iinkai no Keika ni Tsuite" (Concerning the proceedings of the 17th structure committee meeting). Internal memorandum, March 27.

———. 1972c. "Sekitan Tankō Shingikai Dai 35 Kai no Keika ni Tsuite" (Concerning the proceedings of the 35th Coal Industry Council meeting). Internal memorandum, March 31.

———. 1972d. "Dai 18 Kai Taisei Iinkai no Shingi Keika ni Tsuite" (Concerning the proceedings of the 18th structure committee meeting). Internal memorandum, May 13.

———. 1972e. "Dai 19 Kai Taisei Iinkai no Keika ni Tsuite" (Concerning the proceedings of the 19th structure committee meeting). Internal memorandum, May 20.

Zysman, John. 1977. *Political Strategies for Industrial Order: State, Market, and Industry in France.* Berkeley: University of California Press.

———. 1983. *Governments, Markets and Growth: Financial Systems and the Politics of Industrial Change.* Ithaca: Cornell University Press.

List of Acronyms

AGIP	Azienda Generale Italiana dei Petroli
AIST	Agency for Industrial Science and Technology
AMA	Administrative Management Agency
ANRE	Agency for Natural Resources and Energy
APOC	Anglo-Persian Oil Company
ATIC	Association de l'Importation Charbonnière
BNOC	British National Oil Corporation
BP	British Petroleum
CANDU	Canadian heavy water reactor
CDF	Charbonnages de France
CFP	Compagnie Française des Pétroles
CFR	Compagnie Française de Raffinage
DC	Christian Democrats
DONG	Dansk Olie os Naturgas
DSP	Democratic Socialist Party
EDF	Electricité de France
ENEL	Ente Nazionale per l'Energia Elettrica
ENI	Ente Nazionale Idrocarburi
EPDC	Electric Power Development Corporation
ESB	Economic Stabilization Board
FRG	Federal Republic of Germany
GATT	General Agreement on Tariffs and Trade
IBJ	Industrial Bank of Japan
IEA	International Energy Agency
ILO	International Labor Organization
IRI	Istituto per la Recostruzione Industriale
JAEC	Japanese Atomic Energy Commission
JAERI	Japan Atomic Energy Research Institute
JAIF	Japan Atomic Industrial Forum
JAPCO	Japan Atomic Power Company

JAPEX	Japan Petroleum Exploration Company
JDB	Japan Development Bank
JNOC	Japan National Oil Corporation
JPDA	Japan Petroleum Development Association
JPDC	Japan Petroleum Development Corporation
LDP	Liberal Democratic Party
MCI	Ministry of Commerce and Industry
MITI	Ministry of International Trade and Industry
MMPC	Metal Mining Public Corporation
NEDO	New Energy Development Organization
NFPC	Nuclear Fuels Public Corporation
NSC	Nuclear Safety Commission
NSKR	Nihon Sekitan Kōgyō Rengōkai
OAPEC	Organization of Arab Petroleum Exporting Countries
OECD	Organization for Economic Cooperation and Development
ÒNCL	National Liquid Fuels Office
PAG	Petroleum Advisory Group
PARC	Policy Affairs Research Council
PCI	Communist Party of Italy
PIL-I	First Petroleum Industry Law
PIL-II	Second Petroleum Industry Law
PNC	Power Reactor and Nuclear Fuel Corporation
RFB	Reconstruction Finance Board
SCAP	Supreme Commander for the Allied Powers
SIAP	Società Italo-Americana per il Petrolio
SKR	Sekitan Kōgyō Rengōkai
SNEA	Société Nationale Elf-Aquitaine
STA	Science and Technology Agency
TEPCO	Tokyo Electric Power Company
TVA	Tennessee Valley Authority
VEBA	Vereinigte Elektrizitäts und Bergwerke

Index

Abegglen, James C., 19n
Addison, Paul, 56n
Adelman, M. A., 18n, 218
Administrative tradition, 16–17, 283–84
Advanced thermal reactor. *See* Nuclear
   power industry
Alimenti, Cesare, 60n, 61n
Allen, G. C., 20n, 145n
Allison, Graham, 287
Almond, Gabriel, 4n, 9n
Alternative Energy Law of 1980, 230–32
American Occupation, 289–90
  in coal industry, 90–95
  in electric power industry, 151–61, 166
  in oil industry, 186–91
  See also ESB; Priority production
Anderson, Irvine H., Jr., 18n, 178n, 179n
Andō, Yoshio, 92n, 95n, 99n, 101n, 155n
Anglo-Persian Oil Company, 53–56, 263
Arabian Oil Company, 195, 201n, 204–5
Athos, Antony G., 22n

Banks. *See* Finance
Becker, David, 4
Bell, Joel, 46
Berger, Suzanne, 6n, 9n
Bisson, T. A., 20n
Boltho, Andrea, 278n
Brown, Mark S., 188n–207n
Bruce, Harry J., 25n
Bureaucracy, 21, 258–63
  See also Administrative tradition; Cen-
   tralization, bureaucratic; MCI; Minis-
   try of Communications; MITI
Business, belief in free market, 261–62
  See also Industry associations

Business-government relations. *See* Point
  of compact; Reciprocal consent, politics of
Bye, Maurice, 31n, 40n

Calder Hall reactor, 238, 240, 248
Caldwell, Martha, 108n–9n, 113n, 118n–
  219
Cameron, David, 10n, 16
Campbell, John C., 9n, 207n, 287n
CANDU reactor, 245, 248–51, 289
Carnoy, Martin, 4n
Cartels, 261
  in coal industry, 75, 80–84
  in electric power industry, 140–43
  in oil industry, 179–85, 190
  See also Haitan Kōdan; Ruhrkohle syn-
   dicate; Shin Shōwa Sekitan; Shōwa
   Sekitan
Centralization, bureaucratic, 14–15, 270–
  2, 284
CFP, 57–59, 264
Chandler, Alfred D., Jr., 14n, 17n
Coal industry, 264
  attempts at state control, 84–90, 95–
   101
  comparative state ownership, 24–32,
   264, 266
  Fifth Coal Program, 131–32
  First Coal Program, 113–16, 282
  Fourth Coal Program, 124–30
  and labor, 70, 89–92, 97, 114, 117
  market composition, 80
  Miike strike, 91, 114, 281
  Occupation organization, 90–102
  origins, 68–75

Coal industry (*cont.*)
  privatization, 70–73
  production, 88–89, 102–3, 105, 111,
    117, 131
  rationalization, 108–12
  Second Coal Program, 116–20
  Sixth Coal Program, 132
  small mine owners (gojokai), 81–82,
    86–87, 104, 271
  Third Coal Program, 120–24
  See also Great Britain; Germany, and
    Ruhrkohl; Italy
Cohen, Jerome B., 20, 21n, 90n, 99,
    178n–86n, 230n, 259n, 264n
Colitti, Marcello, 62n, 63n
Cottino, Gastone, 61n
Craig, Albert M., 272n
Critical case, Japanese energy as, 9, 17–
    22, 265

Daum, Arnold R., 136n
Deutsch, Karl, 7n
Developmental timing, 7, 15, 273–77, 284
Di Palma, Guiseppe, 42n
Doern, C. Bruce, 11n
Dore, Ronald, 7n, 22n
Downstream. *See* Oil industry
Dupuy, A., 14n
Duus, Peter, 20n, 146n–47n, 290n
Duvall, Raymond D., 10n

Ebinger, Charles K., 244n
Eckstein, Harry, 17n
Einaudi, Mario, 31n
Electric power industry:
  and coal, 113, 115–16, 123, 149–50
  comparative state ownership, 32–45
  and labor, 151
  origins, 135–41
  regulation, 138–41, 164
  reliance on foreign capital, 141, 278
  state control, 143–51, 163
  wartime organization, 152
  See also France; Great Britain; Italy
Electric Power Industry Advisory Council,
    164–65
ENEL, 41–44, 66, 264, 280
Energy Roundtable Report, 198–200, 204
Energy technology, 228–45, 254
ENI, 42, 62–63
EPDC, 32, 123, 135, 160–66 194, 257
  and nuclear power, 239, 245
  See also CANDU reactor
ESB, 92 96–100
Evans, Peter, 5n, 9n, 10n, 289n

Fagan, H., 12n, 28n, 31n
Fauré, Edgar, 57n

Federation of Economic Organizations.
  See Keidanren
Fedi, Publio, 52n–43n, 280n
Feigenbaum, Harvey B., 9n, 11n, 18n,
    56n, 58
Ferrier, R. W., 54n, 55n
Finance:
  and coal industry, 94, 117–18, 120–22,
    129
  and electric power industry, 141–43,
    147–48, 166
  and oil industry, 209–10, 221–23
  public versus private, 274
  and state intervention, 273–77
  See also IBJ; Ministry of Finance; RFB
Fontaine, Pierre, 59n
Foreign capital. *See* Electric power indus-
  try; Nuclear power industry; Oil
  industry
Foreign competition. *See* Openness
France:
  and electric power industry, 40–41
  and Japan, 259–69
  and oil, 56–59
Freeman, J. Leiper, 9n
Freeman, John R., 4n, 10n, 11n, 14n
Friedman, David, 22n, 261n, 276, 288
Frost, Robert L., 6n, 31n, 40n–41n
Fugen. *See* Nuclear power industry, ad-
  vanced thermal reactor
Fujita, Keizō, 20n
Fukuda, Takeo, 121, 125, 242
Fukui, Haruhiro, 20n, 262n

Gale, Roger W., 161n, 255
Gelinas, Andre, 10n
Germany, and Ruhrkohl, 31–32, 82, 127,
    264
Gerschenkron, Alexander, 11, 12n, 15,
    273
Gillingham, John R., 31n, 82n, 264n
Gilpin, Robert, 4n
Gojokai (Association of small
  mineowners), 81–82, 86–87, 104
Goldthorpe, John H., 7n
Goodermote, Dean, 46n
Gould, Stephen Jay, 7, 290
Gourevitch, Peter, 4n–7n, 9n–10n, 12n
Gracey, Don, 52n
Gramsci, Antonio, 9n
Grassini, Franco A., 52n
Grayson, Leslie E., 52n, 57n, 58, 177n
Great Britain:
  and coal, 28–31
  and electric power, 39–40
  and oil, 52–56
Greenway, Charles D., 53–55
Gusfield, Joseph R., 7n

Hadley, Eleanor M., 20n
Hagiwara, Kichitarō, 114n, 120, 125–27
Haiden (electric power distribution firms),
     150, 154–58
Haitan Kōdan, 93, 103, 108
Harada, Taneo, 90n, 98n
Hasegawa, Shoishi, 173n, 183–84
Hashimoto Keizaburō, 171n–72n, 179n,
     180, 187
Heclo, Hugh, 9n
Hein, Laura, 91n, 94n, 186n
Heller, C. A., 46n, 53n
Hilferding, Rudolph, 14n, 274
Hirschman, Albert O., 106n
Hoffman, Stanley, 12n
Holland, Stuart, 11n, 52n
Homan, P. T., 18n
Horie, Yasuzō, 72
Horikubō, Masaji, 74
Horiuchi, Akiyoshi, 129n, 222n, 276n
Horne, James, 20n
Horwitch, Mel, 25n
Hoshino, Yoshirō, 20n
Huntington, Samuel P., 7n

IBJ, 221, 222n
Idemitsu, Sazō, 182, 189
Idemitsu Kōsan, 190, 203
Ikenberry, G. John, 5n, 12n, 17, 18n,
     264n, 278n
Imai, Kōzō, 68n, 70n, 73n, 90n, 101n–
     16n
Imperial Oil, 184, 267–68, 187–88, 192–
     93
     and JAPEX, 193
Important Industries Control Law, 82–84,
     174, 178, 263
Inayama Yoshihiro, 131–32
Industry associations:
     Confindustria, 43, 63
     Denryoku Renmei, 141–43, 274
     Japan Coal Association, 104–31
     Japan Coal Mining Industrial Associa-
        tion, 92–99
     JPDA, 201
     NSKR, 104, 110
     Petroleum Association of Japan, 198–
        214, 271
     SKR, 80
Inoguchi, Takashi, 21n, 258n, 288
Inokuchi, Tōsuke, 169n, 173n–87n,
     193n–94n, 225
Ishikawa, Ichirō, 235–37
Ishikawa, Kinya, 244, 247n–51n
Ishimura, Zensuke, 68
Italy:
     and electric power industry, 41–44, 280
     and oil industry, 59–63

Jacoby, Neil H., 46n
JAEC, 236, 239–43, 247, 249–52
JAERI, 235, 237, 240–43
"Japan, Inc.," 19–20, 283
Japan Coal Company. *See* Nittan
JAPCO, 239–40
JAPEX, 193–94, 209, 213–14
     and JNOC, 214
JDB, 94
JNOC, 64, 214–16, 257
Johnson, Chalmers, 20n, 21, 82n, 92n, 95,
     96n, 102n, 108n, 134n, 135, 145, 156,
     157n, 191, 193n, 233n, 258–59,
     260n, 276n, 290n
Jōyō. *See* Nuclear Power Industry, fast
     breeder reactor
JPDC, 208, 210

Kamiō, Kyōichi, 234n, 251n–52n
Kanazawa, Yochio, 236n
Kaplan, Eugene, 19n
Karl, Barry D., 9n
Katayama, Tetsu, 95–101, 152, 187
Katzenstein, Peter J., 4n–5n, 9n, 10n,
     13n, 16, 258n, 260
Kawi, Takeshi, 235n–39n
Keck, Otto, 33n
Keeny, Spurgeon, M., 244n, 246n
Keidanren, 282
     and alternative energy, 231–37, 250
     and coal industry, 109n, 113–16, 123,
        128
     and oil industry, 201–2, 205–6, 208
Kelf-Cohen, R., 28n, 31n, 39n
Kent, Marian, 41n
Kirby, M. W., 28n, 30n, 31, 65n, 268–69
Kiso Shigeyoshi, 74–101, 124–25, 271
Kiyomiya, Ichirō, 73n, 83n, 87n–88n
Klapp, Merrie G., 12n, 46n
Kojima, Keizō, 95n–96n, 99n, 101n
Komamura, Yosaburō, 142n, 148n
Kondō, Kanichi, 74n, 87n, 98n–126n,
     190n–208n
Kono, Ichirō, 239
Krasner, Stephen D., 4n–6n, 14n, 18n,
     259n
Krauss, Ellis, S., 9n, 20n, 258n, 281–89n
Krieger, Joel, 28n, 269n
Kuboyama, Yozō, 69n, 81n, 82n
Kuisel, Richard F., 58n
Kunisaki, Shinsui, 89
Kurth, James, 5n, 12n, 15

Labor, 260, 280–82
Labor unrest:
     and coal industry, 74–75, 91–92,
        105–6
     and electric power industry, 151–52

Labor unrest (*cont.*)
  and nuclear power industry, 241
  and oil industry
Laux, Jeanne Kirk, 11n
LDP, 121–22
  and alternative energy, 233–34
  and PARC, 121, 125
  See also Nakasone, Yasuhiro; Ohira,
    Masayoshi; Tanaka, Kakuei
Lerner, Daniel, 7n
Lesbriel, S. Hayden, 246n
Levy, Brian, 46n
Liberal party, 97–99, 110–11
  See also Yoshida, Shigeru
Lindblom, Charles E., 9n, 10
Lockwood, William, 20n, 65, 74, 136, 141,
  170n, 258n, 288n, 290n
Lovejoy, W. F., 18n
Lowi, Theodore, J., 13n, 262–63

Magini, Manlio, 60n, 61n
Mandel, Ernest, 12n
Manke, Richard B., 46n
Mansfield, Harvey, 11n
Market-conforming, 2, 168, 257–60
Market structure, 64–67, 191, 266–70
  in coal industry, 80, 107, 133, 266
  in electric power industry, 166, 266
  horizonal isolation, 266
  in nuclear power industry, 234, 238,
    252–55
  in oil industry, 216, 218, 266
  vertical fragmentation, 266–69
Market transformation, as unit of analysis,
  285–96
Marshall, Byron K., 20n, 23n, 70
Matsukata Kōjirō, 175
Matsukata Masayoshi, 72, 169
Matsumoto Kenjirō, 83, 85–88.
Matsunaga Yasuzaemon, 140–61, 235
Matsuzaka, Naomi, 145n, 155n
Matsuzaki, Tetsuhisa, 289n
Mattei, Enrico, 62–63, 265
MCI:
  and coal, 83–88, 96–102
  and oil, 173–75, 180–83
  and synthetic fuels, 230
  Yoshino Plan, 83–85, 90
Meiji period:
  in coal industry, 69–74, 133, 271
  role of state in, 19
  ruling coalition of, 280
Middle East. *See* Arabian Oil Company
Miliband, Ralph, 3n–4n, 12
Military. *See* Oil industry, Imperial navy
    and; Oil industry, strategic concerns
Milward, H. Bunton, 9n

Ministry of Communications, 137–49
Ministry of Finance:
  in alternative energy, 231–33
  in coal industry, 121–22
  in oil industry, 193–95, 206
Minseitō, 139, 146
MITI, 21, 258–59
  divisions within, 203–4, 272
  in coal industry, 105–6, 108–11, 114–
    30
  in electric power industry, 156, 160–62
  energy forecasts, 195
  intra-bureaucratic conflicts, 272
  in nuclear power industry, 234–52
  in oil industry, 190–94, 211, 217–27
  and oil restructuring, 196–97
  in synthetic fuels, 230–34
Mitsubishi, 70, 244
  and coal, 101, 126–28
  and oil, 174n, 180, 184
Mitsui, 70–72
  Mitsui Bussan, 70–72, 82, 178
  and coal, 74–75, 101, 126–30
  bank, 141–43, 147–48
Miyazaki, Isamu, 84n, 88n, 147n, 148n,
  174n
Mochizuki, Kiichi, 211n, 213n, 219n
Moe, Ronald, 10n
Monsen, R. Joseph, 10n, 24n
Moore, Barrington, 12n, 20
Moore, Joe, 91n
Morozumi Yoshihiko, 211, 248
Mosley, Oswald, 56n
Muramatsu, Michio, 9n, 259n, 281–82,
  288, 289n
Murat, Daniel, 56n
Myrdal, Gunnar, 10n

Nagai Ryūtarō, 145–46
Nagasue, Toshio, 68n, 83n–84n, 89n
Naitō, Hisahiro, 169, 173n
Nakajima, Tokunosuke, 236n–37n, 241n
Nakamura, Takafusa, 20n, 84n–92n,
  102n, 116, 147n–48n, 174n, 290
Nakasone Yashuhiro, 113n, 200, 234, 236
NEDO, 233–34, 255, 272
Neff, Thomas, 18n
Nettl, J. P., 3, 12n
Nezu, Tomoyoshi, 83n, 85, 87, 89n
Nihon Sekitan Kōgyo Rengokai, 104, 110
Nippatsu, 85, 148–60, 266, 268
  transfer to EPDC, 160
Nippon Oil, 169–84
Nittan, 85–89, 93, 26
Noguchi, Yōichirō, 120n, 290n
Noguchi, Yukio, 233n
Nordhauser, Norman, E., 18n

Nordlinger, Eric A., 4n, 9n, 19n, 287n
Nowell, Gregory P., 53n, 56n–58n
Nuclear power industry:
  advanced thermal reactor, 241–55
  attempts at state control, 234–40
  fast breeder reactor, 241, 243, 251–55
  foreign interests, 244
  labor strikes, 241
  privatization, 244
  security concerns, 228–29
Nueño, Pedro, 25n

O'Connor, James, 4n, 12n
Offe, Claus, 4n, 12n
Ōhira, Masayoshi, 231, 233
Ōi, Ryōaki, 114n, 175n, 177n, 191n, 198–202n
Oil industry, 264–65
  attempts at state control, 177–208
  comparative state ownership, 45–53, 266–67
  consolidation, 220–25
  downstream, 168, 179, 188–92, 207–8, 216–17, 267
  foreign interests, 168–78, 279
  fragmentation, 65, 217–20
  Imperial Navy and, 170, 173, 177, 226, 229
  origins, 268–77
  production, 171, 174
  restructuring, 179–86, 204–8
  Russian import, 175–76
  strategic concerns, 45–46, 55, 64, 226
  upstream, 168, 182–88, 192–95, 204–7, 216, 267
  wartime organization, 177–85
  See also France; Great Britain; Italy
Okamoto, Ryōzō, 170n, 178n
Okamura, Kiwao, 143–45
Oki, Yōichi, 74n, 81n–110
Okimoto, Daniel I., 20n, 258–89
Okuda, Hideo, 177n, 180n
One Company Plan, 120, 125–26
Openness, 64–67, 277–79, 284
Osanai, Hiroshi, 74n, 87n, 98n–126n, 190n–208n
Otake, Sokuichi, 135n–45n, 148n, 153, 154n
Ōtani, Ken, 136n–58n, 163n
Ouchi, William, 22n
Ozawa, Etsuji, 138n, 141n–44n

Parsons, Talcott, 3, 7n
Pascale, Richard T., 22n
Patrick, Hugh, 19n, 261n, 276n
Pempel, T. J., 20–21, 258n, 259n, 281n
Pepper, Thomas, 19n, 261n

Petroleum. *See* Oil industry
Petroleum Council, 202–4, 221
Petroleum Distribution Control Company, 182–86
PIL-I, 84, 177–79
PIL-II, 196–204, 222–23, 282
Piore, Michael J., 6n, 7n
PNC, 242–44, 251
Point of compact, 9–13, 23, 64–67, 257
Porges, Amelia, 190n, 218, 226
Posner, Alan R., 43
Potsdam Ordinance, 157, 166
Poulantzas, Nicos, 4n
Pratt, Larry, 52n
PRDC, 275
Priority production, 92–95
Prodi, Romano, 41n
Przeworski, Adam, 12n
Public corporations, 23–24
  See also Coal industry; Electric power industry; Oil industry; Point of compact; State
Public Utilities Commission, 157–61
Pye, Lucian, W., 7n

Ratiglia, Fabio, 61n
Reciprocal consent, politics of, 2, 8–9, 260–62, 287–90
  in coal, 133–34
  in electric power, 166–67
  in nuclear power, 255–56
Reed, Steven, 272n
Refining Industry. *See* Oil industry, downstream
Regini, Marino, 14n, 285
Regulation. *See* State intervention
RFB, 92, 94, 102–3
Robson, William A., 28n, 39n
Rondot, Jean, 58n
Rossi, Ernesto, 31n, 42
Rueschemeyer, Dietrich, 5n, 9n
Ruhrkohle syndicate, 31–32, 82, 127, 264
Ruling coalition, 66, 279–83
  effect in coal case, 65–66, 110–11, 133

Sabel, Charles F., 7n
Saitō, Masatoshi, 95n, 99n, 100n, 110n
Sakai, Yoshio, 95n, 137n–39n, 145n–46n
Sakakibara, E., 290n
Sampson, Anthony, 18n
Sasaki, Jōtarō, 120n
Satō, Hideo, 234n, 236n, 239n–40n, 242, 248n
Satō, Seizaburō, 289n
Satō, Taiji, 224
Saxonhouse, Gary, 19n, 261n, 276n
Scalapino, Robert, 74n

SCAP. *See* American Occupation
Schmitter, P. C., 6n, 9n
Seidenstecker, Edward, 136
Seidman, Harold, 11
Seiyūkai, 139, 146
Sharkansky, Ira, 11n
Sheahan, John B., 24n, 52n
Shinobu, Seizaburō, 99n, 156n
Shin Shōwa Sekitan, 112, 290
Shonfield, Andrew, 11
Shoriki, Matsutarō, 235–39
Shōwa Sekitan, 82, 87, 290
Silberman, Bernard, 20, 133n, 258
Skocpol, Theda, 3n–6n, 8, 284n
Smith, Thomas C., 20n, 23n, 70, 72
Sonoda, Minoru, 94, 102n–30
Spindler, J. Andrew, 277
Squarzina, Federico, 61n–62n
STA, 236, 247–49, 255, 272
State:
   autonomy, 3–5, 19–20, 287
   bureaucratic centralization, 133, 270–72
   capacity, 5–6, 19
   development, 7–8, 20–21
   as guarantor, 133–34, 258–63, 276, 283
   identity, 3–5
   jurisdiction versus control, 8–9, 20, 167, 260–61, 286
   leadership, 258–59
   as market-conforming, 1–2
State enterprise, 1, 9–13, 23
   See also Coal industry; Electric power industry
State intervention, 2, 13–17, 64–67
   and market structure, 14, 166, 266–70, 284
   and centralization, 14–15, 255, 270–72, 284
   and development timing, 15, 134, 273–77
   and openness, 15, 277–79
   and ruling coalition, 16, 279–83
   and administrative tradition, 16–17, 283–84
Steel industry, and coal, 103, 123, 131
Steiner, Kurt, 20n, 163n, 270n
Sugihara, Keiji, 214n
Suleiman, Ezra, 6n
Sumiya, Mikio, 19n, 68n, 70n, 71–73, 74n
Suttmeier, Richard P., 243, 246–47n
Suzuki, Tatsuru, 163n
Sweezy, Paul 7n
Synthetic fuels, 229–34
   security concerns, 228–29
   state control, 229–31

Taira, Koji, 19n
Takai, Yochio, 224n
Tanaka Kakuei, 98, 101, 121, 132, 161, 192, 202, 212n, 220, 246
Tarrow, Sidney, 6n
Tiedemann, Arthur E., 20n, 140, 290n
Tōhata, Seiichi, 20n
Trezise, Philip, 19n, 261n
Truchil, B., 14n
Tsunekawa, K., 20, 21, 281n
Tsurumi, Yoshi, 21n, 217
Tuchman, Barbara, 101n
Tupper, Allan, 11n

Uehara, Masuo, 169n, 170–71
Uemura Kōgorō, 115, 125, 122, 127–30
Uemura Program, 124–30, 269
Upstream. *See* Oil industry
Usami, Shōgō, 145n, 155n

Vernon, Raymond, 11n, 18n, 70, 198n, 202, 259, 283
Vining, Aidan, R., 33
Vittas, Dimitri, 277n
Vogel, David, 17n
Vogel, Ezra, 21n–22n, 117n, 133n, 259n, 283n
Votaw, Dow, 62n, 63

Wallerstein, Immanuel, 7n
Walsh, Annamarie Hauk, 11n
Walters, Kenneth D., 10n, 24n
Wamsley, Gary T., 9n
Weber, Max, 3
Wildavsky, Aaron, 272n
Williamson, Harold F., 53n, 136
Wilson, Carroll L., 25n
Wilson, Ernest, 14n
Wilson, Frank L., 9n
Woolf, S. J., 43

Yada, Toshifumi, 68n, 72n–73n, 87n–89n, 106n 269n
Yamada, Ichitarō, 149n, 151n, 164n
Yanaga, Chitoshi, 20n, 98n, 235n, 237n
Yoshida, Shigeru, 95–98, 106, 157, 159. 161
Young, Michael, 21n, 212n, 261n, 287, 288n
Yuki, Hajime, 173n

Zysman, John, 5n, 6, 12n, 14n, 259, 276n, 277

Library of Contress Cataloging-in-Publication Data

Samuels, Richard J.
  The business of the Japanese state.

  (Cornell studies in political economy)
  Bibliography, p.
  Includes index.
  1. Energy industries—Japan. 2. Industry and state—Japan. I. Title. II.
Series.
HD9502.J32S27 1987   338.4'7621042'0952   87-5230
ISBN 0-8014-2022-9 (alk. paper)
ISBN 0-8014-9462-1 (pbk. : alk. paper)